I0805306

APPROACHING THE BIBLE IN MEDIEVAL ENGLAND

MANCHESTER 1824

Manchester University Press

Manchester Medieval Studies

SERIES EDITOR Professor S. H. Rigby

The study of medieval Europe is being transformed as old orthodoxies are challenged, new methods embraced and fresh fields of inquiry opened up. The adoption of inter-disciplinary perspectives and the challenge of economic, social and cultural theory are forcing medievalists to ask new questions and to see familiar topics in a fresh light.

The aim of this series is to combine the scholarship traditionally associated with medieval studies with an awareness of more recent issues and approaches in a form accessible to the non-specialist reader.

ALREADY PUBLISHED IN THE SERIES

Pacemaking in the middle ages: Principles and practice
Jenny Benham

Money in the medieval English economy, 973–1489
James Bolton

Reform and the papacy in the eleventh century
Kathleen G. Cushing

Picturing women in late medieval and Renaissance art
Christa Grössinger

The Vikings in England
D. M. Hadley

A sacred city: consecrating churches and reforming society in eleventh-century Italy
Louis I. Hamilton

The politics of carnival
Christopher Humphrey

Holy motherhood
Elizabeth L'Estrange

Music, scholasticism and reform: Salian Germany 1024–1125
T. J. H. McCarthy

Medieval law in context
Anthony Musson

The expansion of Europe, 1250–1500
Michael North

Medieval maidens
Kim M. Phillips

Gentry culture in late medieval England
Raluca Radulescu and Alison Truelove (eds)

Chaucer in context
S. H. Rigby

The life cycle in Western Europe, c.1300–c.1500
Deborah Youngs

MANCHESTER MEDIEVAL STUDIES

APPROACHING THE BIBLE IN MEDIEVAL ENGLAND

Eyal Poleg

Manchester University Press

Published by Manchester University Press
Altrincham Street, Manchester M1 7JA, UK
www.manchesteruniversitypress.co.uk

British Library Cataloguing-in-Publication Data is available

Library of Congress Cataloging-in-Publication Data is available

ISBN 978 1 7849 9374 0 *paperback*

First published by Manchester University Press in hardback 2013

This edition first published 2016

Printed by Lightning Source

For Stav,
אהבה עזה אהבת מישור
Rashi on the Song of Songs 1:4

CONTENTS

PLATES

Colour versions of the images within the plates section of this paperback edition can be found at www.manchesteruniversitypress.co.uk/approaching-the-bible-in-medieval-england/

Plates appear between pages 74 and 75.

FIGURES

MUSIC EXAMPLES

TABLES

PREFACE

A certain degree of *chutzpah* is necessary when writing a book about the medieval Bible. Any work on such a topic must omit more than it can include, leaving entire areas unexplored and touching only lightly on others. Rather than taking the obvious path of concentrating on a specific medium or a biblical episode, I have chosen to examine the problem in multiple media, approaching the Bible as a complex object, a collection of sacred texts and narratives. Such a choice is at the heart of the concept of biblical mediation, which this book introduces. Mediation is my key to the understanding of the Bible within its medieval contexts. Through four test cases this book follows the Bible as it was sung and carried in city streets, as it was studied and preached in medieval England. It explores the concept of biblical mediation and its theoretical underpinning, in the hope of achieving a fuller appreciation of the medieval Bible, and of contributing to the study of sacred Scripture in other times and places.

The challenges of exploring the Bible in diverse fields, ranging from liturgy and jurisprudence to palaeography and preaching, were met with the help of friends and colleagues. I wish to thank especially Bill Cambell, Sarah Carpenter, the late David Chadd, Rita Copeland, J. Cornelia Linde, Pino di Luccio, SJ, and Sam Mirelman. Early chapters were read by David d'Avray, Nicole Bériou, Susan Boynton, Eamon Duffy, Alun Ford, Sarah Hamilton, Laura Light and Paul Saenger. Sam Worby has provided advice and support beyond the call of friendship and collegiality. Their comments have made this a better book. Any mistakes remain, entirely, my own. Steve Rigby, the series editor, has helped to bring the book to fruition, and at Manchester University Press, Emma Brennan, John Banks and Greg Thorpe have overseen its taking of material form. Aliza Poláček, Michael and Riki Poleg have stood by me throughout the long process.

My desire to understand liturgy deeply has led me, time and again, to unexpected places. I gratefully thank the communities of Latrun Trappist monastery, Downside Abbey, Mount St Bernard Abbey, and St Hugh's Charterhouse, Parkminster, for their generous hospitality and for sharing with me their unique ways of living the Bible. In consulting manuscripts I benefited immensely from kind, patient, and knowledgeable manuscript librarians at the British Library, the Bodleian Library, Cambridge University Library, St John's College, Cambridge, Trinity College, Cambridge, the Archives of New College, Oxford, St Paul's Cathedral Library (and especially Mr Wisdom, its most resourceful librarian), Guidlhall Library, London, Lambeth Palace Library, and the National Art Library at the Victoria and Albert Museum (and especially Rowan Watson, curator of Western manuscripts). The generous support of several trusts and institutions has enabled me to devote the necessary time to research and revise. I am grateful for the support of Queen Mary College University of London's Westfield Trust and the Overseas Research Students Award Scheme (ORSAS), the Royal Historical Society Marshall Fellowship, The Spalding Trust, and a British Academy Postdoctoral Fellowship. The book's colour plates, indispensable for its analyses, were reproduced with the support of the Marc Fitch Fund. Lastly, I wish to thank Miri Rubin, who (apart from reading this book time and again) has shown me the value of academic life, and Stav, for reminding me there is life beyond academia.

NOTE ON TRANSCRIPTION

In the transcriptions I have tried to adhere to original spellings. In general c/t and v/u are modernised and Middle English thorn and yogh are written as th and y, but otherwise orthography is preserved. Abbreviation are expanded silently and punctuation kept to a minimum. When more than one manuscript is examined, variant readings which do not alter meaning are silently omitted. Biblical references in parentheses or brackets are an editorial addition, while biblical references made by the original scribe (particularly in Chapter 4) are presented as part of the text, keeping to the scribe's abbreviations. Biblical references follow the *Chicago Manual of Style*, with the four Latin Books of Kings divided into 1 and 2 Samuel and 1 and 2 Kings. The numbering of the Psalms follows the Gallican Psalter. Biblical quotations are from the 1969 edition of the Clementine Vulgate, while English translation follows the Douai–Rheims edition with Challoner Revisions.

LIST OF ABBREVIATIONS

BL	The British Library, London
CCCM	Corpus Christianorum, continuatio mediaevalis (Turnhout, 1966–)
CCSL	Corpus Christianorum, seria Latina (Turnhout, 1953–)
DNB	*Oxford Dictionary of National Biography*, ed. H. C. G. Matthew and Brian Harrison (Oxford, 2004 = http://oxforddnb.com, accessed 10 June 2012)
EETS OS / ES / SS	Early English Text Society Original Series (1864–); Extra Series (1867–1921); Supplementary Series (1970–)
Glossa ordinaria	*Biblia latina cum glossa ordinaria: Facsimile Reprint of the editio princeps Adolph Rusch of Strassburg 1480/81*, 4 vols, ed. Karlfried Froehlich and Margaret T. Gibson (Turnhout, 1992)
HBS	Henry Bradshaw Society (1891–)
MED	*Middle English Dictionary*, gen. ed. Hans Kurath (Ann Arbor, MI, c.1952–c.2001 =http://quod.lib.umich.edu/m/med, accessed 10 June 2012)
OED	*The Oxford English Dictionary*, 3rd edn (Oxford, 2005 =http://oed.com, accessed 10 June 2012)
PL	*Patrologiae cursus completus, seria Latina*, 217 text vols, gen. ed. Jacques-Paul Migne (Paris, 1844–55)
RS	Rolls Series: Rerum Britannicarum medii aevi scriptores (London, 1858–1911)
Stegmüller	*Repertorium Biblicum Medii Aevi*, 11 vols, ed. Friedrich Stegmüller (Madrid, 1950–80)

INTRODUCTION

The digital era has brought Bibles to a wider public than ever before. Bibles are now available in hundreds of languages and appear in their entirety in cheap prints or on websites to match every taste and bandwidth. Yet, knowledge of the Bible is far from the norm in most Western societies. Secularisation and cultural vogues have left people to rely on films, television programmes or Sunday Schools for knowledge of biblical stories and ideals. Such mediated access and second-hand knowledge is far from a modern innovation. In medieval Europe it was the cost of manuscripts, degrees of literacy, or social boundaries that determined people's access to the Christian Scripture. Devoid of close contact with the biblical text, the majority of men and women experienced the Bible through a carefully structured array of rituals and images, sermons and chants. These media are at the core of this book as it follows the ways the Bible was sung and preached, revered and studied in medieval England; as it traces how the Bible was mediated and known across the social and cultural boundaries of literacy and piety.

At the heart of this book is biblical mediation, a concept both widely familiar – in practice if not in as an explicit theory – and surprisingly elusive. That images and literature, liturgy and sermons were all central in explicating the Bible to the medieval populace is beyond doubt. How such access was constituted or what was its impact, is less evident. Did all media, whether illuminated on a page, sung by a choir, or preached by a friar transmit the Bible in the same way? Were different facets of the Bible more likely to appear in oral, performative, or material forms? Were particular media aimed at specific audiences? What was the impact of mediated access on the way the Bible was retained in the memory of lay and religious, men and women? These questions allow us to explore whether biblical mediation was a carefully guided project led by the clergy and a means to reinforce social boundaries and church hierarchy, and how active lay men and women were in this endeavour. Such questions are at the heart of our understanding of the place of the Bible in the medieval world, and this book constitutes a step in their analysis.

Mediation emerges from the very nature of the Bible. A complex and sacred text, written and edited over a long period of time in remote eras and places, it did not easily fit with the prevailing values of those societies that held it dear. Taken at face value, the dietary laws of Leviticus, the love lore of the Song of Songs, or the visions of Revelation had little to do with the values of Christian (or Jewish) medieval culture. Keeping these archaic narratives relevant and alive was thus a necessity. It led to a high degree of creativity in expounding and exploring the Bible, making biblical mediation a dynamic part of society, ever changing and bringing new texts, tunes, objects, and monuments into its ambit. The Bible was made all things to all people, in a process that was often veiled and hidden. The subtle mechanisms which made its narratives present for medieval society were masked in the Bible's sacrality, as up-to-date theological teachings were presented as an immutable biblical truth. A thorough investigation into transmission and reception is therefore necessary if the dynamics of biblical mediation are to be revealed. Such an investigation is made difficult by the sheer multitude of objects and procedures that facilitated biblical knowledge, by the sheer number of sources of biblical bearing that testify to biblical mediation in medieval Europe.

So far, the two most common means of exploring the place of the Bible within the medieval world have been collections of articles or works on specific media. The former bring together the works of experts across disciplines and eras.[1] The latter analyse specific media, as in the use of biblical imagery in medieval art and literature or the way exegesis and preaching engaged with the biblical text (and often one another).[2] Such works have demonstrated the complexity of biblical transmission and the ways different media functioned simultaneously. Time and again medieval examples show oral, visual, textual, and material means of dissemination in convergence: liturgy and preaching were performed at the same time, sharing space and actors; visual imagery reflected dramatic re-enactments; exegetes were often preachers too; and literary narratives employed biblical and liturgical tags interchangeably. These juxtapositions necessitate extending the study of mediation horizontally as well as vertically. Exploring a single medium has the advantage of offering an in-depth analysis, while concentrating on a specific biblical episode enables a well-focused analysis of multiple media. Both, however, also hinder the emergence of an integral view grounded in the medieval experience. An investigation into biblical mediation must take into account not only multiple media but also the multiplicity of the Bible itself. For the Bible is more than a collection of sacred narratives. It is also a complex and challenging text, with books of poetry and law, history and wisdom; its words are sacred, but so is the object itself. All this makes it necessary for the study of biblical mediation to assume a new theoretical framework, one that addresses both Bible and society, and that forms an integrated field of investigation.

The relationship between society and Scripture has been explored most fruitfully by Brian Stock. In his study of heretical sects in the high Middle Ages he identified 'textual communities', groups which clustered around a charismatic individual whose oral mediation of the sacred text became dogma.[3] Stock's analysis reveals that it was the mediation of the text, rather than the text itself, which brought such groups together. His important insight extends far beyond the study of medieval heresies. In monasteries and parish churches communities were brought together by the interpretation and celebration of sacred texts. Beyond the role of a single person, the dynamics of cultural transmission are now being explored by the growing school of *Mediologie*, which analyses the presentation of sacred Scripture to communities of believers. Introduced by Régis Debray and practised primarily by French-speaking scholars, this approach offers important theoretical framework for understanding how meanings are transmitted within cultures.[4] An understanding of the way media technology evolved to present core social values over generations combines with an acute awareness of the role of the mundane as well as the sublime in shaping culture, to shed new light on scripturalist religions. Christianity, primarily in Late Antiquity, serves to exemplify time and again Debray's analyses:

> Aujourd'hui même, le message évangélique opère encore sur les esprits par les cantiques et les fêtes, les ors et les orgues des églises, l'encens, les vitraux et les retables, les flèches des cathédrals et les sanctuaires, l'hostie sur la langue et le chemin du calvaire sous les pieds – et non par l'exégèse individuelle ou communautaire des textes sacrés.[5]

An array of material artefacts and sensory experiences underpins *médiologie*'s investigation of culture and society. Although Debray's Marxist orientation often makes *médiologie* of particular interest to social historians, its key concepts are invaluable in the analysis of mechanisms of transmission within any society. This can be done by moving away from the diachronic analysis advocated by Debray, and into a more synchronic investigation, one that draws into its ambit a variety of sources, moments, and objects. This type of investigation combines the theoretical merits of *Mediologie* with a more accurate historical and contextual underpinning. It follows in the footsteps of Miri Rubin and Eamon Duffy, juxtaposing ritual and performance, object and text in the study of the religious experience of medieval people.[6]

A more synchronic model enables in-depth examination of the two sides of the mediated divide. Mediation is the constant effort to bridge between a text and its reception, between society and its Scripture. These two sides – Bible and society – are far from monolithic. The Bible is both single and plural, a collection of historical and literary narratives, preserved in papyri and manuscripts hallowed over time. All biblical texts were seen as the word of God, and shed their authority on church and society. Not all biblical books, however, are the same. The Gospels underpinned liturgical spectacle and their narrative of Christ's life was widely turned into visual images; the Psalms were chanted day and night by the religious (and increasingly often by pious lay men and women) in monasteries and in homes; the historical books appealed to monarchs with their morality of kingship, while in the poetry of the Song of Songs monks found the image of the Virgin. The need to reconcile Christian belief with Hebrew texts gave rise to intricate allegorical interpretations. The Bible was often understood as an archaic hypertext, with elements of the Old Testament prefiguring the New, a link made visible in marginal annotations in manuscripts and organised in exegetical works and concordances. The Bible was both narrative and text, a source of exemplary stories, as well as a repository of sacred vocabulary. In its material form, the Bible was also a sacred object, processed and venerated in complex rituals which took place in churches and in courts of law, employing the Bible's sacrality and authority to uphold social and religious order.

Society was far from uniform in its mediation of the Bible. The Bible reverberated in vernacular literature, as well as in the Latin of exegetes and divine office. Its scenes were depicted in richly illuminated manuscripts, but also on less refined murals in parish churches. Religious drama and liturgical processions welcomed believers from across the social spectrum to experience the Bible. Some exposure to biblical stories was shared by all. Yet, biblical knowledge was distributed unevenly. The higher echelons of society benefited from a dynamic and rich manuscript culture (as in books of hours or illuminated Apocalypses), from private chapels and clergy to serve their needs and respond to their devotions and interests. Nor did the sacrality of the Bible affect all equally. Priests were the mediators par excellence and enjoyed a unique proximity to sacred books and biblical narratives. Self-fashioned angels, they bridged the mediated gap in sermons and chant, and above all in the Mass, when the biblical past was literally brought to life. With carefully constructed boundaries of space and ritual separating them from the laity, priests and other religious nevertheless experienced the Bible through biblical media of their own, learning of its texts and narrative in extensive libraries or the incessant chanting of Psalms in the divine office.

Mediation extends to biblical manuscripts. Mise-en-page and rubrics, binding and script, all facilitated specific understandings of the Bible. In tracing how biblical manuscripts, which were available to only a few beyond the clerical elite for most of the Middle Ages, mediated the Bible, I have used the growing and powerful insights offered by the discipline of book studies. Book historians trace reading patterns within social and cultural contexts, and their analyses (primarily regarding printed books) are invaluable in the study of the medieval evidence. The concept of *paratext*, coined by Gérard Genette, describes the layers of meaning embedded into the physical appearance of texts; how choice of ink and type, paper and size, facilitated specific reading strategies.[7] In the study of the medieval Bible, its external features have long stood in the shadow of its transmission and textual accuracy. Nevertheless, an emphasis on appearance is still discernible from sixteenth-century descriptive narratives to Christopher de Hamel's recent comment that the thirteenth-century Bible was 'the turning point of the whole story (of the Bible's history), for then the Bible was for the first time assembled into a size, order and format which is still in use'.[8] Beyond layout and addenda, the study of medieval Bibles leads also to the territory of medieval bindings, whose precious materials and religious iconography portrayed the Bible's sacrality without the need to turn a single page.

Medieval England during the thirteenth and fourteenth century provides a fertile ground for the present study. At the time biblical mediation evolved in a period of stability circumscribed by two bursts of hectic creativity.[9] Building on the cultural achievements of the twelfth century, the early thirteenth century saw the rise of the mendicant orders and of the first universities, alongside the codification of the basic tenets of faith in the Fourth Lateran Council of 1215. In dialogue with these events, biblical mediation was changing as well. An innovative type of biblical manuscript was produced and disseminated widely while a new form of preaching was practised by a growing cadre of dedicated preachers. A period of stability followed. For almost two centuries biblical manuscripts were used and copied, but remained virtually unchanged; preachers employed old and new forms simultaneously, with sermons composed at its beginning delivered also at its end. Liturgical rites were less changeable and the uses established after the Norman Conquest were employed all through the period, with local customs gradually succumbing to the hegemonic use of Sarum.[10]

For most of the period under consideration the Bible was rarely available in the vernacular. Only a handful of Old English texts were preserved in monastic libraries, and translations into French and Anglo-Norman remained a noble exception. This language gap enhanced the laity's reliance on visual, performative, and oral media. By the end of the fourteenth century English was beginning to occupy a prominent place in culture and society. The Lollards' ideal of lay access to the Bible then took the form of an English Bible, whose rich manuscript culture (surviving in *c.* 250 manuscripts, primarily from the first quarter of the fifteenth century) catered for orthodox and heterodox audiences alike.[11] The introduction of a vernacular Bible changed biblical discourse in late medieval England. It led to a period of raised anxiety regarding religious orthodoxy and vernacular Bibles. A strong official position developed in the late fourteenth and early fifteenth century, manifested in Arundel's Constitutions of 1407/9, and associated English Bible and vernacular theology with heresy. Such a dichotomous view of biblical access and knowledge was embraced by later reformers. Recent studies have likewise explored questions of translation, access, and control at the expense of a more nuanced understanding of biblical mediation.[12]

England serves as the field of enquiry. It was an important centre of biblical studies and dissemination, where innovations in the layout of biblical manuscripts and new forms of preaching were practised. The Anglo-Saxon past was evident in Gospel books used in monasteries and cathedrals, as in the ancient stone crosses towering over churchyards. Common law treatises and Middle English literature convey unique insular traditions with a distinct iconography. The English example, however, was never detached from the wider European setting. The biographies of Stephen Langton (d. 1228) or the preacher Odo of Cheriton (d. 1246) tell of lives shared between England and the Continent. Similarly, liturgical chants were sung on both side of the Channel, with the most memorable element in insular Palm Sunday processions – the *Gloria, laus et decus* – written by Theodulf of Orléans (d. 821) and chanted, with minor variations, throughout Western Europe. Liturgical commentaries, canon law treatises, and model sermons written on the Continent were consulted in England, while English scribes made their living in France and Italy, and English Gospel books and Bibles were transported to the Continent, legally or illegally.[13] English and French biblical manuscripts are all but indistinguishable, a testimony to mass-production within an international book market. The English example is thus both unique and part of a wider phenomenon, rendering its study viable for contextualisation but also broadly significant.

The English example furnishes a snap-shot of society in a specific era and unearths the complex and dynamic qualities of biblical mediation. This book seeks to explore the mundane uses of the Bible, the daily contact with the divine in four instances: liturgical spectacles, talismanic uses, the layout of biblical manuscripts, and sermons. These instances weave a single narrative, which moves between antiquity and change, performance and material culture; liturgical rites are explored for their texts, as for their use of sacred books; innovative biblical manuscripts, intrinsically different from the sacred books of the liturgy, were tied with medieval sermons, the obverse of liturgical rites. The book thus begins with Palm Sunday, an important liturgical celebration, which provided an opportunity for many to integrate joy and participation into the biblical narrative. The second chapter continues to examine the Bible in liturgical spectacles, but in another manifestation. Not only text and narrative, Bibles were also sacred objects, employed in Masses and oath rituals (as well as making a brief appearance in the Palm Sunday procession itself). Many of these hallowed objects were ancient, venerated for their antiquity as well as for their appearance. Innovative forms of biblical manuscripts, however, emerged at the beginning of the thirteenth century. These mass-produced Bibles are examined in the third chapter for their carefully structured array of ink and scripts, rubrics and addenda, for their specific means of engaging with the biblical text. They were utilitarian objects, employed by trained professionals. The last chapter finds a prime audience of these manuscripts among late medieval preachers. Three Advent Sunday sermons demonstrate how the format of biblical manuscripts corresponded to the rise of the new form of preaching, and how a new facet of the Bible unfolded in these elaborate sermons to engage with biblical words and texts.

Liturgical rites and talismanic uses drew upon time-honoured traditions, while biblical manuscripts and preaching techniques introduced novel means of engaging with the biblical text. Such changes were not always accepted unquestionably, and already in the Middle Ages comments were made regarding the nature and authenticity of biblical mediation. The transformation of biblical manuscripts and sermons at the beginning of the period under investigation (explored at length in Chapters 3 and 4) incurred the opposition of some contemporaries, who saw in them the decay of biblical knowledge and dissemination. Writing in 1267, Roger Bacon criticised the inaccuracy of the new biblical manuscripts, placing the blame on the 'illiterate and wifely' stationers of Paris who produced many of them. He claimed that they had falsified the biblical text, relying on inferior specimens and disseminating them far and wide.[14] A century later another Oxford scholar, John Wyclif (d. 1384), claimed that the rhetoric of preachers' was a mere guise for pride and vainglory; employing Christ's Parable of the Sower (Lk 8:4–15) he enumerated their sins and accused them of preferring the style of the new form of preaching to the Word of God.[15]

Bacon and Wyclif saw recent innovations as drawing one away from the biblical truth. Such criticism has had an extremely long afterlife. It was practised by generations of scholars, who attached a moral undertone to biblical mediation, and hence marginalised late medieval biblical manuscripts and sermons. As part of the rise of textual criticism at the end of the nineteenth century, scholars of the medieval Bible have followed Bacon's quest for textual accuracy; involved in the creation of a critical edition of the Vulgate endorsed by the Vatican, they examined biblical manuscripts for signs of antiquity and textual authority.[16] Such studies elevated text over paratext, and the rare biblical manuscripts of the early Middle Ages at the expense of the multitude of late medieval ones. In the twentieth century, and especially in recent years, biblical paratext received growing attention, and the hundreds of Bibles from the later Middle Ages are now being explored without condescension.[17] The study of late medieval sermons follows a similar trajectory. A celebrated return to the ancient homiletic form of preaching in the Renaissance and the Reformation made the late medieval sermon an outdated specimen, often scolded by Reformers and researchers.[18] In recent years the derogatory view of late medieval preaching has been replaced by an understanding of sermons as an important part of medieval religious culture, a touchstone of interaction between laity and clergy, and, for my interests here, a vital channel of biblical transmission.[19]

The study of manuscript and sermons has traditionally been conducted diachronically and dominated by the search for origins. This tendency has been even stronger in studies of liturgy and the Bible. One of the most important works on Bible and liturgy took place against the background of the papal committees that paved the way for the reforms of the Second Vatican Council: Jean Daniélou's study moves between Late Antiquity and modern rituals to employ proximity to the Bible as way of assessing the antiquity of Catholic rite – thus putting aside medieval liturgy.[20] A similar approach has guided the editors of a recent article collection on liturgy and the Bible: the articles make invaluable contributions to the understanding of the way liturgy transformed the biblical text, from early Christian rites to their modern equivalents, but sadly omit the Middle Ages altogether.[21] The place of the Bible in medieval liturgy has been addressed in a few introductory essays, which have charted early medieval uses and identified the importance of performance to biblical mnemonics.[22] A notable exception is Evelyn Birge Vitz's exploration into liturgy and the Bible, which follows literary and liturgical accounts to argue for the appearance of biblical allusions in their liturgical guise.[23] The links between Bible and liturgy can extend beyond word and act into talismanic uses of Bibles, a facet which has rarely been explored in research. This meeting point of biblical paratext and liturgical rites has only recently been evoked in Richard Firth Green's study of Middle English literature and legal documents, as well as in a few articles which have challenged the distinction between Bibles and reliquaries and between books and icons.[24]

The current book concludes with an appreciation of biblical mediation at large. The four test cases demonstrate how discrete media functioned simultaneously. Liturgy and preaching are the two sides of the same coin, and their similarities and discrepancies are manifested in their use of the same biblical lesson (Mt 21:1–9, read on Palm Sunday and Advent Sunday alike). Both sermon and procession were occasions to employ the sacrality of biblical books, as Gospel books shed their authority on the liturgy and on priests in their subsequent sermons. Preachers made use of the unique features of biblical manuscripts in weaving their sermons, while talismanic uses of sacred books was a practice shared by priests and court officials alike. Discrete media corroborated one another in presenting an image of the Bible both challenging and appealing to the medieval populace; rituals, images, objects and texts converged in portraying biblical stories gowned in medieval attire. The study of biblical mediation challenges the lay–clerical divide and brings into question the Reformation emphasis on *sola scriptura*. The function of biblical mediation in a specific time and place thus sheds light on the wider historical context and explains, for instance, the survival rate of Anglo-Saxon Gospel books or how the layout of Late Medieval Bibles (see Chapter 3 for explanation of this term) weathered the advent of print and the Reformation. More importantly, this study attests to the importance of biblical mediation as a historical phenomenon, one which did not wither with the Middle Ages, but is rather an integral part of the link between societies and their sacred Scripture.

Notes

1 *Le Moyen Age et la Bible*, ed. Pierre Riché and Guy Lobrichon, Bible de tous les temps 4 (Paris, 1984); *The Cambridge History of the Bible: Vol. 2, The West from the Fathers to the Reformation*, ed. G. W. H. Lampe (Cambridge, 1969), supplanted by *The New Cambridge History of the Bible: Vol. 2, From 600 to 1450*, ed. Richard Marsden and E. Ann Matter (Cambridge, 2012); *The Practice of the Bible in the*

Middle Ages: Production, Reception, and Performance in Western Christianity, ed. Susan Boynton and Diane J. Reilly (New York, 2011); *Retelling the Bible: Literary, Historical, and Social Contexts*, ed. Lucie Doležalová and Tamás Visi (Frankfurt am Main, 2011). Addressing more specific points are: *The Early Medieval Bible: Its Production, Decoration and Use*, ed. Richard Gameson (Cambridge, 1994); *La Bibbia del XIII secolo. Storia del testo, storia dell'esegesi: Convegno della Società Internazionale per lo studio del Medioevo Latino (SISMEL) Firenze, 1–2 Giugno 2001*, ed. Giuseppe Cremascoli and Francesco Santi (Florence, 2004). (Of special interest is the introductory essay: Louis-Jacques Bataillon, 'La Bible au XIIIe siècle. Un incitation aux recherches de demain', pp. 3–11); *Form and Function in the Late Medieval Bible*, Library of the Written Word: The Manuscript World, ed. Eyal Poleg and Laura Light (Leiden, 2013).

2 On the link between preaching and exegesis: Beryl Smalley, *English Friars and Antiquity in the Early Fourteenth Century* (Oxford, 1960), pp. 28–44; Louis-Jacques Bataillon, 'Similitudines et exempla dans les sermons du XIIIe siècle', in *The Bible in the Medieval World: Essays in Memory of Beryl Smalley*, ed. Katherine Walsh and Diana Wood, Studies in Church History, Subsidia 4 (Oxford, 1985), pp. 191–205; Bataillon, 'De la lectio à la praedicatio. Commentaires bibliques et sermons au XIIIe siècle', *Revue des sciences philosophiques et théologiques* 70 (1986), 559–75; Bataillon, 'Early Scholastic and Mendicant Preaching as Exegesis of Scripture', in *Ad Litteram: Authoritative Texts and Their Medieval Readers*, ed. Mark D. Jordan and Kent Emery, Jr, Notre Dame Conferences in Medieval Studies 3 (Notre Dame, IN, 1992), pp. 165–98; Gilbert Dahan, *l'exégèse chrétienne de la Bible en Occident médiéval: XIIe–XIVe siècle*, Patrimoines christianisme (Paris, 1999), pp. 7–33. And to a lesser extent Marie Anne Mayeski, 'Reading the Word in a Eucharistic Context: The Shape and Methods of Early Medieval Exegesis', in *Medieval Liturgy: A Book of Essays*, ed. Lizette Larson-Miller (New York, 1997), pp. 61–84; Harry Caplan, 'The Four Senses of Scriptural Interpretation and the Mediaeval Theory of Preaching', *Speculum* 4 (1929), 282–90 (= *Of Eloquence: Studies in Ancient and Mediaeval Rhetoric*, ed. Anne King and Helen North, Ithaca and London, 1970, pp. 93–104); William J. Courtenay, 'The Bible in the Fourteenth Century: Some Observations', *Church History* 54:2 (1985), 176–87; Pim Valkenberg, 'Readers of Scripture and Hearers of the Word in the Mediaeval Church', in *The Bible and Its Readers*, ed. Wim Beuken, Sean Freyne, and Anton Weiler, *Concilium* 233:1 (London, 1991), pp. 47–57. For the Bible in medieval literature: Nicholas Perkins, 'Reading the Bible in Sawles Warde and Ancrene Wisse', *Medium Aevum* 72:2 (2003), 207–37; John A. Alford, 'Bible in Middle English Literature', in *Medieval England: An Encyclopedia*, ed. Paul E. Szarmach et al. (New York and London, 1998), pp. 126–8; David C. Fowler, *The Bible in Early English Literature* (Seattle, 1976) followed by Fowler, *The Bible in Middle English Literature* (Seattle, 1984); *A Dictionary of Biblical Tradition in English Literature*, gen. ed. David L. Jeffrey (Grand Rapids, MI, 1992); *The Bible in the Middle Ages: Its Influence on Literature and Art*, ed. Bernard S. Levy (Binghamton, NY, 1992).

3 Brian Stock, *The Implications of Literacy: Written Language and Models of Interpretation in the Eleventh and Twelfth Centuries* (Princeton, 1983), pp. 88–240.

4 There is now a growing corpus of works dedicated to *médiologie*, including a

journal – *Cahiers de médiologie*. An introduction to the concept is Régis Debray, *Transmettre* (Paris, 1997), translated as: *Transmitting Culture*, tr. Eric Rauth, European Perspectives (New York, 2000, with a comprehensive bibliography).

5 'To this day, for example, the Gospel's message makes its appeal to followers via canticles and holy days, the church's swell of organ notes and glitter of gold, the colours of its stained glass and altarpieces, the perfumes of its incense, the soaring spires of its cathedrals and shrines, the wafer's placement on the tongue and the foot's tread on the road to Calvary [...] rather than individual or group exegesis of sacred texts', Debray, *Transmettre*, p. 16 (and slightly revised in *Transmitting Culture*, p. 2). The reference to Cavalry – especially in its modern stone-encased re-creation – enhances rather than diminishes the importance of individual and communal exegesis.

6 For example: Miri Rubin, *Corpus Christi: The Eucharist in Late Medieval Culture* (Cambridge, 1991); Eamon Duffy, *The Stripping of the Altars: Traditional Religion in England c.1400–c.1580*, 2nd edn (New Haven and London, 2005).

7 Gérard Genette, *Paratexts: Thresholds of Interpretation* (orig. *Seuils*, Paris 1987), tr. Jane E. Lewin (Cambridge, 1997). Such an examination is in tune with the recent emphasis on 'new philology' and especially the significance of manuscript reception in the study of religious phenomenology (as in Eamon Duffy, *Marking the Hours: English People and Their Prayers 1240–1570* (New Haven and London, 2006)).

8 John Bale, *Illustrium maioris Britanniae, scriptorum, hoc est, Angliae, Cambriae, ac Scotiae summarium ...* (Wesel, 1548), fol. 102v, and in his footsteps Humphrey Hody, *De Bibliorum textibus originalibus, versionibus Græcis et Latina Vulgata libri IV* (Oxford, 1705), p. 430; P. Martin, 'Le texte Parisien de la Vulgate Latine', *Le Muséon* 8 (1889), 444–66; 9 (1890), 55–70, 301–16; Christopher de Hamel, *The Book: A History of the Bible* (London, 2001), p. ix.

9 Periods of change and stagnation in conjunction with the medieval Bible were suggested by: Smalley, *English Friars*, pp. 30–2; for the centrality of the early thirteenth century for the English church: W. A. Pantin, *The English Church in the Fourteenth Century, Based on the Birkbeck Lectures, 1948* (Cambridge, 1955), pp. 2–3.

10 Nigel J. Morgan, 'The Introduction of the Sarum Calendar into the Dioceses of England in the Thirteenth Century', in *Thirteenth Century England VIII*, ed. Michael Prestwich, Richard Britnell, and Robin Frame (Woodbridge, 2001), pp. 179–206. A more nuanced reading is: Richard W. Pfaff, *The Liturgy in Medieval England: A History* (Cambridge, 2009), pp. 365–87.

11 Mary Dove, *The First English Bible: The Text and Context of the Wycliffite Versions*, Cambridge Studies in Medieval Literature 66 (Cambridge, 2007); Eyal Poleg, 'Wycliffite Bibles as Orthodoxy', in *Instructing the Soul, Feeding the Spirit and Awakening the Passion. Cultures of Religious Reading in the Late Middle Ages*, ed. Sabrina Corbellini, Utrecht Studies in Medieval Literacy (Turnhout, 2013), pp. 71–91.

12 Christina von Nolcken, 'Lay Literacy, The Democratization of God's Laws and the Lollards', in *The Bible as Book: The Manuscript Tradition*, ed. John L. Sharpe III and Kimberly Van Kampen (London, 1998), pp. 177–95; Fiona Somerset, *Clerical Discourse and Lay Audience in Late Medieval England* (Cambridge, 1998); Kantik Ghosh, *The Wycliffite Heresy: Authority and the Interpretation of Texts* (Cambridge, 2001); Richard Marsden, 'Cain's Face, and Other Problems: The

Legacy of the Earliest English Bible Translations', *Reformation* 1 (1996), 29–51 (available on www.tyndale.org/Reformation/1/rmarsden.html, accessed 10 April 2012); and very prominently: David Daniell, *The Bible in English: Its History and Influence* (New Haven and London, 2003), ch. 4: 'Romance and Piety, 1066–1350', pp. 56–65. A notable exception is Margaret Deansely, *The Lollard Bible and Other Medieval Biblical Versions* (Cambridge, 1920, repr. 1966), whose discussion of pre-Wycliffite Bibles (pp. 156–224) sheds light on the Bible in its broadest definition.

13 For an example of a team of an English scribe and French illuminators working in thirteenth-century Italy: Richard H. and Mary A. Rouse, 'Wandering Scribes and Traveling Artists: Raulinus of Fremington and His Bolognese Bible', in *A Distinct Voice: Medieval Studies in Honor of Leonard E. Boyle, O.P.*, ed. Jacqueline Brown and William P. Stoneman (Notre Dame, IN, 1997), pp. 32–67. Gospel books taken to the Continent: Patrick McGurk and Jane Rosenthal, 'The Anglo-Saxon Gospelbooks of Judith, Countess of Flanders: Their Text, Make-Up and Function', *Anglo-Saxon England* 24 (1995), 251–308 (= Patrick McGurk, *Gospel Books and Early Latin Manuscripts*, Ashgate, 1998, §15); Books (including Bibles) stolen from Ely in 1332 and traced to Paris: Ernest A. Savage, *Old English Libraries: The Making, Collection, and Use of Books during the Middle Ages* (London, 1911), p. 86.

14 Roger Bacon, *Opus minus*, ed. John S. Brewer, RS 15 (London, 1859), p. 333; *Fratris Rogeri Bacon, ordinis minorum, Opus majus ad clementem quartum*, ed. Samuel Jeb (London, 1733), p. 49. For analysis: Laura Light, 'Roger Bacon and the Origin of the Paris Bible', *Revue bénédictine* 111 (2001), 483–507. Bacon's comment was recently evoked in a volume, whose subtitle was taken from the very same comment: Richard H. Rouse and Mary A. Rouse, *Manuscripts and Their Makers: Commercial Book Producers in Medieveal Paris, 1200–1500; Illiterati et uxorati*, 2 vols (Turnhout, 2000), i:32–3.

15 *Iohannis Wyclif Sermones: Now First Edited from the Manuscripts*, 4 vols, ed. Iohann Loserth (London, 1887–90), iv:256–62, 262–75 (Latin sermons §30, §31).

16 Samuel Berger, *De l'histoire de la Vulgate en France: Leçon d'ouverture faite à la Faculté de Théologie Protestante de Paris le 4 Novembre 1887* (Paris, 1887); *Histoire de la Vulgate pendant les premiers siècles du moyen âge* (Paris, 1893); Henry Quentin, *Mémoire sur l'établissement du texte de la Vulgate: 1ère partie Octateuque*, Collectanea Biblical Latina 6 (Rome and Paris, 1922).

17 Hans H. Glunz, *History of the Vulgate in England from Alcuin to Roger Bacon: Being an Inquiry into the Text of Some English Manuscripts of the Vulgate Gospels* (Cambridge, 1933, repr. 2010); Josephine Case Schnurman, 'Studies in the Medieval Book Trade from the Late Twelfth to the Middle of the Fourteenth Century with Special Reference to the Copying of Bibles' (B.Litt. Thesis, St Hilda's College, Oxford, 1960); Laura Light, 'Versions et révisions de texte biblique', in *Le Moyen Age et la Bible*, pp. 55–93; 'The New Thirteenth-Century Bible and the Challenge of Heresy', *Viator* 18 (1987), 275–88; 'French Bibles c. 1200–30: A New Look at the Origin of the Paris Bible', in *The Early Medieval Bible*, pp. 155–76; 'Roger Bacon'; Robert Branner, *Manuscript Painting in Paris during the Reign of St Louis: A Study of Styles* (Berkeley, 1977); Rosanna Miriello, 'La Bibbia portabile de origine italiana del XIII secolo. Brevi considerazioni e alcuni esempi', in *La Bibbia del XIII secolo*, pp. 47–77. These build upon the earlier work of: P. Martin,

'La Vulgate latine au treizième siècle d'après Roger Bacon', *Le Muséon* 7 (1888), 88–107, 169–96, 278–91, 381–93; 'Texte Parisien'. More recent is the collection *Form and Function in the Late Medieval Bible.*

18 John Hooper, 'A Declaration of the Ten Holy Commandments of Almighty God', in *Early Writings of John Hooper, D.D., Lord Bishop of Gloucester and Worcester, Martyr, 1555*, ed. Samuel Carr, Parker Society 11 (Cambridge, 1843), pp. 249–430 (325–6); G. R. Owst, *Literature and Pulpit in Medieval England: A Neglected Chapter in the History of English Letters and of the English People*, 2nd edn (Oxford, 1961), pp. 66–7. A more extreme criticism was adopted by: *Middle English Sermons Edited from British Museum MS. Royal 18B. xxiii.*, ed. Woodburn O. Ross, EETS OS 209 (London, 1940), p. l. The connection between Hooper and Owst was made by H. Leith Spencer, *English Preaching in the Late Middle Ages* (Oxford, 1993), ch. 8. 'The Sermons' Later History: A Postscript', pp. 321–34. On re-embracing the homiletic form in the Reformation: John W. Blench, *Preaching in England in the Late Fifteenth and Sixteenth Centuries: A Study of English Sermons 1450–c.1600* (Oxford, 1964), pp. 87–94.

19 Most prominently Nicole Bériou, *L'avènement des maîtres de la Parole: La prédication à Paris au XIIIe siècle*, 2 vols (Paris, 1998), ch. VII 'Communiquer la Parole de Dieu (1272–1273)', i:475–595.

20 Jean Daniélou, *The Bible and the Liturgy* (Notre Dame, IN, 1956, orig. *Bible et liturgie* (Paris, 1951)).

21 *Studia Liturgica* 22:1 (1992), and in particular: Paul De Clerck, '"In the Beginning was the Word": Presidential Address', 1–16; Klauss-Peter Jörns, 'Liturgy: Cradle of Scriptures?', 17–34; Paul F. Bradshaw, 'The Use of the Bible in Liturgy: Some Historical Perspectives', 35–52.

22 Pierre-Marie Gy, 'La Bible dans la liturgie au Moyen Age', in *Le Moyen Age et la Bible*, pp. 537–52; Susan Boynton, 'The Bible and the Liturgy', in *The Practice of the Bible in the Middle Ages*, pp. 10–33. I thank Susan Boynton for supplying me with an early version of the article. To a lesser extent: Mayeski, 'Reading the Word in a Eucharistic Context'; Evelyn Birge Vitz, 'The Liturgy and Vernacular Literature', in *The Liturgy of the Medieval Church*, ed. Thomas J. Heffernan and E. Ann Matter, 2nd edn (Kalamazoo, MA, 2005), pp. 503–63 (562–3); S. J. P. van Dijk, 'The Bible in Liturgical Use', in *The Cambridge History of the Bible: Vol. 2*, pp. 220–52.

23 'Liturgical Versus Biblical Citation in Medieval Vernacular Literature', in *Tributes to Jonathan J.G. Alexander: The Making and Meaning of Illuminated Medieval & Renaissance Manuscripts, Art & Architecture*, ed. Susan L'Engle and Gerald B. Guest (Turnhout, 2006), pp. 443–9.

24 Richard Firth Green, *A Crisis of Truth: Literature and Law in Ricardian England* (Philadelphia, 1999); Klaus Schreiner, 'Das Buch im Nacken: Bücher und Buchstaben als zeichenhafte Kommunikationsmedien in rituellen Handlungen der mittelalterlichen Kirche', in *Audiovisualität vor und nach Gutenberg: zur Kulturgeschichte der medialen Umbrüche*, ed. Horst Wenzel et al., Schriften des Kunsthistorischen Museums, Band 6 (Vienna, 2001), pp. 59–103; Jean Vezin, 'Les livres utilisés comme amulettes et comme reliques', in *Das Buch als Magisches und als Repräsentationsobjekt*, ed. Peter Ganz, Wolfenbütteler Mittelalter-Studien 5 (Wiesbaden, 1992), pp. 101–15.

1

The Bible and liturgy: Palm Sunday processions

Introduction

> And when they drew nigh to Jerusalem, and were come to Bethphage, unto mount Olivet, then Jesus sent two disciples; Saying to them: Go ye into the village that is over against you, and immediately you shall find an ass tied, and a colt with her: loose them and bring them to me. And if any man shall say anything to you, say ye, that the Lord hath need of them: and forthwith he will let them go. Now all this was done that it might be fulfilled which was spoken by the prophet, saying: Tell ye the daughter of Sion: Behold thy king cometh to thee, meek, and sitting upon an ass, and a colt the foal of her that is used to the yoke. And the disciples going, did as Jesus commanded them. And they brought the ass and the colt, and laid their garments upon them, and made him sit thereon. And a very great multitude spread their garments in the way: and others cut boughs from the trees, and strewed them in the way: And the multitudes that went before and that followed, cried, saying: Hosanna to the son of David: Blessed is he that cometh in the name of the Lord. (Mt 21:1–9)

The Gospel of Matthew was read during the Palm Sunday procession and served as the rationale for the day's liturgy. A comparison between the biblical narrative (with parallels in Mk 11:1–11; Lk 19:28–38; Jn 12:12–16) and its liturgical re-enactment, however, may result in a few raised eyebrows. If 'The liturgy was the primary context within which medieval Christians heard, read and understood the Bible',[1] then why are many of the liturgy's crowning moments nowhere to be found or marginalised in the biblical narrative; where are elements that defined the day in medieval England: the children and the palms, the ornate gates and the familiar hymns? These liturgical traits reveal a gap between the Bible and its re-creation; they appear, time and again, in visual images and literary narratives and attest to the way liturgy has shaped the knowledge of biblical events. This chapter traces the gap between Bible and liturgy through a close analysis of the liturgical event, to reveal how texts, locations, performances and objects brought the Bible to life while simultaneously subjecting it to the demands of faith and exegesis. Beyond the seamless unity of the liturgy, we can appreciate how the Gospel narrative was joined with other biblical episodes, as well as apocryphal or extra-biblical texts presented in biblical guise.

Palm Sunday provides a fertile ground for the study of biblical mediation. Located at the end of Lent and the beginning of Holy Week, it combined joy and sorrow, the unmasking of images and contemplation of the Passion. In the form of a procession, it brought the Bible into a local landscape and made parishioners into active participants in re-creating the Gospel narrative. Palm Sunday was widely depicted on church walls and lavish manuscripts; its texts reverberated in Middle English literature; and its performance was re-created in civic processions. What makes the day even more significant for the study of biblical mediation is the fact that this memorable biblical story does not lend itself easily to liturgical re-enactment. Liturgical processions were made to emulate Christ's reception at the outskirts of Second-Temple Jerusalem in the towns and villages of medieval Europe. Transforming the biblical event into a liturgical spectacle required a high degree of creativity and led to unexpected logistical problems, such as the need to procure palms in cold climates. The liturgy sustained ancient Hebrew words and Graeco-Roman rituals within the medieval world, long after the reasons for their existence had ceased to exist. Liturgical ingenuity preserved the peripatetic nature of the biblical event as a procession, and came up with solutions to problems of protagonists, location and emotional response, inherent in the Gospel narrative. This chapter follows the course of the Palm Sunday procession in late medieval England. It begins with its spatial dimension, then the liturgical paraphernalia are considered, as are the stations: the chants of the first station; the *Gloria laus* and its spectacle that follows; a para-liturgical moment in the speech of Caiphas at the third station; and the move into liturgical time in the fourth. The chapter ends with a model for the evolution of Bible and liturgy.

Palm Sunday was celebrated in variety of liturgical elaborations, from those performed in modest parish churches to those in wealthy cathedrals.[2] Recreating these requires use of a range of sources. Liturgical manuscripts, such as processionals, customaries, missals and breviaries, contain a wealth of information on the medieval ritual with its texts, tunes, and performance. Nevertheless, these manuscripts have two shortcomings.

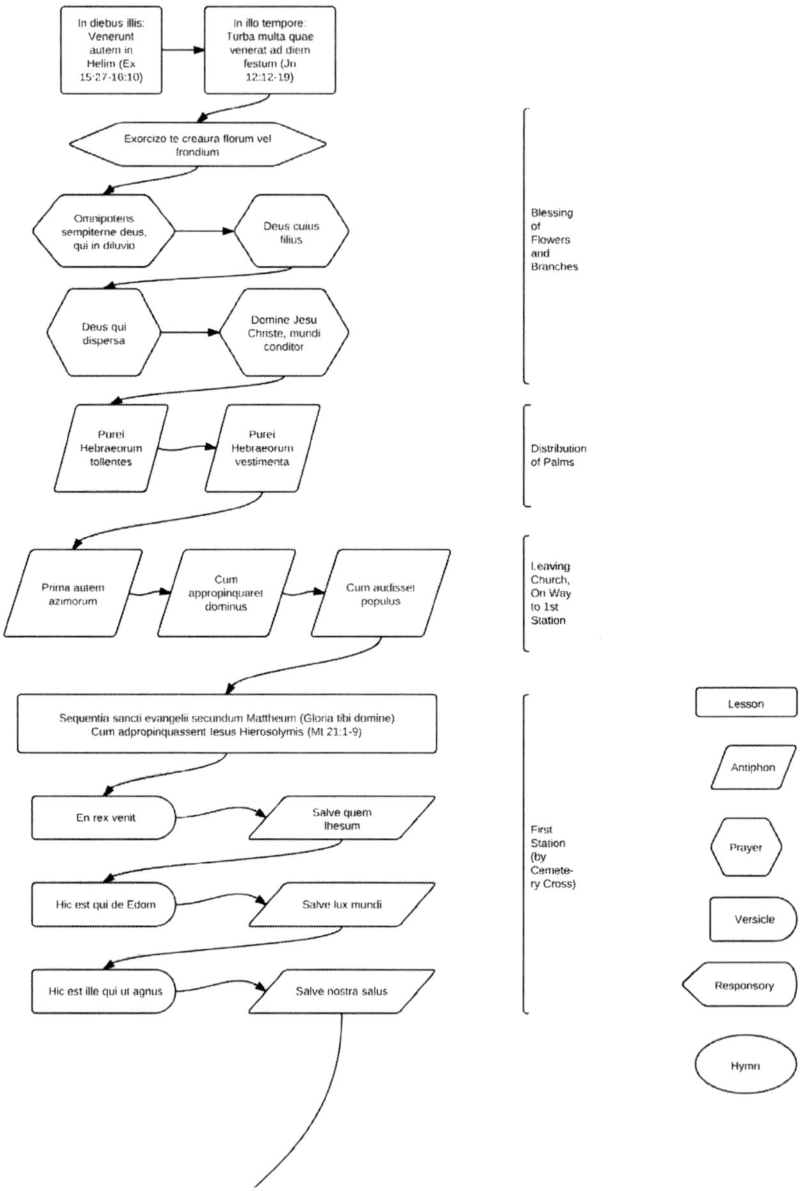

Figure 1 Palm Sunday procession according to the use of Sarum

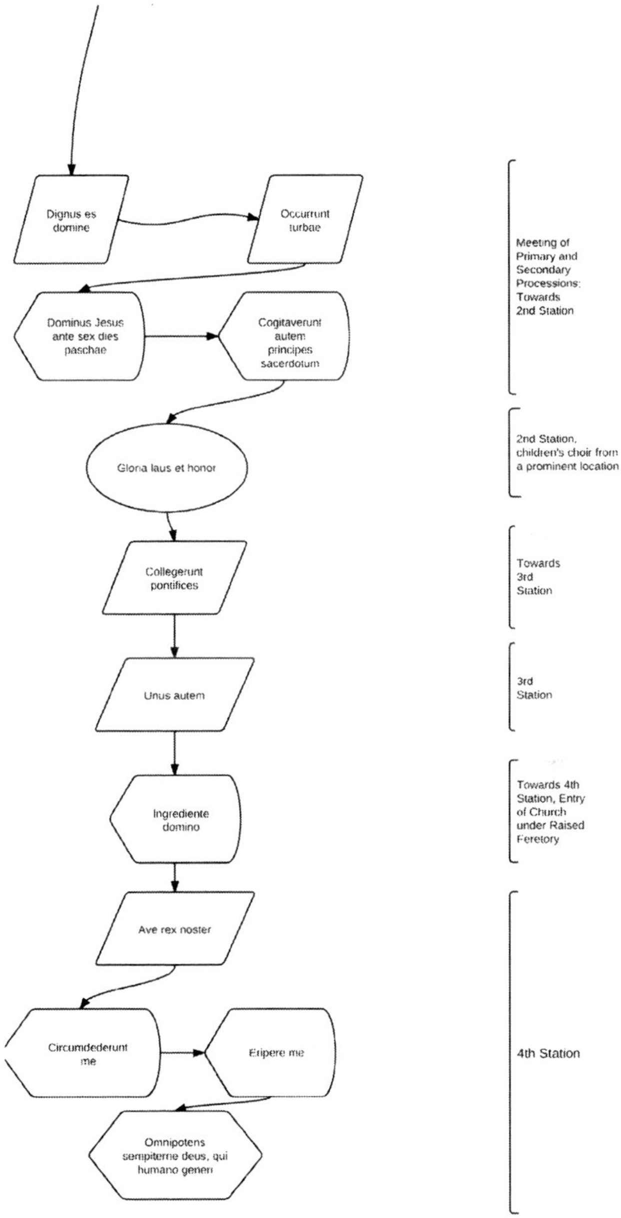
Dignus es domine
Occurrunt turbae
Dominus Jesus ante sex dies paschae
Cogitaverunt autem principes sacerdotum
Gloria laus et honor
Collegerunt pontifices
Unus autem
Ingrediente domino
Ave rex noster
Circumdederunt me
Eripere me
Omnipotens sempiterne deus, qui humano generi
Meeting of Primary and Secondary Processions: Towards 2nd Station
2nd Station, children's choir from a prominent location
Towards 3rd Station
3rd Station
Towards 4th Station, Entry of Church under Raised Feretory
4th Station

First, they usually describe the rituals of monasteries and cathedrals; only a handful of surviving manuscripts belonged to parish churches, and even these often portray a liturgy designed for a larger community. Rather than evidence of performance, these liturgical manuscripts witness attempts to impose hegemonic uses on local communities.[3] Secondly, the practicalities of the performance, from dress and actors to paraphernalia and locations, are discussed only briefly in rubrics that are few and far between. These manuscripts were commissioned by trained professionals for their peers, and much information regarding the practicalities of recurring rituals was taken for granted.

In order to provide a fuller picture of the day's liturgy, this analysis draws on a variety of sources both within and without the immediate remit of liturgical manuscripts. In illuminated manuscripts, church murals, literary narrative or chronicles, ample evidence exists for the liturgical celebration, often intertwined with a description of the biblical event itself. Beyond the simplicity of printed editions, the manuscript evidence is complex. It tells of local variations and bears witness to unfamiliar customs and hidden controversies, all of which help to trace the hidden facets of the medieval rite. This survey gives precedence to the use of Sarum, the liturgical rite performed in the Cathedral of Salisbury that became hegemonic in the later Middle Ages, while also addressing local uses and variations from religious houses in Norwich, Lincoln, York, Hereford, and Barking Abbey.[4] The overwhelmingly textual nature of the ritual described by the liturgical manuscripts should not divert one's attention from the performance of these texts. As argued by Tom Elich, the sensory qualities were key to the medieval liturgy.[5] In order to encompass the richness of this experience, the actors, gestures, locations and objects – whenever known – are portrayed. Similarly, the musical qualities of the text are examined, to demonstrate how these served to highlight specific components or preserve the integrity of a liturgical scene. The performative strata corroborate written texts to create a complex and challenging picture of the biblical event, which was presented to lay and clerical audiences alike.

Locating Palm Sunday

Attempts to follow the path of Christ and his followers raised an obvious question, where was one to commemorate Palm Sunday? Other biblical stories such as the Last Supper, Crucifixion, and Resurrection took place in identifiable locations: the places which came to be known as *Cenaculum*, *Golgotha*, or the Holy Sepulchre. Re-enactment within the confines of a church posed little difficulty. Yet, Palm Sunday took place on the road between the Mount of Olives and Jerusalem. This is not merely an unnamed location, but one outside the city of Jerusalem. The peripatetic nature of the event was modified already in the emerging liturgy of the early Christian Church. In late fourth-century Jerusalem, the Spanish pilgrim Egeria witnessed a liturgy that preserved the transitional essence of the day, and re-created the acts of Christ in the very places where he trod. Even this early liturgy tied the day's performance to sacred landmarks, which had more to do with the theology of the emergent religion than with the biblical narrative. The crowning moment of the day took place on the slopes of the Mount of Olives, where the biblical narrative was re-created in its original setting with hymns and the carrying of palms. Unlike the biblical story, the day began and ended within the city of Jerusalem, at the churches of the *Golgotha* and the Holy Sepulchre.[6] The joy of welcoming Christ was linked to the memory of his Passion, manifested for all to see in the places of the Crucifixion and Resurrection.

In medieval Europe a less literal route had to be employed in the re-creation of the biblical narrative. A sacred procession came to dominate the commemoration of the day, preserving the biblical narrative and wording (*procedere*, Jn 12:13), while introducing an array of fixed locations to ground the biblical event in the local landscape and to ease in its dissemination. This was a gradual transition. The Constitutions of Lanfranc (*c.* 1070), which introduced a new monastic liturgy to Canterbury and St Albans after the Norman Conquest, combined stationary and transitory elements by referring to the activity of 'statio facere' (making a station).[7] Later uses omit the accompanying verb, as stations became the places where the bulk of the liturgy was performed. Two types of processions emerged in post-Conquest England: one circled a church, and the other had entered through a city's gate. In Sarum, where the former prevailed, there were four stations: the graveyard cross, a prominent location for *Gloria laus*, the west door of the church, and in front of the rood. In Hereford and Lincoln, the procession went further afield, and the town's gate became the place of the second or third station. Some variations were permissible owing to church size or weather, and the York processional offers the option of leaving the city or staying near the church. The two variants shared more than their differences suggest. When the procession exited a city, it was often done nearby its main church, as in York or Lincoln, where the procession remained by the Minster, keeping mostly within the close.[8] Both variants preserved the outdoors element, emphasised the idea of entry (either to a city or church) and designated a raised platform for the chant of the *Gloria laus*.

In the common use of Sarum the first station took place at the cemetery found adjacent to churches or cathedrals. There the congregation assumed the role of the crowd of Jews awaiting the coming of Christ. The link between liturgy and landscape endowed the graveyard cross with a new meaning. The 1229 constitutions of William de Blois, Bishop of Worcester, refer to Palm Sunday procession in their discussion of cemeteries:

> De Coemeterio. Cap V.
> nulla pars coemeterii aedificiis occupata sit, nisi tempore hostilitatis. Crux decens et honesta, vel in ipso coemeterio erecta, ad quam fiet processio ipso die Palmarum, nisi in alio loco consuevit fieri.[9]

The graveyard cross was firmly linked to the celebration of Palm Sunday. When the dean of Sarum visited the chapel of St Nicholas in Earley, Berkshire, in 1224 he witnessed a Palm Sunday cross set to mark a plot of land in a (failed) attempt to make it into a cemetery.[10] Palm Crosses became an integral part of the liturgical landscape of medieval England. Such crosses, however, had existed long before the Norman Conquest and the introduction of the Palm Sunday procession of the high Middle Ages. Still present in churchyards throughout the British Isles, they tower over their surroundings and are carved with narrative scenes, marking the place of preaching and worship.[11] These sacred stone crosses did not originate with the post-Conquest liturgy, but were rather a remnant of its Anglo-Saxon past. They were incorporated into the route of the procession as a local interpretation for the meeting place of Christ and the welcoming crowd.

Palm Crosses served an important symbolic function. They grounded the biblical re-enactment in the landscape and provided a location both hallowed and familiar. At the next station, a marginal location in the Gospel narrative became central. Having met Christ by the Palm Cross, the combined entourage made its way to a city's gate or a church's west portal, where children sang the *Gloria laus* from above. Not mentioned in the Gospels, this location was nevertheless crucial for the performance of the day's liturgy. Liturgical manuscripts set it apart from other stations by noting its location: above the church's entry ('supra ostium ecclesiae') at York, on top of the city gates ('(portas civitatis) in quarum summitate') at Hereford, and in a very prominent location ('in loco eminentiori') according to the Sarum use, specified in Barking Abbey as above the church's entrance ('in eminentiori loco ultra ostium ecclesie'). The location was properly prepared. Lanfranc's Constitutions state clearly that the place of entry should be adorned with well-decorated hangings ('Locus vero super introitum portarum honeste debet esse paratus cortinis et dorsalibus').[12]

Such a cloth was offered at Lincoln as a gift, to be hung from the Bail Gate for the children's song of the *Gloria laus*.[13] Scholars have argued whether scaffolds were erected for the celebration of this moment in the liturgy. Beyond the brief references in liturgical manuscripts, there is little evidence and it appears that existing landmarks were adorned and employed for the children's song of the *Gloria laus*. The recent study of Carolyn Malone identifies a link between a back passage above the west portal at Wells Cathedral and the children's performance of the *Gloria laus*: sounded from behind the busts of angels, the children's song appeared to be emanating from the angelic choir itself, according to her reconstruction.[14]

The liturgical emphasis on the point of entry with its prominent, well-adorned location and memorable liturgy indicates an important phase in the evolution of Palm Sunday liturgy. In the Gospel narrative and in the emerging liturgy of late fourth-century Jerusalem, the point of entry was of little interest, standing in the shadow of the way from the Mount of Olives to Jerusalem. Yet, gradually and drawing from the subsequent episode of the children's song at the Temple (Mt 21:15–16), the moment of entry became the cornerstone of the day's liturgy. This transformation is evident in the iconography of Palm Sunday: earlier visual images, such as those found on fourth-century sarcophagi or in early medieval manuscripts, display gates in the margins, if at all. With time, however, the gates had moved centre stage, and elaborate structures appear in visual depictions of the biblical narrative. This is evident in images ranging from the late tenth-century benedictional of St Æthelwold to fourteenth-century church murals.[15] In a leaf from a Benedictine Psalter (Chertsey, (Surrey), *c.* 1220–30, Figure 2), the gate occupies a significant part of the drawing, with an open door, windows and crenellations. The actions of the figures follow the biblical narrative and its liturgical re-enactment: branches are waved, gowns cast down, and Christ is welcomed as these were spread on his way. The event takes place at the foot of the gate, reflecting the second station of the Sarum liturgy, rather than the biblical narrative.[16]

Images from parish churches portray similar scenes. Fourteenth-century Passion cycles in East Anglian church murals frequently show the entry into Jerusalem.[17] These images had a wider audience than illuminated manuscripts ever did. While cruder in style, they bear a striking resemblance to manuscript illuminations in their emphasis on the moment of entry and liturgical activities, portraying gates as central and elaborate structures. This is evident even in badly preserved murals, such as those at All Saints, Crostwight (Norfolk) and St Mary, West Somerton (Norfolk), in which one can still identify figures on two distinct planes, attesting to

Figure 2 Entry to Jerusalem, Cambridge, Emmanuel College MS 252, fol. 11v

a gate or raised platform that is no longer visible. At St Botolph, North Cove (Suffolk, Figure 3), the two most prominent features are the gate and Christ the rider, connected visually by the garments spread on the road. Above the gate two figures spread their arms in salutation while the central figure hangs a cloth from the top of the gate – much like the evidence from Lincoln Cathedral. The present state of the mural does not allow further deductions, but in a similar image from late-fifteenth century stained glass windows at St Mary, Fairford (Gloucestershire), the cloth is replaced with a scroll, containing the words and notation for the *Gloria laus*.[18] In St Mary, Fairstead (Essex, Figure 4), the artist had to accommodate the image into the uppermost register of the chancel arch. Forced to depict only the essential components of the scene, he portrayed Christ the rider and a gate with its distinct crenellations.

The increasing importance of the moment of entry in liturgy and iconography had a significant moral undertone that followed a biblical link between gates and justice. Psalm 117, which reverberated in the Gospel crowd's exclamations of hosannas and *benedictus qui venit*, refers to the Temple gates within a liturgical and moral context: 'Open ye to me the gates of justice: I will go in to them, and give praise to the Lord. This is the gate of the Lord, the just shall enter into it' (vv. 19–20). For priests, well-versed in the Psalms, gates had a meaning beyond the practicalities of Christ's entry into Jerusalem. They endowed their own entry with meaning. Besides entering the earthly Jerusalem, in a re-enactment of the

Figure 3 Entry to Jerusalem, St Botolph, North Cove (Suffolk)

Gospel story, this was also a move towards Heavenly Jerusalem, in whose image churches were constructed and to which believers aspired. Such an understanding was made visible in the iconographical scheme of Wells Cathedral, where angels welcomed the believers from above. It was also apparent in the liturgical commentaries of John Beleth (d. after 1165) and William Durand (d. 1296), both likening Christ's entry to Jerusalem to the Israelites' transition from the wilderness into the Promised Land. Both also provided a tropological (i.e. moral) interpretation for Christ's entry, seen as the progression of the righteous soul.[19] The performance of the liturgy presented this understanding for lay and clerical audiences alike: as the procession left the cemetery to re-enter the church (or the town's gate) it moved from an uninhabited and liminal terrain – a cemetery or the edges of a medieval town – and into a religious centre, experiencing through the landscape the complex allegory of liturgical commentaries.[20]

Palms and consecrated hosts: the matter of Palm Sunday

Palm Sunday liturgy endowed the landscape with new meaning, employing existing monuments and transforming the biblical event. It also drew an array of sacred and mundane objects, from palms and branches to relics and Gospel books, into its ambit. The importance of liturgical paraphernalia to the day is attested in its name – Palm Sunday (*Dominica in ramis palmarum* / *Dies palmarum*) – and in the way symbolic objects were used. Early in the day, before the departure of the procession, palms and flowers were blessed by the clergy and distributed to participants. Following two biblical lessons (i.e. readings), in which a brief reference is made to palms (Ex 15:27–16:10, Jn 12:12–19), the words of the benediction departed from the biblical narrative. Presenting a tropological understanding of the procession, they removed all traces of the devil from the branches, thus enabling their use in the liturgy. As made clear by Durand, these palms and branches were active in the struggle against evil, a sign of victory over the devil.[21] This view explains the custom of keeping blessed palms after the procession. When layfolk employed palms and branches as talismans, they were not breaking with the liturgy. Rather, they followed its words and acts in keeping a souvenir of the biblical re-enactment, an amulet against the devil and an aid in their spiritual progression, ascribed by liturgical commentators.

Blessed palms were distributed by the clergy with the chanting of two antiphons, common in insular and Continental uses alike:

> Pueri Hebraeorum tollentes ramos olivarum, obviaverunt domino clamantes: Osanna in excelsis;
> Pueri Hebraeorum vestimenta prosternebant in via et clamabant dicentes: Osanna filio David; Benedictus qui venit in nomine domini[22]

While palms are mentioned briefly in the Gospel of John, the antiphons introduce a scene foreign to the biblical narrative. They draw on a subsequent episode in Matthew to connect Christ's entry with children. While children appear in the words of the chant, it was actually the clergy who were responsible for the distribution of palms and branches in churches. The children still left a strong mark on visual images of the biblical event: Italian images portray children as actively plucking and distributing palms to parishioners with outstretched arms, an amalgam of church ritual and imagined biblical narrative.[23] The liturgical performance even influenced the sacred geography of Jerusalem itself: the twelfth-century account of the Holy Land by Peter the Deacon (of Monte Cassino, d. *c.* 1140) identifies a tree in the valley of Jehosafat from where the children had taken palms, crying hosanna, in a scene that follows the liturgical re-enactment of the Gospel narrative, but is nowhere to be found among its pages.[24]

Palms were mentioned in chants, antiphons and the biblical lessons that preceded their distribution. They were not, however, easily found in late medieval England. 'Real' palms (of the *Palmae* family) were certainly imported at the time, as trade enabled a limited influx of palms from the East. The Middle English term for a pilgrim returning from the Holy Land – a *Palmer* – identifies one such carrier, and bears witness to the sacred value of the plant. The limited supply of palms, however, could not provide all the day's needs. Lanfranc's Constitutions specify that sacrists were to give palms to the abbot, prior and dignitaries, and other branches to everyone else. At St Mary's, York, a more generous distribution ensued: all brothers, together with the prior and abbot, were given palms by the sacrist, while servants distributed branches to the crowd.[25] The social tension embedded into the distribution of palms is reflected in a breviary from Chertsey Abbey, Surrey (Plate 1), where the Apostle carries a real palm, while other participants touch indigenous branches. Ever-reflective, Durand commented upon the various qualities of branches and palms, connecting the latter to giving oneself to acts of peace and mercy, as well as being furnished with vigour, and the former to the struggle against the devil.[26]

How did parishioners refer to the branches they carried? A Middle English speech from the end of the thirteenth century sheds lights on popular attitudes towards these liturgical paraphernalia. It quotes Durand in the Latin and then expounds upon it in Middle English. While the Latin section preserves Durand's differentiation, its vernacular rendering groups all types of branches under the category of palms, and asks the laity to wave them in sign of victory over the devil.[27] This suggests that indigenous branches were therefore used as palms on Palm Sunday and is corroborated by other evidence. Yew and willow (with its catkins) became most popular among the laity, an insular alternative to the biblical plant. They have been used in the liturgy and known as palms for centuries. In the nineteenth century, long after trade had provided for a regular import of 'real' palms, indigenous branches were still being sold at Covent Garden as palms for the celebration of Palm Sunday.[28]

While real or 'indigenous' palms were being distributed, a different array of liturgical paraphernalia was also put into play. In order to re-enact the biblical drama, the waiting crowd had to meet Christ at the first station. Parishioners took the place of that biblical crowd, constituting the primary procession of the day. A secondary procession, however, stood in for Christ and the Apostles: a small group of clerics carrying an array of liturgical paraphernalia. The secondary procession carried cross and relics, gospel books, and a consecrated host, as representatives of Christ: the gospel book contained the narrative of his life and death; it was also, as examined in the following chapter, employed as talisman in civic and ecclesiastical rites; the cross reminded of the looming Passion; and the relics were a manifestation of Christ's legacy and his actions in the world (a sequence similar to that preceding the gospel lessons in the ordinary of the Mass, explored in the next chapter as well). In Germany a very literal depiction of the biblical event took the form of a *Palmesel*, a life-size sculpture of Christ riding the ass, mounted on a wheeled platform. However, as argued by Eamon Duffy, the unique insular custom of the consecrated host elevated the liturgical drama to new heights, surpassing even the German example in its realism. While all the other devices represented Christ and his legacy, the host was Christ in the flesh.[29] Meeting Christ at the first station thus extended beyond a mere liturgical representation of the biblical scene to an event akin to the biblical narrative itself, meeting Christ in person.

We know little of liturgical paraphernalia employed in the remaining parts of the procession. Beyond the injunction that the secondary procession carries the sacred objects, our sources remain mostly silent. One notable exception is to be found in two Sarum processionals, which digress from a description of the first station to address the cross used in the secondary procession:

> Nota quod ad nullam crucem imponunt flores vel frondes in die palmarum apud sarum, ne videantur parare crucem. Sed nam si ista crucis adoratio post passionem lectam esset facta, videretur satis congrue fieri [...] Et si aliquis opponendo dicat quare adoramus denudatam crucem in introitu ecclesie ante passionem lectam, respondendum est quod non crucem sed ipsum crucifixum adoramus, quod evidentur per antiphonam 'Ave rex noster'.[30]

The desire to adorn the cross with flowers emanated from the very essence of Palm Sunday. The joy of welcoming Christ was manifested in the activities of laity and clergy, in the ample use of branches, flowers, and 'singing cakes' (addressed below). The processionals' discussion of liturgical paraphernalia exemplifies the inherent tension of the day. The biblical joy of welcoming Christ (as in Lk 19:37) was understood to stand in the shadow of his Passion and Resurrection. The adoration of the cross was to be done in anticipation of the Passion at the end of the procession, rather than at its beginning, where it would have served as a manifestation for the jubilation in meeting Christ. Much like the route of the fourth-century procession, meeting Christ was subjected to future events in the

Gospels. This tension, however, was not eradicated. A sermon preached at Newcastle on Palm Sunday 1435 expanded upon Proverbs 14:13a ('Laughter shall be mingled with sorrow'), exemplifying the bipolarity of the day.[31] Liturgical paraphernalia thus added a dynamic quality to the Palm Sunday procession. They shaped the experience of clergy and laity and added a new level of realism to the biblical re-enactment. Much like the construction of sacred space in the course of the procession, the delicate undertones of liturgical paraphernalia conveyed social and theological meanings.

Quasi-biblical language at the first station

The layout of liturgical manuscripts presents a specific view of the link between Scripture and liturgy. Beyond clearly demarcated biblical lessons, there is no differentiation between biblical and extra-biblical language; no change in colour or hand, illustrations or rubrication mark biblical quotations and allusions. Nor did liturgical performance distinguish, in gestures or melodies, between biblical and non-biblical components, biblical lessons notwithstanding. As a result, one cannot easily tell apart a purely biblical text, modifications of a biblical text, or an autonomous composition. Such a confusion was not unique to the medieval experience. Modern editors of liturgical texts (medieval and modern alike) have refrained from tracing and identifying all biblical allusions and paraphrases apart from placing direct quotations in italics. The task of identifying each and every biblical allusion would inevitably complicate the structure of editions almost beyond usefulness; it would also go against the grain of liturgical texts. Any distinction between biblical language and later additions seems artificial in a liturgical setting. A detailed analysis of liturgical texts from the first station and their performance even suggests that a conscious act of blurring the two was at play.

Three antiphons and three versicles (two types of short sentences sung antiphonally) constitute the backbone of the first station. As the entire congregation awaited by the Palm Cross, these antiphons and versicles bridged the gap between the Gospel lesson (Mt 21:1–9) and the arrival of Christ and the Apostles in the secondary procession. They unfolded as two parallel monologues, with each versicle followed by an antiphon (creating the sequence of Versicle 1, Antiphon 1, V2, A2, V3 and A3). The analysis of text, music, and performance reveals that each group of antiphons or versicles was distinct and portrayed a strong cohesion: all versicles were sung by three clerks of the second rank (such as presbyters) dressed in their choir

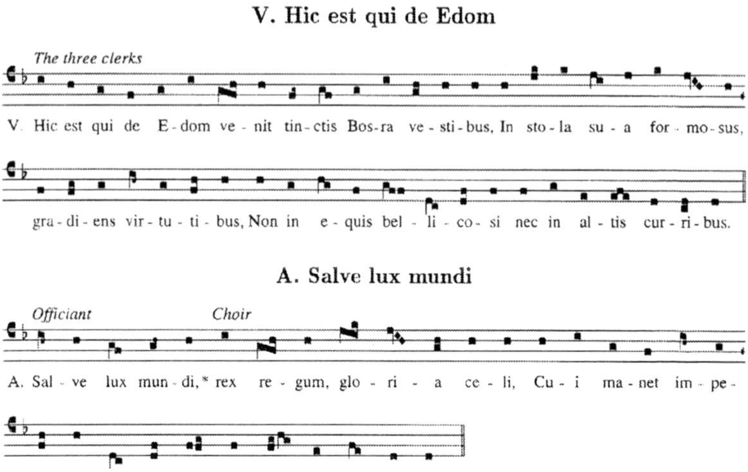

Example 1 *Hic est qui de Edom* (Versicle) and *Salve lux mundi* (Antiphon)

habits; they were chanted around the note D (the Dorian mode)[32] with the pitch specified as B flat; the two latter versicles shared the opening words of *hic est.* All antiphons, on the other hand, began with *salve*, chanted by the officiant who also carried the second word and then picked up by the choir; all antiphons began on B flat, descended to F and rose up again, with the choir picking up either at B flat or at the C above it (Example 1 – a modern rendering of the medieval notation of the second antiphon and versicle).[33]

Musical and performative unity was complemented by content. While all antiphons shared a common theme of praise and petition (echoing the exclamations of the Gospel crowd), the versicles depicted key moments in salvation history, from Christ's entry to Jerusalem through the Passion to the Harrowing of Hell, moving the liturgical plot forward. In order to distinguish between biblical and liturgical elements I highlight (in bold print) the words shared by both liturgy and Bible.

> **V1.** En **rex venit mansuetus tibi Syon filia** mistica humilis **sedens super** animalia quem venturum iam predixit lectio **prophetica**.[34]

The Gospel lesson of Matthew (21:1–9) had just ended, but its words still echoed in the first versicle of the station. A comparison with Mt 21:5 ('Hoc autem factum est ut impleretur quod dictum est per **prophetam** dicentem; Dicite **filiae Sion**: Ecce **rex** tuus **venit tibi mansuetus**, et **sedens super** asinam et pullum filium subiugalis')[35] reveals a clear reiteration of the biblical text. The choice of this specific verse was not accidental.

As demonstrated by modern biblical scholars, it is the axis of the entire biblical narrative and its reiteration of the Old Testament prophecy of Zechariah supplies Christ's entry with its rationale.[36] The wording of the versicle preserves the central sense of Scripture – Christ's entry as a fulfilment of prophecy – through a repetition of key words such as *prophetica*, *Syon*, and *rex venit*. The versicle's words extend beyond associating two biblical stories. They link Zechariah's prophecy to the performance of the liturgy itself. The term *lectio* (*lesson*) appears in the versicle and not in the original Gospel narrative. It alludes to the prophetical lesson of Zechariah but also to the liturgical lesson that had just ended. The connection between liturgy and Bible was rendered similar to that between individual biblical components: just as Matthew's Gospel relied on the Zechariah, so did the versicle rely on the Matthew's Gospel in presenting a key moment in biblical history.

> **A1.** Salve, quem Ihesum testatur plebs hebreorum, obvia cum palmis tibi clamans verba salutis.[37]

This antiphon, much like the other antiphons of the station, does not follow closely any biblical narrative, but conveys the gist of the biblical event and its liturgical re-enactment. Rather than narrating a biblical event, this antiphon offered congregants the opportunity to become part of that very same narrative, to assume the mantle of the biblical crowd. The actor of the antiphon is the Jewish crowd, in whose place now stood the primary procession and the clerks chanting the antiphon. It refers to the palms, carried and waved at that very moment, and to the chanting words of salutation – the very same words of salutation that comprise this antiphon and underpinned the liturgical performance. The use of the present tense and of the second person further indicates the immediacy of the liturgical performance.

The next versicle diverges from the Gospel narrative to present an important biblical allusion. Its first half follows the biblical text closely, but later digresses from it in favour of the imagery of Palm Sunday:

> **V2.** Hic **est qui de Edom venit tinctis bosra vestibus in stola sua formosus gradiens** virtutibus non in equis bellicosis nec in altis curribus.[38]

This versicle relies heavily on the prophecy of Isaiah, whose beginning it shares: 'Quis **est** iste, **qui venit de Edom, tinctis vestibus** de **Bosra**? Iste **formosus in stola sua, gradiens** in multitudine fortitudinis sue? Ego qui loquor justitiam, et propugnator sum ad salvandum' (Is 63:1).[39] Minor alterations simplify the biblical text while retaining its unique characteristics:

the rhetorical question implied in Isaiah's *quis* is altered to *hic*, thereby avoiding the suggestion of dialogue; the preposition *de* before *Bosra* is removed, following the incomprehensibility of the Hebrew term to most clerical and lay audiences. The second part of the versicle extends beyond Isaiah's prophecy to describe the simplicity of God, who uses neither horses nor carriages. This corresponds to the singularity of God's acts in the same chapter of Isaiah (e.g. Is 63:3, 5), and to the biblical trope of defining God apophatically, frequent among Christian mystics.[40]

The modification of the biblical text suppresses much of Isaiah's messianic and apocalyptic tone. It follows Zechariah's original prophecy in contrasting the images of horse and carriage with Christ riding the ass, drawing attention to his divine humility and paving the way for later parts of the liturgy (primarily the concluding prayer of the Sarum use *Omnipotens sempiterne deus*, which addressed Christ's humility in the Incarnation and Crucifixion). A residue of Isaiah's apocalypticism remains in the adjective *tinctis*, whose original meaning of blood-saturated clothes is lost in the new context. The versicle's distinct vocabulary (*Edom*, *tinctis*, *Bosra*, etc.) enabled only a well-versed audience to appreciate the link between blood-stained garments and the Passion. Exegetes placed Isaiah's question in the mouth of an angel, who marvelled at Christ's appearance upon his return to Heaven in the garments of his Passion, a link evident in numerous visual images and in a Middle English commentary from *c.* 1400, which presents vividly the dialogue between Christ and the angel.[41]

> **A2**. Salve **lux mundi**, **rex regum** gloria **celi** cui manet **imperium** laus et decus hic et in evum.[42]

Just like the previous antiphon, this does not follow any biblical text closely, but rather constitutes an amalgam of common biblical attributes to the divinity ('Ego sum **lux mundi**' (Jn 8:12); 'Tu **rex regum** es: et Deus **celi** regnum, et fortitudinem, et **imperium**, et gloriam dedit tibi' (Dn 2:37)).[43] By combining God's praises with a move to the second person, this antiphon expands upon the *verba salutis* (*words of salutation*) of the previous antiphon, once more placing the choir alongside the biblical crowd in their praises of Christ. A close examination of the antiphon's wording reveals that it does not only allude to the Bible. The reference to *laus et decus* echoes the memorable hymn *Gloria, laus et decus* which was chanted in the second station. One of the crowning moments of the procession, this hymn was familiar to lay and clerical members alike. By referring to a later moment in the liturgy, the antiphon weaves a web of allusion beyond the Bible, creating a delicate array of internal references, which serve to link

Bible and liturgy, text and performance.

> **V3**. Hic est ille qui ut **agnus** insons morti traditur mors mortis inferni morsus morte donans vivere ut quondam beati vates promiserunt prophetice.[44]

As the versicle opens with *hic est* and concludes with *prophetice*, its wording closely follows the previous versicle. A new tune, however, indicates a radical transformation of content. Breaking with all previous antiphons and versicles, it begins with a melisma (a group of notes sung to a single syllable) and retains a less syllabic tone throughout. This modification serves to emphasise the introduction of a new theme, moving away from the Gospel narrative with its words of salutations and into the proximity of death. The word death (*mors*) appears four times within this short versicle, in which Christ is described as the innocent lamb which had dealt death a deadly blow. This understanding alludes to the Gospel of John (1:29, '[…] ecce **agnus** Dei qui tollit peccatum mundi') and its prophecy of Christ's redeeming death, most evident in the words of Caiphas (Jn 11:49–52) which reverberated in the antiphon *Unus autem* of the third station.[45]

Such allusions do not mask the fact that the picture evoked in the versicle does not exist in any of the Canonical Gospels. Rather, it follows the Harrowing of Hell from the apocryphal Gospel of Nicodemus. That story, ubiquitous in medieval imagery, drama, literature, and sermons, portrays how by dying Christ had deceived Death and enabled the salvation of all the faithful.[46] This short versicle thus ties seamlessly biblical and liturgical allusions with a reference to a well-known apocryphal story. The allusion to the Harrowing of Hell extended beyond words to the time and place of the procession: Palm Sunday marked the beginning of Holy Week, at whose end, between Passion and Resurrection, the Harrowing took place; in a custom, documented from the fifteenth century, a priest knocked on the door of the church with the processional cross in imitation of Christ's knock on Hell's gates.[47] The centrality of death, moreover, was never far away from this moment in the liturgy: standing by the stone cross in the middle of the cemetery, the surrounding tombstones complemented the repetition of *mors* in the versicle.

> **A3**. Salve nostra salus. Pax vera redemptio virtus ultro qui mortis pro nobis iura subisti.[48]

The concluding antiphon serves as a coda to the entire unit. It combines elements from previous antiphons and versicles: beginning with the *salve*, typical of all three antiphons, it likewise incorporates supplicatory elements; its redemptive theme brings to mind previous antiphons and versicles, while the reference to Christ's redeeming death closely follows the previous versicle and the Harrowing of Hell.

The antiphons and versicles of the first station extend beyond the Gospel narrative to provide an array of biblical, liturgical and apocryphal allusions from Isaiah, Daniel, and the Gospel of John, from the day's liturgy, and from the Gospel of Nicodemus. The merging of biblical and other elements is accomplished seamlessly, making the liturgy an extension of the Bible rather than a separate entity.[49] Beginning with a clear reiteration of the Gospel lesson performed just moments earlier, biblical themes and echoes were carried throughout the station. The use of tense and person, the rendering of the liturgy as part of the biblical narrative (as in the 'words of salutations' of the antiphons) and the expansion of biblical themes (such as divine humility and redeeming death) beyond the liturgy, made Bible and liturgy the same, and shed the authority of the Bible on its liturgical re-enactment. This constitutes the creation of a 'quasi biblical' language, an attempt to emulate biblical text and language in the creation of liturgical narratives. Beyond individual components, such a move is evident in the structure of the station as a whole: beginning in a clear reiteration of the Gospel lesson (V1), evolving through a close reliance on other biblical narratives (A1, V2, A2) to introduce a new idea in self-standing liturgical texts (V3, A3).[50]

In the first station text and performance complemented one another. The location of the first station supplied a crucial interpretative layer to the liturgical performance, one which expanded on the same complex array of versicles and antiphons to create a unique, non-textual exegesis of the Gospel narrative. We cannot assume the audience's familiarity with all chanted texts, and the immediate associations invoked by 'Hic est qui de Edom venit' would have evaded even some clerical audiences. However, these texts were performed just before the arrival of the secondary procession; they were sung by the primary procession as it represented the crowd of Jews awaiting the arrival of Christ. The congregation stood by the Palm Cross in the churchyard, where it was joined by the dead in their graves, awaiting Christ who was to raise them from their tombs. At this moment, past, present, and future merged into a singular liturgical reality: in the past – the procession re-enacted a biblical scene from the life of Christ; in the present – it awaited Christ's immanent arrival with the host and the secondary procession; in an eschatological future – it anticipated the Second Coming, surrounded by graves.[51]

Gloria, laus et honor and an imagined entry scene

Christ's arrival marked the end of the first station. Anticipation subsided as the crowd joined the secondary procession to make its way to the second station, re-enacting the Gospel procession towards Jerusalem. The joy of the crowd, welcoming Christ into its midst in the words of Luke (*gaudentes*, 19:37) became a clear tone for the liturgy. Characterised by a prominent location, memorable performance and a popular hymn – the *Gloria, laus et honor* – this station was the emblem of Palm Sunday processions. The *Gloria laus* was chanted throughout Europe and became the cornerstone of many Continental and insular performances of Palm Sunday. Its origins assisted in establishing its authority: medieval accounts such as Durand's liturgical commentaries and the *Golden Legend* tell how Theodulf of Orléans (d. 821) heard the Palm Sunday procession from his cell, during his imprisonment by Louis the Pious. He composed the *Gloria laus* on the spot, and the hymn had led to his release from prison and restoration to his episcopal see.[52]

The hymn constitutes a unique quasi-biblical creation, whose subtle dialogue with biblical language, text, and genre rendered it memorable and authoritative. It takes its name from its opening line, which serves as the refrain:

> Gloria laus et honor tibi sit rex christe redemptor
> cui puerile decus prompsit osanna pium.[53]

Luke's Gospel, with its description of the crowd's proclamation 'pax in caelo, et gloria in excelsis' ('peace in Heaven, and glory on high'), helps contextualise this hymn within the Gospel scene. Much like the antiphons of the previous station, this hymn incorporates biblical words of salutations into a re-enactment of the biblical event. As well as the Gospels, its wording follows closely the Psalms, and especially Ps 65:2 'Cantate gloriam nomini eius date gloriam laudi eius' ('Sing ye a psalm to his name; give glory to his praise'). Much like the lesser and greater doxologies (*Gloria patri* and *Gloria in excelsis*, two of the most common hymns of praise), this hymn appears at first glance or in cursory hearing to be taken verbatim from the Bible. However, it has no roots in any specific biblical text, nor does it amount to a clear biblical quotation or allusion. It incorporates key biblical words, such as *Gloria*, *laus*, *honor* and *hosanna*, to emulate the biblical genre, creating a quasi-biblical appeal, combining the use of the second person with a reference to the (imagined) biblical narrative of Palm Sunday.

The refrain alludes to the performance of the hymn itself through the activities of children and choir. Children had been seen as active in the liturgy of the day from the distribution of palms. In the *Gloria laus* their performance became the quintessence of the liturgy: the hymn took the form of a dialogue between children singing from a prominent location and an adult choir located below. The children's high voices, engaged in songs of praise, reflected the song of the angels from above. The male choir, its basses answering from below, represented mortals praising God on earth. This was evident in act and word, as the third stanza made clear:

> Coetus in excelsis te laudat coelitus omnis,
> et mortalis homo et cuncta creata simul.[54]

The performative allusion to the song of the angels explains the emphasis on a well-adorned and prominent location for the performance of the *Gloria laus*, ascribed time and again in liturgical manuscripts and expanded in Wells Cathedral to emulate the angelic choir.[55]

The children's song strengthened the link between liturgy and Bible, while simultaneously drawing it away from the Gospel narrative. It follows the subsequent episode in Matthew, in which children welcomed Christ with 'hosanna to the son of David' in the Temple (Mt 21:15). This episode, however, took place only after Christ's arrival at Jerusalem; separated from Christ's arrival by the events in the Temple and Jesus's rebuke of the money-changers, it was not an integral part of the events of Palm Sunday as narrated in the four Gospels. Children, nevertheless, became an inseparable part of the day's liturgy, appearing as early as Egeria's fourth-century account. This performative trait solved an inherent difficulty in the biblical text. The biblical welcoming crowd was composed of Jews, either the citizens of Jerusalem or Passover pilgrims, whose exact identity remains unknown. The crowd – the true protagonist of the event – was inconveniently similar to another Jewish crowd that had answered Pilate on the following Friday by rallying against Christ and asking for his crucifixion (Mt 27:11–26 and parallels). This episode was read in a dramatic fashion on Palm Sunday Mass (following the procession) and supported the medieval identification of Jews as killers of Christ.[56] The problem of reconciling the two Jewish crowds – the one celebrating in Christ's messianic role and the other rejecting him and responsible for deicide – necessitated a means of differentiating the two crowds, and led to the identification of the former with the children. Durand's liturgical commentaries make this move explicit by delineating a boundary between Jews and children: 'Vel deum corde et ore pueri laudabant, sicut iudei corde et ore conviciabant'.[57] Despite the logical flaw of this solution (as Jews placed the blame on themselves *and* their children (Mt 27:25 and parallels)), the image of children dominated the liturgical performance of the *Gloria laus* and influenced the medieval understanding of the biblical event.

A historiated initial D from the breviary of Chertsey Abbey, Surrey (Plate 1), links the biblical event with its liturgical re-enactment – the children's song of *Gloria laus*.[58] Christ's gaze and outstretched hand gesture at a figure at the top of the gate. Unlike all other participants, from the palm-carrying Apostle to the crowd spreading cloth on the road, the elevated figure is beardless. It reminds viewers of the role of children in the day's liturgy and in particular of the chanting of *Gloria laus* from a raised platform. This image reflects the performance of Palm Sunday liturgy by a subtle modification of a long-standing iconographical tradition. Images of Christ's arrival to Jerusalem, dating back to the fourth century, depict a person sitting in a tree beside Christ, commonly identified as Zaccheus, who had climbed on a tree to see Christ better (Lk 19:1–10).[59] Medieval images often preserve both the tree and a person on a raised platform. These, however, replaced a minor biblical event with the performance of the liturgy. As in the Chertsey Abbey breviary, the child taking the place of Zaccheus is both more familiar (through the performance of the liturgy) and more remote from the biblical narrative.

Medieval images portray a variety of activities at the top of the gate, from casting down leaves and branches through hanging cloth and scrolls to waving hands in salutation. These images suggest that at this moment in the procession, a moment of joy and celebration, the children complemented their song by other means. Liturgical manuals, however, give little evidence for the nature of these activities, and one can best turn to other sources. Later and better documented accounts, such as the early sixteenth-century liturgy at Long Melford, tell how children cast flowers and 'singing cakes' (i.e. unconsecrated hosts) from the top of the gate on the awaiting crowd.[60] Another type of source presents a mirror image to the ritual of Palm Sunday, one in which the laity took the initiative. Royal entries constituted one of the most complex civic rituals of the later Middle Ages. In an event infused with liturgical and biblical echoes, a triumphant ruler was greeted by a welcoming crowd. Henry V's 1415 entry to London, following the battle of Agincourt, contained visual and performative echoes to the liturgy of Palm Sunday:

> (by the Tower) erant innumerosi pucri representantes ierarchiam angelicam, vestitu candido, vultibus rutilantibus auro, alis interlucentibus et criminibus virgineis consertis laureolis preciosis, qui concinebant in adventu regio suavi vocis modulatione et organis, litteram prosequentes,

> hanc angelicam cantilenam: Benedictus qui venit in nomine domini [...] (a second boys' choir by the cross in the middle of Cheapside sang) quasi archangelica et angelica multitudo, celesti nitore decori, vestitu candido ... qui emiserunt in caput Regis subgredientis minas aureas cum frondibus lauri.[61]

The scene bore a striking resemblance to the liturgy of Palm Sunday in text, location, and performance. The choirs of children were likened, time and again, to a host of angels: garments, props, arrangement of hair, and face paints served to bring this allusion home to spectators. The singing of the *benedictus qui venit* by the first choir applied the Gospel exclamation to the arrival of a monarch. The second choir threw jewels and laurel branches from a raised platform, in a lavish rendering of the liturgical procession. Its location by Cheapside Cross (demolished during the Civil War) enhanced its affinity to the liturgy of Palm Sunday, in a spatial modification of the Palm Cross of the first station. This had a special appeal to the king, as the cross was one of the 'Eleanor Crosses' constructed by Edward I. The opulence of the pageant extended beyond the liturgy of even the most affluent churches, but its texts, scenery, and joyous nature reflected its liturgical origins. It employed the biblical scene (in its liturgical rendering) to transform the civic ritual; it drew on the comparison between King and Christ, London and Jerusalem to endow the royal ritual with biblical authority. The detailed account of the royal entry suggests that the joyous nature of the liturgical performance of the *Gloria laus* extended to props, costumes, and performance as well, although possibly of a more modest nature.

Royal entries drew upon Palm Sunday liturgy. Palm Sunday, in turn, commemorated a biblical narrative, which was heavily influenced by the civic rituals of Late Antiquity. In Greek and Roman *adventus* processions town dignitaries welcomed a triumphant ruler as a personification of a deity outside the city walls; they carried branches and palms, cast flowers, burned incense and offered sacrifices in his honour.[62] The Gospel narrative was influenced by these rituals, familiar to Gentile audiences, and preserved their key elements in the meeting point outside the city walls, in the use of palms and of flowers. In the later Middle Ages the ritual has come a full circle, as the biblical narrative and its liturgical re-enactment influenced royal entries in an evolution of a tradition, in which the Bible was a link rather than *fons et origo*.

Caiphas

Following the performance of the *Gloria laus*, the procession made its way to the third station, where the antiphon *Collegerunt fontifices* and the versicle *Unus autem* were chanted. These narrated the decision of priests and Pharisees to surrender Jesus to the Romans, following verbatim the Gospel of John (11:47–50, 53). The station linked Christ's entry with the Crucifixion, acting as a stepping stone between the joy of the second station and the grim contemplation in front of the rood at the fourth station.

An unusual source, the Middle English speech of Caiphas the prophet, provides a glimpse into the little-documented world of extra-liturgical activities. The speech survives in a single manuscript (BL, Sloane MS 2478, fols 43r–44v), a miscellany of mostly Latin treatises from the early fourteenth century. It was edited by Carleton Brown, who, on the basis of its south-west dialect and reference to a secular cathedral, suggested its connection to Salisbury or Wells, preferring the latter.[63] The speech itself has attracted little attention from scholars, but its unique way of comically narrating Bible and liturgy, and its reliance on liturgical commentaries, merit a fuller investigation. Furthermore, the performances of boy prophets, which became an integral part of the first station of the Sarum use from the fifteenth century, echo Caiphas's speech and indicate that it is part of a much wider tradition, whose memory is preserved only in segments.[64] All but invisible to the modern scholar, these para-liturgical activities bridged the gap between Bible and laity; light-hearted and in the vernacular, they mediated biblical scenes and narratives, extending beyond the prescribed liturgy to transmit complex texts alongside their allegorical undertones. The bulk of the speech is an address in 160 short repetitive lines in Middle English, with a clear rhyming pattern of *aabccb* throughout. A short Latin address appears between lines 36 and 37, in which the dean and canons (*decane*, *karissimi*) are approached. Both Latin and Middle English link the liturgical paraphernalia of Palm Sunday to personal devotion. Unknown to Carleton Brown at the time, they build upon Durand's liturgical commentaries. A comparison between the speech and the commentaries sheds light on the reception of the *Rationale* in England and its applicability for both lay and clerical audiences; it can also assist in retrieving a lacuna in the Latin address.

In a subtle play on the arrival of Christ in the first station, the performer's arrival leads parishioners on the road to personal devotion and self-improvement. The presenter identifies himself as Bishop Caiphas, who will sing the prophecies of the King of Heaven. Entertaining and befitting oral performance, the address makes frequent use of the second person and conveys a blithe undertone in its expansion of the liturgical occurrence. The presenter is aware of the risk of boring one's audience – a problem seldom acknowledged in liturgical manuscripts. Caiphas therefore assures his audience that his speech will be short, and begs their patience:

> Thy stondeth a stounde and bloweth breth
> And yif icham as yee soeth
> Ichulle bere me bolde
> And synge you sone a lytel song
> Ha schal boe schort and nothing long
> That rather ichadd y-tolde.[65]
>
> (ll. 13–18)

Next follows a brief account of Caiphas, based on the Gospel of John and his role as a high priest in the time of the Crucifixion, with explicit reference to his prophecy of Christ's life after death and its relevance for the medieval audience:

> Ich was bysschop of the lawe
> Th^t yer th^t crist for you was slawe
> Ye mowe boe glade therfore
> Hit com to sothe th^t ich tho seyde
> Betere hit were th^t o man deyde
> Than al volk were y-lore.[66]
>
> (ll. 29–24)

The speech reiterates both the Gospel narrative and the antiphon *Unus autem* of the third station, supplying an English translation of the liturgical performance ('Unus autem ex ipsis Caiphas nomine cum esset pontifex anni illius prophetavit dicens expedit vobis ut unus moriatur homo pro populo et non tota gens pereat. Ab illo ergo die cogitaverunt interficere eum dicentes ne forte veniant Romani et tollent nostrum locum et gentem').[67] The biblical text, however, appears only briefly in the speech, in which it is reserved for the introduction of Caiphas. The remainder of the speech diverges from the Gospel account to develop its own theological message, which comprises most of the Middle English address and all of the Latin. After introducing his aims briefly, the performer moves from Middle English to Latin to engage with a clerical audience.

The Latin address begins with a rhymed appeal, asking the dean to bestow his favour on the performer:

> O Decane reverende
> In adiutorium meum intende

Ad informandum hic astantes
Michi scitis favorante
Si placet bone domine
Iube benedicere.[68]

(Latin Section, ll. 1–6)

This section constitutes an unorthodox biblical allusion. It opens with a reiteration of Psalm 69:2 ('Deus in adiutorium meum intende …'). This, however, is far from a simple biblical allusion and demonstrates the performer's liturgical playfulness. This Psalm was employed in the office of Matins, where the versicle and response *Deus in adiutorium meum intende; domine ad adiuvandum me festina* were chanted daily.[69] The liturgical echo reaches new heights as the performer seeks the dean's favour in words taken from the ordinary of the Mass. In a formula used in Masses throughout Western Christendom, a deacon asked for an officiant's blessing prior to the Gospel lesson in the words *Iube, domine, benedicere*.[70] This was now employed by the performer. However, it is not the Gospel text that follows but rather a jocular Middle English address. This puts the rhymed appeal in a new light. The integration of biblical and liturgical allusion does not endow the performance with biblical authority, as in Mass and office; rather the performer employs these biblical and liturgical allusions comically, out of context, bridging the gap between exulted language and mundane request.

The rhymed address gives way to an interpretation of Palm Sunday procession in Latin prose. Beginning with *Karissimi*, it follows Durand's liturgical commentaries to the letter. We are able now to correct Brown's punctuation and, more importantly, to recover the lacuna in the text.[71] It begins by calling the antiphon *Occurunt turbe* to mind; the Gospel crowd, mentioned in the antiphon, is then linked with the listeners through the liturgical paraphernalia carried by both, flowers and palms. These objects are assigned precise allegorical interpretations: flowers symbolise virtue while palms stand for victory; olives are carried as a sign of giving oneself to acts of peace and mercy, and palms in obtaining victory over sins and the devil; bearing green flowers and boughs is to adorn oneself with virtues, spreading garments is the destruction of the flesh, while plucking branches follows in the footsteps of the saints. The Latin address ends with the performer stating his intention to narrate these interpretations to the laity.

The prolonged Middle English rendering of Durand sheds light on forms of biblical and liturgical mediation to clerical and lay audiences. In Middle English Durand's complex allegorisation of Palm Sunday paraphernalia is condensed to a single aim: victory over the devil. The audience is encouraged to combat sin, from baptism (ll. 67–72) in a daily battle with temptation. The soul is likened to a house, into which Christ should be welcomed (ll. 73–96). This is, as Caiphas explains, the essence of Palm Sunday procession:

> & hwanne ye habbeth overcome thanne voend
> Thanne y-meteth cryst your froend
> Wyth palm & bowes grene
> That ys a token; that alle & some
> Habbeth the develes al overcome
> Ham to sorwe and toene.[72]
>
> (ll. 97–102)

Palms and green boughs, serving different aims in Durand's original commentaries, are presented to the laity as signs of victory over the devil. These paraphernalia are then mentioned in the context of the biblical event, connecting Bible, audience and doctrine through the material culture of the day:

> Nou yee th^t^ bereth today your palm
> [...]
> As dude the chyldren of tholde lawe
> Yyf ye hym lovede ye scholde wel vawe
> Boe by tyme schryuve.[73]
>
> (ll. 127–32)

The audience is treated as an active community: its preparation in confession (in accordance with canon 21 – 'Omnis utrius sexus fidelis' – of the Fourth Lateran Council[74]) and participation in waving palms and singing are key in the liturgy of the day. Having expressed its theological position, the speech nears its end and Caiphas comically reminds his audience of the brevity of his speech. He asks them for the book he carried earlier, as he does not remember it all by heart ('Schewe me the bok th^{t} i^{c} haddydo | The song schal wel an heyy | Ich may noyt synge hym al bi rote' (ll. 146–8)).[75] The speech ends with a contextualisation within the performance of Palm Sunday:

> Nou gawe hom hit is fordays
> Lengere ne tyd you here no pays
> The belle wol sone rynge
> Doth so tht ich cunne you thonkes
> Wyth bordoun hauteyn menamonkes
> Lat me hure you synge.[76]
>
> (ll. 157–62)

Bells are rung at the end of the procession and the audience is tired at the end of a long day. The loud bass (*bordoun*) of performer and audience is strong, accompanying the high pitch of the children's choir, singing the *Gloria laus*. As the performance is nearing its end, Caiphas's last words encourage the audience to join in song, a world away from the passivity of the audience implied by liturgical manuscripts.

All through Caiphas's performance listeners are urged to reflect on the symbolism of the day's liturgy. Through preparation and active participation they achieve spiritual progression. This is Caiphas's ultimate goal for Palm Sunday, made clear in an allegorical interpretation of the liturgical paraphernalia. Caiphas's message accords with the liturgical texts and performances to provide an allegorical interpretation of Christ's entry as a move towards Heavenly Jerusalem. The juxtaposition of Latin and Middle English reveals that lay and clerical audiences alike enjoyed biblical allusions alongside a comic performance. The laity, however, were presented with a simplified understanding of the day's liturgy in comparison to the elaborate allegorisation of Durand.

Entering liturgical time

The arrival of Palm Sunday indicated that the end of Lent was near. Lent was a time of contrition and fasting, when images were veiled and the singing of *Alleluia* and *Gloria in excelsis* prohibited. It was brought to conclusion with a joyous celebration which mirrored the carnivalesque Shrove Tuesday at its beginning. Palm Sunday also marked the beginning of Holy Week, at whose crux was Christ's death on Good Friday and Resurrection on Easter Sunday. The liturgy of the day moved between these two poles, encompassing light-hearted performances alongside allusions to death and redemption. The fourth-century procession described by Egeria, which began and ended at the place of Crucifixion and Resurrection, was not dissimilar to the medieval experience. Prior to the distribution of palms the prayer *Deus cuius filius* narrated Christ's descent to earth for the salvation of humanity; in the first station, the joy of meeting Christ was linked to the textual and tangible manifestations of death; the third station, narrating the decision to surrender Christ to the Romans, paved the way to a more sombre reflection of Christ's torments and Passion.

The shift from joy to sorrow, from welcoming Christ to meditating on the Passion, became evident as the procession entered the church. According to the Sarum use, this took place in the transition from the third station (just outside the church) to the fourth (in front of the rood), when Christ's entry to Jerusalem was invoked in the responsory (liturgical chant that was often sung as a sequence of versicles and responsories) *Ingrediente domino*:

> R: Ingrediente domino in sanctam civitatem, Hebraeorum pueri resurrectionem vite pronuntiantes. cum ramis palmarum osanna clamabant in excelsis
> V: Cumque audisset populus quia Jesus venit Hierosolymam exierunt obviam ei
> R: Cum ramis palmarum osanna clamabant in excelsis.[77]

The responsory ended the outdoors part of the procession and summarised the biblical event in its liturgical guise, referring to the children, the text and performance of the *Gloria laus*, the hosannas and the carrying of palms. The opening phrase, which gave the responsory its name, attests to the inversion which occurred at that moment in the procession: the ablative absolute of *Ingrediente domino* shows that by the time the responsory was chanted Christ had already entered the church. During the third station the secondary procession was likely to make its way into the church, prior to the arrival of the primary procession. As parishioners made their way into the church they passed underneath a feretory (i.e. a portable shrine) with relics and Eucharist, which was held high above the doorway. An inverted sequence was thus established: first the crowd welcomed Christ into their midst, at the end of the first station and at the second station; then Christ, in the form of relics and a consecrated host, welcomed the congregation as it entered the church, his symbolic body.

The end of the outdoor part of the procession marked a move from memorable images and tunes to a darkened church and complicated chants.[78] The congregation left behind the joy of welcoming Christ and entered the more sombre contemplation of the Passion in front of the rood, the place of the fourth station. There a dialogue was performed between priest and choir, both on their knees. The liturgy of this station differed slightly between the various uses, but typically included the responsory *Circumdederunt me*, which elaborates upon Christ's torture and redemption. The theme of torments was reflected in the injunction, found in liturgical manuscripts, for priest and choir to genuflect and kiss the ground – a stark contrast to the upwards projection of the second station.[79] More information on the behaviour of the laity is found in Reginald Pecock's *The Repressor of Over Much Blaming of the Clergy* (*c.* 1455), which provides a detailed description of Palm Sunday liturgy 'as y have red in dyverse oolde ordinalis of cathedrale chirchis and of monasteries in Ynglond'.[80] Pecock's account describes not only the clergy kneeling to the ground in front of the rood, but also 'al the lay peple in the processioun knelen doun and knocken her brestis and summe fallen so doun that her brestis and mouthis touchen the grounde'. This description of parishioners' behaviour enabled Pecock to demonstrate the merits of worshipping the cross, rejected by the Lollards who are confronted throughout the treatise. The value of his evidence is corroborated by Pecock's contemporary Margery Kempe (d. *c.* 1438). Her account provides insight into the feelings of a lay woman on Palm Sunday: she combined the joy of meeting Christ with contemplation of the Passion and broke down in tears after the entrance into the church, when she saw Christ's agony on the cross. This led to a lengthy meditation on the Passion, which she visualised in her mind's eye.[81]

The crucifix that inspired Margery Kempe so deeply was another visual manifestation of Palm Sunday. Images and crucifixes that had been veiled all through Lent were revealed on Palm Sunday. The re-appearance of the crucifix was a vivd reminder of the Passion and Christ's suffering. The tribulation and surrounding menace of *Circumdederunt me* joined by the plea for liberation from one's enemies in *Eripere me* to provide a textual echo for Christ's agonies. The grim undertone of previous parts in the liturgy had become a strong presence. The coda of this station's liturgy, the prayer *Omnipotens sempiterne deus*, told of Christ's life, death, and Resurrection. It led believers away from the procession and towards the subsequent Mass with its dramatic reading from Matthew 26:1–27:61, narrating the Last Supper, betrayal, trial, Passion, Crucifixion, and burial.[82] The reading assigned different voices for Christ, Jews and narrator, vividly re-creating the last events of Christ's life and bringing the connection between Christ's entry to Jerusalem and the Crucifixion to new dramatic heights.

Much like the first station at the beginning of the procession, the fourth station at its end provided textual and non-textual means to portray a specific view of the Bible for clergy and laity alike. The link between the joy of Christ's entry and his torments on the cross reverberated in the text of responsory and prayer, in the unveiled crucifix, and in kneeling or lying on the floor. The liturgy led believers on an emotional journey, contextualising Palm Sunday within the events of Holy Week and salvation history. It began with the preparatory blessing of flowers and branches, proceeded through the anticipation of the first station to the joy of the second, and from there gradually descended to the grim contemplation of the fourth station. The array of biblical narratives underpinning the liturgical performance and the dramatic Gospel reading were made clear to parishioners at St Mary, Fairstead (Essex, Figure 4). There, at the uppermost register

Figure 4 Holy Week images (Entry, Last Supper, Flagellation, Crucifixion), St Mary, Fairstead (Essex)

of the chancel arch, Christ's entry to Jerusalem was portrayed as part of a Passion cycle alongside images of the Last Supper, betrayal, arrest, flagellation, and trial. The rood was probably positioned on that very arch, supplying a visual echo to the liturgy of the fourth station and the contemplation of the events of Holy Week.[83]

Concluding hosannas

The Liturgy of Palm Sunday enabled lay and clerical audiences in medieval England to take an active part in a re-creation of the biblical event. This was done in a land remote from Jerusalem, with plants that had little to do with the indigenous flora of the Holy Land, and employed texts which were not to be found in the Bible. Liturgy accommodated the biblical event into a new reality and transformed the way the Bible was known and recalled. It created a complex and challenging web of allusions, locations, chants, and paraphernalia, which emulated biblical genre and language to the extent that renders futile any separation between biblical and liturgical. These quasi-biblical creations seamlessly tied biblical narrative with exegesis and theology to present the medieval populace with a memorable rendering of the way biblical events should have looked. Children – external to the biblical scene – were thus seen to welcome Christ on the slopes of the Mount of Olives, or singing the *Gloria laus* from atop gates. These performative traits assisted in delineating social boundaries (as in the distribution of palms) or in avoiding the association of the welcoming crowd with the Jews of Jerusalem. Performance and text conveyed similar ideals, allowing the laity to become active participants in the liturgy and to glimpse at its delicate subtexts, as in the messianism of the first station or the emotional transition from joy to sorrow of the fourth. Liturgical performance became an integral part of the biblical event. The most memorable scenes of Palm Sunday were not necessarily those closest to the biblical narrative. Rather, it was tunes and actors, performance and location that influenced the popularity of a certain scene, and made the performance of the *Gloria laus* tantamount to the biblical event.

The liturgy of the day wove a web of internal allusions, which rendered it a single liturgical occurrence. As the biblical event enfolded, references to past and future moments preserved liturgical cohesion while the audience progressed from joy to sorrow, from welcoming Christ to contemplation of the looming Passion. The liturgy of the day provided, as much in lighthearted speech as in the grim presence of death, a new understanding of the Bible, and linked Gospel narrative with liturgical occurrence. The

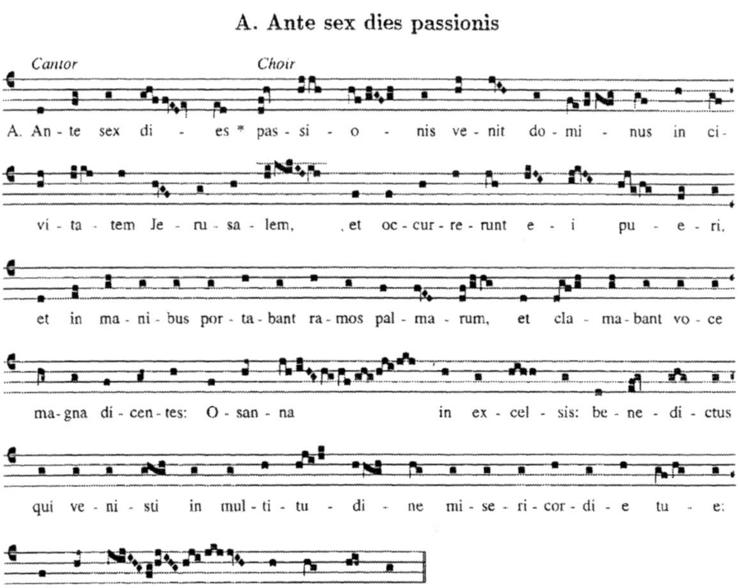

Example 2 Ante sex dies passionis (antiphon)

analysis of the liturgical texts of the procession with their performative and musical strata reveals, however, that not all texts carried the same weight. A single word stood out in biblical and liturgical accounts of Palm Sunday, and was almost interchangeable with it: *hosanna*. In Palm Sunday processions of the Sarum use *hosanna* was the most frequent biblical word: it appears twice in the Gospel lessons and seventeen times in antiphons and responsories, interspersed throughout all the crowning moments of the procession. The *hosanna* also plays a prominent role in the well-known hymn of the *Gloria laus*, repeated four times in the recurring versicle.[84]

The *hosanna* did not only appear throughout the procession, but was also emphasised by its music. In antiphons such as *Ante sex dies solemnitatis* and *Ante sex dies passionis* the word *hosanna* was sung in an elaborate melisma around the last syllable of the word against the background of a mainly syllabic tune, as can be seen from a modern rendering of the medieval notation (Example 2).[85] The mainly syllabic tune for the beginning of the word highlighted the word without infringing on its recognition. The musical similarities helped linking the two appearances of the word; they also assisted in differentiating between the *hosanna* and less elaborate melismas (such as that of Jerusalem).

In literary narratives the word *hosanna* likewise takes a prominent place. *The Story of the Three Cocks* from the Middle English *Gesta Romanorum* (an early fifteenth-century translation of a late thirteenth- to early fourteenth-century Latin text) retells the events of Palm Sunday: as the audience followed Christ into Jerusalem, they cried: 'Osanna filio david! benedictus qui venit in nomine domini! The sone of david make us safe! blessid be he that comythe in the name of the lord.'[86] Palm Sunday was encapsulated in the *hosanna*, though knowledge of the word's meaning (as distinct from its sound) was not taken for granted, and its translation provided.[87] Similar patterns appear in the Middle English *Gospel of Nicodemus*, extant in manuscripts from the fourteenth century. In a dialogue between Pilate and the Jews the *hosanna* once more appears alongside its translation: '"Osanna", quod pilate, "what es it forto say?" Quod the Iewes, "it menes thusgate 'Lord, save us, we the pray'."'[88]

The *Vision of Piers Plowman*, composed in three (or four) distinct versions in the second half of the fourteenth century, provides an elaborate account of Palm Sunday and has been studied as a source for late medieval liturgy.[89] The eighteenth passus of the work (lacking in the A version and passus twenty in the C and the Z manuscript) is a dream vision, which narrates the events of Holy Week and ends with the dreamer waking up to the bells of Easter Sunday (mirroring the bells at the end of

Caiphas's performance). The vision commences at the end of Lent and at Palm Sunday, which is described as: 'Of gerlis and of gloria, laus gretly me dremed' (Passus 18 line 7).[90] This short reference is liturgically saturated, combining both textual and performative traits: children are firmly connected to *Gloria laus* at the moment of entry, mirroring the centrality of children in visual images of the day. The text continues in a like manner: 'And how Osanna by organye olde folk songen' (18:8).[91] The *hosanna* is intertwined with an identification of its performers (*olde folk* – in contrast with the above-mentioned children) and its musical performance (*organye*, referring either to a musical instrument or harmonised singing). The term *hosanna* in the text refers to the liturgical act of singing the *hosanna* in Palm Sunday liturgy, subordinating the biblical text to its liturgical performance.

A synthesis between liturgical and biblical events is established in *Piers Plowman*. Faith and the Jews of Jerusalem welcome Christ with the Latin exclamations *At Fili David* (similar to *Osanna Filio David* of Mt 21:9) and *Benedictus qui venit in nomine domini* – Latin elements common in both biblical narrative and liturgical performance. The end of the account employs chivalric vocabulary to connect biblical events and medieval reality: Christ is likened to a knight who has come to be dubbed in Jerusalem, receiving spurs in an allusion to the Passion ('Withouten spores other spere; spakliche he loked | As is the kynde of a knyght that cometh to be dubbed | To geten hym gilte spores on galoches ycouped' (18:12–14)).[92] This analogy follows both Bible and liturgy in placing Palm Sunday in the shadow of the Passion and Resurrection.

The centrality of the word *hosanna* in the liturgy, as well as in Middle English literature, is reminiscent of the link between royal entries and the liturgy of Palm Sunday: the preservation of liturgical elements which predated the compilation of the Gospel narrative, and could be traced back to the earliest strata of the biblical text. The word *hosanna* did not originate with the Gospels. Rather, it transliterates the Hebrew petition *hosha na – save us we pray* – in the Gospels, both in the original Greek and in later Latin translations.[93] This, alongside the phrase *Benedictus qui venit*[94] *in nomine domini* in all four Gospels, reveals the liturgical undertone of the crowd's exclamations, and its origins. These texts were taken from the Old Testament, from Psalm 117:25–6 ('Obsecro domine salva obsecro obsecro domine prosperare obsecro, Benedictus qui venit in nomine domini; Benediximus vobis de domo domini').[95] This Psalm was central to Jewish liturgy, above all the feasts of Tabernacles and Passover, and the proclamation hosanna became the cornerstone of liturgy of the seventh day of Tabernacles, known as *Hosanna Raba* – the Great Hosanna.

The verse *Benedictus qui venit in nomine domini* was employed at times of pilgrimage to the Temple, such as Passover – the season of Christ's entry to Jerusalem. In the Gospels it establishes a connection between Christ's arrival and pilgrimage, a link acknowledged by medieval exegetes.[96]

The work of Paul Ricoeur offers a new way of understanding how the preservation and diffusion of liturgical undertones in the Bible influenced their appearance in medieval chant and ritual. Ricoeur combines general and biblical hermeneutics to produce a model for the reception and mediation of the Bible as a composite text.[97] He argues for the simultaneous co-existence of two paradigms, in which the Bible is an intermediary rather than the point of origin. The first can be summarised as speech-writing-speech: a speech-act, such as the words of the prophets, was then written down and codified, to later bestow its authority on subsequent speech acts, as in the words of a sermon. The second paradigm is writing-speech-writing, in which a charismatic orator, such as Christ, grounded his speech in the authority of a written canon; in turn, his own words were written down and integrated into a new canon, such as the Gospels. This understanding extends beyond Brian Stock's exploration of textual communities, to ask what happens to such a textual community and its Scripture once the charismatic oral dissemination becomes integrated into the textual canon. Ricoeur's theory is grounded in examples from the New Testament and early Christianity, and is highly applicable to the complexity of biblical texts and their medieval mediation.

Ricoeur's exploration of the evolution of Scripture in tandem with its mediation lends itself to a new understanding of the connection between Bible and liturgy. This can be summarised as the coexistence of textual and liturgical elements: liturgy-text-liturgy. Liturgy predated the compilation of the canon. Liturgical customs were known and practised by the time both Old and New Testaments were written and edited, and as such were embedded into the biblical fabric. One can discern distinct liturgical elements, either in their entirety or in truncated allusions; in full books or in passing references. These include descriptions of liturgical performances, references to paraphernalia, melodies, and actors, as well as liturgical texts that preserve their distinct performative traits (e.g. rhythm, short and memorable catch-phrases, inter-biblical allusion etc.). The most obvious example is the Psalter, whose poetic structure, distinct imagery, and use of supplications and petitions attests to liturgical origins that predated the codification of the Bible.

Once codified, the Bible served as the basis for the creation of a new liturgy. In a growingly literate society, written texts provided liturgy with a textual anchor and endowed its performance with authority. Importantly, in this move towards the creation of new chants and rituals, the Bible's embedded liturgical traits were employed time and again; in Jewish and Christian liturgies alike, their popularity exceeded other parts of the biblical canon. The Psalms became the cornerstone of the divine office, as well as of the Jewish liturgy. Smaller liturgical components underwent a similar process: the phrase *Benedictus qui venit*, originally connected to Temple pilgrimage, was applied to Christ in the Gospels and chanted time and again in medieval Christian liturgy. In a similar manner liturgical terms such as *hosanna* or *Amen* found their way into prayers and became, for the former, an embodiment of the liturgy of Palm Sunday, and for the latter an essential part of the vocabulary of prayer. In parts this can be seen as the appeal of an extra-temporal supplicatory and edifying language, one that is removed from the immediate historical context of the biblical narrative; in other instances it was the remoteness of foreign words, no longer understood in the language of the liturgy, which created a gap between utterance and meaning.

The re-appearance of subdued liturgical elements is a testimony to the enduring power of the liturgy. It is evident in the preservation of liturgical texts, in the diffusion of Hebrew and Greek words (such as *hosanna*, *Amen*, and *Kyrie Eleison*) in the Latin liturgy, and even in the afterlife of Latin in post-Reformation English liturgy.[98] This phenomenon extends to acts and objects. *Adventus* processions were made into royal entries, linking civic rituals over a millennium apart, while the use of palms in the Christian liturgy followed obsolete Jewish and Graeco-Roman traditions. Nowadays, the use of indigenous plants as 'palms' on Palm Sunday is a manifestation of the same phenomenon, of liturgical customs whose *raison d'être* had long ago vanished. Liturgy is therefore a form of biblical mediation, which is far from evident. An in-depth analysis of performance, text, and image reveals the link between Bible and liturgy. One of the most influential ways in which lay and clerical audience learned, and experienced, the Bible, liturgy was never a simple reiteration of biblical texts. Liturgical spectacles drew on texts, objects, tunes, and landscapes to engage the eyes and minds of participants, to present biblical scenes through exegetical and doctrinal prisms. A complex network of meaning was thus created and presented the same message through word and act, while making biblical and extra-biblical into a singular, living recreation of the Bible in the towns and villages of medieval England.

Notes

1 Mayeski, 'Reading the Word in a Eucharistic Context', p. 61. Similar conclusions were made by: Vitz, 'The Liturgy', pp. 562–3; Boynton, 'Bible and Liturgy', p. 27.

2 Prominent works on Palm Sunday are: Henry J. Feasey, *Ancient English Holy Week Ceremonial* (London, 1897), pp. 53–83; Herbert Thurston, *Lent and Holy Week: Chapters on Catholic Observance and Ritual*, 2nd edn (London, 1914), pp. 191–237; Dom H. Philibert Feasey (OSB), 'Palm Sundays', *American Ecclesiastical Review* 38:4 (April 1908), 361–81; Edmund Bishop, 'Holy Week Rites of Sarum, Hereford and Rouen Compared', in *Liturgica Historica: Papers on the Liturgy and Religious Life of the Western Church*, ed. Bishop (Oxford, 1918), pp. 276–300; Mark Spurrell, 'The Procession of Palms and West-Front Galleries', *Downside Review* 119:415 (2001), 125–44; Carolyn Marino Malone, *Façade as Spectacle: Ritual and Ideology at Wells Cathedral*, Studies in Medieval and Reformation Thought 102 (Leiden, 2004), pp. 133–40, 225–7; Duffy, *Stripping the Altars*, pp. 22–7. The best introduction to the variety of English uses is Pfaff, *Liturgy in Medieval England.*

3 David Chadd, 'The Ritual of Palm Sunday: Nidaros in Context', in *The Medieval Cathedral of Tronheim: Architectural and Ritual Constructions in Their European Context*, ed. Margrete Syrstad Andås et al. (Turnhout, 2007), pp. 253–78.

4 There are several editions of Palm Sunday liturgy in the Sarum use. Most of them leave something to be desired. I have used *The Sarum Missal: Edited from Three Early Manuscripts*, ed. J. Wickham Legg (Oxford, 1916, repr., 1969) in conjunction with the modern musically oriented *The Use of Salisbury, vol. 4: The Masses and Ceremonies of Holy Week*, ed. Nick Sandon (Newton Abbot, 1996). This was corroborated with the following manuscripts: BL, Harley MSS 2911, fols 117r–118r, 2942, fols 31r–41r, and 2945, fols 30v–41r; Cambridge University Library, MS Ee.2.3 – probably of Winchester; Oxford, Bodleian Library, MS Bodley 637 (2024) – probably of Winchester; Oxford, Bodleian Library, MS Liturgical 408 (= add. B20), fols 33v–47v; Oxford, Bodleian Library, MS Rawlinson Liturgical e. 47, fols 1r–8r. Variants of the Sarum use were employed in Norwich: *The Customary of the Cathedral Priory Church of Norwich: Ms 465 in the Library of Corpus Christi College, Cambridge*, ed. J. B. L. Tolhurst, HBS 82 (London, 1948, repr. 2010), pp. 76–8; BL, Additional MS 57,534, fols 32r–41v (Carole Rawcliffe, *Medicine for the Soul. The Life, Death and Resurrection of an English Medieval Hospital: St Giles's, Norwich, c. 1249–1550* (Stroud, 1999), p. 120). The English translation is based on *The Sarum Missal in English*, 2 vols, tr. Frederick E. Warren, The Library of Liturgiology and Ecclesiology for English Readers 8–9 (London, 1911), i:217–29. For the use of York: *Missale ad usum insignis ecclesiae Eboracensis*, ed. W. G. Henderson, Surtees Soc. 59 (Durham, 1874), pp. 84–90; *The Ordinal and Customary of the Abbey of St Mary York*, 3 vols, ed. J. B. L. Tolhurst and Abbess of Stanbrook, HBS 73, 75, 84 (London, 1936–37, 1951), ii:264–6; BL, Additional MS 35,285 (the Augustinian Priory of Gisburne), fols 344r–345r. For the use of Hereford: *Missale ad usum percelebris ecclesiae Herfordensis*, ed. W. G. Henderson (Leeds, 1874, repr. Farnborough, 1969), pp. 79–82; BL, Harley MS 2983, fols 27v–28v, 59r. For Barking Abbey: *The Ordinale and Customary of the Benedictine Nuns of Barking Abbey*, 2 vols, ed. J. B. L. Tolhurst, HBS 65–6 (London, 1927–28), i:84–8. An interesting attempt at

charting the route of Palm Sunday processions in smaller churches was made by Feasey, *Ancient English Holy Week*, p. 63.

5 'Using Liturgical Texts in the Middle Ages', in *Fountain of Life: In Memory of Niels K. Rasmussen, O.P.*, ed. Gerard Austin (Washington, DC, 1991), pp. 69–83. On the importance of the musical element in the understanding and reception of the liturgy see: Owain Tudor Edwards, 'Dynamic Qualities in the Medieval Office', in *Liturgy and the Arts in the Middle Ages: Studies in Honour of C. Clifford Flanigan*, ed. Eva L. Lillie and Nils Holger Petersen (Copenhagen, 1996), pp. 36–63; and to a lesser extent: Gabriela Ilnitchi, 'Music in the Liturgy', in *The Liturgy of the Medieval Church*, pp. 589–612.

6 *Itineraria et alia geographica*, ed. A. Franceschini and A. Weber, CCSL 175–6 (Turnhout, 1965), 175:76–7. An English translation is: *Egeria's Travels to the Holy Land*, ed. and tr. John Wilkinson, rev. edn (Jerusalem and Warminster, 1981), pp. 132–3. For analysis: Ora Limor, *Holy Land Travels: Christian Pilgrims in Late Antiquity* (in Hebrew, Jerusalem, 1998).

7 *The Monastic Constitutions of Lanfranc*, ed. and tr. David Knowles (London, 1951); rev. edn, ed. Christopher N. L. Brooke (Oxford, 2002), pp. 34–41.

8 Compare Spurrell, 'Procession of Palms', 132, with a map and information on medieval Lincoln: Francis Hill, *Medieval Lincoln* (Cambridge, 1948, repr. 1965), pp. 122–3.

9 'Chap. V. on the Cemetery: no part of the cemetery shall be occupied with structures, unless in times of hostility. A fitting and worthy cross has been indeed built in the cemetery, to which a procession will be made on Palm Sunday, unless it was customary to happen in another place.' *Concilia magnae Britanniae et Hiberniae, a synodo Verolamiensi A.D. CCCXLVI ad Londinensem A.D. (MDCCXVII): Accedunt constitutiones et alia ad historiam Ecclesiae Anglicanae spectantia*, ed. David Wilkins (London, 1737), i:623–4.

10 *Vetus registrum sarisberiense, alias dictum Registrum S. Osmundi episcopi: The register of S. Osmund*, 2 vols, ed. W. H. Rich Jones, RS (London, 1883–34), i:307. The record for the chapel of St Bartholomew in Earley repeats this account almost verbatim (i:309).

11 Richard Morris, *The Church in British Archaeology*, Council for British Archaeology Research Report 47 (London, 1983), pp. 52–3; G. H. Cook, *The English Mediaeval Parish Church*, 3rd edn (London, 1961), p. 34; G. R. Owst, *Preaching in Medieval England: An Introduction to Sermon Manuscripts of the Period c.1350–1450* (Cambridge, 1926), pp. 195–9. On specific crosses: Éamonn Ó Carragáin, 'At Once Elitist and Popular: The Audiences of the Bewcastle and Ruthwell Crosses', in *Elite and Popular Religion: Papers read at the 2004 Summer Meeting and the 2005 Winter Meeting of the Ecclesiastical History Society*, ed. Kate Cooper and Jeremy Gregory, Studies in Church History 42 (Woodbridge, 2006), pp 18–40; Meyer Schapiro, 'The Religious Meaning of the Ruthwell Cross', *Art Bulletin* 26:4 (December 1944), 232–45.

12 *Monastic Constitutions of Lanfranc*, p. 38.

13 *Lincoln Cathedral Statutes*, ed. H. Bradshaw and C. Wordsworth, part i (Cambridge, 1892), p. 292, used by Spurrell, 'Procession of Palms', 132.

14 For discussion of architecture and Palm Sunday liturgy: Feasey, *Palm Sundays*, pp.

377–8. Advocating a more cautious approach is: Spurell, 'Procession of Palms', 138–9. A detailed analysis of Wells Cathedral which rejects (implicitly) Spurrell's conclusions is: Malone, *Façade as Spectacle*, pp. 133–40, 225–7.

15 Gertrud Schiller, *Iconography of Christian Art* (orig. *Iconographie der christliche Kunst*, Gütersloh, 1968), tr. Janet Seligman, *vol. II The Passion of Jesus Christ* (London, 1972), pp. 18–23; pl. 2, 31–50; St Æthelwold benedictional: BL, Additional MS 49,598 fol. 45v; C. M. Kauffmann, *Biblical Imagery in Medieval England, 700–1550* (London, 2003), pl. 121; Kristine Edmondson Haney, *The Winchester Psalter: An Iconographic Study* (Leicester, 1986), image 18, p. 57.

16 Cambridge, Emmanuel College MS 252, fol. 11v. On the manuscript: *Early Gothic Manuscripts, 1250–1285*, 2 vols, ed. Nigel Morgan, A Survey of Manuscripts Illuminated in the British Isles 4 (London, 1988), §52 i:99–100. On the workshop, responsible also for the Queen Mary Psalter: Linda Dennison, '"Liber Horn", "Liber Custumarum" and Other Manuscripts of the Queen Mary Psalter Workshops', in *Medieval Art, Architecture and Archaeology in London*, ed. Lindy Grant, The British Archaeological Association 10, Conference Transactions for the Year 1984 (Leeds, 1990), pp. 118–34.

17 St Mary, Fairstead (Essex); St Mary the Virgin, Wissington (Suffolk); St Botolph, North Cove (Suffolk); All Saints, Crostwight (Norfolk); St Mary, West Somerton (Norfolk). These images are discussed briefly in E. W. Tristram, *English Wall Painting of the Fourteenth Century* (London, 1955); *Medieval Wall Painting in the English Parish Church: A Developing Catalogue*, ed. Anne Marshall, http://paintedchurch.org/subinx2.htm (accessed 8 June 2012). The nature of the images prevents exact dating. I am grateful to the Central Research Fund of the University of London for a grant enabling the examination of these images, and for Rev. John Hall of Fairstead and Mrs Aldridge of Crostwight for their assistance.

18 *Life, Death and Art: The Medieval Stained Glass of Fairford Parish Church, A Multimedia Exploration*, ed. Sarah Brown and Lindsay MacDonald (Stroud, 1997), Window 5, analysed by M. D. Anderson, *Drama and Imagery in English Medieval Churches* (Cambridge, 1963), p. 21.

19 *Iohannis Beleth Summa de Ecclesiasticis officiis*, 2 vols, ed. Herbert Douteil, CCCM 41, 41A (Turnhout, 1976), 41A, p. 165 (Cap. 94); *Guillelmi Duranti Rationale divinorum officiorum*, 3 vols, ed. A. Davril and T. M. Thibodeau, CCCM 140, 140A, 140B (Turnhout, 1995, 1998, 2000), 140A p. 324 (vi.67.9). This supports Malone's understanding of the iconography of the western entrance as a rood screen, hence creating the emotional experience of entering the holy of holies (*Façade as Spectacle*, pp. 225–7)

20 For the move between a religious centre and liminal locations see: Mircea Eliade, *The Sacred and the Profane*, tr. Willard R. Trask (Harcourt, 1959, repr. 1987), pp. 20–59.

21 Durand, *Rationale*, vi.67.9 (Davril ed. 140A p. 324). The text and its reception are explored below: 'Caiphas'.

22 'The children of the Hebrews carrying olive branches went forth to meet the Lord crying: hosanna on high. The children of the Hebrews spread garments in the way and cried saying: hosanna to the son of David; blessed is he that cometh in the name of the Lord.'

23 Such as the image accompanying these antiphons in a gradual of *c.* 1400 (Glasgow University Library MS Gen. 999, fol. 1 = http://special.lib.gla.ac.uk/exhibns/treasures/gradual.html (accessed 8 June 2012)). A similar image from early fourteenth-century Siena is Schiller, *Iconography*, figure 49.

24 *Itineraria et alia geographica*, p. 96.

25 'Accedentes secretarii distribuant ea; palmas abbati et prioribus et personis honestioribus; flores et frondes caeteris' (*Monastic Constitutions of Lanfranc*, pp. 36–7); 'Distribuuntur palme a sacrista Abbati, Priori et confratribus, et frondes turbe a servientibus ecclesie' (*Ordinal and Customary of the Abbey of St Mary*, ii:264).

26 Durand, *Rationale*, vi.67.8–9 (Davril ed. 140A p. 324).

27 Carleton Brown, 'Caiphas as a Palm Sunday Prophet', in *Anniversary Papers by Colleagues and Pupils of George Lyman Kittredge*, Boston, 1913, pp. 105–17.

28 *Notes and Queries* (1st Ser.) 8:210 (5 Nov. 1853), 447–8; (2nd Ser.) 5:124 (15 May 1858), 391–2. For a more systematic discussion: Ronald Hutton, 'The English Reformation and the Evidence of Folklore', *Past and Present* 148:1 (Aug. 1995), 89–116 (98–101); Herbert Thurston, 'Palms', *The Month: A Catholic Magazine and Review* 86 (April 1896), 373–87. I witnessed the popularity of catkins myself in a Palm Sunday procession held on 20 April 2005, at the Abbey Church of St Benedict's, Ealing Broadway, London.

29 Duffy, *Stripping the Altars*, p. 26.

30 'Note that at Sarum flowers or branches are not placed on the cross, so that they shall not be seen to prepare the cross. But if that cross was adorned after the Passion lesson, it seems to be done fittingly enough [...] And if someone says in opposition, why do we worship a bare cross at the entrance to the church before the Passion lesson, it should be answered: that we worship not the cross but the crucified one himself, as is evident in the antiphon "Ave rex noster".' BL, Additional MS 57,534, fol. 38v, copied in BL, Harley MS 2942, fol. 37r.

31 Siegfried Wenzel, *Latin Sermon Collections from Later Medieval England: Orthodox Preaching in the Age of Wyclif*, Cambridge Studies in Medieval Literature 53 (Cambridge, 2005), p. 295.

32 An introduction to the medieval modes is: Andrew Hughes, *Medieval Manuscripts for Mass and Office: A Guide to Their Organization and Terminology* (Toronto 1995), pp. 111–16.

33 This musical cohesiveness is evident from a comparison with the later insertion of the boy prophet prophecies (which lack the B flat). The notes are reproduced from Sandon, *Use of Salisbury 4*, p. 11, by permission of Antico Edition (anticoedition.co.uk). For general information: David Hiley, *Western Plainchant: A Handbook* (Oxford, 1993), pp. 88–99.

34 'Behold O Sion, mystical daughter, thy gentle king cometh to thee, sitting humbly upon beasts, of whose coming the prophetic lesson hath foretold.'

35 'Tell ye the daughter of Sion: Behold thy king cometh to thee, meek and sitting upon an ass and a colt, the foal of her that is used to the yoke.'

36 Paul Foster, 'The Use of Zechariah in Matthew's Gospel', in *The Book of Zechariah and Its Influence*, ed. Christopher Tuckett (Aldershot, 2003), pp. 65–85 (74–5).

37 'Hail, thou whom the people of Hebrews bear witness to as Jesus, so as to meet thee with palms, shouting words of salutation.'

38 'This is he that cometh from Edom, with dyed garments from Bosra; he is beautiful in his robe, walking in the greatness of his strength; not on war horses, nor in lofty chariot.'

39 'Who is this that cometh from Edom, with dyed garments from Bosra? This beautiful one in his robe, walking in the greatness of his strength. I, that speak justice, and am a defender to save.'

40 E.g. Zec 4:6; I Kgs 19:11; Denys Turner, *The Darkness of God: Negativity in Christian Mysticism* (Cambridge, 1995).

41 *Glossa Ordinaria*, III:91; James H. Marrow, *Passion Iconography in Northern European Art of the Late Middle Ages and Early Renaissance: A Study of the Transformation of Sacred Metaphor into Descriptive Narrative* (Kotrijk, 1979), pp. 50–2, 83–94; David C. Fowler, 'A Middle English Bible Commentary (Oxford, Trinity College, Ms 93)', *Manuscripta* 12:2 (1968), 67–78 (75).

42 'Hail, light of the world, king of kings, glory of heaven, with whom abideth dominion, praise and honour, now and for ever.'

43 'I am the light of the world' (Jn 8:12); 'Thou art a king of kings: and the God of heaven hath given thee a kingdom, and strength, and power, and glory' (Dn 2:37).

44 'Here is he, who as the innocent lamb is consigned to death, the death of death, the bite of hell, by death giving life, as the blessed prophets once promised prophetically.'

45 'Behold the Lamb of God, behold him who taketh away the sin of the world.' In a slight modification of the biblical narrative, the antiphon *Unus autem* replaces *said* (*dixit*) with *prophesied* (*prophetavit*) and thus enhances its link with the prophecies of Christ's death.

46 *The Middle-English Harrowing of Hell and Gospel of Nicodemus*, ed. William H. Hulme, EETS ES 100 (London, 1907).

47 Duffy, *Stripping the Altars*, p. 25.

48 'Hail our salvation, our true peace, redemption, strength, who voluntarily did submit to the dominion of death on our behalf.'

49 This view differs from the separation of the two suggested by Vitz, 'Liturgical Versus Biblical'.

50 This understanding merges the categories offered by Paul Bradshaw ('Use of Bible') for the place of Bible within the liturgy, to demonstrate how a doxological function (as of the antiphons) coexisted with a kerygmatic or anamnetic function (of the versicles), in an amalgam of linguistic borrowing and typologicalinterpretation.

51 This merging of times was explored by Malone (*Façade as Spectacle*, pp. 138, 225–6) in reference to the entrance to the church.

52 Jacobus a Voragine, *Legenda aurea: Vulgo historia lombardica dicta*, ed. Th. Grässe (Dresden and Leipzig, 1846), p. 837; Durand, *Rationale*, vi.67.6 (Davril ed. 140A p. 323). For the origin of the antiphon: Andreas Heinz, 'Gloria, laus et honor', in *Lexikon für Theologie und Kirche*, 3rd edn, gen. ed. Michael Buchberger and Walter Kasper, vol. iv (Freiburg, 1995), p. 752.

53 'All glory, praise and honour to thee, Christ the king, Redeemer | to whom the pious virtue of children brought forth hosannas'.

54 'On high, the entire host is praising thee from Heaven | And mortal man and all things created likewise.'

55 Above, pp. 21–3.

56 Jeremy Cohen, 'The Jews as Killers of Christ in the Latin Tradition, from Augustine to the Friars', *Traditio: Studies in Ancient and Medieval History, Thought, and Religion* 39 (1983), 1–27. Cohen's argument for the growth in the intentionality of the Jews' act during the Middle Ages concords with the liturgical separation of the two crowds.

57 'The children praised God in heart and mouth, just as the Jews reviled (God) in heart and mouth.' *Rationale*, vi.67.1 (Davril ed. 140A p. 322).

58 Oxford, Bodleian Library, MS Lat. liturg. d. 42, fol. 8r. For information on the manuscript: *Gothic Manuscripts, 1285–1385*, 2 vols, ed. Lucy Freeman Sandler, A Survey of Manuscripts Illuminated in the British Isles 5 (London, 1986), §62a ii:70–1, which connects this manuscript to the Queen Mary Workshop (see above, n. 16).

59 Schiller, *Iconography*, pp. 19–21. Schiller's claim that 'The children and often the tree, are missing from the western image of the High Middle Ages' (p. 21) does not correspond with many insular visual images.

60 William Parker, *The History of Long Melford* (London, 1873), p. 72; Feasey, *Ancient English Holy Week*, pp. 57–9.

61 '(by the Tower) were innumerable boys representing the hierarchy of angels, clad in pure white, their faces glowing with gold, their wings gleaming, and their youthful locks entwined with costly sprays of laurel, who, at the king's approach, sang together in sweet sounding chant accompanied by organs, following their texts, this angelic anthem: (Benedictus qui venit in nomine domini) [...] (a second boys' choir by the cross in the middle of Cheapside sang) like a host of archangels and angels, beautiful in heavenly splendour, in pure white raiment ... and they let fall upon the king's head as he passed beneath golden coins and leaves of laurel.' *Gesta Henrici Quinti: The Deeds of Henry the Fifth*, ed. and tr. Frank Taylor and John S. Roskell (Oxford, 1975), pp. 104–11. Compare with the account of the pageant formerly ascribed to Lydgate – and the editors' source for the missing hymn: 'Besyde hym an angell bright, | "benedictus" thei gan synge, | "qui venit in nomine domini" Goddes knyght, | "Gracia Dei" with yow doth sprynge.' (ibid., p. 191) ('Beside him an angel bright, | "Benedictus" they did sing | "Qui venit in nomine domini" God's knight, | "Gratia Dei" with you does spring.' See Mary C. Erler, 'Palm Sunday Prophets and Processions and Eucharistic Controversy', *Renaissance Quarterly* 48:1 (1995), 58–81 (76–7).

62 Sabine MacCormack, 'Change and Continuity in Late Antiquity: The Ceremony of Adventus', *Historia: Zeitschrift für alte Geschichte* 21:4 (1972), 721–52, based on Ernst H. Kantorowicz, 'The King's Advent and the Enigmatic Panels in the Doors of Santa Sabina', *Art Bulletin* 26:4 (December 1944), 207–31; and *Laudes Regiae: A Study in Liturgical Acclamations and Medieval Ruler Worship* (Berkeley, 1946), pp. 71–5. For visual images: *The Roman Imperial Coinage, Vol. II Vespasian to Hadrian*, ed. Harold Mattingly and Edward A. Sydenham (London, 1926), pl. 16. The connection between royal entries and Palm Sunday liturgy was denied, though with little reference to its performance, by Gordon Kipling, *Enter the King: Theatre, Liturgy, and Ritual in the Medieval Civic Triumph* (Oxford, 1998), especially pp. 22–5.

63 Brown, 'Caiphas'. Parts of the speech were brought in: *Reliquiæ Antiquæ: Scraps*

from Ancient Manuscripts, Illustrating Chiefly Early English Literature and the English Language, 2 vols, ed. Thomas Wright (London, 1845), ii:241–5.

64 Erler, 'Palm Sunday Prophets', recounts the history of the Boy Bishops and is one of the few articles to refer in passing to the speech of Caiphas.

65 'Therefore stand a while and draw breath | And if I am as you see | I shall bear myself boldly | and sing you now a little song | It shall be short and nothing long | So that I shall sooner have told it.' Text and numbering follow Brown's edition, corroborated by an examination of the manuscript.

66 'I was bishop of the law | That year that Christ was slain for you | You should be glad therefore | It came true that I said then | Better is were that one man died | Than all the people were lost.'

67 'But one of them, named Caiphas, being the high priest that same year, prophesied saying: it is expedient for you that one man should die for the people, and that the whole nation perish not. Therefore from that day onwards they have thought to kill him saying: lest the Romans shall come and take our place and nation.'

68 'O Reverend Dean | Come to my assistance | to inform those standing by. | You know me favourably, | If it shall please you, good Lord | Grant to bless.'

69 Jeanne E. Krochalis and E. Ann Matter, 'Manuscripts of the Liturgy', in *The Liturgy of the Medieval Church*, pp. 393–430.

70 Legg, *The Sarum Missal*, p. 218. For a discussion of this formula see the next chapter 'The Bible as talisman: *textus* and oath-books'.

71 Durand, *Rationale*, vi.67.8–9 (Davril ed. 140A, p. 324); ll. 94–5 of Durand's text fill the lacuna on fol. 43v.

72 'And when you have overcome the devil | Then you go to welcome Christ your friend | With Palm and green bows | That is a token; that one and all | Have quite overcome the devils | To their (i.e. the devils') sorrow and pain.'

73 'Now you that bear today bear your palm | [...] As did the children of the old law | If you love him, you should very joyfully | Make confession promptly.'

74 *Decrees of the Ecumenical Councils: Vol. i, Nicaea I to Lateran V*, ed. Norman P. Tanner, SJ (London, 1990), p. 245.

75 'Show me the book so that I can have done | The song shall (sound) up to Heaven | I cannot sing it all from memory.'

76 'Now go home, it is late in the day | Do not stand here any longer | The bell will ring right away | Do so that I give you thanks | with the loud bass all together | Let me hear you sing!'

77 'R: The Lord having entered the sacred city, the children of the Hebrews, proclaiming the resurrection of life, with branches of palms cried hosanna on high; V: When the people heard that Jesus had come to Jerusalem they came out toward him; R: With branches of palms they cried hosanna on high.'

78 As in the difference between the syllabic nature of the *Gloria laus* and the frequent melismas of the *Ingredient domino*.

79 'et in ipsa statione executor officii incipiat antiphonam cum genuflectione osculando terram incipiat executor officii antiphonam' (BL, Additional MS 57,534, fols 40v–41r = BL, Harley MS 2942, fol. 40v) ('and in that station the minister shall begin the antiphon with genuflection, kissing the ground the minister shall begin the antiphon'); *York*, fol. 28v.

80 Reginald Pecock, *The Repressor of Over Much Blaming of the Clergy*, 2 vols, ed. Churchill Babington, RS 19 (London, 1860), i:202–7.

81 *The Book of Margery Kempe*, ed. Barry Windeatt (Harlow, 2000), pp. 340ff.

82 Red marks in a thirteenth-century Bible from Worcester (Cambridge University Library MS Kk.2.6, fols 81vb–84va), were aimed at facilitating the dramatic reading.

83 I thank Rev. John Hall of Fairstead for indicating this important fact to me.

84 This is true both for uses which repeated the entire verse, starting with *Gloria laus* (such as Sarum), and also for those which repeated only its second part – *Cui puerile decus prompsit osanna pium* (such as York)

85 The notes are reproduced from Sandon, *Use of Salisbury 4*, p. 9, by permission of Antico Edition (anticoedition.co.uk).

86 'Osanna filio david! benedictus qui venit in nomine domini! The son of David make us safe! Blessed is he that comes in the name of the Lord.' *Early English Versions of the Gesta Romanorum*, ed. Sidney J. H. Herrtage (London, 1879), p. 178. In the second rendering only an abridged English version was brought.

87 This demonstrates how Bradshaw's understanding of linguistic borrowing ('Use of Bible', 43) extends beyond the liturgy to the scattering of biblical words and phrases in vernacular literature.

88 '"Osanna", said Pilate, "what does it mean?" Said the Jews "it means as follows, 'Lord, save us, we pray."' *The Middle-English Harrowing of Hell and Gospel of Nicodemus*, ed. William H. Hulme, EETS ES 100 (London, 1907, repr. Oxford, 1961), p. 29. For the various editions and dates: James H. Morey, *Book and Verse: A Guide to Middle English Biblical Literature* (Urbana and Chicago, 2000), pp. 216–24. A parallel text is found in the York Play (*The York Plays*, ed. Richard Beadle (London, 1982), p. 264).

89 Ralph Hanna III, 'On the Versions of Piers Plowman', in *Pursuing History: Middle English Manuscripts and Their Texts* (Stanford, 1996), pp. 203–43; Bruce Harbert, 'Langland's Easter', in *Langland, the Mystics and the Medieval English Religious Tradition: Essays in Honour of S. S. Hussey*, ed. Helen Phillips (Cambridge, 1990), pp. 57–70; John A. Alford, *Piers Plowman: A Guide to the Quotations* (Binghamton, NY, 1992), pp. 20–1 (advocating a more cautious approach); Bruce W. Holsinger, 'Langland's Musical Reader: Liturgy, Law, and the Constraints of Performance', *Studies in the Age of Chaucer* 21 (1999), 99–141. Langland's acquaintance with, and dependence upon, the Sarum use was established by: Robert Adams, 'Langland and the Liturgy Revisited', *Studies in Philology* 73:3 (July 1976), 266–84.

90 'I dreamed continuously about children crying out *Glory, praise and honour*.' William Langland, *The Vision of Piers Plowman: A Critical Edition of the B-text Based on Trinity College Cambridge MS B.15.17 with Selected Variant Readings*, ed. A. V. C. Schmidt (London and New York, 1978), pp. 219–20. Translated by: William Langland, *Piers Plowman: A New Translation of the B-Text*, tr. A. V. C. Schmidt (Oxford, 1992), p. 210. This section is almost identical in the B and C versions: *Piers Plowman: A Parallel-Text Edition of the A, B, C and Z Versions*, ed. A. V. C. Schmidt (London, 1995), pp. 660–1.

91 'and about older people chanting Hosanna to the accompaniment of the organ (or harmonised singing)'.

92 'He had no spurs or spear, but he seemed spirited and alert | as a young man should be on the day he comes to be dubbed as a knight | and win the right to adorn his slashed shoes with spurs of gold.'

93 On the use of the *hosanna* in Jewish and Early Christian worship: Donald McIhagga, '*Hosanna*: Supplication and Acclamation', *Studia Liturgica* 5:3 (1966), 129–50.

94 In the Gospel of Matthew the verb is declined as *venturus est*. Both declinations derive from the Hebrew participle *h.b.a*, which can be interpreted both in the past and in the future. The version in Matthew corresponds to the Greek translation of the Psalms, as could be seen in Ps 117:26 in the Septuagint.

95 'O Lord, save me: O Lord, give good success. Blessed be he that cometh in the name of the Lord. We have blessed you out of the house of the Lord.' Jerome's translation of the Psalm does not preserve the original Hebrew, but rather translates it as *salva obscero*.

96 Sigmund Mowinckel, *The Psalms in Israel's Worship* (orig. *Offersang og Sangoffer*, Oslo, 1951), tr. D. R. Ap-Thomas (Oxford, 1962, with several reprints), pp. 120–1; *Glossa ordinaria*, II:606.

97 'Herméneutique philosophique et herméneutique biblique', in *Du text à l'action: Essais d'herméneutique II* (Paris, 1986), pp. 133–49 (translated as 'Philosophical Hermeneutics and Biblical Hermeneutics', in *From Text to Action: Essays in Hermeneutics II*, tr. Kathleen Blamey (London, 1991), pp. 89–101). The importance of this theory for understanding liturgy is briefly asserted by Bridget Nichols, *Liturgical Hermeneutics: Interpreting Liturgical Rites in Performance* (Frankfurt am Main, 1996), p. 150.

98 As can be seen, for example, in references to Latin Psalmody in English Bibles and Books of Common Prayer up until the nineteenth century, discussed in the Conclusion.

2

The Bible as talisman: *textus* and oath-books

Introduction: Bibles on the fringe

The previous chapter followed the Bible as it was chanted and re-enacted by churchyard crosses and city gates. Liturgical texts endowed biblical narratives with a new meaning, while emulating the Bible in word and genre. In the course of the procession, however, another facet of the medieval Bible was put into play. Among the array of liturgical paraphernalia carried by the secondary procession in imitation of Christ and his entourage was a Gospel book. This book, much like the relics and the cross, was seen to represent Christ. Its symbolic value had been asserted already by the tenth century, when Pseudo-Alcuin's *Liber de divinis oficiis* described it as: 'sanctum evangelium, quod intelligitur Christus'.[1] Its later use retained this sense. Analysis of the medieval procession reveals that the Gospel book was not put into practical use: the only Gospel lesson of the procession (Mt 21:1–9) was read at the beginning of the first station *prior* to the arrival of the secondary procession. The Gospel book carried by the secondary procession was therefore a symbolic object, a prop in the liturgical re-enactment of the biblical narrative. Such use of Bibles, one that employed sacred books as icons, and put aside readability in favour of sacrality, is at the core of this chapter. This chapter follows Bibles as they were employed as talismans in the most mundane rituals, both civic and ecclesiastical, and questions how the Bible was put to use as a sacred object. This exploration of the material culture of the medieval Bible reveals the interaction between appearance and function, between religion and society. But first, a short survey of the uses biblical books were put into will help contextualise this investigation and identify the unexpected books that were employed in churches and courts, as amulets and in graves.

Talismanic use of Scripture predates the Middle Ages. The Bible, or part of it, was employed talismanically in customs that date back to biblical times (e.g. Dt 6:8–9). Archaeological findings have unearthed biblical verses that were used as amulets, such as the minute, seventh-century BC silver scrolls of the priestly blessing (Nm 6:24–6) or the more common phylacteries, with evidence for their use ranging from the Second Temple to the present.[2] The emerging Christian communities of Late Antiquity were not oblivious to the matter of their Bibles. They made use of the codex – the technological avant-garde of their time – and saw the move away from scrolls as a tangible manifestation of the new message recorded in their sacred books.[3] Much like their Graeco-Roman and Jewish neighbours, Christians also employed sacred scriptures as talismans: Coptic communities placed Gospel books and psalters in graves to accompany the dead, while Jerome reproached 'superstitious little women' for carrying small Gospel books on their bodies.[4] Both uses, as evident in Jerome's derogatory language, preferred the symbolic to the functional and assumed little or no actual reading of these sacred texts.

In the Middle Ages the Bible was employed time and again as talisman, extending far beyond the incantations and divinations that existed on the outskirts of licit practice. When the Venerable Bede described how Irish codices were put to use against snake bites, scraped and immersed in water, their symbolic function superseded (and even prevented) their legibility.[5] Irish book-shrines (*Cumdach*) provided a luxurious repository for Gospel books and Psalters; they were venerated and recorded as performing miracles, much like reliquaries. And much like reliquaries, *Cumdach* were sealed off and their books were never to be read again.[6] In medieval England, a corner stone was laid for the construction of the Lady Chapel in the Abbey of Peterborough in 1272. The Prior, William Paris, instigated the construction and laid the cornerstone with his own hands. As he placed underneath it numerous 'Gospels' (probably quires), he used the book in a clear echo of Acts 4:11 ('This (Christ) is the stone which was rejected by you the builders, which is become the head of the corner.'), with the Gospels standing in for Christ.[7] The entombed Gospels were, once more, employed for their symbolic value, with any possibility of readership as remote as for those buried in Coptic graves. Another sacred book – the *textus* (i.e. Gospel book, examined at length below) of St Mildred – miraculously led a perjuring countryman from the Isle of Thanet to lose his sight in the account of Thomas of Elmham.[8] These occurrences demonstrate how the practical textual qualities of sacred books were put aside in favour of their use as sacred objects, akin to icons and relics. As argued by Jean

Vezin, the sacrality of these books emanated from their sacred text, linked to a hallowed scribe (often a saint) and iconic appearance.[9]

The exact nature of the books used in these rituals deserves a second look. We cannot assume that these sacred books were comprised of all books of the Old and New Testaments, especially as single-volume Bibles (pandects, explored in the following chapter) were a rarity up until the end of the twelfth century. Of the books processed, worn, or entombed in book shrines and graves, one part of the Bible stands out. The Gospels, much like in the Palm Sunday liturgy, was the book employed talismanically as a representation of Christ. Containing the crux of Christian faith, it is of little wonder that in the inner hierarchy of biblical books used talismanically the Gospel presided. Their place of honour is also attested in solemn rituals which were at the heart of the Catholic Church, as explored by Klaus Schreiner. A late ninth-century Byzantine manuscript depicts an open Gospel book set on a throne, presiding, in the full sense of the word, over the First Council of Constantinople (381).[10] In a custom that appeared in church councils from Ephesus (431) to Constance (1414–18), the book served both symbolic and practical aims. The image, however, does not depict the book during one of the readings which occurred at the Council, but rather as it lies open on a throne. In the First Council of Constantinople, the Council that ended the Arian controversy and condemned Apolloniarianism, the open Gospel book was a tangible symbol of the desired unity of the church, a constant reminder of the human element of Christ, rejected by Apollonius. The consecration of Gregory of Nazianzus, appointed bishop that very same year (381, though he quickly resigned his see), is depicted in the same manuscript. There, in a ritual practised in medieval Europe as well, a Gospel book was employed.[11] The open book was held or placed over the neck and head of the ordinand, if he was to become a bishop, or shoulder, if pope. The book filled both functional and symbolic roles. It provided a physical link between the Gospel lessons read in the ordination and the body of the ordinand. Liturgical commentaries, from Amalarius of Metz's (d. 850/1) *Liber officialis* to Durand's *Rationale* (studied and preached in late medieval England), likened the book to Aaron's tiara (Ex 28:36–40), to the word of God (Is 61:1, frequent in ordinations), or to the Holy Ghost descending as a dove (Lk 3:22).[12]

Church rituals open a window on to the use of Bibles as sacred objects in the Middle Ages. They direct our attention away from questions of biblical language and textual accuracy, and into the realm of appearance and gestures. This chapter engages with the Bible as a sacred object, to reveal a book that was judged primarily by its covers and venerated as an icon. The evidence leads to the little-explored world of oath-books and *textus*, two books that employed the text of the Gospels, but whose definition as biblical books is often tenuous. The two most recurrent rituals which made use of such biblical books were Masses and oaths, examined in this chapter. These rituals, at the core of church and civic culture, enabled priests and parishioners to view, hear, and touch sacred Scripture. Vouchsafing the veracity of witnesses and litigants or reiterating the narratives of Christ's life and his redeeming death, Gospel books were key to the success of civic and ecclesiastical rites alike. The two rituals also display a surprising degree of similarity: both employed sacred books in the course of complex rituals, in which utterances and gestures were key; both delineated subtle non-textual boundaries between lay and religious; both endowed the authority of sacred Scripture on their protagonists, even without the need to read from the book in question; and both were governed by trained professionals, who left little record of these most common of rituals in our sources. Liturgy and law, however, have rarely been studied together. The comparative examination of literature and law has benefited the study of both disciplines immensely.[13] In a similar manner, a comparative study of law and liturgy – two of the most complex and challenging systems to the modern student – presents mirror rituals that reinforced social boundaries through performance and material objects.[14] Moreover, convergence of the two spheres sheds new light on the medieval Bible, in the complex and rarely recorded links between religious houses and courts of law for the supply of sacred books, or in the merging of quires from liturgical and legal books into a single, sacred object.

These two types of rituals, repetitive and supervised by trained professionals, left little record in our sources regarding gestures and the exact nature of the books used. Only a handful of oath-books and Gospel books survive in their medieval attire, and we have to resort to sources outside their immediate remit to shed additional light on ritual and material culture. The next part of the chapter examines the medieval Mass through liturgical manuscripts and their vernacular renderings. To corroborate these, library catalogues, sacrists' records, and visitation records furnish the following section with a new understanding of the *textus* – the Gospel book that was used in rituals. Two such *textus* were employed by Hubert de Burgh (d. 1243), and link Masses with oath-rituals, leading us into the realm of courts of law and oath-books. Court records, canon and common law treatises, and Middle English literary narratives all portray the elusive nature of oath-books, which were used in complex rituals. A few surviving manuscripts, and the oaths of medieval Jews, assist in defining the nature of these books, which followed appearance and antiquity. After exploring each of these issues, the conclusion of this chapter questions the transition of such talismanic uses into modernity, addressing the similarities between modern and medieval uses, as well as the changes that were ushered by the coming of moveable-type print and the Reformation.

The Mass: the Gospel book goes centre-stage

The re-creation of the biblical past engaged all the senses during Mass.[15] Much like the liturgy of Palm Sunday, in which parishioners and clergy experienced the Bible in text and tune, key location, and paraphernalia, during the Mass they heard the Bible chanted, smelled the incense, saw sacred books processed and elevated, and consumed the body of Christ. Liturgy was a sensual experience and modern scholars have explored the way it transmitted Bible and doctrine, often presenting it as an overwhelmingly oral and aural experience.[16] Far from being merely a modern idea, this awareness of the involvement of the senses in the liturgy was itself recognised in the Middle Ages. The twelfth-century theologian John Beleth (d. after 1165) saw the injunction for the laity to bare their heads during Gospel lessons as emphasising its appeal to all five senses (with the implicit supremacy of its aural qualities): 'Viri revelato capite debent audire evangelium, ut quinque sensus patuli sint ad audiendum'.[17] Beleth identified the moment prior to the reading of the Gospel as a moment in which all senses should be opened to receive God's words. His comment suggests that not all biblical elements carried the same weight: the Gospel lesson was signalled out in gestures and paraphernalia, indicating its supremacy over all other biblical texts read during Mass.

An explicit comparison between Gospels lessons and those of the Old Testament was made by the Comestor (d. 1178/9) in his first lecture on the Gospel of Matthew. The gestures addressed by Beleth enabled the Comestor to develop an allegorical interpretation:

> Unde ewangelium veteri testamento in tribus antecellit, scilicet in revelatione figuratorum, in impletione promissorum, in magnitudine premiorum. Ad insinuandam hanc triplicem ewangelii preeminentiam, tria facit ecclesia cum legitur ewangelium. Ad ostendendum enim quod per ewangelium facta est figurarum revelatio, audit ewangelium capite revelato; ad ostendendum quod in ewangelio facta est promissorum impletio, audit ewangelium cum silentio, ac si ipso silentio dicat: iam optineo promissa. Solent enim pueri silere postquam tenent poma. Ad ostendendam amplitudinem promissorum, terminat ewangelium voce

> elevata plenum gratie et veritatis, contra lectiones veteris testamenti terminentur voce remissa; ac si dicatur ibi promittebantur, hic superna.[18]

The Comestor's allegorization makes explicit the supremacy of the Gospels in the inner-biblical hierarchy of talismanic uses. The activities of the laity (standing in silence, heads bare) and of clergy (ending on a higher note) manifested the prominence of the Gospels over any other part of the Bible. This emanated from the nature of the Gospels themselves, containing the crux of Christian faith. The Comestor's description of parishioners' activities is corroborated in liturgical manuscripts, in which they are required to stand up, unsupported if possible, and uncover their heads (women being exempt for reasons of modesty) for the duration of the Gospel lesson.[19] The *Lay Folk Mass Book*, a Middle English translation of a late twelfth-century manual for lay participation in the Mass (possibly from Rouen and York), commented upon the required mindset and guided lay devotions: during the Gospel reading lay men and women ought to 'speke thou noght, bot thenk on him that dere the bought' and to pray for Christ's grace, filled with dread and love; they were to cross themselves before and after the reading, imitating the acts of the deacon at that very same moment.[20]

The Comestor's reference to the rising tone of the Gospel lesson was to a slight vocal modification that marked the end of the lesson. Apart from this marker, all biblical lessons often shared a simple, mainly syllabic, chanting tone that did not single out the Gospel lesson from other lessons of Mass and office during ordinary time (i.e. apart from major feasts).[21] Instead, another set of liturgical activities marked the Gospel lesson; this was done by drawing attention to the book from which it was to be read, the *textus*. The first glimpse of the *textus* introduced its central role. After the confession and the collect the *textus* was carried ceremoniously to the lectern. In a small procession, a deacon holding a *textus* was preceded by acolytes carrying incense, candles, and a cross.[22] Unlike the array of liturgical paraphernalia on Palm Sunday, in which the *textus* was secondary to the relics and Eucharist, here it dominated the procession. Durand saw its position at the rear as one of veneration, the culmination of a narrative which unfolded in the preceding objects: the incense – representing Christ's deeds that had introduced his doctrine; the acolytes bearing candles – the Apostles entering cities before Christ (Lk 10:1 and parallels); the cross – the end of Christ's earthly life and its essence.[23] Church dignitaries merited a place of honour at the rear of processions; this, according to Durand and Rupert of Deutz (d. 1129), emphasised the supremacy of the Gospel reading over any other lesson read during Mass.[24]

The *textus* was carried ceremoniously, laid upon the altar, and censed (i.e. passed over with a vessel of burning incense) prior to reading. The deacon then made the sign of the cross on the book and on his person, linking speaker and object. Some uses presented a threefold crossing on the brow, mouth, and chest, allegorically removing one's shyness of proclaiming the Gospels (cf. Rom 1:16), preparing to utter the text, and displaying a sign of faith and a measure against the devil.[25] Next the deacon asked for the officiant's blessing 'Iube domine benedicere'. The reply mirrors the tripartite crossing, in blessing the deacon that God should dwell in his heart and mouth for the reading: 'Dominus sit in corde tuo et in ore tuo (*or* labiis tuis) ad pronuntiandum sanctum Evangelium Dei. In nomine Patris et Filii et Spiritus Sancti. Amen.'[26] In York an extended blessing emphasised the sensory qualities of the liturgy even further. It addressed both oral (*sonantem*) and aural (*aures*, *audientibus*) senses and extended beyond the mouth of the deacon to the ears of clergy and laity:

> Officiant: Dominus aperiat tibi os ad legendum et nobis aures ad intelligendum sanctum evangelium Dei [...] Amen.
>
> Deacon: Da mihi, domine, sermonem rectum et bene sonantem in os meum ut placeant tibi verba mea et omnibus audientibus propter nomen tuum in vitam eternam. Amen.[27]

In word and act the blessing forged a link between God, the reader, and the text of the Gospels as contained in the *textus*. Such a link was absent from the preceding epistle reading and served to assert the supremacy of the Gospel lesson. This supremacy was made evident for all, as during the lesson the laity stood up, with bare heads; the place of the reading itself brought this point home, with liturgical manuscripts emphasising that the Gospels were to be read from a step higher than that of previous lessons.

At the lesson's end the deacon kissed the book, taking the relationship between divinity, reader and text to new heights.[28] The kiss connected the spoken word with the book from which it was read. It also constituted an intimate link between deacon and book, and delineated a boundary between clergy and laity. While parishioners could only witness from a distance, the clergy enjoyed unmediated access to the sacred book. Much like the use of different types of palms on Palm Sunday, access to the sacred was not shared by all.[29] The Gospel lesson and its supremacy were encapsulated in the body of the *textus* – key to the medieval ritual. Such a book is often described in liturgical manuscripts as 'textum, scilicet librum evangeliorum' ('textus, namely a Gospel book'). This link, however, can often be misleading, and its place within the array of books used during the Mass unclear.[30] A search for *textus* in parish churches, monasteries, and cathedrals will complicate matters even further, and lead to a new definition that sees *textus* as sacred books dominated by use and appearance.

Provenance I: parishes

Which biblical books were employed in medieval Masses? Liturgical manuscripts paint a uniform picture in which missals and breviaries were used alongside Gospel books or *textus*. They present the latter as quintessential for the performance of the liturgy, a notion commonly adopted by modern scholars.[31] This understanding concurs with missals from large monastic establishments, as it does with the few surviving specimens from chapels and parish churches (such as the missals from Colwich, Staffordshire, and Maldon, Essex, currently BL, Harley MSS 4919 and 2787). These manuscripts, however, may indicate the depth of the problem rather than a solution. Both missals, although linked to parish churches, follow not Low Mass, in which a sole priest officiated over a rudimentary ceremony with no music, but rather High Mass, more typical of religious houses, where deacon and subdeacon aided the priest, with incense and music; these manuscripts assign the full array of liturgical paraphernalia (including a *textus*) even to minor feasts such as the first Sunday of Advent (fols 15v and 13v respectively). Such elaborate rituals would have been beyond the reach of most parish churches in the country. As argued by David Chadd, one should be wary of seeing liturgical manuscripts as a mirror into the reality of the medieval rite, and the two missals probably reflect the dominant liturgical use of Sarum, rather than opening a window on to the worship of their parishes.[32]

The gap between practice and theory, between biblical manuscripts and liturgical needs, follows a transformation in the nature of liturgical books. Bibles, in full or in part, are most cumbersome for use in liturgical rites. The identification and retrieval of Psalms, hymns, and lessons requires numerous bookmarks, frequent leafing and much preliminary preparation in consultation with calendars and tables of readings.[33] In the early and high Middle Ages designated liturgical books were compiled to ease the way of priests through the array of biblical and extra-biblical materials: biblical lessons were re-structured according to their liturgical sequence into lectionaries (often combining biblical lessons from Old and New Testaments, the Epistles and the Gospels), while the all-embracing missal provided officiants with a single book for the prayers, hymns and biblical readings of the Mass.[34] Such books enabled a sole officiant to celebrate

Mass and had a special appeal for parish churches, where Low Mass was practised. The need for Bibles and *textus* in the medieval rite is therefore unclear. As designated liturgical books supplied liturgical chant and lessons, one may wonder whether Bibles and *textus* were deemed necessary for liturgical performance and how often they were put in use in parish libraries, monasteries, or cathedrals.

The landscape of sacred books in medieval England is mostly hidden. The evidence from the well-endowed libraries of cathedrals, monastic establishments, or colleges (addressed below) is fragmentary; that of parish churches is all but invisible to the modern scholar. Their manuscripts, often cheap and heavily used, seldom survive; book-lists and churchwarden accounts are exceptional before the fifteenth century.[35] The evidence we do possess, however, puts the place of Bibles and *textus* in question. Out of over a hundred manuscripts assigned by Neil Ker and Andrew Watson to parish churches and chapels, there is only a single Gospel book (of St Mary's Great Bedwyn, Wiltshire, currently Cambridge, Jesus College MS 31) and four Bibles (which befitted public recitation, as indicated in the size and table of lessons in the Bibles of St Peter-upon-Cornhill, London, currently London, Guildhall MS 4158A and St John the Baptist Bredgar, Kent, currently London, Lambeth Palace MS 1362).[36] As expected, the vast majority of manuscripts are more liturgical in nature, with a proliferation of missals and psalters.

Visitation records are indispensable for tracing books in thirteenth- and fourteenth-century parish churches. As the bishop's representatives recorded their inquiry into the the state of the church, its clergy and possessions, they provided a snapshot of the parish church at a specific moment in time. Records from the dioceses of Ely, Exeter, Salisbury, London, and Norwich give evidence for the possessions of 576 parishes in the thirteenth and fourteenth centuries.[37] As expected, an overwhelming majority of churches held liturgical books, including psalters and lectionaries. By contrast, Bibles and Gospel books were owned by only a tiny fraction. Scarcely more than one per cent of churches held a Bible (six churches, all from the affluent diocese of Norwich); these churches ranked among the better-endowed parish churches in the country, holding more than fifteen books, some even beyond thirty.[38] Only twelve churches (about 2 per cent) were recorded as holding a *textus* or a Gospel book. These churches likewise were better endowed and possessed more books than most.[39] The lack of Bibles could be explained by their liturgical impracticality, as well as their price; the lack of *textus*, however, stands at odds with liturgical manuscripts and their prescribed rituals. This was noted by the modern editor of the Norfolk visitation record, who commented that the *textus* – a book necessary for celebrating Mass – was almost nowhere to be found; he also noted that several churches, with no *textus* and only a lectionary, hold *tabula textus*, possibly covers or bindings for lectionaries.[40]

The bishop's representatives did not simply come to register and document the state of a given church but rather to ensure that it lived up to required standards in its buildings, the capacities of its clergy and the array of its possessions. In some instances, such as a visit to the church of Clyst Honiton (Devon), the bishop's representatives commented upon the lack of psalters, antiphonaries, and chalices and noted down deficiencies in its lectionary and missal.[41] No such comments were ever made regarding the lack of Bibles and *textus*. This is far from accidental. In their requirements, officials abided by book-lists which had been prescribed in church legislation. The late thirteenth-century statutes attributed to John Pecham, Archbishop of Canterbury (d. 1292), followed the synodal statutes of Worcester III (1240) and Wells (*c.* 1258) in laying down the liturgical paraphernalia and books necessary for parish churches.[42] They list seven books: lectionary, antiphonary, gradual, psalter, troper, ordinal, and a missal (with an additional manual in York). These statutes were re-confirmed in subsequent church councils and guided bishops' representatives in their visits, with copies inserted into visitation records and bishops' registers.[43] Visitation records demonstrate that parish churches on the whole abided by these requirements both in the positive and the negative: a profusion of liturgical books combines with an absence of Bibles and *textus* to accord with prescriptive lists and liturgical pragmatism.[44] Private ownership presents a similar pattern of book possession. A survey of privately owned books gives evidence for thirty-six Latin Bibles prior to 1409, most owned by the upper echelons of church and society with a single Bible owned by a chaplain.[45] Three *textus* appear: one donated by Martin of St Cross (d. 1259), master of the hospital of Sts Lazarus, Mary and Martha at Sherburn (Co. Durham), for use at the altar there and two bequeathed by John de Grandisson, Bishop of Exeter (d. 1369), for the high altar at his cathedral.[46]

Visitation records and wills provide insight beyond quantitive analyses. The nature of their entries calls for a new definition of *textus*. Such records commonly describe liturgical books according to their liturgical applicability: psalters are said to be *grosse litere* (large script that enabled reading at a distance); missals are fitting or unsuitable for liturgical rite. *Textus*, however, are *always* described according to their outside appearance, commenting time and again on their binding: St Andrew, Sonning-on-Thames (Berkshire) had a silver gilt *textus* containing the readings in a liturgical, rather than consecutive, sequence (*Unus textus coopertus argento continens Evangelia anni*); a golden *textus* embossed with crystals was at the church of Burgh, Cambridgeshire (*unus textus deauratus cum lapidibus cristalinis, ex dono domini Iohannis de Borw*)[47], and one with gilt images at the church of Fowlmere, Cambridgeshire (*textus bene apparatus de imaginibus deauratis*). The silver *textus* bequeathed by Martin of St Cross to the hospital at Sherburn (*Textum meum argentum*) was in all probability encased in a silver binding, rather than written in silver characters, as suggested by a modern editor.[48] Even in less well-endowed churches, *textus* are still described according to their appearance: an old and weathered (*vetus et attritus*) Gospel book at Mere, Wiltshire, or a decent (*decentes*) one at Sidbury, Devon; the church of Furneaux Pelham, Hertfordshire, had a 'wooden textus' (*textum de ligno*), referring to the boards of its binding. The supremacy of appearance over contents is evident even in the classification of visitation records: *textus* were often noted down not among other service books but rather as part of the liturgical paraphernalia.

The supremacy of appearance has been accepted by the modern editors of visitation records. In the Sarum visitations record, the *textus* is defined as: 'a complete copy of the four Gospels, though the terms, especially the latter (evangeliarium), are applied also to the book containing such portions of them, as were read at some time or other through the year. The volume was not only beautifully illuminated, but its binding was most costly', and the modern editors of Ely visitations implicitly accepted such a supremacy of form in interpreting a lavish lectionary (*Lectionarium* (?) *cum v gaud' in rasura*) from the church of St John in Mill Street, Cambridge, as 'i.e. a textus (q.v.) with 5 jewels or enamelled bosses on the cover'.[49] Such an understanding is present in the early works of du Cange (and adopted by Brian Stock), who saw the *textus* as '*Textus*, liber seu codex Evangeliorum, qui inter cimelia Ecclesiastica reponi solet, auro gemmisque ut plurimum exornatus, aureis etiam interdum characteribus exaratus'.[50] This suggests that *textus* were inherently different from Bibles or liturgical books. It was their appearance and use – lavish bindings, processed and exulted – that defined the *textus*, rather than the text of the Gospels.

Provenance II: monasteries and cathedrals

The gap between Bibles, liturgical books, and *textus* is further revealed as we move away from parish churches to cathedrals and well-endowed monasteries. These religious institutions had the most comprehensive collections of books in late medieval England, rich in biblical books and liturgical manuscripts. The places where these books were kept attest to their use, and at this point we need to extend our gaze beyond libraries to appreciate the tripartite division of biblical books. Books for consultation and study were kept in libraries. The library catalogues of Reading Abbey, Dover Priory, York Austin Friars or Christ Church, Canterbury, record numerous Bibles; interestingly, none of these was defined as *textus* and they typically befitted scholarly rather than liturgical use.[51] Liturgical books such as lectionaries and psalters were kept in the choir from where they were taken out for Mass and office. *Textus* were stored in treasuries among relics, jewelled crosses and chalices. Such a location accorded with their sacral and monetary value. In the 1222 register of St Osmund, Sarum, *textus* were recorded as 'inventa in Thesauraria' and enumerated in descending order of opulence:

> Textus unus aureus magnus continens saphiros xx., et smaragdos vi., et thopasios viii., et alemandinas xviii., et gernettas viii., et perlas xii.
> Item unus Evangelicus bene deauratus cum lapidibus viii.
> Item textus unus parvus cum ymagine beatae Mariae cum lapidibus xix.
> Item texti [*sic*] quatuor cooperti argento, deaurati omnes praeter unum
> Item texti [*sic*] duo sine argento[52]

The splendour of the first *textus* listed here surpassed any found in parish churches and attests to a truly spectacular object, covered in gold and silver and embedded with dozens of precious stones. The record, however, reflects the evidence from parish libraries in describing *textus* among liturgical paraphernalia primarily according to their appearance.

A supremacy of form over content is evident in other inventories as well. Opulent *textus* were recorded in the inventories of St Paul's, Durham Abbey, Canterbury Cathedral, Westminster Abbey and the smaller, though well-endowed, St George's Chapel at Windsor Castle.[53] The most detailed account is probably the 1315/16 catalogue and inventory of Christ Church, Canterbury (BL, Cotton MS Galba E.iv, fols 112r–47v).[54] This record preserves the tripartite division of biblical books: general books in the library, liturgical in the choir and *textus* in the treasury. Once more *textus* are described following their appearance, in terms of image and material (e.g. 'Item textus argento deaurato coopertus, cum crcifixo, Maria & Iohannes pictortis [...] Item textus cupro deaurato coopertus cum mayestate in medio & tribus ymaginibus in tabernaculis & duobus angelis argentis & de auro cum iiij evangelistis in quatuor angulis de cupro de auro').[55] Some of the *textus* were further identified by their donor or were given a unique name (e.g. 'Item textus magnus qui dicitur domus dei argento coopertus & gemmis ornatus [...]; Item textus Edmundi Comitis Cornubie argento deaurato coopertus et gemmis ornatus [...]').[56]

The *textus* in the Canterbury inventory concur with other inventories in descriptions of precious metals and stones, as well as of sacred iconography. Three items in the inventory expand our understanding of *textus* even further. Although made of precious metals, and incorporating images of Christ's life and Thomas Becket, these were noted as *textus sine libro*, a book-less *textus*:

> Item textus sine libro in medio auro coopertus & gemmis ornatus cum crucifixo eburneo et Maria et Iohannes eborneis et auro fibulatus.
>
> Item textus ligneus sine libro. argento deaurato coopertus et gemmis ornatus cum annunciatione oblatione in templo et aliis ymaginibus de nativitate Christi argenteis et deauratis.
>
> Item textus ligneus sine libro coopertus argento deaurato cum martyrio sancti Thome.[57]

Much like the *textus*-boards from the diocese of Norwich, these were empty bindings made of precious metals and stones. The entries in the Canterbury inventory reveal that the standard text of a *textus* was that of the Gospels, as any disparate examples were clearly identified; they also demonstrate that text was secondary to appearance, and that 'book-less *textus*' were not rejected by sacrists.

Most *textus* displayed a common iconography. In Canterbury, as elsewhere, these typically included Christ in Majesty (on twelve *textus*) and the Crucifixion with Mary and St John (on seven), surrounded by angels and the Four Evangelists. Object and function, text and image were tied together, as images on *textus* mirrored the ritual narrative of the Mass. The Crucifixion is the cornerstone of every Mass, while the image of Christ in Majesty surrounded by cherubim is a visual representation of the *Sanctus* – the clergy's imitation of the heavenly songs of praise (Is 6:3, Rev 4:8) during the canon of the Mass. A unique exception to this iconography is the image of the martyrdom of Thomas Becket on a Canterbury 'book-less *textus*'. This *textus* was part of the emerging cult of Becket in Canterbury and can be associated with another exceptional *textus* in the inventory: 'Item Textus cum psalterio Sancti Thome argento deaurato coopertus gemmis ornatus in circumferentia cum mayestate eburnea tenente librum in medio, & .iiij. evangelistis sculptis'.[58] Displaying the common iconography of Christ in Majesty and Four Evangelists, the latter *textus* encompassed the psalter of no other than Thomas Becket himself. One of the very few *textus* to contain a text other than the Gospels, this book's sacrality emanated not only from its text and appearance. In accordance with the categories offered by Jean Vezin, its sacred text and iconic appearance were overshadowed by its hallowed patron. It was an object of devotion which offered access to the saint himself, much like his relics which were noted down in the same sacrist's record.[59] The centrality of Becket to the community at Canterbury explains the break with common contents and iconography, as two of the four non-Gospel *textus* had a close affinity to Thomas Becket. Vezin's analysis of Gospel books as reliquaries of the sacred text supports a new understanding of the Becket-*textus* at Canterbury, and may assist in reconstructing their use. The psalter, relics, and book-less *textus* all brought the martyrdom and memory of Thomas Becket to mind. They were of special use in the evolving liturgy of the saint, celebrated on the days of his martyrdom (29 December) and translation (7 July). On these days they could have supported the saint's liturgy – either in Psalmody or as an ad-hoc binding for liturgical manuscripts.[60]

The memory of Becket preserved in the treasury of his cathedral corresponds with Eric Palazzo's understanding of treasury books as the collective memory of a religious establishment.[61] The iconography of Becket's martyrdom and his book-relic were given a place of honour in the community's memory as well as in its treasury. Another link between a *textus* and communal identity is to be found in record of Rochester Cathedral. The Cathedral's 1202 inventory records a beautiful golden *textus* containing the life and history of St Andrew, its patron saint ('textum pulchrum deauratum, in quo vita et historia sancti Andree').[62] Of special value on the saint's day, the *textus* of St Andrew mirrors that of Canterbury in providing a material link between the community and its past. Such a connection extended to the incorporation of donors' names, charters, and inventories into the *textus* examined by Palazzo. It made *textus* part of the living memory of the community, akin to the relics that cohabited its treasury.

The connection between *textus* and relics extended beyond co-occupying a treasury. The two categories of sacred objects, precious and symbolic, even merged together in a handful of occurrences. Such is a fourteenth-century sacrist's inventory from Glastonbury Abbey. Between the records for King Arthur's grave and a reliquary given to the abbey by King Edmund, two *textus* appear. Not out of place among these sacred containers, their description extends beyond precious metals and iconography to enumerate the relics which were embedded within, or affixed to, their binding. One of these *textus* contained three relics and the other no fewer than fifty-two:

In textu cuius superiori parte et inferiori sunt ymagines regum et in utroque latere ymagines virginum continentur hee reliquie:

de Apostolis:

- de Sancto Petro
- de Sancto Paulo [...]
- de Sancto Georgio
- de Sancto Gildardo

de martiribus et de confessoribus:

- de Sancto Edmundo archiepiscopo
- de Sancto Augustino Anglorum apostolo [...]
- de Sancto Dunstano
- de Sancto Aidano

de virginibus:

- de Sancta Margareta [...]
- de Sancta Edburga

In textu cum leonibus et aquilis in auro continentur hee reliquie:

- de Sancto Oswaldo rege
- de Sancta Hylda
- de Sancto Vincentio.[63]

No reference is made to the content of these books. They appear to have functioned as any other reliquary, supporting an unexpected twist on Vezin's understanding of Gospel books as reliquaries, this time not only following the sacred text contained in them. Such books were far from the norm, but similar *textus* did also exist elsewhere. Such was a golden *textus* with relics (*textus de auro cum reliquiis*) which Nigel, Bishop of Ely, carried with him on his way to Rome (*c.* 1140). As a supporter of Empress Matilda during the civil war, he was stopped by the soldiers of King Stephen who took possession of the *textus* alongside other liturgical paraphernalia.[64] The Bishop's *textus* was a unique vademecum, supplying both relics and Gospels for liturgy and veneration; its theft reminds us that relics were cherished not only for their sacral but also for their monetary value. Much like gold and gems, relics made these *textus* dear to their owners.

The splendour of *textus* endangered their survival, for they were often pawned, sold, or stolen.[65] In England most were seized at the Dissolution, melted for gold, and taken apart for their precious stones. Very few *textus* of English origins have escaped this fate intact. Two rare survivals are currently New York, Pierpont Morgan Library MSS M.708 and M.709, and their appearance assists in corroborating sacrists' records. The front binding of M.708 (Plate 2) fits perfectly with the written evidence: Christ in Majesty occupies the upper register, sitting in mandorla flanked by two seraphim, while the Crucifixion with Mary and St John is in the lower register; silver gilt and precious stones rank this *textus* among the more lavish examples of its time. Patrick McGurk's analysis sheds light on their provenance and use, showing that their appearance was more important than their contents.[66] These two *textus* were compiled in mid-eleventh-century England under the patronage of Judith of Flanders (d. 1094/5), then wife of Tostig Godwinson, Earl of Northumbria. They were part of a group of four Gospel books (with Fulda, Hessiche Landesbibliothek MS Aa 21 and Monte Cassino, Archivio della Badia MS 437, both lacking their original binding). The four manuscripts share the narratives of Crucifixion and Resurrection, but only M.709 contains the full text of the four Gospels. MacGurk's dating of the textual gaps to the time of composition, combined with numerous uncorrected scribal errors and a lack of Eusebian canons, led him to conclude that 'the books may have been made essentially for a symbolic or ceremonial use for the members of a household or capella'.[67] Such use agrees with evidence from cathedrals and parish churches, and is corroborated by the books' subsequent history: when Judith went into exile to her father's court in 1065 she took these manuscripts with her; shortly before her death she bequeathed them among other liturgical books and paraphernalia to the Benedictine abbey of Weingarten, where they remained until the end of the eighteenth century. McGurk's detailed analysis reveals that during that time they were put into partial use, once more primarily for iconic purposes. Both the Fulda manuscript and M.708 contain donations and charters, showing that they may have been used to facilitate oaths in a use that relied less on textual accuracy, and more on the object's appearance and sacrality.

Other *textus* have survived without their original binding. They bear close resemblance to the *textus* of Judith of Flanders in their compilation and likely use. The York Gospels, another Anglo-Saxon Gospel book once encased in lavish bindings and used to facilitate oaths at York Minster, is discussed below. BL, Royal MS 1 B.xi was written at Canterbury in the second half of the twelfth century and held at St Augustine's Abbey there. It contains (fols 145v–147v) administrative addenda, such as revenues, knight's fees, and tithes wrongly withheld, which attest to a possible use in oath-taking. BL, Royal MS 1 D.iii was written in Canterbury a century earlier, in the first half of the eleventh century. It presents the four Gospels in a clear Caroline minuscule with Eusebian canons and illuminated initials. Its liturgical use is attested by prayers and short treatises inserted between the Gospels, and by an *Exultet* (the Easter Proclamation, chanted before the paschal candle during the Easter Vigil) with musical notation added in a twelfth-century hand on fols 7v–8r. Much like other *textus* there are no textual corrections, and it was probably employed primarily on solemn occasions, when it was processed and venerated. The book's known history attests to times when it was kept outside the treasury. Written at

Plate 1 Entry to Jerusalem, Oxford, Bodleian Library, MS Lat. Liturg. d. 42, fol. 8r

Plate 2 Christ in majesty and Crucifixion, Pierpont Morgan Library, MS M.708, front binding

Plate 3 Crucifix, BL, Stowe MS 15, back binding

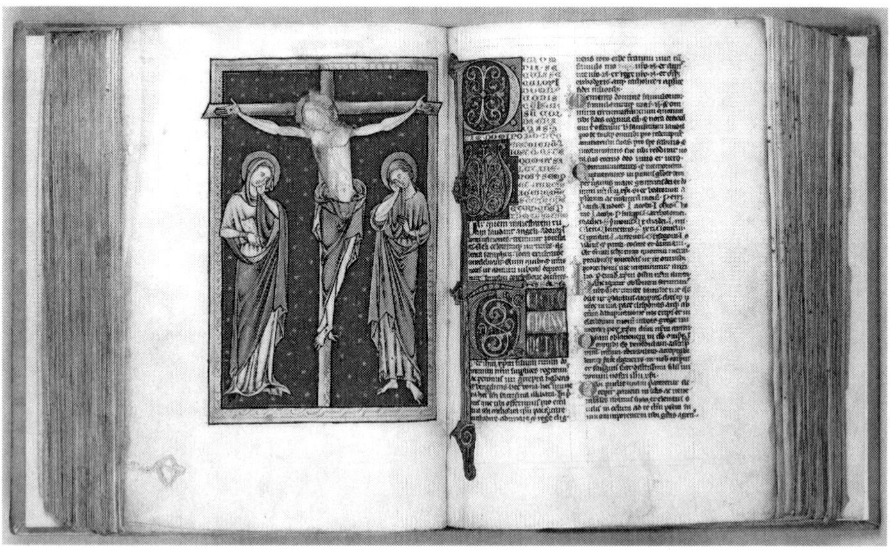

Plate 4 Crucifixion and prefaces of Mass, Huntington Library, MS HM 26061, fols 178v-179r

Plate 5 Late Medieval Bible, Edinburgh University Library, MS 4, fols 170v–171r

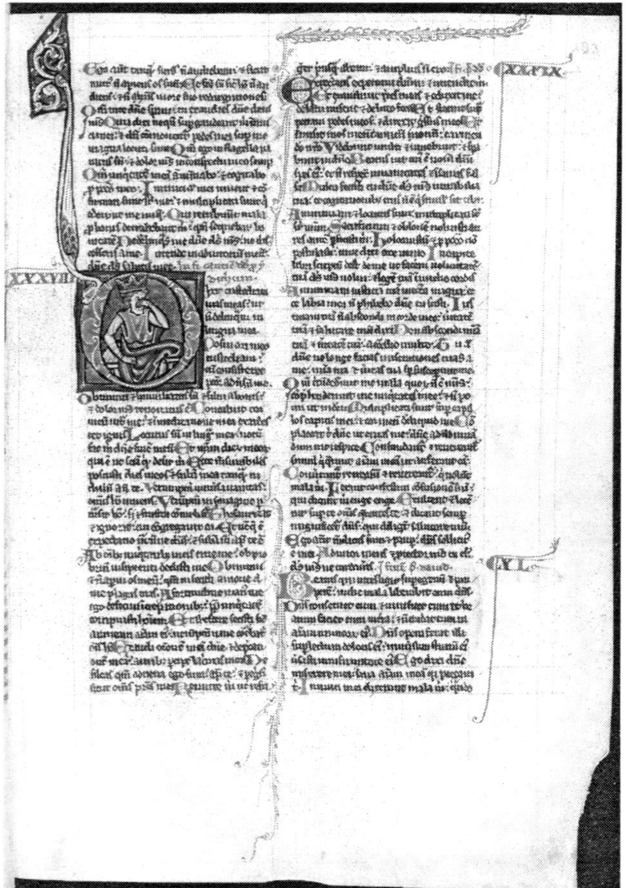

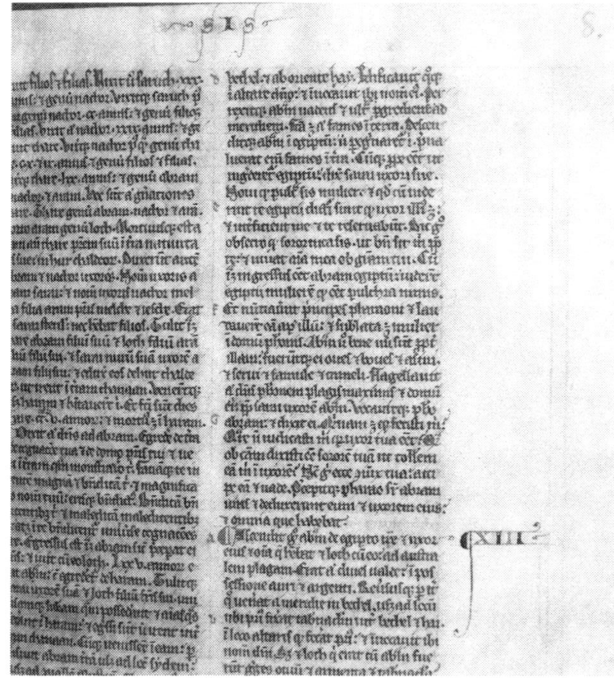

Plate 6 Layout detail, Victoria and Albert Museum, Reid MS 21, fol. 8rb (detail)

Plate 7 Psalm 38, Oxford, Bodleian Library MS Lat. bib. e. 7, fol. 183r

Canterbury for Countess Godgifu (or Gode, d. *c.* 1049), sister of Edward the Confessor, it was given to the Benedictine priory at Rochester, where it was bound with gold and gems. In was subsequently placed in pawn and redeemed by Prior Helyas, *c.* 1200, who was then recorded as giving the golden *textus* back to the cathedral.[68] Another to pawn a precious *textus* was Nigel, Bishop of Ely, whose stolen *textus* is discussed above (p. 73) and who pledged a 'golden *textus*' to the Jews of Cambridge.[69] *Textus* were thus dynamic objects that were adorned, pawned, stolen, used, and cherished not only by religious communities but also by lay men and women who commissioned and bequeathed them.

Transition: *textus* and the career of Hubert de Burgh

The register of Sarum Cathedral notes that on 2 October 1225 Hubert de Burgh (d. 1243), the Chief Justiciar and possibly the most powerful man in the kingdom at the time, donated a golden *textus* with precious stones and relics in honour of the Virgin Mary to the cathedral ('textum aureum cum lapidibus pretiosis & reliquiis diversorum sanctorum, ad honorem beatae Virginis'). The following day the dean went to collect the *textus* from London and offered it over the new altar. It was then decided by the bishop and canons that it would be placed in the church's treasury for safe-keeping, with the key given to the dean of Sarum.[70] At the end of that year the same *textus* was recalled. After attending the Mass of the Holy Innocents at Salisbury, Henry III, still a minor, ordered that his gift to the cathedral – a precious stone and gold from a ring – be inserted into the *textus*. The justiciar asked for the *textus* to be brought, carried between them, and then laid with great devotion on the altar.[71] A complex ritual unfolded, which drew king, justiciar, and *textus* into its ambit. The medium of the *textus* facilitated a dialogue between the two laymen, demonstrating how donating and adorning a *textus* extended beyond mere pious deeds. Although the motives of Hubert and the young king accord with devotional practices and acknowledge the sanctity of the Cathedral, the Virgin Mary, and the text of the Gospels, the connection between the two acts also reflects a temporal balance of power. At the time the rivalry between Hubert and Peter des Roches, Bishop of Winchester (d. 1238), had nearly escalated into a civil war.[72] Hubert was victorious in this contest and became one of the most influential men in Henry's court. Accordingly, the attachment of Henry's ring to the *textus* donated by Hubert expressed Henry's affinity with Hubert.[73] It was treasured by the cathedral and the 1536 Dissolution inventory describes it as: 'A Text after John, gilt with gold, having precious stones and the relicks of dyvers saints, *Ex dono Huberti de Burgo Justiciarij* Domini regis Henrici III'.[74]

The *textus* preserved in Sarum may have served as a reminder of the height of Hubert's career. Another *textus*, however, bears witness to his downfall. On 2 July 1232, Henry lodged at Hubert's house at Burgh (Norfolk) on his way back from pilgrimage to the relic of the True Cross at Bromhold. The king had a special affinity to the relics of Bromhold and had made the pilgrimage on at least four other occasions. In 1232 it was taken in a new political climate, following the readmission of Peter des Roches to the affinity of the king.[75] During his travels (either at Bromhold or Burgh) Henry promised various honours to both Hubert and his wife, taking a solemn oath on a *textus*.[76] This was not to last. A month later Henry wrote to Pope Gregory IX seeking the oath's annulment. Hubert fell from grace, his lands were confiscated, and he was imprisoned. In this shift of temporal power, a *textus* once more played a key role. In light of these events it is noteworthy that Henry's oath was not taken on the relics of the True Cross, to which he had had access on the previous day. Rather, the choice to take an oath on a *textus* suggests an attempt to modify the oath's sanctity. The use of a *textus* to facilitate an oath, although sacred and customary, had enabled Henry to avoid employing the few precious remnants of the True Cross for an oath he was quickly to break. Showing the links between the mundane and the secular, the religious and the civic spheres, the two *textus* attest to a variety of talismanic uses of Scriptures and their delicate undertones.

Oaths and sacred books in courts of law

The sanctity of the *textus* and its iconic use were employed outside the immediate remit of the liturgy. Other highly structured rituals took place daily in churches, as well as in courts of law, and made use of the link sacred books forged between mortals and the divine. Oath rituals present a mirror image to Masses, and their analysis likewise benefits from tracing gestures, speech, and paraphernalia to reveal the complexity of books, their nature, and their use. Much like their liturgical counterparts, legal manuscripts make only passing reference to recurring rituals, and unearthing the nature and use of oath-books requires a wide array of sources, within and without the legal system. Written by and for trained professionals, court records and legal treatises presuppose much knowledge of legal practice, and most often simply note that an oath was taken. In instances when the oath is expanded upon, the language is succinct and highly formulaic. Two records go briefly beyond the mere acknowledgement of an oath, to refer to the nature of the sacred book employed. They present similar emphases in different languages, showing the same patterns of use across the legal sphere. During a prolonged dispute between the Prior of Newton Longville (Buckinghamshire) and his unfree tenants, the latter were charged with defaming the prior and came before the manor court of Great Horwood on 8 April 1356. The accused informed the court that in order to clear themselves from this allegation they had appeared before the prior at Newton Longville and placed themselves in his grace, swearing: 'Johannes et alii tacti sacrosanctis ewangeliis corporaiter prestiterunt sacrum, quod de cetero erint iusticabilis domino suo secundo quod statum suum et tenura sua requirit'.[77] A similar description appears in the records of a private indenture from 1316, in which Peter de Uvedale was retained to the service of Henry Despenser in an oath of alliance 'sur les seintz Evangelies Dieu corporament touchez de sa mayn destre toute nouve'.[78] Both records present a common legal formula in different languages: they identify the book in question as the Gospels, its sacrality asserted by the adjective 'sacrosanct' (*seintz* / *sacrosanctis*); they further emphasise the physical (*corporaliter* / *corporament*) touch with the book.

A common law treatise preserved in BL, Egerton MS 656 provides instructions for administering an oath given by a seneschal to a bailiff. In order to instruct the seneschal in due conduct, it expands upon the necessary requirements while taking an oath. Thus, the seneschal is instructed to put his hand on the book, say the oath, and kiss the book thereafter ('et mettra (le seneschal) sa meyn sur le lyvere et dirra issinc: Serement – "Ceo oyex vous Baylyf [...] si deu mey eyde et ly seynx" et puys beysera le lyvere et s'en irra').[79] The value of these physical acts is further asserted, rendering them paramount to the validity of the oath. The treatise proceeds to list the circumstances in which the oath would be invalid: if the hand was removed from the book during oath, or the book was not kissed afterwards, or the wrong words were used, the oath could be annulled. The ritual was therefore not a mere embellishment; it was at the heart of the administration of the oath and its gestures and utterances were key to its success.

A common law treatise from the fourteenth century presents a tripartite explanation of the activities of an oath-taker, in a manner not dissimilar to the Comestor's understanding of the medieval Mass, discussed above:

> Qui jurat super librum tria facit. Primo quasi diceret: omnia que scripta sunt in hoc libro nunquam mihi proficiant, neque lex nova neque vetus, si mentiam in hoc juramento. Secundo apponit manum super librum: quasi diceret nunquam bona opera que feci michi proficiant ante faciem

> Jesu Christi, nisi veritatem dicam quam per manum significantur opera. Tercio et ultimo osculatur librum quasi diceret nunquam (oraci)ones neque preces quas per os meum dixi mihi ad salutem animi valeant si falsitatem in hoc juramento michi apposito dicam.[80]

The intimacy between book and oath-taker evolved gradually: at first he acknowledged the existence of a book which contained both old and new law (a slightly ambiguous attribution that could refer to either a legal document or a full Bible). Then the touch of the book brought to mind the Last Judgement, when Christ would preside over a court and judge all men's deeds. This eschatological moment had a special appeal for participants in the legal drama, as the present court session was a mere reflection of the one to come. The third level was manifested in a kiss. Much like the deacon's kiss of a *textus* during Mass, this was an intimate act in a public sphere. It joined together oath-taker and book, with references to the orality of one's prayers and petitions, while simultaneously strengthening the act's liturgical parallels.

The link between oath rituals and the liturgy, especially the ordinary of the Mass, are evident on multiple levels. Both instances were public ritual acts under the examination of a senior member (officiant or judge and clerics), in which the utterance of the actor (deacon or witness and jurors) linked book and divinity to ensure the veracity of his utterance (lesson or oath), culminating in the intimacy of a kiss. Unlike the liturgy, in which only the clergy enjoyed unmediated access to the book, in courts of law it was experienced by the laity and supplied them with a unique opportunity to physically touch a sacred book. Such a breach of social boundaries was curbed by canon lawyers, whose alternative inverted the roles of clergy and laity in the two rituals. Problems stemming from the appearance of priests in courts of law were a cause of continuous friction between the church and secular authorities.[81] A solution was therefore devised to enable priests to take oaths. John of Bologna (*Iohannes Bononiensis*), a notary of the papal curia, joined the staff of the Archbishop of Canterbury and accompanied him to England in 1279. In a treatise intended for the education of English notaries, written after his return to the Continent, he commented upon priests' oaths to conclude that 'si vero presbyter est qui iurat, non debet tangere librum, sed tantum manum apponere super librum'.[82] Priests, unlike laymen, enjoyed direct contact with sacred books in the course of the liturgy and had merely to acknowledge their existence when giving oaths. This restored the boundary between clergy and laity, implicitly suggesting that contact with the sacred book, which priests enjoyed daily, was not necessary to assure the veracity of their oaths.

John of Bologna's treatise was devised for lawyers engaged in the study and practice of canon law, the legal system practised within the established church but touching upon many facets of lay life. Canon law treatises and court records complement the two other legal systems of medieval England, common law and manorial courts, in employing the same words and gestures. This is evident in brief records, such as the one made by the representatives of the Bishop of Exeter, when they visited the church of Aleborne in 1309, recoding an oath made in the course of an inheritance dispute in words similar to those of common and manor courts: 'jurans ad sacrosancta dei evangelia, coram nobis corporaliter tacta'.[83] John of Bologna discussed at length the manner in which a notary must question a witness to conclude: 'Dicat notarius actori in hunc modum: "tu iurabis ad sancta Dei evangelia, dicere et respondere puram veritatem [...] sic Deus te adiuvet et hec sancta Dei evangelia." Et faciat notarius quod tam actor quam reus tangendo librum in propria persona proferat dicta verba.'[84] Much like the common law treatise of the Egerton manuscript, utterance and touch are key to the oath's success; as in common law, the precise oath-formula concludes with the phrase 'Sic me Deus adiuvet et hec sancta Dei evangelia' ('So help me God and these sacred Gospels'). John of Bologna instructed that even when a group of people swore together (hence employing an abbreviated statement), each was still to utter this phrase in full.[85] This formula is full of meaning: similar to the deacon's proclamation prior to the Gospel lesson, it equated between God and Gospels through the medium of the book (manifested in the pronoun *hec*). Such equation, far from a linguistic trifle, incurred the wrath of those who found swearing on the Gospels a form of idolatry.

Gratian's *Decretum*, the cornerstone of canon law from *c.* 1140, attests to a heated argument which saw oaths on the Gospels as detracting from divine worship and violating the third commandment (as well as Mt 5:36 and Jas 5:12). These unnamed opponents are answered: '(after a prohibition of swearing by creatures, God's hair, or his head) Si aliqua causa fuerit, modicum videtur facere, qui iurat per Deum. Qui autem per evangelium, maius aliquid fecisse videtur. Quibus dicendum est: Stulti, scripturae propter Deum sanctae sunt, non Deus propter scripturas.'[86] The *Decretum*'s solution was to deny the Gospels any inherent sacrality, beyond that of God. This, however, does not mask the fact that it was church ritual itself which had endowed the physical object with an aura of sacrality. Much like the palms and flowers of Palm Sunday, ritual activities presented oath-books as sacred objects which would cause the oath-breaker's eternal damnation. The solemnity of the occasion, seen by

Gratian's unnamed opponents to stretch the boundaries of monotheism, was devised to instil fear in the heart, a means to ensure the veracity of litigant in an echo of the early medieval ordeal.[87]

Heterodox groups' objection to the use of Gospel books in courts of law, based on the Third Commandment, challenged the basic tenets of the legal system. Crucial to the medieval court and evidence culture, as well as means of assuring or enforcing loyalty, the oath's infringement posed a threat which was treated with vigour.[88] John Wyclif warned against swearing in God's name in vain and his followers' rejection of oaths incurred the wrath of English crown and church.[89] On Palm Sunday 1405, a chaplain named John Edward was forced to recant his suspected Lollard convictions publicly outside Norwich Cathedral. In the record each heretical article in Latin is followed by the chaplain's English statement:

> I sey that this article is fals and erronee and by fals informacion y held it [...] renounce and aske foryevenesse ther of and swere to these holi evangelies by me bodily touched that fro this tyme forward y shal it never prechin techin ne holdyn priveliche ne in apert.[90]

Outside the cathedral John Edward renounced his heretical beliefs in word and act. One of the articles which he professed to be erroneous declared that no priest, apart from the pope, had the power to force a person to take an oath on God's creatures or on the Gospels ('Item quod pape nec aluquis prelatus neque ordinarius potest aliquem compellere ad iurandum per aliquam creaturam dei nec ad sancta dei evangelia').[91] As John Edward made this statement while being forced to swear on the Gospels, its errors were evident to all those around. Moreover, as we note that John Edward was a chaplain, an additional layer of meaning to the ritual unfolds. Priests were exempt from touching the oath-book, but this was not the case in this chaplain's denunciation of heresy; a ritual in which a clergyman was forced to touch the Gospels had the additional aspect of public correction, if not humiliation.

Provision and nature of oath-books

Medieval legal documents, much like their liturgical counterparts, present a uniform image of oath rituals and the books used in them. As with the liturgy, sources outside their immediate genre shed more light (and add more questions) on the nature of these books and their provision. Middle English literary narratives display succinct descriptions of oath-rituals, akin to those in legal manuscripts. Such is the early fourteenth-century verse romance *Richard Coeur de Lion*, in which three knights swear an oath of alliance not to forsake the King:

> On the book they layde here hand,
> To that forewarde for to stand
> And kyste hem thenne alle three
> Trewe sworn for to bee.[92]
>
> (ll. 605–8)

This brief account resembles court records and legal treatises in stating that the knights placed their hand on the book while uttering the oath, although – in keeping with chivalric ideals – they kissed one another afterwards; its rhymes assist in merging ritual acts (lines 605, 607) with the essence of the oath (606, 608). Other literary oaths further expand on the use of books, their nature, and their ritual activities, and forge a stronger link between law and liturgy.

In Chaucer's *Canterbury Tales*, the 'Man of Law's Tale' narrates how a knight falsely accused Constance of murder. To judge in the case, King Alla asks for a book. A Gospel book is brought, upon which the knight swears his false oath and is immediately struck from the heavens:

> 'Now hastily do fecche a book,' quod he,
> 'And if this knyght wol sweren how that she
> This womman slow, yet wol we us avyse,
> Whom that we wole, that shal been oure justise.'
> A Britoun book, written with Evaungiles,
> Was fet, and on this book he swoor anoon
> She gilty was, and in the meene whiles
> An hand hym smoot upon the nekke-boon,
> That doun he fil atones as a stoon.[93]
>
> (lines 662–70)

The narrator, well-versed in legal procedure, presents an ideal oath-ritual: the oath's veracity is asserted by divine intervention (in a distant echo of the custom of placing a Gospel book on the neck of ordained bishops) and punishment is handled by the secular authorities. Following the miracle the king executes the perjurer and converts with his household. Chaucer followed a well-trodden path in assigning miraculous powers to Gospel books, especially in oath rituals. The particulars of the 'Man of Law's Tale', however, require an explanation: how did a Gospel book make its way to the pagan court of King Alla? What was the nature of that 'Britoun book'? Don-John Dugas's analysis concludes that the 'Britoun book' supplied King Alla with imperial and divine authority through an allusion to a glorified past (Felix Brutus), dignified present (the 'natural Christianity' of the king), and pious future (predating Augustine's arrival to England).[94] The use and appearance of medieval *textus* supports this understanding: much like its use within medieval liturgy or oaths, the king employed the *textus* as a talisman, relying less on its text and more on its symbolic value; such use explains the *textus*'s appeal to a non-Christian. Furthermore, the reference to a 'Britoun book' concurs with the appearance of oath-books (discussed below), in which antiquity was part and parcel of their sanctity.

Chaucer presented a very different oath in the 'Shipman's Tale', in which a pact is signed between the monk and the merchant's wife:

> 'For on my portehors I make an ooth
> That nevere in my lyf, for lief ne looth,
> Ne shal I of no conseil yow biwreye.'
> 'The same agayn to yow', quod she, 'I seye.
> By God and by this portehors I swere,
> Though men me wolde al into pieces tere,
> Ne shal I nevere, for to goon to helle.'[95]
>
> (ll. 131–7)

The oath presented by the Shipman echoes the usage in medieval courtrooms in stating the consequences of breaking an oath and explicitly acknowledging God and the sacred book. The differences between Chaucer's two oaths are nevertheless striking: the *textus* is used in a solemn oath in the presence of a king and induces divine punishment for the perjurer; the breviary (*portehors*), on the other hand, vouchsafes an oath between a lascivious monk and unfaithful wife. Both wife and monk cunningly use the wording of the oath to further their acts of deceit and adultery. The oath is still legitimate and binding. It is kept to the end, although subsequent events change the way the oath and its takers are seen. These accounts tell of two types of oaths: one performed in a royal court and the other a private transaction between two parties; the distinction between the two is made by employing two discrete categories of manuscripts: a *textus*, characterised by appearance and antiquity; and a breviary, a personal book, a liturgical vademecum for the daily performance of divine office.

The affinity of oath-rituals to the liturgy, implied in the use of *textus* and breviary, is manifested in other literary oaths. The late thirteenth-century *Havelok the Dane* recounts how King Athelwold prepares various instruments of Mass to facilitate Earl Godric's oath to protect the king's young daughter:

The king was payed of that rede;
A wel fair cloth bringen he dede,
And theron leyde the messebok,
The caliz, and the pateyn ok,
[...] (promising to give his daughter to the best man)
That dede he him sweren on the bok.[96]

(ll. 184–201)

Once more under the royal aegis, a solemn oath is performed. An array of liturgical paraphernalia is presented: cloth, mass-book (a missal), chalice, and paten. The use of a missal reflects the legal custom and suggests a new category of oath-books. Its popularity is attested in the similar account of the fourteenth-century English rendering of Chrétien de Troyes's *Ywain and Gawain*. There Lunet has also prepared an array of sacred objects to facilitate an oath. The text expands upon the previous account by adding relics to the chalice and missal ('Lunet than riche relikes toke; The chalis and the mes-boke').[97] Despite the obvious sanctity of the relics, the oath is taken on the book, which is kissed at its end ('Hir hand opon the boke sho laid [...] The boke sho gert hir lady kys').[98] Much like Henry III at Burgh, Lunet follows common legal practice in preferring book to relics, suggesting a new interpretation of Henry's activities. As in the 'Shipman's Tale', the oaths administered on these liturgical books are presented as solemn and binding.

The link between oaths and the liturgy stands behind the proverb *to swear by book and bell*. In the late fourteenth-century *Earl of Toulouse*, the Earl's oath makes use of this proverb without designating a specific book: 'Y swere by boke and by belle' (l. 190).[99] Curses, the oath's counterpart, made use of this very same saying. In the *Cursor Mundi*, a curse is laid on those who withhold the book from its rightful owner: 'Curced in kirc than sal thai be | wid candil, boke, and bell'.[100] The liturgical paraphernalia of the latter example – book, bell, and candle – alongside the reference to the church indicate the proverb's reliance on the ritual of the Mass, when the bell is rung, the book read, and the candle lit. The connection between oath and Mass becomes explicit through liturgical paraphernalia, not least the sacred book. As seen here, both in Masses and oaths this was not a Bible, but rather a Gospel book or its liturgical derivative.

The link between liturgy and oaths, matter and appearance, was employed in a set of prescriptions that aimed to answer a unique challenge to the medieval legal system. Jews were the only licit religious minority in medieval England until their expulsion in 1290. Their oaths on Christian scriptures were deemed ineffectual if not offensive. On the fringes of common practice, special arrangements were therefore made to enable Jews to take an oath. A charter of liberties to the Jews, preserved in the records of the Exchequer of the Jews for 1201, specifies the ways in which Jews were to take an oath: 'Et si Judeus ab aliquo appellatus fuerit sine teste, de illo appellatu erit quietus solo sacramento suo super Librum suum. Et de appellatu illarum rerum que ad Coronam nostram pertinent similiter quietus erit solo sacramento suo super Rotulum suum'.[101] The charter omits the common oath formula, which was of no avail to a Jewish audience. It employs two distinct physical objects for two types of oaths. Cases against the crown were deemed superior to private litigation, as manifested in their respective oath-books: a scroll for the former and a book for the latter, both unspecified. The distinction between book and scroll, nevertheless, reflects a boundary of sacrality within Judaism. The scroll of the Pentateuch is revered as a sacred object, surpassing in its sanctity any other book, including other parts of the Bible, and a different set of rituals governs its compilation and use.[102] The book, on the other hand, might have been a copy of the Talmud or a designated Jewish oath-book, as suggested by Joseph Ziegler.[103]

The Jewish oath was employed in courts of law. In 1275 Abraham son of Deulecresse the Jew of Norwich took an oath against a Christian, placing his hand on his own book: 'Et quia dictus Judeus fecit legem suam, sicut Judeus facere debet versus Christianum, videlicet, se sola manu super Librum suum, ideo consideratum est, quod predictus Abraham inde recedat quietus'.[104] Even in the turbulent times preceding the expulsion, due procedure led to Abraham's acquittal. Producing oath-books appears to have been the responsibility of the Jewish community. In late April 1278 the Royal Justice, Hamo Hauteyn, visited the Jewish community of York and placed the sergeant (*serviens*) of the York Jewry in mercy for not having the books of Jewish law used in oaths.[105] It appears that the mechanism of producing oath-books, through officials of the Jewish community under the supervision of the Crown, was clear and any deficiencies were punished. As Dobson has remarked, however, the content of Jewish oath-books remains a mystery. None of these books has survived, and the sources are silent regarding their exact nature.[106]

Christian oath-books, much like their Jewish counterparts, are all but invisible to the modern eye. Court records and legal treatises instruct and record gestures and utterances, but omit almost any reference to the supply and contents of these books. Some sources identify these books as the 'sacrosanct Gospels', although much like the medieval *textus* one cannot take such an identification at face value; others simply make reference to a book (*liber / livere*), seen by modern editors to represent the Bible. Such an understanding may be too based on modern customs rather than medieval. I have yet to find a single concrete example of the use of Bibles in courts of law (the above-mentioned common law treatise with its vague reference to old and new law notwithstanding).[107] A survey of Late Medieval Bibles (Appendix) supports this assumption. No Bible bears witness to such a use prior to the sixteenth century, although an officer at the ecclesiastical court of York bequeathed a 'lavish book called a Bible' ('unum librum largum vocatum Bibliam') to the Austin priory at Drax (Yorkshire) in 1440.[108] The use of Gospel books in oath rituals likewise remains unclear. It is evident that large monastic establishments employed Gospel books for oaths, but the lack of evidence for Gospel books in courts of law and parish churches puts in question such use beyond monasteries and cathedrals.

The supply of oath-books was at times the responsibility of oath-takers, as in two occurrences presented by Paul Brand. In the Warwickshire eyre at 1212 essoiners (those presenting excuses for the non-appearance of a person in court) were required to bring the book upon which they would swear ('debet secum deferre librum super quem iurare debet'); in Gloucestershire an attorney presenting an essoin brought his book with him ('venit cum libro suo').[109] Oath-books could also be supplied by local religious establishments. During a session of the county court of Chester on 10 December 1398 litigants were unable to take their oaths and due procedure was interrupted. This resulted from the lack of an oath-book; a specific book, clearly identified by the record, it had been provided by the abbots of the nearby St Werburgh's Abbey in a custom that was said to be generations old:

> (problem of inability to swear emanating from) quod non habetur librum vocatum Jurybook ... (all those present in court said) quod Abbbas Monasterii sancte Werburge Cestr' et omnes predecessores sui abbates loci predicti predictum librum ad serviendum in Curia domini Regis hic ad omnes Comitatus hic tentos sive tenendos invenire tenentur; Et quod dominus Rex Anglie modo princeps Cestr' et omnes progenitores sui Comites Cestr' necnon omnes comites Cestr' tempore quo non extat memoria de predicto libro ad serviendum hic in Curia (supplied by the Abbot and his predecessors).[110]

This is a rare account of how a county court was provided with its oath-book, and of the collaboration between religious and secular establishments. The 'Jurybook' was defined not by its contents but rather by custom; no other book could replace it and its absence inhibited legal procedures and led to the abbot being placed in mercy and fined. The 'Jurybook' and its provision appear to be well known to all those present at court, the antiquity and popularity of the custom attested in the words of the record ('tempore quo non extat memoria'), as in the preservation of the book's English name ('Jurybook') in the Latin record. No library catalogue nor sacrist's record survives from St Werburgh's Abbey and the exact nature of the 'Jurybook' remains unknown.[111] Another oath-book provided by a local religious establishment appears in the 1220 visitation records for the church of Mere, Wiltshire. There, one of the church's books is described as 'Item liber vetustissimus habens crucem superpositam super quam juratur'.[112] This book is described solely by its physical characteristics and applicability for oaths. While it resembles descriptions of *textus* in the supremacy of its binding, its labeling as a 'most ancient book' brings the Chester 'Jurybook' to mind. The exact identification of the Mere oath-book becomes even more complex as we note that the church of Mere was one of the few to possess a Gospel book, described as old and worn ('item liber evangeliorum vetus et attritus'). The connection between this oath-book and the text of the Gospels cannot therefore be taken for granted.

Evidence of oath-books is rare, leaving one to wonder how to reconcile references for Gospel books, the *liber* of courtrooms and the missals and breviaries recalled in Middle English literature. Thirteenth- and fourteenth-century oath-books would have served as an ideal solution, but I have yet to find a single insular specimen in its original binding (with the possible exception of BL, Stowe MS 15, discussed below). Several fifteenth-century oath-books, however, combine with earlier incomplete books to suggest an interesting solution to the problem, one that recalls the oath-book of Mere church. BL, Stowe MS 15 once belonged to the Exchequer, where it was used for oath-taking. Its contents cannot be described as anything else than a textual mishmash. It integrates leaves from several liturgical manuscripts: noted chants for the vigils of the Ascension, St Catherine, and St Nicholas (fols 9v–12r, fourteenth-/fifteenth-century hand); a calendar (fols 20r–25v) in a fourteenth-century hand with fourteenth- and fifteenth-century additions ranging from dates of Easter and obits of chancellors, monarchs, and Lords of the Exchequer, to historical events (for instance the marriage of Richard II and Anne of Bohemia (20 January 1382) or the coronation of Richard III (6 July 1483)). This is followed by Gospel lessons in a twelfth-century hand, depicting primarily Christ's birth and Passion, alongside a nearly complete Gospel of John.[113] This array of sacred texts is interspersed with miscellaneous notes in hands ranging from the thirteenth to the sixteenth: extracts from the Red Book of the Exchequer (fols

13r–15r, 83r–84v), dues from various counties (fols 15v–18v, 85r–88v), pen-tests, signatures and historical information (such as the capture of Berwick on 30 March 1296, fol. 19r).[114] The manuscript thus combines sacred and secular elements to stand between the liturgical, the biblical and the legal; its jumbled contents concur perfectly with the various denominations of oath-books in our sources. The haphazard nature of Gospel and liturgical snippets suggests that the compilers of the manuscript made use of easily available materials that endowed the manuscript with an aura of sacrality, rather than facilitating liturgical services or biblical reading.

Upon viewing and touching this manuscript it is evident that the contents were secondary to appearance. Its pages are encompassed by a thick binding (the text is only a third of the breadth of the volume) and an impressive crucifix takes up almost all of the back binding (Plate 3).[115] Two leaves of a late thirteenth- or fourteenth-century theological treatise provided the binder with pastedowns and supply a *terminus a quo* for the binding. The appearance of this manuscript bears a strong resemblance to the oath-book of Mere church, and its entry, 'An old book, on which a cross is superimposed', could easily describe the Stowe manuscript as well. The position of the crucifix on the back binding is reminiscent of luxurious liturgical books which were left closed on a lectern, and its imagery of the iconography of *textus*.[116]

Another fifteenth-century oath-book in its original binding is BL, Additional MS 22,573. It contains sixteen folios, most taken from liturgical manusripts: a calendar (independent quire, fols 3r–8v, without added entries apart from pen-tests and signatures) and several Gospel lessons in a thirteenth- or fourteenth-century hand.[117] The Gospel lessons are on a separate quire (9–14), in which the second part of each bifolium (11v, 12, 13, 14) was left blank and later interspersed with signatures, pen-tests, and oath-formulae in various hands, which appear also in empty spaces in pastedowns, in flyleaves, and in between liturgical texts and calendar entries. The manuscript retains its original leather binding, lacking any attachment. A close examination of the binding reveals, nevertheless, traces of a device previously affixed to it. Several holes and dents on the back binding were made by its removal; metal pins which once held the device were sawn off but their traces are still visible.[118] Two such pins form a horizontal line in the upper half of the back binding, while three other form a vertical line approximately in its middle (Figure 5, indicated by circles). This alignment corresponds with the way crucifixes were affixed, and is similar to the pins used to support the crucifix on the Stowe oath-book. The attachment of a cross is less likely as it would have required an addi-

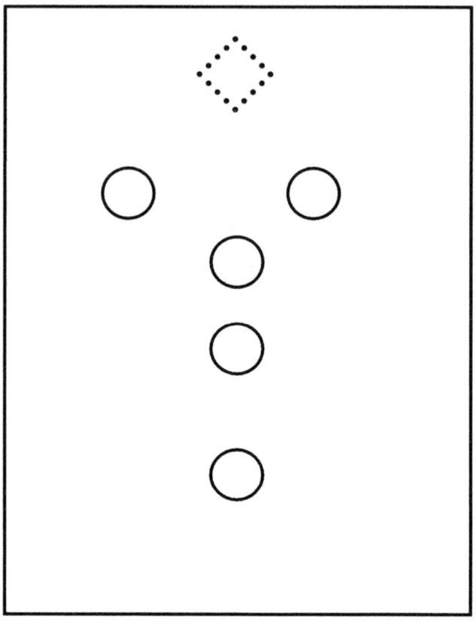

Figure 5 BL Add. MS 22,573, back binding

tional pin on the upper part of the binding (indicated by a dotted diamond in Figure 5). Thus the scant evidence for oath-books outside cathedrals and monasteries presents a single image of books whose appearance was dominated by a cross or crucifix attached to their binding.

Two secular oath-books have survived without their medieval binding: BL, Royal MS 9 A.vii and 9 A.xii. The former was employed by a court clerk in the early fourteenth century. Its 241 folios contain Gospel lessons and a calendar (fols 13r–14v, 15r–17v, with historiated initials of the emblems of the four Evangelists preceding each lesson, an image of Mary with Christ the Child taking the empty space at the end of the lessons (in blue, gold, pink, and green, 6 × 5.5 cm, fol. 14v), and the Crucifixion with the two Marys (same colours, full-page, fol. 18r)), but primarily encompasses legal tracts on essoins, statutes (with an affinity to Gloucestershire), and charters of liberties primarily from the reign of Edward I. Royal MS 9 A.xii is a very different fifteenth-century manuscript. Its twenty-two folios are taken up by a calendar and Gospel lessons (2r–7v, 8r–15r), as well as oath formulae for ships' masters, porters, accountants (*tellours*), and weigher – attesting to a use within a custom house. Both manuscripts, however, share an important feature. Unlike the Stowe and Additional oath-books, the Gospel lessons in these manuscripts were written in the same hand as oath-formulae and legal treatises. These were therefore elements of the Gospels envisioned as appropriate for oath-books. The two manuscripts share the same lessons (in different orders): the beginning of the Gospel of John (1:1–14), Annunciation (Lk 1:26b–38), Adoration (Mt 2:1–12), and Christ's Commission and Ascension (Mk 16:14–20). These passages therefore constitute a single unit, which facilitated oath-swearing. These are almost identical to the lessons written in the Additional oath-book (whose blank folios suggest that these were likewise commissioned for the oath-book) and appear in variation in the Stowe oath-book.

Swearing on the 'sacrosanct Gospels' did not necessitate a full Bible or even a single Gospel in its entirety. Biblical snippets (combined with an iconic binding) sufficed to make these manuscripts hallowed objects and to ensure their efficient use as talismans. The choice of lessons was not accidental: they pertained to key episodes in salvation history. Known at times as the *Cursus evangelii*, the four Gospel episodes of the Royal oath-books are commonly found in books of hours, where they likewise summarised the Gospels to lay men and women. A slightly different selection appears in another fifteenth-century oath-book. When admitting new members to their ranks, guilds and livery companies employed their books as oath-books, containing sacred texts and oath-formulae, as well as ordinances, charters, and records of the guild or company. One such book is the fifteenth-century oath-book of the Company of Weavers (London, Guildhall Library MS 04645, lacking its original binding). It contains, apart from matters relating to the Company, the oaths of a bailiff (unnumbered, inserted on the first leaf) and journeymen (fols 7v, 13v, 28v), as well as extracts from the Gospels (fols 10–11).[119] The Gospel extracts, copied by the original scribe, contain a slightly modified version of the *Cursus evangelii* (Mk 8:15–26; Mt 20:17–19; Lk 1:26–38; Jn 1:1–14). A comparison between the manuscript and the Vulgate reveals uncorrected errors, similar to those found in the Gospel books of Judith of Flanders.[120]

The last oath-book to be examined allows us to come full circle to *textus* and cathedrals, with a modern rendering of the medieval rite. Nowadays, York Minster, Additional MS 1 lives a double life. It spends its days locked in a safe and seen only by the few scholars whose interest in Anglo-Saxon art and palaeography (or late medieval rituals) has convinced the archivist that it cannot be satisfied by examining a facsimile. One of few surviving Anglo-Saxon Gospel books, it is the most treasured manuscript of York Minster Library and Archives. Unlike other manuscripts of its time and value, York Add. MS 1 is taken periodically outside the library precinct. Known as the York Gospels, it is processed in the Minster and vouchsafes the oath of all new archbishops of York (and from 1984 the Minster's canons as well).[121] The manuscript's binding, boards and brown morocco, fits its use within the Anglican rite but bears little resemblance to its medieval counterpart. In line with other medieval *textus* the York Gospels was once encased in a silver gilt binding, described in the Minster's 1500–10 inventory as: 'Item unus textus ornatus cum argento non bene deaurato, super quem juramenta Decani et aliarum dignitatum ac canonicorum in principio inseruntur'.[122] The contents of the manuscript correspond with its function: the text of the Anglo-Saxon Gospels (fols 10r–156r, written probably at Canterbury *c.* 1000) is circumscribed by oath-formulae, legal and administrative documents, dating from *c.* 1020 (when the manuscript arrived at York) to the sixteenth century (fols 3r–9v, 156v–167v). These insertions are explored in the essays accompanying the facsimile, which explain the smudges on some of its folios as emanating from generations of priests touching and kissing the book while taking their oaths.[123] Both *textus* and oath-book, the York Gospels is an iconic object which has been used talismanically for a millennium.

In line with the 1500–10 survey, the York Gospels records the oaths of an archdeacon, deacon, subdeacon, canon and prebendary, treasurer and vicar choral, in person or by proxy. The book's function as an oath-book rendered it most valuable for the medieval Minster and explains its unique survival: it retained its importance even after the Dissolution, when its bindings were taken apart and all other treasured manuscripts were removed from the Minster. One oath-formula, however, is lacking from its pages. This lack is most striking given the book's modern use. The omission of the archbishop's oath was seen by Bernard Barr as evidence that the archbishop had taken his oath on a much more lavish object than the worn *textus* used by dean and canons; this was possibly the sumptuous two-volume Gospel book, bequeathed by Archbishop Wilfrid in the seventh century, its binding made of gold and silver with images of the Crucifixion, Trinity, and Christ in Majesty. If so, the archbishop's preferences for an ancient and luxurious book over a (relatively) worn and (relatively) recent one, made antiquity and material culture key in the ritual. It mirrors the hierarchy explicit in Jewish oaths and implicit in Chaucer's narratives, as the archbishop's choice was determined by the appearance of the book, rather than its contents, as means of delineating a boundary of sacrality and ritual.[124] A preference for appearance and ritual activities is evident in the modern use of the York Gospels. Nowadays, an ancient manuscript whose text (Latin in Caroline minuscule) has little to do with the Anglican rite, endows the ceremony with an aura of a glorified past and a sense of continuity. This is a matter of appearance and allusion, as the modern ritual (and its choice of book) bears little resemblance to the medieval rite.

Conclusion

The juxtaposition of legal and liturgical accounts allows a single story of books and rituals to emerge at Masses and oath rituals, where sacred books were employed to endow civic and religious spectacles with an aura of sacrality. The sacred object, *textus* or oath-book, validated the words of a priest or vouchsafed the veracity of witnesses and litigants. This link between speech acts and the divine was accomplished through carefully structured rituals, which employed gestures, utterances, and objects to transform books into talismans. Time and again the physical touch was deemed crucial to the medieval rite and enabled the sacred book to function almost independently of the text contained in it. In a society in which oaths were gradually taking the place of ordeals as means of ascertaining innocence, such talismanic use was key to ecclesiastical hierarchy and civic governance. These ritual gestures delineated subtle though pervasive social boundaries. A touch or a kiss was a means of displaying one's place within society, as priests were exempt from touching oath-books, while simultaneously benefitting from direct access to Mass-books, only seen from afar by the laity.

Appearance was central to the sacrality of books in medieval courts and churches. Although oath-books and *textus* were both seen as biblical, their identity cannot be taken at face value. The nature of the sources denies us exact knowledge of most books employed in rituals. However, sacrists' descriptions of *textus* with their elaborate metalwork and precious stones, surviving oath-books, historical records, and Jewish oaths join to demonstrate how such books were judged primarily by their covers. Appearance was of supreme importance to the compilers of visitation records and inventories, in which *textus* were described almost solely by their binding, and a book-less *textus* did not constitute a conundrum. Appearance, age, and custom determined how these books were employed, with specific books reserved for important saints' days, the oaths of dignitaries, or matter pertaining to the Crown. The appearance of these books, with crosses and crucifixes, scenes of Christ in Majesty, and the Crucifixion, transformed them into icons, identified and venerated beyond their texts.

Surviving *textus* and oath-books rarely present a full and accurate biblical text. Their text, however, was not chosen at random. Book-less *textus* did exist but were clearly identified, as were non-Gospel *textus*. In the world of medieval rite, one part of the Bible stood out: the Gospels. More than any other biblical book, the Gospels were employed as talismans in Coptic graves, Irish book shrines, or late medieval Masses and oath-rituals, surpassing in their sanctity any other part of the Bible. Seen as the crux of Christian faith, their narratives were reflected not only in the texts of *textus* and oath-books but also in the iconography of their bindings. When parts of the Gospels were chosen, this was also far from accidental. Narratives of Christ's birth, Crucifixion, and Resurrection (known also as the *Cursus evangelii*) were clearly preferred and appear in oath-books, partial *textus* (such as those of Judith of Flanders), and books of hours. When compared with a wider sample, as with oath-books of guilds and livery companies, a singular biblical excerpt appears time and again: the opening verses from the Gospel of John. The study of talismanic use of Scriptures reveals an inner-biblical hierarchy: the Gospels were set apart from any other biblical book; within the Gospels the *Cursus evangelii* was seen as paramount; and at the very core of this use were the opening verses of the Gospel of John (typically Jn 1:1–14, beginning with 'In principio erat verbum' ('In the beginning was the Word')). Such hierarchy accords with uses on the fringes of orthodoxy, in which these very same verses were recalled time and again in talismanic uses, chanted in incantations and engraved on amulets.[125]

The nature of oath-books, their appearance and proximity to the Bible, can shed additional light on late medieval English religion. In the late fourteenth-century the followers of John Wyclif rejected the custom of swearing on the Gospels, and were subsequently persecuted by church and civic authorities. Lollard sources reveal that they did not always exercise a wholesale rejection of oaths.[126] Their acts therefore take an unexpected twist when we note the reality of oath-books in late medieval England. Could it be that what incurred the wrath of Lollards was not only the theoretical problem of swearing on the Gospels but the more concrete nature of the oath-books they were presented with? Not only highlighting the physicality of the Bible (its lowest manifestation according to Wyclif), these books truncated the biblical text to present only snippets, at times based only on liturgical manuscripts; they were encompassed within precious bindings whose lavish iconography was resented by the Lollards. The few *textus* which contain relics, a custom seen as pure idolatry by Lollards, no doubt did little to improve their opinion of these sacred books and their use.

The legal and religious spheres mirrored one another in oaths and Masses. They also converged in their use of sacred books. The use of liturgical manuscripts in oath-rituals is narrated in Middle English literature, which brings together oaths, curses, and Masses. In a similar fashion oath-books incorporate excerpts from liturgical manuscripts, and Gospel books contain charters and oath formulae. Religious and legal institutions could even function in tandem: (extremely scant) evidence exists for the supply of oath-books by the religious community, as in the oath-book of Mere church, the county court of Chester, or the Jewish community of York. The relationship between church and courts was potentially a symbiotic one. Oath-rituals depended upon religious institutions to provide sacred books which would instil fear in the heats of potential perjurers, while priests benefited from their role of mediators of the divine in their dual function in oath and Mass rituals.

The appearance of sacred books has been central to Christian communities and employed in their rituals beyond the Middle Ages. The successful assimilation of codices by early Christian communities led to the evolution of lavish bindings and their iconography; whereas in Judaism the ancient format of the scroll was reserved to the most sacred of books, the Torah, Western Christianity employed luxurious bindings or ancient traditions as marks of sacrality. The move from ordeal to the modern oath was assisted by the sanctity of oath-books, evident in their iconic appearance, gestures, and utterances, as well as in their use of biblical texts; in a similar vein the medieval *textus*, often an ancient Gospel book processed and venerated in Mass, linked the medieval rite with its past. The importance of the material culture of the Bible was not abandoned with the Reformation. Mass-production of Bibles in the sixteenth century placed them in parish churches, courtrooms, and private homes; it has transformed our understanding of the Bible and influenced researchers' depictions of medieval sacred books. The physicality of these early modern Bibles continued to play a prominent role in their definition and use. From the time of the Great Bible of 1539/40, parish Bibles became synonymous with large and immaculately printed volumes. After the Geneva Bible of 1560 introduced cheaper quartos, such a distinction became even more prominent, with the subsequent Bishops' Bible (1568) boasting an even larger size and a higher grade of paper, extending beyond functionality to a symbolic value and marking a boundary between church Bibles and family Bibles.

Talismanic use of Bibles likewise did not cease with the Middle Ages. When Pope John Paul II visited Canterbury in 1982, the St Augustine Gospels (Cambridge, Corpus Christi College, MS 286, still used for the oath of the Archbishop of Canterbury) was placed on the chair of St Augustine. In a moment similar to that of medieval church councils, the Gospel book presided over the meeting and emphasised the link between Rome and Canterbury in the first papal visit to England since the Reformation. On a more mundane level, in courtrooms nowadays one often swears on a Bible, identified less by its contents (which are still rarely consulted or registered in court records) but rather by its iconic appearance. Specific Bibles and their saintly patrons still carry special weight. In the inauguration of President Barack H. Obama in January 2009, a Bible from the Library of Congress was used. This was the very same Bible that Abraham Lincoln had used at his first inauguration. The message Obama sent is clear. Much like the modern use of the York Gospels, this choice was devised to reflect continuity and sacrality based not on the biblical text but rather on its appearance, antiquity, and custom. Like the use of *textus* and oath-books in late medieval England, this was a link between the secular and the religious spheres, made through the medium of a sacred book.

Notes

1 'the sacred Gospel, that is understood as Christ', Pseudo-Alcuin, *Liber de divinis oficiis*, c.14 (PL 101:1201B); J. Joseph Ryan, 'Pseudo-Alcuin's *Liber de divinis officiis* and the *Liber 'Dominus vobiscum'* of St Peter Damiani', *Mediaeval Studies* 14 (1952), 159–63.

2 Timothy H. Lim, 'Deuteronomy in the Judaism of the Second Temple Period', in *Deuteronomy in the New Testament: The New Testament and the Scriptures of Israel*, ed. Steve Moyise and Maarten J. J. Menken, Library of New Testament Studies (London, 2007), pp. 6–26 (15–18). I thank Timothy Lim for supplying me with a copy of this article.

3 Christopher Clarkson (with an introduction by John Sharpe), 'Some Representations of the Book and Book-Making, from the Earliest Codex Forms to Jost Amman', in *The Bible as a Book: The Manuscript Tradition*, ed. John L. Sharpe III and Kimberly Van Kampen (London, 1998), pp. 197–203; C. H. Roberts and T. C. Skeat, *The Birth of the Codex* (Oxford, 1987); Yvonne Johannot, *Tourner la page: Livres, rites et symboles*, 2nd edn (Grenoble, 1988), pp. 29–40, 45–6.

4 'superstitiosae mulierculae', *Sancti Hieronymi presbyteri Opera. Pars I, Opera exegetica. 7, Commentariorum in Matheum libri IV*, ed. D. Hurst and M. Adriaen, CCSL 77 (Turnhout, 1969), p. 212 (Mt 23:5); translation and analysis which links this attack with the Jewish phylacteries: Hillel I. Newman, 'Jerome's Judaizers', *Journal of Early Christian Studies* 9:4 (2001), 421–52 (425).

5 *Bede's Ecclesiastical History of the English People*, ed. Bertram Colgrave and R. A. B. Mynors (Oxford 1969, repr. 1992), p. 20 (I:1). Such use carries interesting (and to the best of my knowledge unexplored) parallel to the biblical custom of the bitter water (Nm 5:23–8).

6 Paul Mullarkey, 'Some Observations on the Form and Date of the Soiscéal Molaise Book Shrine', in *Irish Art Historical Studies in Honour of Peter Harbison*, ed. Colum Hourihane (Dublin, 2004), pp. 124–40; Eamonn P. Kelly, 'The Lough Kinale Book Shrine: The Implications for the Manuscripts', in *The Book of Kells: Proceedings of a Conference at Trinity College Dublin, 6–9 September 1992*, ed. Felicity O'Mahony (Aldershot, 1994), pp. 280–9, and a detailed description of the same book shrine by Kelly, 'The Lough Kinale Book Shrine', in *The Age of*

Migrating Ideas: Early Medieval Art in Northern Britain and Ireland, ed. R. Michael Spearman and John Higgit (Edinburgh, 1993), pp. 168–74.

7 *Monasticon anglicanum: A History of the Abbies and Other Monasteries, Hospitals, Frieries, and Cathedral and Collegiate Churches …*, ed. William Dugdale, 2nd edn, 6 vols (London, 1817–30), i:357 (referred to in Deanesly, *Lollard Bible*, p. 170). This corresponds to the use of letters in church consecration (Schreiner, 'Buch im Nacken', pp. 86–90).

8 *Historia Monasterii S. Augustini Cantuariensis by Thomas of Elmham, formerly Monk and Treasurer of that Foundation*, ed. Charles Hardwick, RS 8 (London, 1858), pp. 97–8.

9 'Livres utilisés'.

10 Bibliothèque nationale de France Cod. Graec. 510, fol. 355r (Constantinople 879–883) = http://visualiseur.bnf.fr/Visualiseur?Destination=Mandragore&O=0 8001305 &E=1&I=112375&M=imageseule (accessed 8 June 2012). This was noted by Frauke Steenbock, *Der kirchliche Prachteinband im frühen Mittelalter: von den Anfängen bis zum Beginn der Gotik* (Berlin, 1965), p. 53, and explored in-depth by Schreiner, 'Buch im Nacken', pp. 83–6.

11 Bibliothèque nationale de France Cod. Graec. 510, fol. 452r (excerpt), http://visualiseur.bnf.fr/Visualiseur?Destination=Mandragore&O=08007767&E=1&I =112478&M=imageseule (accessed 8 June 2012); Roger E. Reynolds, 'Image and Text: The Liturgy of Clerical Ordination in Early Medieval Art', *Gesta* 22:1 (1983), 27–38 (30). A late medieval Continental example is the Metz Pontifical (*The Metz Pontifical: A Manuscript Written for Reinhald von Bar, Bishop of Metz (1302–1316), and now Belonging to Sir Thomas Brooke, Bart., F.S.A.*, ed. E. S. Dewick (London, 1902), pl. 89).

12 Amalarius of Metz, *Liber officialis*, 2:14 (*Amalarii episcopi opera liturgica omnia*, ed. Jean-Michel Hanssens, vol. 2, Studi e testi 139 (Vatican City, 1948), pp. 233–6); Durand, *Rationale*, ii.11.7–8 (Davril ed. 140, p. 173).

13 Green, *Crisis of Truth* (building on Michael T. Clanchy, *From Memory to Written Record: England 1066–1307*, 2nd edn (Cambridge, MA, 1993)); *The Letter of the Law: Legal Practice and Literary Production in Medieval England*, ed. Emily Steiner and Candace Barrington (Ithaca, NY, 2002), especially Steiner and Barrington, 'Introduction', pp. 1–11; Emma Lipton, 'Language on Trial: Performing the Law in the N-Town Trial Play', pp. 115–35.

14 This was suggested by John Witte, Jr, 'Introduction', in *Christianity and Law: An Introduction*, ed. Witte and Frank S. Alexander (Cambridge, 2008), pp. 1–32 (29).

15 Much like the sources for Palm Sunday liturgy, discussed in the previous chapter, printed missals are often remote from the manuscript evidence. For the Sarum use I have consulted the following: *The Use of Salisbury, vol. 1: The Ordinary of the Mass*, ed. Nick Sandon (Amersham, 1984), pp. 21–3; *Tracts on the Mass*, ed. J. Wickham Legg, HBS 27 (London, 1904), pp. 4, 219–20; *The Sarum Missal: Edited from Three Early Manuscripts*, ed. J. Wickham Legg (Oxford, 1916, repr. 1969), pp. 216–18, which is probably the closest to the manuscript evidence; BL Harley MS 4919, fol. 15v (*c.* 1400); BL Harley MS 2787 fols 13v–14r (*c.* 1400); Cambridge University Library, MS Dd.1.15, fol. 99v (London, *c.* 1450); Cambridge University Library, MS Ff.2.31, fol. 95r (Norwich?, third quarter of

fifteenth century). Hereford: *Missale ad usum percelebris ecclesiae Herfordensis*, pp. 116–17. York: *Missale ad usum insignis ecclesiae Eboracensis*, p. 170; BL Add. MS 43,380, fol. 110r (early-fifteenth century); *Ordinal and Customary of the Abbey of St Mary*, i:103–4 (instruction for the priest), i:117–20 (deacon). Eynsham Abbey: *The Customary of the Benedictine Abbey of Eynsham in Oxfordshire*, ed. Antonia Gransden (Siegburg, 1963), p. 47. Westminster: *Missale ad usum ecclesie Westmonasteriensis*, 3 vols, ed. J. W. Legg, HBS 1, 5, 12 (London, 1891, 1893, 1897), ii:col. 498.

16 William A. Graham, *Beyond the Written Word: Oral Aspects of Scripture in the History of Religion* (Cambridge, 1987); Daniel J. Sheerin, 'Sonus and Verba: Varieties of Meaning in the Liturgical Proclamation of the Gospel in the Middle Ages', in *Ad Litteram: Authoritative Texts and Their Medieval Readers*, ed. Mark D. Jordan and Kent Emery, Jr, Notre Dame Conferences in Medieval Studies 3 (Notre Dame, IN, 1992), pp. 29–69; Debray, *Transmettre*, p. 16 (slightly revised in *Transmitting Culture*, p. 2).

17 'Men must hear the Gospel with bare heads, so that the five senses should be wide open to listen', *De ecclesiasticis officiis* 39:i (Douteil ed., 41A, p. 73).

18 'Hence the Gospel surpasses the Old Testament in three points, that is in the revelation of prefigurations, in the fulfilment of promises, in the magnitude of the rewards. To make known this triple preeminence of the Gospel, the church does three things when the Gospel is read: for in order to indicate that through the Gospel the revelation of prefigurations was made, (the church) hears the Gospel with bare head; in order to indicate that in the Gospel the fulfilment of promises was made, (the church) hears the Gospel in silence, as if it said with this silence: now indeed I obtain the promise. For children are usually quiet after they hold an apple. To indicate the magnitude of the promises, the Gospel, full of grace and truth, ends with a raised voice, in opposition the lessons of the Old Testament shall end with falling voice; as if to say there the godly things were promised, here the godly things are', Beryl Smalley, *The Study of the Bible in the Middle Ages*, 3rd rev. edn (Oxford, 1983), p. 240, based on a marginal note in Oxford Bodleian Library MS Laud Misc. 291, fol. 1ra. Smalley's transcription was truncated two-thirds through the quotation. The Comestor's understanding follows that of Rupert of Deutz, who saw the supremacy of the New Testament to the Old manifested in the activities of clergy: *Liber de divinis officiis* 1:36 (*Ruperti Tuitiensis liber De divinis officiis*, ed. Hrabanus Haacke, CCCM 7 (Turnhout, 1967), pp. 29–31).

19 *Missale ad usum percelebris ecclesiae Herfordiensis*, pp. 116–17; *Missale ad usum insignis ecclesiae Eboracensis*, p. 170; Beleth, *De ecclessiasticis* 39:i (Douteil ed., 41A, p. 73); Durand, *Rationale* iv.24.24 (Davril ed., 140, p. 351).

20 'speak you not, but think on him that dearly paid for you.' *The Lay-Folks Mass-Book or the Manner for Hearing Mass, with Rubrics and Devotions for the People, in Four Texts and Office in English According to the Use of York from Manuscripts from the Xth to the XVth Century with Appendix, Notes, and Glossary*, ed. Thomas F. Simmons, EETS OS 71 (London, 1879), pp. 16–19. For a short summary see: Pfaff, *Liturgy in Medieval England*, pp. 460–2.

21 Sandon, *Use of Salisbury, vol. 1*, pp. 22–3; Hiley, *Western Plainchant*, pp. 54–8. In this respect I disagree with Sheerin ('Sonus and Verba', p. 37), whose reliance on

modern chant renders his argument on the centrality of music less relevant for the medieval example.

22 In York the procession took place after the reading and during the Creed.

23 Durand, *Rationale* iv.24.12–16 (Davril ed., 140, pp. 346–8).

24 Durand., *Rationale* iv.24.3 (Davril ed., 140, p. 341); Rupert of Deutz, *Liber de divinis officiis* 1:37 (Haacke ed., p. 31).

25 *Ordinal and Customary of the Abbey of St Mary*, 1:118, corresponding with Beleth, *De ecclessiasticis* 39:d (Douteil ed., 41A, p. 71); Durand, *Rationale* iv.24.27 (Davril ed. pp. 352–3) – based on Innocent III, *De sacro altaris mysterio* II:43 (PL 217:824).

26 'Command, lord, to bless ... The Lord be in thy heart and in thy mouth (*or* lips) to proclaim God's holy Gospel. In the name of the Father, and of the Son, and of the Holy Ghost. Amen.'

27 '(Officiant) The Lord shall open your mouth to read, and our ears to understand God's sacred Gospel [...] Amen. (Deacon) Give me, o Lord, right and well sounding speech in my mouth so that my words shall please you and all hearers, on account of your name in eternal life. Amen.'

28 Most works on kisses in medieval culture engage less with inanimate objects, but nevertheless substantiate the role of kisses as a ritual gesture that delineates social boundaries: Yannick Carré, *Le baiser sur la bouche au Moyen Age: Rites, symboles, mentalités, à travers les textes et les images XIe–XVe siècles* (Paris, 1992); Nicolas J. Perella, *The Kiss Sacred and Profane: An Interpretative History of Kiss Symbolism and Related Religio-Erotic Themes* (Berkeley, 1969), p. 278, n. 27; Michael Penn, 'Ritual Kissing, Heresy and the Emergence of Early Christian Orthodoxy', *Journal of Ecclesiastical History* 54:4 (2003), 625–40. Kisses of inanimate objects as a mark of sacrality are rife in Judaism, as in kisses of Bibles, liturgical books, articles of clothes and *mezuzahs*.

29 The *Lay Folk Mass Book*'s injunction to 'make a cross, and kiss hit sone' at the end of the lesson (pp. 18–19) should thus be seen to refer to the hand or a *Pax*, rather than the *textus* itself (the latter argued by Joseph A. Jungmann, *The Mass of the Roman Rite: Its Origin and Development* (orig. *Missarum Solemnia*, Vienna, 1949), 2 vols, tr. Francis A. Brunner (New York, 1951), i:449).

30 This can be seen from the reference to two books, *textus* and a Gospel book, in Sandon, *Use of Salisbury, vol. 1*, pp. 21, 23. Such use is at odds with missals both in manuscript and in print form, and might have been caused by the use of two *textus* or relics in double feasts, noted in the first prints of the Sarum missal (e.g. *Missale ad usum insignis ac preclare ecclesie Sarum* (London: Richard Pynson, 1512), fol. 70v).

31 Lesley Smith, 'The Theology of the Twelfth- and Thirteenth-Century Bible', in *The Early Medieval Bible: Its Production, Decoration and Use*, ed. Richard Gameson (Cambridge, 1994), pp. 223–32 (231); s.v. 'Textus', *Mediae latinitatis lexicon minus*, ed. Jan F. Niermeyer and Co van de Kieft, 2nd rev. edn by J. W. J. Burgers (Leiden, 2002); Christopher Wordsworth and Henry Littlehales, *The Old Service-Books of the English Church*, 2nd edn (London, 1910), pp. 198–203 (dividing gospel books into three kinds, based on their arrangement according to the biblical or liturgical order); Robert N. Swanson, 'Medieval Liturgy as Theatre: The Props', in *The Church and the Arts*, ed. Diana Wood, Studies in Church

History 28 (Oxford, 1991), pp. 239–53; and the definitions adopted by the modern editors of the visitation records discussed below.

32 Chadd, 'Ritual of Palm Sunday'.

33 I thank Father Pino di Luccio, SJ, for his assistance in this matter.

34 Hughes, *Manuscripts for Mass and Office*, pp. 22–3, 143; Eric Palazzo, *A History of Liturgical Books: From the Beginning to the Thirteenth Century* (orig. *Le Moyen Age: Des origines au XIIIe siécle*, Paris, 1993), tr. Madeleine Beaumont (Collegeville, MN, 1998), pp. 107–10.

35 John Shinners, 'Parish Libraries in Medieval England', in *A Distinct Voice: Medieval Studies in Honour of Leonard E. Boyle, O.P.*, ed. Jacqueline Brown and William P. Stoneman (Notre Dame, IN, 1997), pp. 207–30.

36 *Medieval Libraries of Great Britain: A List of Surviving Books*, ed. Neil R. Ker, 2nd edn, Royal Historical Society Guides and Handbooks 3 (London 1964), supplemented by: *Supplement to the Second Edition*, ed. Andrew G. Watson (London, 1987).

37 *Vetus liber archidiaconi Eliensis*, ed. C. L. Feltoe and Ellis H. Minns, Cambridge Antiquarian Society, Octavo Ser. 48 (Cambridge, 1917); *The Register of Walter de Stapeldon, Bishop of Exeter (A.D. 1307–1326)*, ed. F. C. Hingeston-Randolph (London, 1892); *Vetus registrum sarisberiense*, i:273–314; *Visitations of Churches Belonging to St Paul's Cathedral in 1297 and in 1458*, ed. W. Sparrow Simpson, Camden Society NS 55 (London, 1895), pp. 1–64; *Inventory of Church Goods temp. Edward III*, 2 vols, ed. Dom Aelerd Watking, Norfolk Record Society XIX, I–II (Norwich 1947–48). Partial summary for the fifteenth century was offered by Deansely, *Lollard Bible*, pp. 391–8.

38 St Peter, Mancroft (*Inventory of Church Goods*, i:2); St Michael, Coselan, Norwich (i:6); St Peter, Mancroft (i:18); Itryngham (i:56); Salthous (i:81); Tiryngton (ii:127); Walsokne (ii:129).

39 Ely: St Benedict, Cambridge (*Vetus liber archdiaconi Eliensis*, p. 37); Burgh, Cambridgeshire (ibid., p. 53); Fowlmere, Cambridgeshire (p. 89); St John Melnestrete, Cambridge (p. 34); Wycham, Cambridgeshire (p. 146); Chateriz, Cambridgeshire (p. 143). Exeter: Sidbury, Devon (*Register of Walter de Stapeldon*, p. 368). Salisbury: St Andrew's at Sonning-on-Thames, Berkshire (*Vetus registrum sarisberiense*, i:276); Mere, Wiltshire (i:291) London: Furneaux Pelham, Hertfordshire (*Churches belonging to St Paul's*, p. 41).

40 *Inventory of Church Goods*, i:xxxv, xcvii.

41 *Register of Walter de Stapeldon*, p. 107.

42 *Councils and Synods, with other Documents Relating to the English Church, vol. 2, A.D. 1205–1313*, ed. Frederick M. Powicke and Christopher R. Cheney (Oxford, 1964), pp. 1385 N.o (Variant – J), 1387 (the Statutes of Pecham); 296 (Worcester III); 379 (Salisbury II); 599 (Wells); 1005–6 (Exeter II); Christopher R. Cheney, 'The So-Called Statutes of John Pecham and Robert Winchelsey for the Province of Canterbury', *Journal of Ecclesiastical History* 12 (1961), 14–34 (18–19).

43 *Vetus liber archdiaconi Eliensis*, p. 150; *Liber pontificalis Christopheri Bainbridge, archiepiscopi Eboracensis*, ed. William G. Henderson, Surtees Society 61 (Durham, 1875), pp. 371–2.

44 The argument that visitation records misrepresent the actual book possession of

parish churches (Stacey Gee, 'Parochial Libraries in Pre-Reformation England', in *Learning and Literacy in Medieval England and Abroad*, ed. Sarah Rees Jones (Turnhout, 2003), pp. 199–222) carries little weight for orthodox books.

45 Susan H. Cavanaugh, 'A Study of Books Privately Owned in England 1300–1450' (PhD Thesis, University of Pennsylvania, 1980), p. 227.

46 *Wills and Inventories Illustrative of the History, Manners, Language, Statistics, etc. of the Northern Counties of England, from the Eleventh Century Downwards*, ed. James Raine, Surtees Society 2 (London, 1835), p. 7; Cavanaugh, 'Study of Books', p. 378.

47 John de Borw died in 1384. The effigy of Catherine, his second wife, is still to be found in the same church (St Augustine's) to which the *textus* was donated (*Vetus liber archdiaconi Eliensis*, p. 232; C. H. Evelyn-White, *The Churches of Cambridgeshire and the Isle of Ely*, Country Churches (London, 1911), pp. 11–12.

48 'Hospitals: SS Lazarus, Mary & Martha, Sherburn', in *A History of the County of Durham*, ed. William Page, Victoria County History, Durham 2 (London, 1907), pp. 115–17 (www.british-history.ac.uk/report.asp?compid=39888, accessed 6 June 2012).

49 *Vetus registrum sarisberiense*, i:117 n. 1; *Vetus Liber Archdiaconi Eliensis*, p. 35.

50 'Textus, a book if not a codex of the Gospels that is habitually kept in church treasuries, many adorned with gold and gems, sometime written in golden letters as well', *Glossarium meidae et infimae latinitatis*, 10 vols, ed. Charles du Fresne du Cange et al., new edn (Paris, 1883–87), viii:91–2 s.v. textus (http://ducange.enc.sorbonne.fr/TEXTUS%201, accessed 8 June 2012), adopted by: Brian Stock, *Listening for the Text: On the Uses of the Past* (Baltimore, 1990), pp. 41–2. For a broader use of the term *textus* see: Deanesly, *Lollard Bible*, p. 3 n. 2.

51 Alan Coates, *English Medieval Books: The Reading Abbey Collections from Foundation to Dispersal* (Oxford, 1999); *The Friars' Libraries*, ed. K. W. Humphreys, Corpus of British Medieval Library Catalogues 1 (London, 1990), pp. 11–154; *Dover Priory*, ed. William P. Stoneman, Corpus of British Medieval Library Catalogues 5 (London, 1999); Canterbury Christ Church library catalogue was printed by: E. Edwards, *Memoirs of Libraries*, 2 vols (London, 1859), i:122–235.

52 'One big golden *textus* containing 20 saphires, 6 emeralds, 8 topazes, 18 almond-shaped (?), 8 garnets and 12 pearls; Item, one Gospel book well-gilt with 8 stones; Item, one small *textus* with the image of the Blessed Mary with 19 stones; Item, four silver gilt *textus*, gilt all but one; Item, two *textus* without silver', *Vetus registrum sarisberiense*, ii:127 (= *Ceremonies and Processions of the Cathedral Church of Salisbury, edited from the Fifteenth Century ms. no. 148, with Additions from the Cathedral Records and Woodcuts from the Sarum Processionale of 1502*, ed. Christopher Wordsworth (Cambridge, 1901), p. 169).

53 Neil R. Ker, *Books, Collectors and Libraries: Studies in the Medieval Heritage*, ed. Andrew G. Watson (London, 1985), pp. 215–36 (1295 inventory of St Paul); *Extracts from the account rolls of the Abbey of Durham, from the original mss*, 2 vols, ed. Joseph T. Fowler, Surtees Society 99–100 (Durham, 1898–99), ii:426; John David Chambers, *Divine Worship in England in the Thirteenth and Fourteenth Centuries, Contrasted with and Adapted to that in the Nineteenth*, rev. edn (London, 1877), pp. 275–6 (Canterbury); Wordsworth and Littlehales, *Old Service-*

Books, pp. 202–3 (Westminster); *The Inventories of St George's Chapel, Windsor Castle, 1384–1667*, ed. Maurice F. Bond (Windsor, 1947), p. 34.

54 The library catalogue: Edwards, *Memoirs of Libraries*, i:122–235. The church inventory was printed and analysed by: *Inventories of Christchurch Canterbury*, ed. J. Wickham Legg and W. H. St John Hope (London, 1902).

55 'Item, silver *textus* gilt with a crucifix and the images of Mary and John; item, copper *textus* silver gilt with (Christ in) Majesty in the middle and three images in tabernacles and two silver angels and four golden evangelists in four corners of gilt copper' (fol. 122v).

56 'Item, a great *textus* that is called House of God of silver gilt and ornate with gems with a crucifix and Mary and John of ivory, and a white cameo beneath the foot of the Crucifix, with the four Evangelists in the four corners; Item, *textus* of Edmund the Count of Cornwall of silver gilt and ornate with gems' (fol. 122r). The last entry probably refers to Edmund of Almain, second Earl of Cornwall (d. 1300), whose other bequest – a precious stone – is recorded in the same inventory. Canterbury is also unique in recording an English *textus* (the Wessex Gospels), as noted by Deanesly, *Lollard Bible*, p. 137.

57 'Item, *textus* without a book, in the middle gilt and ornate with gems with an ivory crucifix and Mary and John in ivory and a golden clasp; Item wooden *textus* of silver and gilt without a book, ornate with gems with the Annunciation, Presentation in Temple and other images of Christ's nativity in silver and gold; Item, a wooden *textus* without a book of silver gilt with the martyrdom of St Thomas' (fols 122r–v). This fact was briefly noted by by Legg, *Inventories*, pp. 28–9, and Chambers, *Divine Worship*, p. 276, without further comments.

58 'Item, *textus* with the psalter of St Thomas, covered with silver gilt and ornate with gems round the edges, with an ivory (Christ in) Majesty holding a book in the middle, and four engraved Evangelists' (fol. 122v).

59 Vezin, 'Livres utilisés'.

60 I thank Marie-Pierre Gelin for suggesting this possibility.

61 Eric Palazzo, 'Le livres dans trésors du Moyen Age: Contribution à l'histoire de la Memoria médiévale', *Annales: Histoire, Sciences Sociales* 52:1 (1997), 93–118.

62 W. B. Rye, ed., 'Catalogue of the Library of the Priory of St Andrew, Rochester, AD 1202', *Archaeologia Cantiana* 3 (1860), 47–64 (62–3).

63 'In the *textus* in whose upper and lower parts are images of kings and in both sides images of virgins are held these relics: of the Apostles: of St Peter, of St Gregory, of St Paul [...] of St Godard; of martyrs and confessors: of St Edmund Archbishop, of St Dunstan, of St Augustine, Apostle of the English [...] of St Aidan; of Virgins: of St Margaret [...] of St Edburga; In the *textus* with lions and eagles in gold are held these relics: of St Oswald, King, of St Hylda, of St Vincent.' BL, Cotton MS Titus D.vii, fols 9v–10r (James P. Carley and Martin Howley, eds, 'Relics at Glastonbury in the Fourteenth Century: An Annotated Edition of BL, Cotton MS Titus D.vii, fols 2r–13v', *Arthurian Literature* 16 (1998), 83–129 (111–12)).

64 *Liber Eliensis* iii:78 (Latin: *Liber Eliensis*, ed. E. O. Blake, Camden Society 3rd ser. 92 (London, 1962), p. 325; English: *Liber Eliensis, A History of the Isle of Ely from the Seventh Century to the Twelfth, Complied by a Monk of Ely in the Twelfth Century*, tr. and ed. Janet Fairweather (Woodbridge, 2005), p. 400). On

relics in binding: Steenbock, *Kirchliche Prachteinband*, pp. 53–4. At times relics were affixed to other books: Hanns Swarzenski, *The Berthold Missal, the Pierpont Morgan Library ms 710 and the Scriptorium of Weingarten Abbey* (New York, 1943), p. 65.

65 As noted, alongside the example of Bishop Nigel, by Deanesly, *Lollard Bible*, p. 169.

66 McGurk and Rosenthal, 'Anglo-Saxon Gospelbooks of Judith', complemented by: Jane Rosenthal and Patrick McGurk, 'Author, Symbol, and Word: The Inspired Evangelists in Judith of Flanders's Anglo-Saxon Gospel Books', in *Tributes to Jonathan J. G. Alexander: The Making and Meaning of Illuminated Medieval & Renaissance Manuscripts, Art & Architecture*, ed. Susan L'Engle and Gerald B. Guest (Turnhout, 2006), pp. 185–202. Additional information can be found in: Marvin C. Ross, 'An Eleventh-Century English Bookcover', *The Art Bulletin* 22:2 (1940), 83–5; Frauke Steenbock, *Kirchliche Prachteinband*, §77 (pp. 169–71); Howard M. Nixon and Mirjam M. Foot, *The History of Decorated Bookbinding in England* (Oxford, 1992), pp. 19–20; Paul Needham, *Twelve Centuries of Bookbindings, 400–1600* (New York, 1979), pp. 33–8.

67 McGurk and Rosenthal, 'Anglo-Saxon Gospelbooks', p. 275.

68 'Textus de ecclesia Roffensi per Godam comitissam III' on fol. 9r, corresponding to 'Textum Aureum Gode comitisse' in BL, Cotton MS Vespasian A.xxii, fol. 89r; Rye, 'Catalogue of Library', 63; *Registrum Roffense: Or a Collection of Ancient Records, Charters and Instruments of Divers Kinds Necessary for Illustrating the Ecclesiastical History and Antiquities of the Diocese and Cathedral Church of Rochester*, ed. John Thorpe (London, 1769), pp. 119–20.

69 Noted, alongside another incidents in which ten *textus* were unmade by the newly appointed abbot of Hide Abbey in 1141, in: S. R. Maitland, *The Dark Ages: A Series of Essays, Intended to Illustrate the State of Religion and Literature in the Ninth, Tenth, Eleventh, and Twelfth Centuries. Reprinted from The British Magazine', with Corrections and Some Additions* (London, 1844), pp. 218–20.

70 *Vetus registrum sarisberiense*, ii:43–4.

71 '(28.12.1225, after the king gave a golden ring with a ruby) Celebrata Missa, dixit rex decano, quod voluit quod lapis ille quem optulerat, simul et aurum annuli insererentur textui quem justitiarius dederat alia vice. De cuppa vero, non expressit voluntatem suam. Et tunc etiam fecit justitiarius afferri textum quem antea dederat, et per suos, ut predictum est, transmiserat, et ipsum cum magna devotione optulit super altare' (*Vetus registrum sarisberiense*, ii:44).

72 David Carpenter, *The Reign of Henry III* (London, 1996, repr. 2006), ch. 3: 'The Fall of Hubert de Burgh', pp. 45–60; Fred A. Cazel, Jr, 'Intertwined Careers: Hubert de Burgh and Peter des Roches', *The Haskins Society Journal* 1 (1989), 173–81.

73 Personal affinity of a different type was expressed through the medium of sacred books and their adoration by Malcolm III of Scotland (d. 1093). Although he was illiterate, his affection for his wife, Queen Margaret (d. 1093) had led him to adorn a gospel book with gems and precious stones, offering her the book as a gift (Richard Gameson, 'The Gospels of Margaret of Scotland and the Literacy of an Early Medieval Queen', in *Women and the Book: Assessing the Visual Evidence*, ed.

Lesley Smith and Jane H. M. Taylor (London, 1996), pp. 149–71 (158–9)). Such use recalls Palazzo's understanding of how a *textus* which was donated to Bamberg by Henry II in 1007 was later employed by Henry the Lion, Duke of Saxony, as sign of inheritance ('Livres dans trésors', pp. 109–10).

74 Wordsworth, *Ceremonies and Processions*, p. 168.

75 Frederick M. Powicke, 'The Oath of Bromholm', *English Historical Review* 56:224 (1941), 529–48 (531–3)

76 *Calendar of the Charter Rolls Preserved in the Public Record Office: Vol. I Henry III A.D. 1226–1257* (London, 1903), pp. 164–5. It is discussed by Carpenter, *Reign of Henry III*, pp. 52–5, and Powicke, 'Oath of Bromholm'.

77 'Touching the sacred Gospels bodily, John and others kept the sacrament that of the others they were justifiable concerning their lord, according to what their statutes and tenure required', Oxford, New College Archives 3914 m. 62d. A similar instance appears in the preceding entry for 5 Feb. 1356 (Oxford, New College Archives 3914 m.62). I thank Chris Briggs for this reference and his assistance.

78 'with his bare right hand laid physically on God's holy Gospels', Michael Jones and Simon Walker, eds, 'Private Indentures for Life Service in Peace and War 1278–1476', *Camden Misc.* 22, Camden Soc. 5th ser. 3 (London, 1994), pp. 1–190 (56), analysed and translated by Green, *Crisis of Truth*, p. 159.

79 'and he (the seneschal) will put his hand on the book and will say the oath "Hear this you Bailiff [...] if God and the saints help me" and then he will kiss the book and will go away' (fol. 191r). The treatise was presented in John S. Beckerman, 'Procedural Innovation and Institutional Change in Medieval English Manorial Courts', *Law and History Review* 10:2 (1992), 197–252 (204, 211). I thank Marigold A. Norby for her kind assistance in transcription and translation.

80 'He who swears on a book does three (acts): first, as if said "all that is written in this book shall never be of use to me, not the new nor the old law, if I shall lie in this oat"; second he lays his hand on the book, as if he said "good deeds that I have done will never be of use to me in front of Jesus Christ, if I do not say the truth which is signified in acts through the hand"; third and last he kisses the book as if he said "no orations nor prayers that I have said in my mouth on my behalf will ever be efficient for the deliverance of my soul, if I shall lie in this oath, which was applied to me."' Cambridge, Trinity College MS O.1.71, fol. 2v (with minor alterations, Cambridge, St John's College MS B.14, fol. 28v col. a). I am grateful for Paul Brand for this reference and his assistance.

81 A. K. McHardy, 'Church Courts and Criminous Clerks in the Later Middle Ages', in *Medieval Ecclesiastical Studies in Honour of Dorothy M. Owen*, ed. M. J. Franklin and Christopher Harper-Bill, Studies in the History of Medieval Religion 7 (Woodbridge, 1995), pp. 165–84.

82 'If a priest takes an oath, he does not have to touch the book but only to place the hand close-by above the book', Iohannes Bononiensis, 'Summa notarie de hiis que in foro ecclesiastico coram quibuscumque iudicibus occurunt notariis conscribenda', in *Briefsteller und Formelbücher des elften bis vierzehnten Jahrhunderts*, 2 vols, ed. Ludwig Rockinger, Quellen und Erörterungen zur bayerischen und deutschen Geschichte 9 (Munich, 1863–4, repr. New York, 1961), ii:593–712 at ii:663. In several manuscripts *episcopo* is written instead of *presbyter*. This builds

upon Gratian *Decretum* II:c.ii:q.5 (*Corpus Iuris Canonici*, 2 vols, ed. Emil Friedberg (Leipzig, 1879, 1881, repr. Graz, 1959), i:455–65).

83 'swearing on God's sacred Gospels, before us physically touched' (*Register of Walter de Stapeldon*, pp. 29–30).

84 'The notary shall say to the plaintiff thus: "Will you swear by God's sacred Gospels to say and answer the absolute truth [...] so help you God and these sacred Gospels" and the notary shall make both plaintiff and defendant utter the said words while touching the book in person.' Bononiensis, 'Summa notarie', ii:664 (repeated pp. 671–2). Information on author and treatise: ii:595–8; Christopher R. Cheney, *Notaries Public in England in the Thirteenth and Fourteenth Centuries* (Oxford, 1972), pp. 26–7, 31–2, 47, 52, 135–7.

85 Bononiensis, 'Summa notarie', ii:672.

86 'If another case should exist, he who swears by God seems to do a moderate mis-deed, while he who swears by the Gospels seems to have done something worse. To them one should say: "fools, Scriptures are sanctified because of God, not God because of Scriptures!"' (II:c.xxii:q.1:c.xi, Friedberg ed. i:864).

87 On the medieval oath as replacing the ordeal: Mathias Schmoeckel, 'Proof, Procedure, and Evidence', in *Christianity and Law*, pp. 143–62 (160); R. C. van Caenegem, *Legal History: A European Perspective* (London, 1991), pp. 77, 93.

88 John Spurr, '"The Strongest Bond of Conscience": Oaths and the Limits of Tolerance in Early Modern England', in *Contexts of Conscience in Early Modern Europe, 1500–1700*, ed. Harald E. Braun and Edward Vallance (Basingstoke, 2004), pp. 151–65.

89 Margaret Aston, 'Devotional Literacy', in *Lollards and Reformers: Images and Literacy in Late Medieval Religion*, ed. Aston (London, 1984), pp. 101–33 (109–11); Henry G. Russell, 'Lollard Opposition to Oaths by Creatures', *The American Historical Review* 51:4 (July 1946), 668–84. For a more general negation of talismanic use of Scripture: *An Apology for Lollard Doctrines Attributed to Wicliffe; Now First Printed from a Manuscript in the Library of Trinity College, Dublin*, ed. James Henthorn Todd, Camden Society 1st ser. 20 (London, 1842), pp. 90–2.

90 'I say that this article is false and heretical, and by false information I held it [...] renounce and ask forgiveness thereof and swear by these holy Gospels by me bodily touched that from this time forward I shall never preach it, teach it or hold it privately or publicly', *The Register of Thomas Arundel, Archbishop of Canterbury*, Lambeth Palace, vol. i, fols 390r–v. An analysis of the record is: Ian Forrest, *The Detection of Heresy in Late Medieval England* (New York and Oxford, 2005), pp. 145–50; 217–18 (for a later incident). I thank Ian Forrest for bringing this record to my attention.

91 'Item, that the pope and not any prelate nor regular clergy can compel anyone to swear by any of God's creatures nor to God's holy Gospels', *Register of Thomas Arundel*, fol. 390r; Forrest, *Detection of Heresy*, p. 150 n. 19.

92 'On the book they laid their hands, | To stand by that agreement | And then all three kissed each other | To be true sworn.' *Der mittelenglische Versroman über Richard Löwenherz: Kritische Ausgabe nach allen Handschriften mit Einleitung, Anmerkungen und Deutscher Übersetzung*, ed. Karl Brunner, Wiener Beiträge zur englischen Philologie 42 (Vienna and Leipzig, 1913), pp. 108–9.

93 '"Now lose no time, but fetch a book," said he, | "And of this knight will swear that it was she | Who killed this woman, then we will consider | Whom to appoint as her executioner." | A Gospel, written in the British tongue [inconclusive translation], | Was brought, and on this book he swore the guilt | Was hers; that she had murdered Hermengyld. | At which a hand smote him on the neck-bone | So that he fell that instance, like a stone'. Origin: *The Riverside Chaucer*, gen. ed. Larry D. Benson, 3rd edn (Boston, MA, 1988), p. 96; translation: Geoffrey Chaucer, *The Canterbury Tales: A Verse Translation*, tr. David Wright, new edn (Oxford, 2011), p. 134. For the legal knowledge of Chaucer and the centrality of the narrator in the 'Man of Law's Tale' see: Maura Nolan, '"Acquiteth yow now": Textual Construction and Legal Disclosure in the Man of Law's Introduction', in *Letter of the Law*, pp. 136–53.

94 'The Legitimization of Royal Power in Chaucer's "Man of Law's Tale"', *Modern Philology* 95:1 (1997), 27–43 (34–8).

95 '"See, I take an oath here on my prayer-book | That never while I live by hook or by crook, | Shall I betray what you confide in me." | "I swear the same again to you," said she. | "By God and by this prayer-book I swear, | Though I were to be torn to pieces here, | I'll never, even if I go to hell.' *Riverside Chaucer*, p. 204; *Canterbury Tales*, p. 345.

96 'The king was please with that activity | A very fair cloth he caused to be brought, | And thereon laid the Mass-book, | The chalice, and the paten too.| [...] That he made him swear on the book.' *Middle English Metrical Romances*, ed. Walter Hoyt French and Charles Brockway Hales (New York, 1930), pp. 81–2.

97 'Lunet then took precious relics, | The chalice and the Mass-book.' *Sir Perceval of Galles and Ywain and Gawain*, ed. Mary Flowers Braswell (Kalamazoo, MI, 1995), lines 3907–8 (=http://lib.rochester.edu/camelot/teams/ywnfrm.htm, accessed 8 June 2012).

98 'Her hand upon the book she (the lady) laid | [...] She (Lunet) made her lady kiss the book.' (lines 3911, 3922)

99 'I swear by book and bell ...', *The Middle English Breton Lays*, ed. Anne Laskaya and Eve Salisbury (Kalamazoo, 1995), p. 324 (= http://lib.rochester.edu/camelot/TEAMS/erltofrm.htm, accessed 8 June 2012).

100 'Then they shall be cursed in church with candle, book and bell', *Cursor Mundi (the Cursor of the World): A Northumbrian Poem of the XIVth Century in Four Versions*, vol. 2, ed. Richard Morris, EETS OS 62 (London, 1876), p. 979. See also the entries for Book (n §5b) and Bell (n.1 §8) in the OED.

101 'And if a Jew be appealed by any man without witness, he shall be quit from that appeal by his bare oath upon his Book. And in like manner he shall be quit of an appeal touching those things which pertain unto our crown, by his bare oath upon his Roll.' *Select Pleas, Starrs, and Other Records from the Rolls of the Exchequer of the Jews, A.D. 1220–1284*, ed. J. M. Rigg, Selden Soc. 15 (London, 1902), p. 1; translated in: *English Economic History: Select Documents*, ed. A. E. Bland, P. A. Brown, and R. H. Tawney (Norwich, 1914), p. 44. For information on the Jewish oath: Joseph Ziegler, 'Reflections on the Jewry Oath in the Middle Ages', in *Christianity and Judaism*, ed. Diana Wood, Studies in Church History 29 (Oxford, 1992), pp. 209–20; F. A. Lincoln, 'The non-Christian Oath in English Law', *The*

Jewish Historical Society of England – Transactions 16 (1945/51), 73–6. I thank Zefira Entin Rokeah and Yossi Ziegler for their assistance and guidance in this field, and Stephen Rigby for his sharp eye.

102 See the highly influential composition of Maimonides (d. 1204), *Mishneh Torah*, the Book of Love, the Laws of Tefilin, Mezuzah and the Book of the Torah, chs 7–9, and especially chapter 10, on laws regarding usage and veneration of the torah scroll (Maimonides, *The Mishneh Torah: Edited according to the Bodleian (Oxford) Codex*, ed. Moses Hyamson (New York, 1949), pp. 129a–140a).

103 Ziegler, 'Reflections on the Jewry Oath', pp. 209–10, 217–18; Ziegler, 'Oath, Jewish', in *Medieval Jewish Civilization: An Encyclopedia*, ed. Norman Roth, Routledge Encyclopedias of the Middle Ages 7 (New York, 2003), pp. 483–7 (486), refers to an image from Lérida, showing Jews swearing on the codex of the Ten Commandments. The confusion between books used by Jews for oaths is evident in other sources. Such is the narrative of a well-poisoning accusation from the time of the Black Death in Geneva, in which the scroll used by the tortured Jew to verify his testimony was understood by the seventeenth-century editor to be the Talmud: 'Et haec omnia per ea quae in quinque libris moysi & Judaeorum rodulo continentur, confessus fuit esse vera = Und daß dieses alles macht sein hat er behaht ben allen was in den funff Büchern Mosis und der Juden ihrem Rodel (Talmud) enthalten' (*Die älteste Teutsche so wol allgemeine als insonderheit Elsassische und Strassburgische Chronicke. Von Jacob von Königshofen … von Anfang der Welt biss ins Jahr … 1386 beschrieben*, ed. Johann Schiltern (Strassburg, 1698), p. 1043). This caused a heated reaction of a later editor (here in square brackets): 'And now by all that which is contained in the five books of Moses and the scroll of the Jews, he declared that this was true, and that he was in now wise lying, no matter what might happen to him [This Jew does not seem to know that the books of Moses and the scroll of the Jews are identical!]' (*The Jew in the Medieval World: A Source Book, 315–1791*, ed. Jacob R. Marcus (New York, 1938), rev. edn with introduction and updated bibliographies by Marc Saperstein (Cincinnati, 1999), p. 51).

104 'And because the said Jew has made his own law, as a Jew should do against a Christian by placing his bare hand on his book, therefore it was considered that the said Abraham retired acquitted' (Rigg, *Select Pleas*, pp. 88–9).

105 'Idem Meyrot (de Staunford judeus) quia serviens est judaismi Ebor' et non habuit librum legis judaice super quem judei potuerunt sacramentum (suum) facere in misericordia' (*The Plea Rolls of the Exchequer of the Jews, Preserved in the Public Record Office, vol. V: Edward I, 1277–1279*, ed. Sarah Cohen (London, 1992), p. 46). Analysis and translation are brought in Barrie Dobson, 'The Medieval York Jewry Reconsidered', in *Jews in Medieval Britain: Historical, Literary and Archaeological Perspectives*, ed. Patricia Skinner (Woodbridge, 2003), pp. 145–56 (151–2).

106 The possibility that these books were copies of the *Torah* (*Oxford Dictionary of Medieval Latin from British Sources*, gen. ed. D. R. Howlett, Fascicule v (Oxford, 1997) p. 1597 s.v. 'Liber'; Rigg, *Select Pleas*, p. xii) is at odds with the above-mentioned distinction between scrolls and codices and the implied hierarchy of oaths.

107 This understanding is evident in: R. Steward-Brown, 'The "Jurybook" of the County Court of Chester', *The English Historical Review* 48:190 (1933), 268–9

(though with some caution); Paul Brand, *Kings, Barons and Justices: The Making and Enforcement of Legislation in Thirteenth-Century England* (Cambridge, 2003), p. 104, n. 132; Green, *Crisis of Truth*, pp. 78–9; *Oxford Dictionary of Medieval Latin*, v:1597 (although none of its examples refers explicitly to a Bible).

108 *Testamenta Eboracensia: A Selection of Wills from the Registry of York, vol. 2*, ed. James Raine the Younger, Surtees Society 30 (Durham 1855), p. 79.

109 Brand, *Kings, Barons*, p. 104 n. 132. See also *Curia Regis Rolls of the Reigns of Richard I and John preserved in the Public Record Office: vol. 6: 11–14 John*, ed. C. T. Fowler (London, 1932), p. 229.

110 '(problem of inability to swear emanating from) because the book called "Jurybook" was not held ... (all those present in court said) that the abbot of the monastery of St Werburgh at Chester and all the abbots his predecessors of the said place are known to procure the said book to serve in the court of the Lord King here to all the assembly, here held or to be held. And that the Lord King of England, who is now the earl of Chester and all his predecessors who were earls of Chester, along with all the earls of Chester from a time beyond memory [were known to procure] the said book to serve here in court' (Steward-Brown, 'Jurybook'). The fact that between 1397 and 1399 Chester became the first, and only, principality in England has important links to the document's ideals of continuity and authority.

111 *English Benedictine Libraries: The Shorter Catalogues*, ed. Richard Sharpe et al., Corpus of British Medieval Library Catalogues 4 (London, 1996), pp. 104–6.

112 'Item a most ancient book having a cross superimposed, over which [one] is sworn' (*Vetus registrum sarisberiense*, i:291).

113 fols 26r–82v = Mt 1:1–18a, 1:18b–1:21, 3:13–17, 26:1–27:66; Mk 1:1–8, 16:1b–7, 16:14–20; 14:1–15:46; Lk 1:5–17, 1:26b–38b, 3:21–4:1a, 22:1–23:53; Jn 1:1–20:18, where it ends abruptly.

114 Description of the manuscript: http://bl.uk/catalogues/manuscripts/HITS0001.ASP?VPath=html/20176.htm&Search=15&Highlight=F (accessed 8 June 2012)

115 The width of the text is slightly below 2 cm, that of the covers is 1.4 (front) and 2 (back). The crucifix measures 14.3 × 10.5 × 1.9, from a cover sized 18.5 × 11.7 × 2.

116 Nixon and Foot, *Decorated Bookbinding*, p. 19.

117 Fols 9r–9v = Jn 1:1–14; 9v–10r = Lk 1:26b–38a; 10r–11r = Mk 16:14–20; 11r = Mt 20:17–19. The numbering of the folios is lacking. 1 and 17 are pastedowns, while a blank folio between 14 and 15 is unnumbered.

118 For the use of cut pins and holes to identify a previous binding: Nixon and Foot, *Decorated Bookbinding*, pp. 22–3

119 The manuscript is described in: Frances Consitt, *The London Weavers' Company, vol. 1: From the Twelfth Century to the Close of the Sixteenth Century* (Oxford, 1933), pp. 175–6, with the oaths transcribed as appendices 9 and 10 (pp. 202–4, without any specific reference to the contents of the book). There are some inaccuracies in this edition.

120 As in the following comparison between Mk 8:15–17 in the manuscript and the Vulgate:

Guildhall MS 04645	*Vulgate*
(I)N illo tempore. Dixit Ihesus d. s. venite, et cavete a fermento pharise-orum, et fermento Herodis. Et cogitabant ad alterutrum, dicentes: quia panes non habemus. Quo agnito, Ihesus ait illis Quid cogitatis, quia panes non habetis? non dum cognoscitis nec in telligitis? ad huc cecatum habetis cor vestrum?	Et precipiebat eis, dicens: Videte, et cavete a fermento phari-seorum, et fermento Herodis. Et cogitabant ad alterutrum, dicentes: quia panes non habemus. Quo cognito, ait illis Jesus Quid cogitatis, quia panes non habetis? nondum cognoscetis nec intelligitis? adhuc cecatum habetis cor vestrum?

121 Reproduction and information on compilation and use: *The York Gospels: A Facsimile with Introductory Essays by Jonathan Alexander, Patrick McGurk, Simon Keynes & Bernard Barr*, ed. Nicholas Barker (London, 1986).

122 'Item one *textus* ornate with sliver not well-gilt, over which the oaths of dean, other dignitaries and canons are inserted in (its) beginning' ('Excursus I: Inventory of Treasures at York Minster 1500–10', in *York Gospels*, p. 121). The grammar is lacking in the Latin original.

123 'Excursus IV: Oaths', in *York Gospels*, pp. 127–31; Bernard Barr, 'The History of the Volume', in *York Gospels*, pp. 101–17.

124 A comparison between the text of the York Gospels and the Vulgate reveals a general textual accuracy.

125 Don C. Skemer, *Binding Words: Textual Amulets in the Middle Ages* (University Park, PA, 2006), pp. 88–9, 216 (the latter of an amulet of the full *Cursus evangelii*); Morton W. Bloomfield, 'The Magic of *In principio*', *Modern Language Notes* 70 (1955), 559–65; Spencer, *English Preaching*, p. 89.

126 Russell, 'Lollard Opposition', p. 670.

3

Paratext and meaning in Late Medieval Bibles

Introduction

The *textus* and oath-books of the previous chapter conveyed in their physicality a particular view of the Bible. Medieval records and surviving manuscripts attest to the great effort invested in lavish and iconic binding, even at the expense of the biblical text. The use of these books and their sacrality relied on a backward glance: the glorified past of Chaucer's 'Britoun book', the 'time beyond memory' of the Chester 'Jurybook', or the antiquity of the oath-books of the archbishop of York (as well as that of President Obama) all show these books being employed as relics from a glorified past, in whose authority those present wished to share. In late medieval England such Gospel books were becoming an archaic remnant. While they were used in liturgy and ritual, another type of Bible emerged. Adhering to a revolutionary paratext, these new full Bibles (or pandects) became a standard for Scripture, replicated in Bibles in manuscript and printed forms for centuries to come. A far cry from silver gilt and jewelled bindings of earlier texts, these were mundane objects encased in boards and skin. They presented the biblical text through a careful array of layout and addenda which forms the subject of this chapter.

At the end of the twelfth century and the beginning of the thirteenth a new type of Bible was developed. This was the period when the first universities were established, in which a growing number of students and lecturers engaged in the study of theology and law through the analysis of key texts and their glosses, from Gratian's *Decretum* to the Bible. They produced study aids which relied on textual clarity and easily locatable textual divisions, benefitting from the availability of cheaper and portable books. Their needs were met by urban and lay workshops, where professional scribes practised a minute Gothic hand, written on exceptionally thin vellum. The combination of need and expertise led to the creation of a new type of Bible, small in size and with aids to assist use and reference. The new pandects became an immediate success. They emerged from the centres of learning in Paris and Southern England to spread rapidly throughout Western Europe. Hundreds of manuscripts nowadays bear witness to one of the most prolific books of the later Middle Ages. The proliferation of Latin Bibles did not reach all strata of church and society indiscriminately. The survey conducted in Chapter 2 from select dioceses showed that only a small fraction (about 1 per cent) of parish churches held a Bible, and that only four extant manuscripts could be assigned to such churches. Combined evidence from English wills prior to 1409 records thirty-six privately owned Latin Bibles.[1] Out of these, one was owned by Elizabeth de Burgh, Lady of Clare (d. 1360, founder of Clare College, to which the Bible was bequeathed); six by princes and princesses (such as Isabella of Castile, daughter of Pedro the Cruel (d. 1392), and Thomas of Woodstock, son of Edward III (d. 1397, who also owned a Wycliffite Bible)); one by a knight in Yorkshire; another by a London embroiderer (*Brouderer*) and yet another by chaplain. The remaining twenty-six Bibles were owned by monks, friars, bishops, and university masters. This strongly suggests that in late medieval England Latin Bibles rarely existed beyond the realm of universities, cathedrals, monasteries, and friaries, in whose library records they appear time and again. Among the primary users of these manuscripts were the friars, whose education, poverty and itinerant life helped spread these Bibles far and wide.

Biblical paratext underwent a major transformation at the turn of the thirteenth century. Its legacy is felt to the present day. However, the identity of this group of manuscripts, which I have chosen to name 'Late Medieval Bibles' (for reasons detailed below), is still unclear. Scholars of biblical manuscripts have followed primarily questions of origins and accuracy, rather than reception and readership. An interest in the origins of this new type of Bibles has led researchers to concentrate on the end of the twelfth century and the beginning of the thirteenth, when these biblical manuscripts took form. A closely knit group of manuscripts was therefore delineated, to assist in ascertaining the evolution of biblical manuscripts. Studying especially the university of Paris, a well-known hub of biblical creativity at the time, Paris Bibles have been seen as witnesses to the early thirteenth century as a watershed in the history of the medieval Bible.[2] These Paris Bibles adhere to strict textual and paratextual criteria: they follow a historical sequence (Heptateuch, Ruth, 1–2 Samuel, 1–2 Kings, 1–2 Chronicles, 1–2 Ezra, Tobit, Judith, Job, Psalms, Sapiential Books, Major and Minor Prophets, Maccabees, Gospels, Pauline Epistles, Acts, Catholic Epistles, and Apocalypse), with books preceded by a specific prologue, based on the works of Jerome or later exegetes; these Bibles also exclude the earlier Eusebian canons (a Late Antiquity division of the Gospels to assist in locating parallel narratives) and biblical summaries, and introduce the modern chapter division and a biblical glossary, the *Interpretations of Hebrew Names*. These characteristics are of use in tracing the origins of the Late Medieval Bible. They do, nevertheless, omit numerous biblical manuscripts which share their main characteristics, produced and used in England, France, Italy, Spain, and Germany. Moreover, the very nature of the Paris Group has been recently put in question, with challenges to its links with the university of Paris, with Bacon's assertion of university-stationers' dissemination, and the place of Paris in the introduction of the chapter division.[3]

The study of Paris Bibles has nevertheless asserted how paratext became a form of biblical mediation. The sequence of books and prologues indicative of the Paris Group attests to changes in biblical exegesis. Jerome's sequence, which was based on the Hebrew Bible, was replaced by the Septuagint order and its historical continuity, in tune with the literal sense of Scripture.[4] Thus, for example, in the Old Testament the new sequence attempted to present a single historical narrative from Creation to the second century BC (1–2 Maccabees), with stories such as that of the Book of Ruth re-integrated on the basis of their historical background. New trends in medieval exegesis underlay the modification of prologues, and so Jerome's writings were replaced by more contemporary authors, whose spiritual reading of Scripture was indicative, as argued by Laura Light, of a transformation in the nature of biblical exegesis.[5] Gilbert Dahan has suggested that the prologues added layers of interpretation to provide readers with a link between Bible and Christian dogma, and many attest to a revived interest in biblical etymology, also evident in the *Interpretations of Hebrew Names*.[6] In the current chapter this discussion is extended beyond textual interpolations to biblical manuscripts at large. Such link between culture and the appearance of manuscript is at the heart of my investigation. This chapter examines Bibles as the combined creation of scribes, rubricators, and illuminators. Their rubrics, divisions, illumination, and mise-en-page, as well as biblical glossaries and mnemonic aids are analysed as a form of biblical mediation, which engaged in dialogue with other media, such as biblical exegesis, preaching and liturgy. It facilitated discrete reading strategies, and its analysis reveals a time when the Bible's narrative qualities were put in the shadow of the Bible as a composite text.

Such a transformation rendered the Late Medieval Bible a highly efficient reference book, and had an important impact on the way one approached the biblical text.

Once we move away from questions of origins and into mediation and reception, the strict definition of the Paris Bible become of lesser use. Rather, the examination of a wider group of Bibles reveals a staggering paratextual uniformity in script and addenda, mise-en-page and textual division. These Bibles constitute a singular group of manuscripts, whose members' similarity is such that modern scholars often struggle to tell one Bible from the other. The text and paratext of these Bibles are so uniform that ascertaining date and provenance is rarely practised by modern scholars, especially for Bibles without a colophon, calendar, or illuminations. Such Bibles are often catalogued simply as English or French of the mid-thirteenth century, noting their proximity to the group of Paris Bibles.[7] This confusion reflects the medieval reality. Then, these manuscripts were copied, transmitted, and employed throughout Europe, and they bear witness to centuries of subsequent use. They were part of a revolution in mass-communication that took place in the later Middle Ages.[8] Rather than a hinderance in ascertaining date and provenance, this uniformity becomes an important means of tracing biblical paratext and its function as a form of biblical mediation. As more and more Bibles adhered to a uniform layout and integrated fixed addenda, their study can take the place of a singular distinct class of manuscripts. In order to assess such a large corpus of manuscripts, each containing an ocean of information, I have relied on a randomly chosen sample of fifty-six manuscripts, primarily of English or French origins, which date to the thirteenth and fourteenth centuries (listed in the Appendix). The uniformity of layout and addenda they display, both in their general layout and in minute details, over two hundred years and in a variety of locations, shows the applicability of this sampling technique. Unlike the variations apparent in biblical paratext of the early and high Middle Ages, this uniformity shows the Late Medieval Bible to have been a singular cultural artefact, evident in manuscripts in all sizes, produced across Europe. I have named this group Late Medieval Bibles, reflecting the similarity of manuscripts written between 1230 and 1450, which serve as the basis for the current investigation.

The chapter continues with a survey of biblical addenda and traces how biblical manuscripts were made personal, facilitating a variety of reading strategies. The most common addition to the Late Medieval Bible, the *Interpretations of Hebrew Names*, a glossary to the Hebrew, Greek, and Aramaic proper names of the Vulgate, exists in hundreds of manuscripts today, and bears witness to a new way of understanding the Bible. Beyond addenda, the layout of Late Medieval Bibles is then presented as a form of biblical mediation, both in its general appearance and in its major exception – the Book of Psalms. While the general layout of Late Medieval Bibles assisted in the fragmentation of the biblical text and the move away from biblical narratives, that of the Psalms encoded liturgical customs and a unique mnemonics. Yet, the least stable element of the Psalms, their superscriptions, presents a pattern similar to the *Interpretations* in highlighting the Hebrew origins of the Bible. It also breaks away from the common understanding of the Psalms' layout as an echo of liturgical practices. The chapter concludes by demonstrating how these Bibles became the precursors of early modern Bibles, not only in their wide dissemination and uniformity but also in the interest displayed in biblical origins and ancient languages.

A variety of biblical addenda

At the beginning of the thirteenth century Bibles were becoming pandects. Beyond portability and cost, this transformation revolutionised the way Bibles have been read ever since. Whereas the earlier, heavier, multi-volume Bibles were consulted primarily in large monastic libraries, single-volume Bibles were now also taken on the road, to be read without additional volumes of exegesis and theology. The new Bibles became self-sufficient books, volumes that could function as the first and last port of call for biblical study and dissemination. A variety of glossaries, tables, diagrams, tracts, and lists were embedded into their pages and played a prominent role in this transformation. They provided readers with keys to the biblical text. They also facilitated discrete reading strategies, and assisted in further dissemination, in dialogue with biblical mnemonics, exegesis, liturgy, and preaching. While the layout was uniform, the addenda were varied and versatile, accommodating Bibles to personal tastes and rendering them invaluable for the medieval classroom, pulpit, or lectern.[9] Of the myriad addenda to Late Medieval Bibles, liturgy is the single most popular category (the *Interpretations of Hebrew Names*, discussed below, notwithstanding). Calendars are found in over a quarter of the Bibles investigated (sixteen out of fifty-six). Central to the performance of the liturgy, they enabled readers to identify saints' days and the feasts of the *temporale* not dependent on Easter (the non-moveable feasts). In the later Middle Ages calendars became a common feature in liturgical manuscripts as well, often found in breviaries, psalters, and books of hours. Richard Pfaff has traced the rise of calendars in late medieval England and demonstrated how they became a highly versatile element in devotional books: they integrated unique entries, ranging from obits and local saints' days to church dedications and historical events; they facilitated personal, regional, or monastic devotions, incidentally often providing modern scholars with important means of localising these manuscripts.[10]

Such calendars were also integrated into administrative books (such as the oath-books presented in the previous chapter) and scientific treatises, in which they varied in complexity to tie in with astronomical observations. Their primary value, however, was in conjunction with tables of lessons. Such tables are found in nine Late Medieval Bibles of the sample (about 13 per cent) of the sample, often in tandem with calendars) and provide the appropriate biblical lessons for the feasts of the *temporale* and *sanctorale* (as well as votive Masses). They assisted readers in making their way through the array of biblical lessons of the liturgical year. Entries in these long lists follow the liturgical sequence (traditionally commencing with Advent Sunday) to identify the biblical lessons for each feast. This was done by referring to the biblical book and chapter (at times accompanied by a subdivision). Making use of the newly integrated chapter division, these lists facilitated quick and efficient means of identification and retrieval.

Calendars together with tables of lessons linked the biblical text with its liturgical commemoration. In several Bibles they aided public recitation. Cambridge University Library MS Ee.2.23, BL, Additional MS 11,842, and London Guildhall MS 4158A (once the possession of the parish church of St Peter-upon-Cornhill, London) demonstrate such use. These are large volumes with thick parchment, which could be read from a distance even in half-lit churches; liturgical subdivisions, notes, and colophons further support this attribution. Such use, however, did not apply to all Bibles. Bibles were cumbersome books for *in situ* public recitation of the relevant lesson. Finding the right lesson in Bibles, even with the aid of the new chapter divisions and tables of lessons, required much preparatory work and leafing. Instead, this goal was best served by missals and lectionaries, which proliferated from the high Middle Ages. The gulf between Bibles with tables of lessons and the public recitation of Scripture is at its widest in two of the manuscripts examined. BL, Additional MS 35,085[11] and BL, Arundel MS 303 are minute books, whose script and delicate parchment discouraged lengthy readings and public uses. Even in well-lit reading rooms nowadays one often struggles to decipher their diminutive script and abbreviations, showing that their original patrons were unlikely to have intended them to be used for public recitation. The Dominican provenance of these two Bibles reveals another function of calendars and tables of lessons, one rarely evoked by the liturgists who have usually engaged in their study. Priests had to identify specific liturgical lessons not only for communal (or personal) devotion but also in order to prepare their sermons. As explored in the following chapter, the day's pericope would then serve (in full or truncated into a *thema*) as the basis for the sermon. Calendars and tables of lessons were thus of use within liturgical services, but also as preachers' aids, consulted in private well before the public event. Both uses, nevertheless, presented the biblical text in a specific light. Time and again they tied the stories of the Bible with its liturgical commemoration. The liturgical year was thus embedded into Late Medieval Bibles, subjecting biblical manuscripts to the same exegetical gap between text and liturgical occurrence, and blurring the distinction between the written and spoken word.[12]

A handful of Bibles enabled their readers to take an even more active part in liturgical celebrations. In three of the Bibles examined (and in two additional Bibles I was able to locate but not to consult in person) texts for the Mass appear. When written by the original scribe(s), these were placed near the Psalms; when added by a later scribe they were inserted at the end of the manuscript to prevent breaking up existing quires.[13] These texts range from full Masses to prefaces and the canon of the Mass, and their layout from noted texts and full-page illumination to additions made by non-professional scribes. These additions did not transform the Late Medieval Bible into a self-sufficient liturgical book, such as a breviary or a missal. However, they did equip readers with key elements of the most repeatedly celebrated rituals, facilitating occasional prayers or a single Mass. These Bibles enabled a sole priest or an itinerant friar (references to Dominic and Francis are often found among them) to perform liturgical duties on his way and to facilitate private devotion. This is most evident in San Marino, Huntington Library, MS HM 26061, fols 178v–179r (Plate 4).[14] There the image of the Crucifixion was intended for the eyes of the reader, and the smear at Christ's face made as his thumb flattened (or his mouth kissed) the page adjacent to the *Te Deum*, a common practice as the priest read the most solemn part of the Mass.[15]

Liturgical addenda to Late Medieval Bibles linked them to the performance of the liturgy, though not necessarily for public recitation. In a similar vein, elements often described in catalogues as theological treatises or biblical aids should not necessarily suggest a use in a classroom. Although these Bibles originated in the schools and universities of the late twelfth century, they were not an obvious sole sourcebook for students of *sacra pagina*. University students relied upon exegetical works, which circulated independently, or on quires from the *Glossa ordinaria*, a distinct class of manuscripts that were a remnant from the height of twelfth-century scholasticism.[16] Only a few Late Medieval Bibles, typically larger in size, contain exegetical notes and diagrams, with a very small minority displaying the full array of marginal exegetical notes or scholastic commentary typical of a systematic study of biblical exegesis.[17] Biblical addenda to most Late Medieval Bibles commonly simplify or summarise the Bible. In the manuscripts examined, one often finds the *Aurora* (Stegmüller §6823–25), the Song of the Gospels ('quator est primus', Stegmüller §850), Robert de Sorbonne's (d. 1274) *Glosse divinorum librorum* (Stegmüller §7486, relying on the interpretations of biblical names in its presentation of the biblical narrative), a variety of Christ's genealogies (at times accompanied by diagrams), or the *Summarium Biblicum* (Stegmüller §1175–82).[18] Rather than an in-depth analysis of the biblical text, these summaries present a simplified version, befitting mnemonic functions or further dissemination in sermons; their authors and scribes made use of the newly devised textual divisions to tie summary and text together, enabling readers to look up the biblical text by book and chapter references. Their incorporation into Late Medieval Bibles implicitly acknowledged the fact that readers often did not have the time or capacity to read the entire Bible. This realisation later guided Miles Coverdale to integrate summaries into his English Bible, as he made explicit in his introduction.[19]

Beyond readers and patrons, additions to Late Medieval Bibles shed light on the scribes who produced them.[20] Colophons are not often found among the pages of these Bibles, which were commonly written by teams of professional scribes. When found, however, they reflect scribes' achievements, credit them with piety, and follow in a long-established monastic tradition which saw the copying of manuscripts as an act of devotion. London, Victoria and Albert Museum, MS L. 2060–1948 is a mid-thirteenth-century New Testament of English origins, which was probably once part of a pandect. Its monastic origins are shown by a colophon at the end of Revelation that reads: 'Ex thorrentona (Thorton-on-Humber, Austin Abbey, North Lincolnshire) liber hic perscriptus habetur | Qui scripsit dona scriptor de iure meretur | Non laus. nec probitas operis. non gloria rerum | Exigit[ur]. ac caritas solito pro labore dierum'.[21] More light-hearted is the concluding comment in Cambridge University Library, MS Dd.10.29: 'finito libro sit laus et gloria Christo | et nunc pro scripto reddatur cena magistro'.[22] The labour of the latter scribe merited a reward beyond mere charity, and thus diverges from the monastic ideal. This scribe might have been a secular craftsman, one of the professional scribes working in the lay workshops that were often responsible for the minute script and carefully executed layout of the Late Medieval Bible. The mundane world of scribes is reflected in the inclusion of practical notes, such as an ink recipe found among the pages of Cambridge University Library, MS Dd.8.12 (fol. 216v), an insertion common also in books of a more profane nature. Richard and Mary Rouse have traced the work of an English scribe – Raulinus of Fremington, working alongside French illuminators in Italy – who had inserted his laments for his cloak, stolen by *Vilana* the harlot, as well as another lover by the name of Meldina; such profanities notwithstanding, he dedicated the Bible and his labour to the Virgin Mary.[23]

Nowadays the majority of surviving biblical manuscripts include only few extra-biblical materials. This situation raises an obvious question: is it a reflection of actual medieval practice or simply the result of generations of overly zealous owners and binders who trimmed and removed non-biblical addenda? Medieval library catalogues are of little help as they habitually note these manuscripts simply as 'Biblia'. However, a crime committed more than seven hundred years ago sheds unexpected light on the production and personalisation of Bibles in medieval England. Around the feast of St Margaret (20 July) 1253, a Bible was stolen from Reading Abbey. Alured of Dover, the Abbey's sacrist, sent letters to ward off potential buyers. His attempt to prevent the Bible's sale has left a detailed description of a Late Medieval Bible, beyond any entry in a library catalogue.[24] The Bible is first identified by its small measurements: about 15 cm in length ('biblia una parva mensure quasi unius palmi et dimidii'), ranking it among the smallest of Late Medieval Bibles. In order to identify the Bible firmly, Alured enumerated the various addenda in four clusters: in its beginning Robert Grosseteste's *Templum Domini* (Stegmüller §7404, 4), *De sex alis cherubim* (Clement of Llanthony's (?), Stegmüller §949), a treatise on the candelabra, Peter of Poitiers's *Genealogia historiarum* (Stegmüller §6778); between Psalms and Proverbs a calendar; between Ecclesiasticus and the New Testament (showing an order of books not common among the group of Paris Bibles, where Ecclesiasticus precedes Isaiah, and the Books of Maccabees conclude the Old Testament) a list of Gospel and epistle readings for the liturgical year; at the end of the Bible were an excerpt from Peter Riga's *Aurora*, the *Interpretations* (attributed to Remigius of Auxerre), a concordance (possibly Stegmüller §3605–6), *distinctiones* (?) in alphabetical order,[25] verses on the Evangelists, and Pseudo-Augustine's *Liber de spiritu et anima* (PL 40:779–832).

Much like other Bibles, the Dover manuscript contained a calendar, tables of lessons, the *Interpretations*, summaries, and genealogies. Other addenda demonstrate the patron's personal taste and facilitated both private devotion and preaching. The latter is evident in the concordance and *distinctiones*, both popular preaches' aids. The *Templum Domini*, a pastoral manual by Robert Grosseteste, and the emphasis on penance underpinning the allegorical interpretation of the Cherubim's wings (*De sex alis cherubim*), further supports the use of this Bible in the care of souls.[26] The position of addenda in the Dover Bible is typical of other biblical manuscripts. Additional texts are most commonly found at the book's opening, end, or between the Old and New Testaments. However, additions of a liturgical nature often appear after the Psalms, not only providing readers with a convenient location near the middle of the Bible[27] but also agreeing with the Psalms' distinct layout and its liturgical undertones, discussed below.[28]

The stolen Bible sheds additional light on how Bibles were modified following their compilation. Pseudo-Augustine's *De spiritu et anima*, a treatise on the connection between the soul and the body its prison, is not commonly found among the pages of Late Medieval Bibles. In the Dover Bible it likewise did not constitute part of the original manuscript, but was rather added at a later date. A list of labours of 'W. of Wycombe', a brother of the Abbey, enumerates the various tasks he was given while at the daughter priory of Leominster (Herefordshire). Among these was the copying of the above tract and its insertion into a Bible, which had been previously purchased by Alured.[29] The nature of the list, as demonstrated by Alan Coates, suggests that these tasks were performed by the brother unwillingly, possibly as a form of penance; Alured's appearance on that list might explain his interest in retrieving the Bible. The distinct features of the Dover Bible correspond with two other extant Bibles, which display a similar breadth of addenda: Cambridge University Library, MS Dd.8.12 and BL, Royal MS 1 B.x.[30] All three Bibles share the genealogies of Christ, the treatise on the wings of the Cherub (either in full or as part of the *Speculum theologiae*), and verse summaries of the Bible. As both extant manuscripts display parts of these treatises graphically, one can deduce that elements in the Dover Bible such as the treatise on the Cherub's wings and the candelabra were illuminated as well. This small group of manuscripts puts into question the breadth of addenda in most Late Medieval Bible, and raises two alternatives: the Dover Bible and its parallels could be just the tip of an iceberg of biblical addenda, often removed from extant Bibles and not indicated in library catalogues. Alternatively, given the similarity of the works, they might constitute a closely knit group of biblical manuscripts, whose copying relations are currently lost, but whose nature attests to one possible subgroup of the unfathomable multitude of Late Medieval Bibles.

The *Interpretations of Hebrew Names*

A variety of summaries, charts, calendars, and lists equipped readers with tools to consult the Bible, compose sermons, and assist in devotional practices. None, however, comes near the importance and popularity of the *Interpretations of Hebrew Names* (*Interpretationes nominum Hebraeorum*, Stegmüller §7709). This glossary of the Hebrew, Aramaic, and Greek names of the Bible was attributed in the Middle Ages to Jerome, the Venerable Bede, or Remigius of Auxerre. It became the standard addition to the Late Medieval Bible and survives in a large number of manuscripts. Of the fifty-six manuscripts examined, thirty-seven include the *Interpretations*, an impressive 66 per cent. Similar percentages have been put forward by Amaury d'Esneval's and Richard and Mary Rouse's analyses of the catalogue of medieval manuscripts at the Bibliothèque nationale de France.[31] If we allow for frequent removal of the glossary by post-medieval users, the real figures are probably even higher. Although little studied in modern times, this glossary was an important means of unfolding the biblical text and attests to a crucial moment in the evolution of the Late Medieval Bible, a move away from the medieval schools and universities where it had originated.

The sheer number of surviving manuscripts of the *Interpretations* seems to have inhibited its modern investigation. To date there is no critical edition of the *Interpretations*, and only three articles engage directly with the late medieval *Interpretations*.[32] In tracing the evolution and typology of the *Interpretations* these articles shed important light on the links between the rise of the glossary and the schools of the late twelfth and early thirteenth century. The starting point for the study of the *Interpretations* was d'Esneval's identification of three discrete versions, all attributed by him to Stephan Langton and seen as evidence for knowledge of Hebrew at the end of the twelfth century and the beginning of the thirteenth. Responding to these assertions, Gilbert Dahan analysed the entries of several high and late medieval glossaries to confirm the importance of the three versions. He placed the earlier versions a generation before Langton's time and argued that their compiler(s) relied on Latin synonyms and other glossaries, rather than direct knowledge of Hebrew. Recently, Giovanna Murano has provided a more nuanced reading of the glossary, to trace the important sub-categories of d'Esneval's (and Stegmüller's) three major renderings. She has been able not only to demonstrate the appearance of entries from the last rendering in Langton's work but also to trace the medieval attribution to Remigius of Auxerre (d. 908).

The three articles present the inception and evolution of the *Interpretations* in tandem with medieval exegesis. Their emphasis on origins led their authors to address the *Interpretations* as an independent compilation, although acknowledging the place of the latter versions primarily within Late Medieval Bibles. Changes in biblical manuscripts and oral mediation further serve to explain the overwhelming popularity of the last version of the *Interpretations* and to trace how this glossary became important in unfolding the biblical text to which it was attached. The *Interpretations* originated with the works of Jerome. The Vulgate preserves Hebrew, Aramaic, and Greek proper names in transliteration. Jerome drew on Eusebius of Caesarea's (d. *c.* 330) *Onomasticon* to compile the *Liber interpretationis*, a glossary of biblical names.[33] In keeping with the work of Origen, Jerome extended this glossary beyond the *Onomasticon*'s toponyms to encompass personal names, which became the majority of its entries. Jerome's work circulated widely in the Middle Ages and served, by the twelfth century, as the basis for several biblical glossaries. Paris, Bibliothèque de l'Arsénal, MS 97 (possibly from Clairvaux) captures a moment in the evolution of these glossaries, and contains several glossaries with interlinear notes and pasted slips of parchments, alongside biblical genealogies, gazetteers, and an interpretation of the Hebrew alphabet. By the early thirteenth century there were three major renderings of the glossary, commonly identified by the first entry of each glossary: *Adam*, *Aaron* or *Aaz*. Each version employs a different system of classification and diverges in the nature and scope of its entries. One can clearly detect a gradual rise in the scope and breadth of the *Interpretations*, with the *Adam* rendering containing about 1,050 entries, the *Aaron* about 1,425, and the *Aaz* about 5,250. The glossaries came to encompass more and more biblical personae of little significance, and the *Aaz* version ranges from *Aaz* (grandfather of a lower priest in Neh 11:13?) to *Zuzim* (a Canaanite tribe, Gn 14:5).[34]

Jerome's original work follows individual books of the Bible, each subdivided alphabetically (e.g. Genesis A–Z, Exodus A–Z, etc.). This is altered in the first version of the *Interpretations* (*Adam*) to form an alphabetical sequence subdivided by biblical books (A Genesis–Revelation, B Genesis–Revelation, etc.). The two last versions (*Aaron* and *Aaz*) follow a purely alphabetical sequence, without any historical subdivision (A, B, etc.). This modification, and the general appeal of the *Interpretations*, was part of a rise in alphabetical aids and an academic shift towards the systemisation of knowledge which took place during the twelfth century.[35] The evolution of the Late Medieval Bible and the advent of the pandect suggests another explanation. Much like Jerome's *Liber interpretationis*, the *Interpretations* initially circulated independently. The appearance and success of the single-volume Bible rendered the *Liber interpretationis* and the earlier versions of the *Interpretations* obsolete. The division of the glossary into biblical books was compatible with multi-volume Bibles, which had become antiquated by 1230. A purely alphabetical sequence befitted a single-volume Bible perfectly. Such glossaries thus appear in the vast majority of Late Medieval Bibles, where the *Aaz* version is the most popular, the *Aaron* version appears infrequently, and the earlier version of *Adam* is a rarity.

Alongside a movement towards a purely alphabetical order, the glossary entries themselves underwent a radical transformation with the evolution of the *Interpretations*. A few entries from each version exemplify this shift (see Table 1).[36]

The length of the entries and their contents differ considerably. While the *Aaron* and *Aaz* versions introduced a novel sequence to the biblical glossary, it is the earlier *Adam* version whose entries are most revolutionary. The *Adam* version is unique in providing historical information which ties the person with the biblical narrative; this is commonly accomplished by providing a geographical identification or biblical lineage, accompanied by a book identification and a short etymology of the name. The *Aaron* and *Aaz* versions do away with most of the historical information, leaving only a skeletal etymology. The *Aaron* version often contains a biblical reference which made use of the newly devised chapter division (which took shape alongside the evolution of the *Interpretations*). The *Aaz* version is the shortest of all three; it contains no information regarding the biblical narrative and stands at odds with the modern understanding of a biblical glossary. In this version the etymology of the name is the furthest removed from the biblical narrative, and does not lend the reader any assistance in understanding biblical history. It provides short and diverse definitions which remove the word from its narrative and is a far cry from a gazetteer or a biblical genealogy.

The success of this aid and its appeal to medieval audience was unequivocal. The earlier *Adam* version, both in its alphabetical sequence and in a version which followed the biblical narrative (i.e. 'Adam, Eva, Abel, Enoch, etc.', Bibliothèque de l'Arsenal, MS 97, fols 133r–158r), quickly faded away.

Table 1: Sample entries from the *Interpretations of Hebrew Names*

Jerome's Liber Interpretationis (Lagarde ed., pp. 60–1)	**Adam** (Bibliothèque de l'Arsenal MS 97, fols 7ra–8ra)	**Aaron** (BL, Royal MS 1 B.viii, fols 340vb–342ra)	**Aaz** (BL, Stowe MS 1, fols 426rb–431rb
Abel: luctus sive vanitas aut vapor vel miserabilis	Abel: secundus filius Adam; luctus vel vanitas vel vapor vel pavor vel misera-bilis vel Iustus. vel committens. Abel: civitatem vineis consitam legimus in libro Iudicum. Abel: magnum. Super quem ut ibi legitur posuerunt archam domini in primo libro regum. Abel: etiam civitatem in quarto libro regum; & omnium interpretatio est luctus vel commit-tens.	Abel: committens vel commissio aut luctus vel pavor. Gen 4, Mt 23. Abela: committens ei vel commissio eius sive lugens eum aut miserabilis ei. IV Reg 20.	Abel: committens vel commissio Abel: luctus vel vapor seu vanitas aut miserabilis Abela: committens ei vel commissio eius sive lugens eum aut miserabilis ei.
Ada: testimonium	Ada: prima uxor Lamech. Illius qui fuit de genere Chayn; testimonium vel ablata Ada: secundo uxor Esau; filia Helon Hethei; mater Eliphaz; decor vel ornata.	Ada: testificans vel testimonium. Gen 4, 34 (rect. 36).	Ada: testificans vel testimonium
Arfaxath: sanans depopulationem	Arfaxad: tertius flilius Sem, filii Noe. A quo Arfaxad Chaldeorum gens est exorta. Arfaxad: quoque rex Medorum in libro Judith; sanans depopulationem	Arphaxad: sanans vel sonans depopu-lationem. Gen 10, Jud 1.	Arphaxat: sanans vel salvans

Other types of biblical glossaries fared little better, even when presenting an explicit allegorical understanding of Scripture, such as Isidore of Seville's 'Adam figuram Christi gestavit' (Stegmüller §5173, as in BL, Royal MS 2 F.iv, a thirteenth-century Gospel book of Rochester Priory), which became a rarity. Why was the *Interpretations*, especially in the *Aaz* version, so successful? An answer is suggested by a short treatise preceding the *Interpretations* in Bibliothèque de l'Arsenal MS 97:

> Interpretationes igitur nominum scire tam necessaria res est quam clavis domui reserand<a>. Absque tali clave in domum nechotha non introitur, id est domum aromathum; quia scientiam interpretationum non habenti, non est penetrabilis intellegentia vera scripturarum. Sicut enim clavem domus non habenti nec serata domus aperitur, nec penetralia domus ei patent; sic ignoranti nominum interpretationes in hystoria sacra nec allegoricus nec moralis nec anagogycus sensus ad liquidum elucent. (fol. 2ra)[37]

The *Interpretations* is likened to a key, a vital tool for deciphering the mysteries of the biblical text. Drawing explicitly on 2 Kgs 20:13 and implicitly on exegesis of the Song of Songs with its image of the Bible as a closed garden, the *Interpretations* is seen as an insurmountable way to gain true knowledge of the Bible, a prerequisite for acquiring all four senses of Scripture. Not only the literal sense, but also the allegorical, tropological, and anagogical senses were presented in the glossary's entries. As argued by d'Esneval, this treatise was written by a biblical scholar, who employed the Hebrew word *Nechota*, which does not appear in transliteration in Jerome's Vulgate, in which it was rather translated into 'the house of spices'.

This was the true value of the *Interpretations* and the reason for its overwhelming popularity. It did not assist in understanding the Bible as a narrative or history, but provided a basis for the integration of doctrine. Its definitions, which were seen as an integral part of the literal sense of Scripture, enabled readers to connect specific narratives to the tenets of Catholic dogma in ways that opened numerous possibilities, rather than dictating a single alternative. Unlike less popular glossaries or exegetical works, it does not provide a fixed allegorical interpretation which would have limited a user's creativity. Rather it creates a tension between the original text and the interpretation of the word, a tension which could then be utilised by the reader, exegete or preacher for his own needs. In other words, the *Interpretations* does not supply explicit tropological, allegorical, or anagogical exegesis, but rather a basis which could accommodate all three. As shown by d'Esneval and Dahan, the etymologies were frequently employed by medieval exegetes. The usefulness of the *Interpretations* went beyond the confines of universities, and it was used profusely by preachers, an important group of users of the Late Medieval Bible. The mechanisms through which the *Interpretations* were employed in sermons are discussed below (Chapter 4, pp. 166–70). Its intended use on other occasions was suggested by a wishful note in a 1234 Bible, which expresses hopes that this aid will contribute to the conversion of the Jews.[38]

Before going further, it is beneficial to return to d'Esneval's remark on the word *Nechota*. His assertion that the word is not to be found in the Vulgate is corroborated by an examination of biblical search-engines, concordances, and Late Medieval Bibles. The two places in which the Hebrew term appears (Is 39:2 and 2 Kgs 20:13) are translated in the Vulgate: the former as *cellam aromatum* and the latter as *domum aromatum* ('a store-room of spices' or 'a house of spices') . However, if we search the *Interpretations* (in the *Aaz* version) for the term, we discover that the word *Nechota* is given its own entry ('Aroma vel thimiama sive storax eius aut aromatizatio eius')![39] This puts the *Interpretations* in a different light. It is a glossary of Hebrew words attached to the Vulgate, which contains words that are nowhere to be found in its pages. A preliminary investigation of the glossary reveals that this is far from an isolated occurrence, with possibly as many as one-fifth of its entries lacking in the pages of the Bibles they accompany. The *Interpretations*' role as a biblical glossary needs to be expanded; instead of a glossary, to which the reader turned when confronted with a foreign word, it might have functioned also as a first port of call, where a reader interested in authoritative use of the Bible might go. The *Aaron* version enabled readers to trace back an entry by supplying book and chapter reference. The lack of such features in the *Aaz* version merits further investigation. Did readers made use of these 'unsubstantiated' entries as authoritative texts on their own accord? Is it simply a testimony to rote-copying at an era when Hebrew knowledge was all but gone? Further work on the *Interpretations* and its reception is needed before any conclusion can be drawn.

The evolution of the *Interpretations* and the overwhelming popularity of the *Aaz* version attests to an interest in the Bible beyond its narrative qualities. The glossary's entries put individual words centre-stage, and (in a gradual transition of sequence and definition) disconnect them from their biblical context and its historical narratives. Approaching the Bible as text, rather than a narrative, is a feature of the new form of preaching, discussed at length in the following chapter. Unlike the explanatory nature of the *Adam* rendering, or the explicit allegorisation found in glossaries such as the one in BL, Royal MS 2 F.iv, the biblical etymology embedded in the *Aaz* rendering directed readers' attention to the complexity of the Vulgate's text. It celebrates conflicting readings to present multiple definitions, cryptic words and contradictions. It reminded readers that the Vulgate was not the original form of God's words, and served as an important stepping-stone in the rising interest in the origins of the Bible, shared among humanists and reformers in centuries to come.

Uniformity of layout

The *Interpretations of Hebrew Names* was affixed to the majority of Late Medieval Bibles and served to highlight the Bible's textual qualities and complexities. Such a shift in emphasis, a move towards highlighting the textual qualities of the Bible, is discernible in the layout to which these innovative biblical manuscripts adhere. Size, script, mise-en-page, and use of ink and illuminations combined to transform the reading experience these Bibles offered. The novelty of the Late Medieval Bible becomes evident without even opening a single manuscript, its sheer size being a watershed in the history of the Bible. Until the end of the twelfth century, very few single-volume Bibles were in existence. These were large and cumbersome books, such as BL, Additional MS 24,142, written in France 795/800 (the Bible of Theodulf of Orléans, the author of Palm Sunday's hymn *Gloria, laus et honor*, d. 821).[40] Such Bibles, however, were few and far between. Bibles were typically large and expensive manuscripts, written in four or five volumes; their size and price befitted a communal ownership, and marks of use frequently indicate readings for choir and refectory. This changed at the end of the twelfth century and the beginning of the thirteenth, with the proliferation of pandects, some small enough to fit a large pocket. Plate 5, an opening from Edinburgh University Library, MS 4 (fols 170v–171r = Job 39:4b–42:16, Palms 1:1–3:5), written possibly in northern France at the middle of the thirteenth century, exemplifies the features which made this possible.[41] In this manuscript the text area is 11.6 by 8.3 cm, written in double columns, each of fifty lines, at about four and a half lines per centimetre. A new script, the pearl-script (*Perlschrift*) subcategory of the *Textualis*, is both minute and legible. Its modern equivalent is typeset Times New Roman, point 7.5, line-space 0.75 (as can be seen in Plate 6, a true to size reproduction from a Late Medieval Bible). Writing in such a minute hand was practised by professional scribes and benefited from the introduction of magnifying glasses.[42]

The script of Late Medieval Bibles attests to their roots in the medieval classroom. It was originally developed to accommodate the margins of glossed manuscripts, in which prolonged exegetical works were compressed to follow the main text, still written in a spacious protogothic book hand. In Late Medieval Bibles this marginal script moved to centre-stage, and was employed to present the biblical text itself. Joined with an extremely thin vellum (spuriously called *uterine vellum*), it made the text of the entire Vulgate with prologues and the *Interpretations* (in excess of 700,000 words) fit into a single volume. Edinburgh University Library, MS 4 contains 388 folios, and comprises a true pocket Bible, measuring 14.1 × 10.9 × 3.3 cm. Although the manuscript was trimmed by a later binder (as can be seen from the absence of the upper part of the running title, or lower end of the penwork), this size is far from exceptional. Other Late Medieval Bibles are of equal dimensions (such as Cambridge University Library, MS Ii.6.22, 14 × 10 cm) and some are even smaller, measuring as little as 11.5 × 7 cm.[43] The miniaturisation of biblical manuscripts met a growing demand. With the rise of the mendicant orders a new market was born for smaller books, predominantly preachers' aids, breviaries, and Bibles.[44] The place of such books in the satchels of itinerant friars is evident from the clause *De itinerantibus* (II:14) in a Dominican revision of the Benedictine regula, attributed to the third Master General (Raymond de Peñafort, 1238–40): 'Euntes ad predicationis officium exercendum vel alias itinerantes, aurum, argentum, pecuniam aut munera excepto victu et necessariis indumentis et libris, nec accipient nec portabunt'.[45] Poverty dictated that friars would prefer walking, unless in exceptional circumstances.[46] Small manuscripts thus became a perfect companion, easily stored in bags and used on the road. Highly literate and itinerant, friars needed such books for performing the liturgy, biblical study, refuting heretical arguments, and composing sermons. Small and portable Bibles with a highly developed retrieval system suited these tasks perfectly and found a place of honour in the friars' bags.

Josephine Case Schnurman and Rosanna Miriello have each identified a group of Pocket Bibles which measure 20 cm or less in length. Thus they were able to delineate a group considerably more inclusive than that of the Paris Bible. Size, however, is not the whole story. Although these manuscripts attest to the full innovative thrust of the Late Medieval Bible, they are by no means the only witnesses to its novel layout. Some Late Medieval Bibles adhere to the uniform layout, but are folio in size, befitting public recitation in their parchment and script size. Others are atlas volumes, not much smaller than any 'Giant Bible' of preceding centuries. Size became a matter of choice in the later Middle Ages, as evident in a lavish presentation Bible, BL, Royal MS 1 E.ix, written and illuminated in London at the beginning of the fifteenth century (a time when atlas Bibles once more became the vogue) to become the 'Biblia magna' of Henry IV. The royal provenance of this volume is evident in a carefully executed plan of illuminations, in its size (measuring 63 × 45 cm), and in its weight, more than can be carried easily by a single librarian. Other Late Medieval Bibles range from the minute to the monumental, with numerous sizes in between.

The mise-en-page of Late Medieval Bibles suggests that size was not always of the utmost importance to scribes and patrons.[47] The trimming of Edinburgh UL, MS 4 makes it difficult to determine its original dimensions. London, Victoria and Albert Museum, Reid MS 21 (Plate 6), on the other hand, attests to the intrinsic value of marginal space. This manuscript, whose margins are not exceptionally spacious, has a textual area of 74.9 sq cm, while its margins (omitting inner margins necessary for binding and after a slight modern truncation) measure 85.2 sq cm. Such a layout, with more space allocated to margins than to text, suggests a choice not determined by the practicalities of biding and leafing. Rather, with a complex pattern of double and at times triple ruling lines it suggests an interest in marginal space *per se*. At times scribes, readers, and rubricators employed this space for corrections, biblical references, concordances, and exegetical works (such as Grosseteste's marginal signs, evident in Huntington Library, MS HM 26061). In the vast majority of manuscripts, however, margins have been left blank. The contrast between the whiteness of the vellum and the two narrow textual columns of black ink was seen by modern scholars to represent gothic aesthetics and architecture on page.[48] The evolution of the Late Medieval Bible brings another alternative to mind. Twelfth-century glossed books gave Late Medieval Bibles their script and the custom of writing below the top ruling line. In these early manuscripts the marginal space was of the utmost importance, ruled in complex patterns to facilitate the extremely difficult task of accommodating both text and commentary on the same page. An interesting moment of transition between the *Glossa* and the Late Medieval Bible is BL, Additional MS 15,253, written in Paris *c.* 1210–20, in which several books of the Bible are commented upon in several hands: Genesis–Leviticus ch. 7 (fols 1–28v); Job (142r–149r); Prophets (188v–250r, at times partial); Matthew to John (264v–294r). This, however, is the exception. The margins of most Late Medieval Bibles have remained blank. Their emptiness, even in truncated modern bindings, attests to a gap between ideal and practice. These manuscripts retain an academic feature no longer employed in practice. Much like their size and the nature of their addenda, the blank marginal space attests to patterns of use outside the ambit of the medieval classroom.

Late Medieval Bibles emulated the layout of university textbooks not only in their script and margins but in other dominant features as well. Mary and Richard Rouse have shown that running titles, chapter numbers and paragraph marks originated in the University of Paris at the end of the twelfth and the beginning of the thirteenth century, and that these were integrated into biblical manuscripts.[49] Plate 6, a detail from Reid MS 21 (fol. 8rb = Gn 12:8b–13:5), exemplifies these features: above the ruling line at the head of the page a running title in alternating red and blue letters identifies the book, often extending from the verso to the facing recto (in this instance the last three letters of *GENE- SIS*). Red and blue roman numerals in the outer margins mark the chapter division – the most celebrated and long-lasting innovation of the Late Medieval Bible.[50] Until the end of the twelfth century Bibles were still divided in a variety of portions, known as *capitula*: these divisions varied immensely between manuscripts; they were often marked not by a numeral in the text but rather by a paragraph mark, which accorded to a capitula list at the beginning of each biblical book. Stephen Langton, master in the university of Paris and later Archbishop of Canterbury (d. 1228) is credited with the introduction of the chapter divisions, which became an immediate success and spread rapidly throughout Western Europe.[51]

The new chapter divisions facilitated a particular type of reading for the biblical text. Half a millennium after their introduction they were attacked by John Locke (d. 1704). Working his way through the Epistles of St Paul, Locke lamented the division of the biblical text into chapters and verses and its impact on reading:

> If I should divide it (St Paul's to the Romans) into fifteen or sixteen Chapters, and read of them one to day, and another to morrow, etc. it was ten to one I should never come to a full and clear Comprehension of it. [...] till I came to have a good general View of the Apostle's main Purpose in writing the Epistle, the chief Branches of his Discourse wherein he prosecuted it, the Arguments he used, and the Disposition of the whole. This, I confess, is not to be obtained by one or two hasty Readings; it must be repeated again and again, with a close Attention to the Tenor of the Discourse, and a perfect Neglect of the Divisions into Chapters and Verses.[52]

Chapter numbers modified the way the Bible was read. By removing the narrative qualities advocated by John Locke, the new chapter divisions allowed readers, without the leisure or the skill, to locate a biblical passage quickly and efficiently. Much like the minute script and running titles of the

Late Medieval Bible, the chapter division eased browsing at the expense of lengthy reading. On a par with the *Interpretations of Hebrew Names*, the layout of Late Medieval Bibles served to highlight the Bible's textual qualities rather than its narratives.

On these matters Locke's was a voice crying in the wilderness. The biblical chapter division has been an overwhelming success. It worked seamlessly with newly devised concordances and preachers' aids, as well as works of exegesis and devotion, all of which employed book and chapter references to enable quick and efficient retrieval. A good indication for the success of the chapter division is Cambridge, St John's College MS A1. As attested in a rhymed colophon, this Hebrew Bible was written in 1260 for a rabbi Levi by his brother.[53] The manuscript was written for a Jewish patron and intended for personal use, as is evident in its choice of biblical books: Pentateuch, Five Scrolls (the Song of Songs, Ruth, Lamentations, Ecclesiastes and Esther), Job, Proverbs and *Haftarot*. Yet, soon after its production the manuscript was employed by a Christian scholar, possibly a Franciscan. That later reader commented upon the biblical text in Latin and introduced chapter divisions to the Hebrew text in alternating red and blue Roman numerals in its margins. This, together with Latin running titles in alternating blue and red, created a layout similar to that of a Late Medieval Bible. It assisted the Christian reader to consult a Hebrew and Latin Bibles side-by-side and attests to the variety of possible uses for a numerical and uniform chapter division.

Verse division, the other paratextual feature lamented by John Locke, became common in Bibles only from the sixteenth century. In some Late Medieval Bibles verses were indicated by a touch of red at their first letter; of little help in retrieval, this eased readers' way through the biblical text as an expansion of punctuation marks, and serves as a distant echo to the custom of writing Bibles in lines of meaning (*per cola et commata*, common in Late Antiquity). Alternative forms of subdivision predated verse division to appear in Late Medieval Bibles.[54] These are indicated by red or black marginal letters, dividing the text into portions of equal length. Two systems circulated independently in Late Medieval Bibles, having originated at different times and facilitating different uses. The first system is a subdivision of the modern chapters with marginal letters A–G (with A–D for shorter chapters). This is a visible manifestation of a virtual division, utlised by Hugh of St Cher (d. 1263) and found in Dominican concordances as well as preachers' handbooks. It served to improve the accuracy of biblical citations and directed readers to specific elements within a given chapter. Originally these divisions were not marked in biblical manuscripts, and readers were expected to divide the chapters mentally, unaided by any visual markers. As evident in Reid MS 21 (Plate 6) the virtual system received at times a visual representation (in this manuscript by red marginal letters).

Another type of subdivision facilitated a different use and predated the introduction of the modern chapter division. The A–H division corresponds to the reading of the *lectura continua* in monasteries. Cambridge University Library MS Ee.2.23 exemplifies such a use: it is a large volume (measuring 33.3 × 21 cm) whose parchment is thicker than that of smaller Bibles and whose hand is larger than the minute pearl-script. It was probably produced in Oxford to serve in a Carthusian charterhouse,[55] and its paratext reflects its use. The A–H subdivision appears throughout the volume with marginal notes connecting biblical passages to communal reading in the refectory (e.g. fols 17v–18r = Ex 1:1–3:11 for the second Sunday before Ash Wednesday ('Domenica in LX, in refectorio'); fols 30v–31r = Lv 1:1–4:13 for Shrove Sunday ('Domenica in Quinquagesima lectio, in refectorio')). At times the manuscript incorporates more complex subdivisions, as the letters A–C appear infrequently in the margins (though not necessarily for shorter pericopes) as well as the letters P, S, T for 'first', 'second' and 'third' (*Primus*, *Secundus*, and *Tertius*). A note at the beginning of the Book of Ezekiel (fol. 255r) explains the intricacies of this subdivision: the two divisions facilitated refectory reading of the same text in different years. They allowed the text to be broken into sections of varying length (e.g. sixteen and twenty-two parts to Ezekiel) and provided its readings for liturgical times of differing duration.[56] The paratext of this manuscript, its addenda, choice of parchment, script, size, nature of margins, divisions, titles, and rubrics encouraged a specific reading strategy and places it within a refectory, attesting to one of the variety of possible uses to which these Bibles were put.

Beyond a common layout: the Psalms

Late Medieval Bibles display a remarkable uniformity of layout. This, however, did not apply to all books of the Bible. Subtle modifications of ink and script, titles and rubrics, reflected specific books' origins or use, and presented readers with subtle means of interpretation. Not all texts in the Late Medieval Bible were considered as canonical. This was reflected in variations of the standard layout. Prologues to biblical books, which are made up of excerpts from the works of church fathers or medieval exegetes, are often identified by running titles and rubrics, but are only rarely subjected to chapter division or further subdivision. Books of questionable canonical status were treated similarly. The Third and Fourth Books of Ezra were seen as external to the Christian canon, but were often integrated into Late Medieval Bibles. In some biblical manuscripts, such as Reid MS 21, these books are devoid of chapter division and subdivision. Such an omission corresponds with both liturgical practice and medieval exegesis. These books and the prologues attracted less commentary and were rarely read in refectories or employed in sermons. The absence of paratextual elements signalled them out and saved valuable ink and time. At times these omissions attest to tension within Bible production and to different views adopted by the parties involved. Looking again at Reid MS 21, we can discern a disagreement between scribe and rubricator regarding the canonical nature of the Third and Fourth Books of Ezra. When copying the books, the scribe had left blank spaces for the incipit and explicit for these books to be filled by the rubricator. The latter, however, left these wanting (fols 194r, 196r, 202v). He wrote the incipit to 1 Ezra in its proper place, but the explicit to the unequivocally orthodox 2 Ezra (the Book of Nehemiah) appears at the end of 4 Ezra (212v), leaving the rubrics for the end of 2 Ezra, all of 3 Ezra, and the beginning of 4 Ezra wanting. Thus, when looking only at the rubrics, it seems that the Bible contains only the orthodox 1 and 2 Ezra, as intended by the rubricator.

Several books of more orthodox nature were presented in a distinct layout. In the first four chapters of Lamentations each verse is preceded by a consecutive letter of the Hebrew alphabet in Latin transliteration (i.e. *Aleph*, *Beth*, etc.). A handful of manuscripts even present this in Hebrew characters.[57] This feature dates back to the compilation of the Old Testament, when it constituted a mnemonic device to aid in oral recitation: as each verse was marked with a consecutive letter of the Hebrew alphabet, verses were memorised more easily and recalled in liturgical commemoration.[58] The Vulgate no longer followed this alphabetic sequence, with each verse commencing in a different letter of the Latin alphabet (e.g. Lam 1:1 'Quomodo sedet …'; 1:2 'Plorans ploravit …'; 1:3 'Migravit Judas …'). However, the names of the Hebrew letters were preserved, marked in red on the pages of Late Medieval Bibles. They attest to an oral custom whose logic was lost in translation. It was nevertheless replaced by a graphic feature which likewise assisted in memorising the biblical text, albeit by a more visual means, to concur with medieval mnemonic techniques.[59] These letters also allowed a new understanding of Lamentations. Following Jerome, and much in tune with the etymology of the *Interpretations*, medieval exegetes assigned allegorical interpretations to each letter, which were employed to elucidate the subsequent verse (e.g. Lam 1:1 *Aleph* = 'doctrina'; Lam 1:2 *Beth* = 'domus'; Lam 1:3 *Gimel* = 'plenitudo', etc.).[60]

The Song of Songs is another biblical book whose origins and nature have influenced its appearance. This love poem exercised the imagination of generations of exegetes who tried to accommodate its unique imagery within orthodox dogma.[61] In the early Middle Ages some of these commentaries took the form of short rubrics or 'voices', which connect specific verses to events from the life of Christ or to the tenets of Christian faith. These transformed the Song of Songs into a map of salvation history, a narrative of Christ's life, church history, the journey of the soul, or the love song of Mary to her son. Donatien de Bruyne has identified six distinct cycles which appear, at times in a modified form, in several Late Medieval Bibles (Appendix).[62] Thus, for example, BL, Royal MS 1 B.viii, an early thirteenth-century Bible, integrates rubrics which identify the lovers as the church (*Vox ecclesie*) and Christ (*Vox Christi*, fols 252ra–253ra). The popularity of this device emanated not only from the amatory contents of the Song of Songs, but also from its literary style. The text of the Song of Songs with its frequent move between unidentified speakers, is most challenging for the inexperienced reader. The earliest cycle identified by de Bruyne aided such readers by naming the voices according to the biblical narrative (e.g. 'the bride tells the young women about the husband'; 'the bride to the guards'; 'the husband to the bride', etc.). In several Late Medieval Bibles variations on these rubrics appear to assist the reader (Cambridge, St John's College MS N8 or Cambridge University Library, MSS Ee.2.23 and Ii.6.22); other Bibles (such as BL, Burney MS 5 and Cambridge University Library, MS Dd.13.6) omit these voices, but still assist readers by indicating a change of speakers with a touch of red. Such devices appear even in printed and virtual Bibles nowadays, attesting to the complexity and challenges of this biblical poem.[63]

The most significant variant of the biblical layout is within the Book of Psalms. This stems directly from the nature of the Psalms, and from their prominence in biblical mediation. The Psalms have always been a foreign element within the biblical corpus. Their poetry stands out against the background of biblical prose; their vocabulary and imagery diverges from the historical nature of other biblical books; most notably, both Judaism and Christianity made the Psalms the cornerstone of divine worship. It is of little surprise that the Psalms then were subjected to a distinct layout in Late Medieval Bibles. Their unique layout is preserved in the overwhelming majority of the Bibles investigated, with only two manuscripts of the sample presenting the Psalms like any other biblical book.[64]

An emphasis on the innovative features of the Late Medieval Bible has directed scholars' attention away from the Psalms. They were seen as an archaic remnant, leading Christopher de Hamel to suggest that the Psalter was absent from the biblical manuscript which had served as the basis for Langton's revolutionary layout.[65] Paul Saenger's interest in the development of verse numbering in early printed Bibles has led him to re-examine the Psalms in Late Medieval Bibles, using the later innovations to look back on earlier features. He concludes that the seeds of verse numbering lie in the poetry of the Psalms and their distinct layout. A detailed analysis of the Psalms' layout, however, demonstrates that it is a sign not simply of innovation nor of conservatism; rather, it embeds different means of exploring and mediating the Bible, of medieval scholasticism, liturgy, and mnemonics.

Plate 5 exemplifies the unique features of the Psalms' layout (evident in the transition from the common layout of the book of Job in three columns, and that of the Psalms in the right-most column). Two of the most innovative features of the Late Medieval Bible – running titles and chapter numbers – are omitted from the Psalms. This absence renders the layout of the Psalms akin to that of liturgical manuscripts, such as liturgical psalters, breviaries, and books of hours. A move away from other biblical books and into the realm of liturgical manuscripts is evident also in the marking-out of key Psalms. Psalms 1, 26, 38, 52, 68, 80, 97, and 109 begin with a distinct initial, equal in size and grandeur to opening initials of other books of the Bible. In illuminated manuscripts the iconography of these initials commonly follows the text of the Psalm: the initial accompanying Psalm 38, *Dixi custodiam vias meas*, in the 'de Brailes Bible' (Plate 7, Oxford, Bodleian Library MS Lat. bib. e. 7, fol. 183r) depicts David guarding his mouth in a visual representation of its first verse: 'I said: I will take heed to my ways: that I sin not with my tongue. I have set guard to my mouth, when the sinner stood against me.'[66] These initials, especially in the absence of chapter numbers, assisted readers in dividing the longest book in the Bible (at times aided by additional initials at Psalms 50 and 100). They also presented a subtle interpretation for the Psalms, connecting their narratives with King David (their alleged author), the figure of Christ or church worship (the initial of Psalm 97 *Cantate Domino*, 'Sing ye to the Lord' commonly depicts monk in chant, and that of Psalm 109 *Sede a dextris meis*, 'Sit thou at my right hand' the Trinity). The place of the Psalms within medieval liturgy offers an additional rationale for this device. The Psalms punctuated daily life in monasteries, churches, and cathedrals through the chanting of the divine office.[67] Seeking to emulate the angelic unceasing song of praise, clergy recited the Psalter in its entirety in cycles of one or two weeks. Late medieval Bibles reflect this liturgical practice by marking the first Psalm, chanted at matins on Sunday, Psalm 26 on Monday, Psalm 38 on Tuesday, et cetera.[68]

While key Psalms are marked by a large initial, all other Psalms are devoid of those numerical markings which became the hallmark of the Late Medieval Bible. In all but a small fraction of Bibles, the Psalms were not subjected to the Langtonian chapter division, though at times these numbers were added by early modern readers. This absence is most surprising, as the numbering of the Psalter would had been a less arduous task than any other book of the Bible, with each Psalm being a distinct textual entity. Once more, liturgical customs offer an answer. As argued by Saenger, the lack of numbers in biblical manuscripts derives from the way in which the Psalms were known in the Middle Ages. Having recited the Psalms day and night, clergy came to retain them in their memory as liturgical texts, identified by incipit rather than numerical value. Accordingly, the first Psalm was known as *Beatus vir* ('Blessed is the man'), the second *Quare turbabuntur gentes* ('Why have the Gentiles raged') and so forth. Liturgical manuscripts, exegetical works, model sermons, and *ars praedicandi* treatises all follow suit and identify Psalms by incipit rather than number. At this point the reader could turn to Plate 7 and scold the author for supplying an illustration that contradicts his own argument. The numbering of the Psalms in the 'de Brailes Bible' (as in the 'William of Devon Bible' (Royal MSS, 1.D.i) and BL, Arundel MS 303) stands at odd with most Late Medieval Bibles. It does, however, present a different ideal of Psalm mnemonics. Hugh of St Victor (d. 1142) advocated learning the Psalms by their number rather than incipit. At the time, auditory memory was deemed inferior to the visual, the latter enabling not only recollection in sequence but also retrieval of specific elements and recollection out of sequence. Hugh of St Victor thus suggested placing the Psalms according to their numbers on a mental grid. This removed all references to their role in the liturgy, their musical or oral qualities.[69] Two (and possibly three) of the sample manuscripts to number the Psalms originated among the Dominicans of Oxford. Experiments with these new forms of mnemonics, which removed the Psalms from chant and performance and subjected them to a counter-intuitive textual order, fit well into this academic milieu.[70] BL, Burney MS 11 can also be seen as reflecting the desire of Oxford Dominicans to differentiate between the Psalms and their performance, as it contains (fols 2r–v, in a fifteenth-century hand) a table which links each Psalm's incipit with its ordinal number.

The similarity between the layout of the Psalms in biblical manuscripts and that of liturgical manuscripts becomes even greater as we observe the attention given to each and every verse of the Psalms. While omitting running titles or chapter numbers required little work, marking each verse alternately with blue and red capital letters required the combined efforts of scribe and rubricator. This investment in ink, colour, and labour created a layout that echoed antiphonal psalmody, a common practice in which the Psalms were chanted as a dialogue between two choirs or officiant and choir and punctuated by refrains in between each two verses.[71] Marking the beginning of each verse in alternating colours accorded with this liturgical practice, thus replicating on parchment the performance of the Psalms. Such layout corresponds to the structure of the Psalms themselves. In the Hebrew Psalms, as in the Septuagint and the Vulgate, each verse constitutes an independent unit, a discernible line of a poem. In earlier Bibles this was indicated by the more space-consuming custom of writing each verse on a separate line (*per cola et commata*), a feature replicated in lavish Psalters and modern prints.[72] Within each verse an inverted semicolon (*punctus elevatus*) follows the division of verses in the Hebrew Psalter. It accorded with the Psalms' performance, when a distinct pause marked the middle of each verse, a pause whose nature and length were discussed in liturgical and musical commentaries.[73]

The layout of the Psalms was a distinct feature of Late Medieval Bibles, though it was far from innovative. The lack of running titles and chapter numbers, the use of large initials for key Psalms and red and blue initials for each verse, as well as the choice of punctuation, are common in liturgical manuscripts such as psalters, breviaries, and books of hours. This layout, *mutatis mutandis*, was a characteristic of the Psalms in earlier biblical manuscripts, such as the tenth-century BL, Royal MS 1 E.viii and BL, Additional MS 24,142. One feature of the Psalms' layout, however, eludes such an understanding and breaks from liturgical practices and earlier Bibles alike.

The Psalms' superscriptions

If the Psalms are a foreign element within the biblical corpus, then their superscriptions are strangers in a strange land. These short introductory verses have been one of the least stable elements within the biblical canon, and have given rise to numerous questions regarding their use and origins. The superscriptions' unique vocabulary is only loosely connected to the text of the Psalms and their function is unclear; even their very name creates a problem for the modern scholar. They were known as *tituli* in the Middle Ages, but modern scholars of the Hebrew Bible refer to them as *superscriptions* (or *superscripts*), a term commonly employed by modern students of medieval exegesis to denote a very different element – a specific type of exegesis.[74] They have been disregarded by students of the medieval Bible, but their history is most revealing to the history of the medieval Bible; their removal in the liturgy, replacement in earlier manuscripts, and appearance in Late Medieval Bibles challenges assumptions about the Psalms' layout, their antiquity and their liturgical usefulness.[75]

Superscriptions are short verses at the beginning of a Psalm, which constitute a distinct textual unit. The Psalms are typically ahistorical devotional hymns, which make little reference to other biblical events, personae, or rituals. The superscriptions, on the other hand, allude to biblical history, Temple worship, or Israelite literature. Thus, for example, the third Psalm describes God as a shield against one's enemies. It is preceded by the superscription 'The psalm of David when he fled from the face of his son Absalom', alluding to 2 Samuel chapters 15–18. 'Unto the end (*Menatze'ah*); for the octave (*Sheminith*), a psalm for David' precedes Psalm 11, adding elements of Temple worship to a psalm that beseeches God to rise against the impious; Psalm 38, a prayer of petition, is preceded by 'Unto the end, for Idithun himself, a canticle of David', alluding to a lesser family of the Levites (1 Chr 9:16). As can be seen from these examples, the connection between superscription and Psalm is at times tenuous. The origin of the superscriptions is unknown and their vocabulary is often enigmatic and distinct from that of the Psalms. Several hypotheses have arisen regarding their origin and function, seeing them as contemporaneous with the compilation of the Psalms, or as a remnant of a later editorial effort to accommodate Canaanite texts and liturgical customs into the canon of an emergent religion.[76] Even the position of the superscriptions within the Psalter is unclear. Analysis of their location in the Dead Sea Scrolls (2nd century BC to 1st century AD) and similar appearances in Near Eastern literature suggests that they might have served as postscripts for the preceding Psalm.[77] Their unique vocabulary already troubled the translators of the Septuagint in the second century BC, who left some words in transliteration and supplied others with translations that are questioned by biblical scholars nowadays.

The superscriptions attracted the attention of exegetes already in Late Antiquity. Athanasius (d. 373) and Augustine commented upon their function and relevance to the Psalms while Gregory of Nyssa (d. *c.* 395) furnished them with a predominantly christological interpretation in his

Commentary on the Inscriptions of the Psalms.[78] Beyond assigning allegorical interpretation to the superscriptions, biblical exegetes in the early and high Middle Ages emulated them to create a parallel series of short and allegorical verses – the *tituli*. These preceded the Psalms and replaced the superscriptions in biblical and liturgical manuscripts. Pierre Salmon has identified six distinct series of *tituli* in biblical manuscripts up to the twelfth century: Columba (ser. I), Augustine of Canterbury (II), Jerome (III), Eusebius of Ceasarea (IV), Origen (V), and Cassiodorus-Bede (VI).[79] These vary in size and essence, as can be seen from the various *tituli* to Psalm 3, which connect its understanding of God as one's shield to events from the life of Christ, the Church, personal devotion or the End of Days:

I Vox Christi ad Patrem de Judeis dicit
II Ad passionem Chrisi pertinet
III Ecclesia contra Judeos ceterosque hereticos et gentiles interpellat; et Christus de ressurectione sua dicit
IV Prophetatio David de quibus passus est
V Quod ipse pro nobis in mortis somno obdormiat et resurgat
VI Christus ad Patrem de persecutoribus suis loquitur, instruiturque fidelis populus ne mortem formidet, quia actor eius resurgendo spem ei verae resurrectionis exhibuit.[80]

Much like the superscriptions, *tituli* were only loosely connected to the Psalm. They served two functions: first, by replacing the superscriptions they enabled readers to avoid an element of textual uncertainty and unfamiliar terminology that bound the Psalms to obsolete notions of Jewish liturgy and history; second, they then connected the Psalms to a Christian environment. This was done not through lengthy biblical exegesis (though it was based on such). Rather, the *tituli* imitated the original superscriptions in the interpolation of short phrases which tied Psalm, dogma, and liturgy together. *Tituli* were common in manuscripts from the early and high Middle Ages; no new *tituli*, however, were written in the high Middle Ages, and they were rarely copied into manuscripts after the fourteenth century.

Superscriptions presented a problem for medieval exegetes in their archaic vocabulary, the freight of Jewish worship they carried, and in their loose connection to the body of the Psalms. These challenges were addressed in lengthy exegetical tracts, as well as in the brief *tituli*. In the liturgy, moreover, another means was employed: the utter removal of the superscriptions. Although Psalms were chanted in many and diverse liturgical uses, there is very little to suggest that the superscriptions were ever uttered vocally.[81] This is true of Jewish rite as well as a variety of Christian liturgies, and has been a common practice up until modern times.[82] It was thus the first line of the Psalm following the superscription, which began its chant. And it was by the incipit, rather than by the superscriptions, that the Psalms were known all through the Middle Ages and the early modern period.[83] In the performance of the psalmody an oral proclamation, most commonly the Lesser Doxology, accompanied each Psalm. It linked the Psalm to the tenets of Christian belief, and emulated both *titulus* and superscription.

The layout of Late Medieval Bibles breaks away from liturgical manuscripts and practice, as well as from the format of many earlier Bibles. The vast majority of Late Medieval Bibles provide the *masoretic* superscriptions of the Hebrew Bible. These, however, are not incorporated into the body of the Psalms. Rather, they are signalled out as rubrics (Plates 5 and 7). Such a choice created a layout familiar to the medieval reader. It employed a well-known device to signal specific verses, but in doing so turned the pages of the Psalter into a paratextual conundrum. A priest, trained in the days before Vatican II, recalled a liturgical instructor stating that he should 'read out loud and not understand the body of the text', while the rubrics were 'not to be read out loud, but to be understood and followed'.[84] Rubrics were a first port of call, a place to which readers turned for instructions on how to mediate a given text. Such an understanding prevailed in liturgical manuscripts (where rubrics direct performance), while rubricating incipits and explicits in biblical (and non-biblical) books enabled readers to demarcate a specific text quickly and efficiently. For the late medieval Psalter, however, rubrication was a remnant from an earlier era. In earlier Bibles and psalters the *tituli* offered readers a key to understand and meditate upon the Psalms, a logical function of a rubric. Superscriptions, however, did nothing of the kind. Their enigmatic vocabulary and allusions to long-forgotten customs in an unknown language offered little help in terms of Psalm-identification (which relied on the first verse, following the *titulus*) or understanding. Thus, the rubrication of superscriptions probably did little to assist most medieval readers. In fact, the appearance of the superscription was probably unintentional. The superscriptions stretched the limits of devices used by medieval stationers, and their presentation as rubrics came from a lack of other efficient means (apart from rubrics) for signalling out such extraneous texts.

The instability of the superscriptions is evident in their place within Late Medieval Bibles. In some manuscripts they were replaced by a generic superscription, *Psalmus David*, which was applied to all Psalms alike

(Appendix). An earlier Bible, BL, Additional MS 15,253 (Paris, *c.* 1210–20), displays a moment of transition: while most Psalms are preceded by the *masoretic* superscriptions in the ordinary fashion, in places where these are extremely short or lacking in the original biblical text they are replaced or joined by the relevant *tituli* from Salmon's Series I (e.g. 'Vox ecclesie ad populum' ('the voice of the Church to the people') following 'Ipsi David' ('of David') for Psalm 102, fol. 160r). In other manuscripts, such as Cambridge, St John's College MSS I28 and C24, the space left by the scribe in between the Psalms was not filled by the rubricator. A blank space exists therefore in places where the superscriptions should have been written. Such variations did not prevent the superscriptions from becoming an important feature of the Psalms' layout in Late Medieval Bibles. Out of the fifty-one manuscripts in my sample which contain a Psalter, thirty-five (about 66 per cent) present full superscriptions or spaces for these to be written; fourteen (about 25 per cent) omit them altogether and two (about 4 per cent) present generic superscriptions. The re-integration of this unique and cryptic element into the Late Medieval Bible should be seen as part of a larger movement. Much like the celebrated addendum to these Bibles, the *Interpretations of Hebrew Names*, superscriptions presented readers with a deeper and less accessible stratum of the biblical text and reminded them of the birthplace of the Bible in a time and place remote from medieval Christendom.

Conclusion

The paratext of the Late Medieval Bible weathered the advent of print and the Reformation, and has enjoyed a great longevity. Gutenberg's celebrated 42-line Bible merely replicated the layout of the Late Medieval Bible, alongside its major biblical exceptions. The Book of Psalms in a Gutenberg Bible (Mainz, *c.* 1454, Figure 6, Psalms 1–4 in a copy from Niedersächsische Staats- und Universitätsbibliothek Göttingen, fol. 293r) displays the same characteristics as any Late Medieval Bible: lack of running titles and of chapter numbers (which nevertheless appear for all other biblical books), large initials, alternating red and blue capitals for verses and rubrication of superscriptions. Biblical incunabula and early prints followed suit and replicated the appearance of Late Medieval Bibles with their chapter division, alphabetical subdivision and running titles. In England, where Bible printing arrived only in the sixteenth century, the layout of the Late Medieval Bible still served as a template. The unique mnemonics of the Psalms reverberate in the Great Bible of 1539/40, in which each

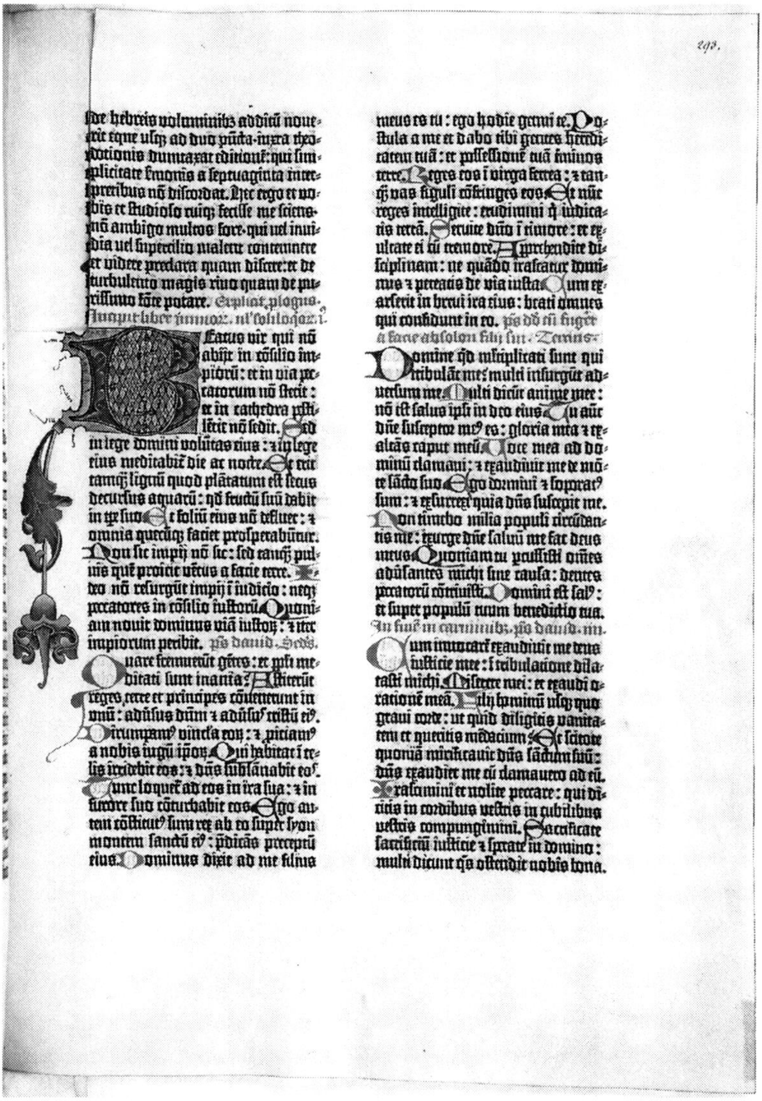

Figure 6 Psalms 1–4, Gutenberg Bible, Niedersächsische Staats- und Universitätsbibliothek Göttingen, fol. 293r

(English) Psalm is preceded by its Latin incipit (in roman capitals on the background of black-letter type), a feature which was replicated in subsequent Bibles, as in the Book of Common Prayer.[85] Modern editions of the Bible likewise display the Bible in a layout of dual columns, running titles, and chapter divisions, and single out the Psalms' superscriptions and the Hebrew alphabet of Lamentations, commonly in italics or small capitals. Not all the unique features of the Late Medieval Bible shared the same fate. *The Interpretations of Hebrew Names*, whose popularity in medieval manuscripts was unsurpassed, disappeared from Bibles at an earlier stage. It appears intermittently in fifteenth-century Bibles and was not included in Gutenberg's Bible; apart for a short spell in Latin and vernacular Bibles of the fifteenth and sixteenth centuries, it gave way to other biblical aids and glossaries, possibly owing to its role in medieval preaching, explored in the following chapter.[86]

The Late Medieval Bible was the first mass-produced pandect, and as such became a template for Bibles ever since. Hundreds of surviving manuscripts nowadays testify to its popularity. The analysis of their paratext, attempted on a test group of randomly chosen manuscripts, can assist in the immensely complex task of ascertaining the relationship between families of manuscripts. This survey merely scratches the surface of the myriad of biblical manuscripts and the information they contain. It nevertheless demonstrates how minor variants in layout and addenda help delineate groups of manuscripts beyond the Paris Group, or beyond the identification of known elements such as the writing of the first line of text below the ruling line, or in the use of integral chapter divisions. Layout variants often appear in clusters, with transitional manuscripts (written *c.* 1230) presenting not only added chapter division but also the voices of the Song of Songs, and the use of generic superscriptions for the Psalms (a feature which lingered in a small group of later manuscripts). The numbering of Psalms in contemporary hands marks off a small group of Bibles; its link to the Dominicans of Oxford concurs with the unique form of biblical mnemonics advocated by Hugh of St Cher. Similarly, biblical addenda of a very specific kind – the genealogies of Christ, *On the wings of the Cherub*, and verse summaries of the Bible – mark another group of manuscripts, including a Bible stolen from Dover Abbey in the thirteenth century.

The paratext of Late Medieval Bibles facilitated a very specific understanding of the biblical text. These Bibles reflect the schools and stationers that were responsible for their production, and encode biblical texts as they were taught, preached, and chanted. The link between the Bible and liturgy, evident in the layout of the Psalms and the nature of its addenda, did not necessitate a use within public performance, nor did the birth of the Late Medieval Bible in the medieval classroom turn these manuscripts into university textbooks. Their scholastic origins, evident in intricate retrieval systems and a significant marginal space, gave way to other uses. Margins were left blank, rather than filled with commentaries. Running titles and numerical chapter division functioned in tandem with concordances and exegetical works, but also eased the access of uninitiated readers. The Late Medieval Bible offered a new reading experience. Its divisions, writing support, script, and addenda, merged to create a highly efficient reference book. It enabled readers to locate a specific passage quickly and accurately, working alongside concordances, preaching manuals, or tables of lessons. Understanding these manuscripts as reference books explains extant minute volumes, which still appear in pristine condition. These Bibles show little sign of wear and tear, but were not necessarily merely decorative objects. Although unsuitable for continuous reading, even with a magnifying glass in a well-lit library, they still enabled readers to follow up a biblical reference or go over the day's pericope, often supplied in the adjacent table of lessons. These manuscripts thus facilitated browsing rather than the reading of lengthy biblical passages.

The innovative layout of the Late Medieval Bible presents the biblical text in a way that eased access for many and was lamented by few. It highlighted the textual qualities of the Bible in layout and addenda. Not only chapter divisions but also the *Interpretations of Hebrew Names* and the Psalms' superscriptions broke away with the biblical narratives. The success of the *Aaz* rendering over earlier glossaries, that of the superscriptions over the *tituli*, and the gradual disappearance of the voices of the Song of Songs all served a similar purpose. They did away with earlier, restrictive paratext, which facilitated specific literal or allegorical interpretation of the biblical text. Rather, these glossaries and rubrics opened up new ways of exploring the biblical text, empowering readers to integrate their own message into their reading of the Bible. In doing so these features brought to mind, time and again, the complexity of the biblical text and celebrated in its conflicting readings and Hebrew (and Greek) origins. Late Medieval Bibles preceded the printing press in achieving a high level of uniformity. Mass-produced and widely disseminated, these manuscripts spread throughout Western Europe and have influenced the shape of Bibles ever since. Originating in the medieval classroom, they were consulted by monks and friars, with a trickle of manuscripts gradually making their way to parish churches.[87] The study of these Bibles demonstrates, however, how even the narrow, Latin-literate elite in medieval England which had access to biblical manuscripts experienced the Bible through modifications of ink and script, addenda and mise en page. Priests, self-proclaimed biblical mediators, were thus never presented with a 'naked text' of the Bible, but rather with manuscripts whose paratext encoded subtle liturgical echoes, mnemonics, technological advancements, and exegetical vogues.

Notes

1 Cavanaugh, 'Study of Books'.

2 The standard description of a Paris Bible is London, Lambeth Palace, MS 1364, in: Neil Ker, *Medieval Manuscripts in British Libraries, vol. I: London* (Oxford, 1969), pp. 96–7. This identification builds upon Martin's 'Texte Parisien'. For further discussion: Light, 'French Bibles', 159–63; Guy Lobrichon, 'Les éditions de la Bible latine dans les universités de XIIIe siècle', in *La Bibbia del XIII secolo. Storia del testo, storia dell'esegesi: Convegno della Società Internazionale per lo studio del Medioevo Latino (SISMEL) Firenze, 1–2 Giugno 2001*, ed. Giuseppe Cremascoli and Francesco Santi (Florence, 2004), pp. 15–34.

3 Light, 'Roger Bacon'; Lobrichon, 'Les éditions de la Bible'; Paul Saenger, 'The British Isles and the Origin of the Modern Mode of Biblical Citation', *Syntagma* 1 (2005), 77–123; idem and Laura Bruck, 'The Anglo-Hebraic Origins of the Modern Chapter Division of the Latin Bible', in *La fractura historiográfica: Las investigaciones de Edad Media y Renacimiento desde el tercer milenio*, dir. Javier San José Lera (Salamanca, 2008), pp. 177–202.

4 Jerome's rationale is presented in his prologue to Kings (Stegmüller §323) and his letter to Paulinus (Stegmüller §3306–7). For the new sequence: Ker, *Medieval Manuscripts in British Libraries*, i:96–7; de Hamel, *The Book*, pp. 120–1. For analysis: Light, 'French Bibles', 159–63.

5 Stegmüller §284–5 (introduction to the historical books); §286–555 (Old Testament, Jerome's and subsequent); §556–842 (New Testament, Jerome's and subsequent). An introduction and survey of the prologues from the sixth to the fifteenth century is the now outdated Samuel Berger, *Les préfaces jointes aux livres de la Bible dans les manuscripts de la Vulgate* (Paris, 1902). Most of Jerome's prologues are printed in *Biblia Sacra iuxta Vulgatam Versionem*, ed. Robert Weber (Stuttgart, 1969). For analysis: Light, 'French Bibles', pp. 163–8.

6 Dahan, *L'exégèse chrétienne*, pp. 9–11.

7 The problem of date is evident from Schnurman's survey ('Studies in the Medieval Book Trade', pp. 40–1), which provides accurate dating for only four manuscripts out of 420; a similar view arises from the handful of entries for datable Late Medieval Bibles in: *Catalogue of Dated and Datable Manuscripts, c.700–1600 in the Department of Manuscripts, the British Library*, ed. Andrew G. Watson (Oxford, 1979) – five entries; *Catalogue of Dated and Datable Manuscripts c.435–1600 in Oxford Libraries*, ed. Andrew G. Watson (Oxford, 1984) – five entries; *Catalogue of Dated and Datable Manuscripts c.737–1600 in Cambridge Libraries*, ed. Pamela R. Robinson (Cambridge, 1988) – one entry. On ascertaining provenance: Jonathan J. G. Alexander, 'English or French? Thirteenth Century Bibles', in *Manuscripts at*

Oxford: An Exhibition in Memory of Richard William Hunt (1908–1979), Keeper of Western Manuscripts at the Bodleian Library Oxford, 1945–1975, ed. A. C. de la Mare and B. C. Barker-Benfield (Oxford, 1980), pp. 69–71.

8 David d'Avray, 'Printing, Mass Communication and Religious Reformation: The Middle Ages and After', in *The Uses of Script and Print, 1300–1700*, ed. Julia Crick and Alexandra Walsham (Cambridge, 2004), pp. 50–70.

9 The most detailed survey of addenda is still Schnurman, 'Studies in the Medieval Book Trade', pp. 143–8.

10 Richard W. Pfaff, 'Why Do Medieval Psalters Have Calendars? in *Liturgical Calendars, Saints, and Services in Medieval England* (Aldershot, 1998), §vi; Pfaff, 'Bishop Baldock's Book, St Paul's Cathedral, and the Use of Sarum', in *Liturgical Calendars*, §xi); Palazzo, *Liturgical Books*, p. 23.

11 Possibly belonging to Gui II de la Tour du Pin, Dominican and Bishop of Clermont (d. 1285), as suggested by Rouse and Rouse, *Manuscripts and Their Makers*, ii:152–3.

12 This exegetical gap underpins the analysis of Chapter 1, and is explored more explicitly in the conclusion of Chapter 4: Beyond Preaching the Liturgy.

13 Of the first type are: *olim* Canterbury Cathedral, Law Society MS 3: prefaces, canon of Mass (notated), votive Masses, prayer and antiphons for burial (thirteenth-century, France); 'De Brailes Bible' (= Oxford, Bodleian Library, MS Lat. bib. e. 7): canon of the Mass (mid-thirteenth century, Oxford); San Marino, Huntington Library, MS HM 26061: collect, secret and postcommunion for various Masses for the dead and full services for parts of the *temporale* and little of the *sanctorale* (mid-thirteenth century, England). Of the second type: Cambridge University Library MS Hh.1.3: canon of the Mass (added late thirteenth- or early fourteenth-century, possibly for a Franciscan); Cambridge St John's MS N1: prefaces and canon of the Mass (thirteenth century, English Gilbertine House). The De Brailes and the St John's Bibles were noted by Pfaff, *Liturgy in Medieval England*, pp. 308, 313–14, identifying an additional Bible (Cambridge, Fitzwilliam Museum, McClean MSS, 16), also of use for an itinerant friar. A forthcoming article by Laura Light will be the first to be devoted to this little-explored class of manuscripts ('The Thirteenth-Century Pandect and the Liturgy: Bibles with Missals', in *Form and Function in the Late Medieval Bible*, ed. Eyal Poleg and Laura Light, Library of the Written Word: The Manuscript World (Leiden, 2013), pp. 185–215.

14 A description of the manuscript accompanied by images is: *Guide to Medieval and Renaissance Manuscripts in the Huntington Library*, ed. C. W. Dutschke with the assistance of R. H. Rouse et al. (San Marino, 1989, available online http://sunsite.berkeley.edu/hehweb/HM26061.html, accessed 8 June 2012).

15 I thank Eamon Duffy for discussing this important custom.

16 Margaret T. Gibson, 'The Place of the Glossa ordinaria in Medieval Exegesis', in *Ad Litteram: Authoritative Texts and their Medieval Readers*, ed. Mark D. Jordan and Kent Emery, Jr, Notre Dame Conferences in Medieval Studies 3 (Notre Dame, IN, 1992), pp. 5–27.

17 Such as Cambridge University Library, MSS Dd.8.12 and Ee.1.16; BL, Additional MS 15,253; Burney MS 2. The exception is Royal MS 1 A.xix, a thirteenth-century Bible which was used at Monk Bretton (Yorkshire) in the fourteenth century. In

this Bible later hands, in all probability those of the monks, added exegetical works in the margins.

18 Christ's Genealogies: Cambridge University Library MS Dd.8.12, fols 461r–467v; BL, Royal MS 1 B.x, fols 8r–33v (the *Genealogia historiarum*, fifteenth-century hand). The Song of Gospels: Cambridge University Library MSS Dd.8.12 fols 459r–460v, Mm.1.2, fols 601v–603r; London, Lambeth Palace MS 533, fols 484r–487v. *Glose divinorum librorum*: BL, Stowe MS 1, fols 466r–478v. *Sumarium Biblicum*: Lambeth Palace MS 534 ('summaria compilatio metrificata'). The *Glose divinorum librorum* was printed in: Giovanni Stefano Menochio, ed., *Commentarii totius Sacræ Scripturæ ex optimis quibusque auctoribus collecti ...*, tom. 3 (Venice, 1758), pp. 429–40. On the *Summarium*: Lucie Doležalová, 'Biblia quasi in sacculo: Summarium Biblie and Other Medieval Bible Mnemonics', *Medium Aevum Quotidianum* 56 (2007), 5–35. A similar function was filled by capitlua lists, a remnant of earlier biblical divisions (as in BL, Royal MS 1 E.ix, fols 338r–350r).

19 'I have considered that every man hath not at al tymes suche leasure as to reade or to tourne the Byble from one chapter to another, whan they shall have a desyre or oaccasion to seke for any speciall matter conteyned herein', from the introduction to the 1550 edition: *The whole Byble. that is the holy scripture of the Olde and Newe testament faythfully translated into Englyshe by Myles Couerdale, and newly ouersene and correcte* (Zurich: C. Froschouer, for Andrewe Hester, London, 1550), Sig. *i.ra.

20 Schnurman, 'Studies in the Medieval Book Trade', pp. 157–69.

21 'This book has been written up out of [a copy of] Thornton | The scribe who copied merits a gift by law. | No praises, nor the goodness of his work | not the glory of all things is asked. | [only] Charity for the habitual labour of days' (fol. 116r). The colophon is in the hand of the original scribe. It is unclear whether the book was copied at Thornton Abbey, or whether it was copied elsewhere from another of the Abbey's Bibles.

22 'The book has ended, praises and glory be to Christ. | And now for having written, dinner shall be rendered to the Magister' (fol. 439v).

23 Rouse and Rouse, 'Wandering Scribes', especially pp. 34–43.

24 The letter is supplied and commented upon by: *English Benedictine Libraries*, pp. 448–51. Additional information is: Coates, *English Medieval Books*, pp. 63–5. The original is Lambeth Palace MS 371, fol. 1.

25 Copied as *diffinciones.*

26 On the Cherubim's wings and their use in the Middle Ages, including their applicability for sermons: Mary Carruthers, 'Ars oblivionalis, ars inveniendi: The Cherub Figure and the Arts of Memory', *Gesta* 48:2 (2010), 1–19.

27 As suggested by Dutschke et al., *Guide to Medieval and Renaissance Manuscripts*, MS HM 26061.

28 Other Bibles to include addenda near the Psalms: London, Lambeth Palace MSS 533 (calendar before the Psalms) and 534 (short liturgical treatise following the Psalms); Cambridge University Library, MS Ee.6.26 (calendar before the Psalms); Cambridge, St John's MSS N8 (hymns before Psalms) and I28 (prayers and pseudo-Augustine's *Canticum Psalmorum animas decorat* (Stegmüller §369) before Psalms); *olim* Canterbury Cathedral, Law Society MS 3 (prefaces and canon

of Mass after Psalms); 'De Brailes Bible' (Oxford, Bodleian Library MS Lat. bib. e. 7, Mass-texts after Psalms); BL, Additional MS 35,085 (ferial readings after the Psalms); San Marino, Huntington Library MS HM 26061 (Mass-texts after Psalms).

29 'scripsit etiam librum perutilem qui dicitur Augustinus de spiritu et anima, super bibliam quam emit Aluredus de Dovera', *English Benedictine Libraries*, p. 462, Coates, *English Medieval Books*, pp. 61–3.

30 In the latter Bible these were added in the fifteenth century, possibly on the basis of an earlier biblical exemplar.

31 d'Esneval estimated that there are more than five hundred copies of the *Interpretations* (the *Aaz* version) nowadays, showing that out of the first two hundred items at the catalogue of the Bibliothèque Nationale about fifty contained the *Interpretations* – Amaury d'Esneval, 'Le perfectionnement d'un instrument de travail au début du XIIIe Siècle: Les trois glossaires bibliques d'Etienne Langton', in *Culture et travail intellectuel dans l'Occident médiéval*, ed. Geneviève Hasenohr and Jean Longère (Paris, 1981), pp. 163–75 (p. 164 n. 12). A similar methodology led Richard H. Rouse and Mary A. Rouse to conclude that the *Interpretations* 'appearing in virtually all Bibles thereafter [1200]' ('Statim invenire: Schools, Preachers, and New Attitudes to the Page', in *Renaissance and Renewal in the Twelfth Century*, ed. Robert. L. Benson et al. (Oxford, 1982), pp. 201–25 (= *Authentic Witnesses: Approaches to Medieval Texts and Manuscripts*, Publications in Medieval Studies 17 (Notre Dame, IN, 1991), pp. 191–219, at p. 221), on the basis of the catalogue of the Bibliothèque Nationale, where 81 out of 91 thirteenth-century pandects contain a version of the *Interpretations*). The discrepancy in numbers is due to the scope of the investigation – the first two hundred items for d'Esneval, and all pandects in the first volume for Rouse and Rouse.

32 The *Interpretations* was in print until the seventeenth century, with varying degrees of accuracy. For the present study I have relied on BL, Additional MS 39,629, fols 560ra–604va, corroborated with BL, Stowe MS 1, fols 426r–465v and London, Victoria and Albert Museum, Reid MS 21, fols 530r–565r. Studies: d'Esneval, 'Instrument de travail'; Gilbert Dahan, 'Lexiques Hébreu-Latin? Les recueils d'interprétations des noms hébraïques', in *Les manuscrits des lexiques et glossaires, de l'Antiquité à la fin du moyen âge*, ed. Jacqueline Hamesse, Textes et études du moyen âge 4 (Louvain-la-Neuve, 1996), pp. 481–526; followed by Dahan, *L'exégèse chrétienne*, pp. 314–25. Giovanna Murano, 'Chi ha scritto le *Interpretationes hebraicorum nominum*', in *Etienne Langton, prédicateur, bibliste, théologien*, ed. Louis-Jacques Bataillon et al., Bibliothèque d'histoire culturelle du Moyen Age 9 (Turnhout, 2010), pp. 353–71. I thank Giovanna Murano for supplying me with an early copy of her article.

33 'Liber interpretationis Hebraicorum nominum', ed. Paul de Lagarde, in *S. Hieronymi Presbyteri Opera. Pars I, Opera Exegetica. 1*, CCSL 72 (Turnhout, 1959), pp. 57–161.

34 The number of entries is conjectural as within each rendering there is much variation, a complex manuscript culture, and the expansion of single entries into multiple items and vice versa. Jerome's *Liber interpretationis* has 3,157 entries.

35 Rouse and Rouse, 'Statim invenire', pp. 210–12; d'Esneval, 'Instrument de travail', p. 166.

36 The entries' extreme brevity renders their translation inconclusive.

Jerome's Liber Interpretationis (Lagarde ed., pp. 60–1)	**Adam** (Bibliothèque de l'Arsenal MS 97, fols 7ra–8ra)	**Aaron** (BL, Royal MS 1 B.viii, fols 340vb–342ra)	**Aaz** (BL, Stowe MS 1, fols 426rb–431rb
Abel: grief or vanity or vapour or miserable	Abel: Adam's second son; grief or vanity or vapour or panic or miserable or just or one who engages/begins. Abel: we read in the Book of Judges of a city of planted vines. Abel: Great. On which, as it is written in the first book of Kings, they placed the Ark of the Lord. Abel: a city in 4 Kings; and the interpretation of all (words) is grief or one who engages/begins.	Abel: one who engages or a beginning, grief or panic (Gen 4, Mt 23) Abela: engages with him or his beginning if not mourning him or miserable by him (2 Reg 20)	Abel: one who engages or beginning Abel: grief or vapour, vanity or miserable Abela: engages with him or his beginning if not mourning him or miserable by him
Ada: testimony	Ada: First wife of Lamech, who was of the sons of Cain; testimony or fetched. Ada: Esau's second wife; daughter of Helon Hethei; mother of Eliphaz; beauty or ornate.	Ada: testifies or testimony (Gen 4, 34 (rect. 36))	Ada: testifies or testimony
Arfaxath: healer of the ravaging	Arfaxad: the third son of Sem, Noa's son. Of whom came the race of Chaldees. Arfaxad: likewise king of Medes in Judith; healer of the ravaging	Arphaxad: healer or speaker of the ravaging (Gen 10, Jud 1)	Arphaxat: healer or saver

37 'To know the interpretations of names is as necessary as a key to open a house. Without such key one does not enter into the house of Nechota, that is the house of spices; because to him who does not have the knowledge of the interpretations, the true knowledge of Scripture is not penetrable. For just as to one that does not have the keys of the house the bolted house is not opened, nor are the innermost parts of the house be accessible; so to the one who is ignorant of the interpretations of names not the allegorical nor the tropological nor the anagogical senses in sacred history shine forth clearly.' The first sentence was transcribed by d'Esneval, 'Instrument de travail', p. 163 n. 5.

38 De Hamel, *The Book*, p. 123.

39 'Spice or incense if not its gum or its sweet smell.'

40 Light, 'Versions et révisions', pp. 59–65. On the 'Giant Bibles' of the early and high Middle Ages: Diane J. Reilly, 'French Romanesque Giant Bibles and Their English Relatives: Blood Relations or Adopted Children?' *Scriptorium* 56:2 (2002), 294–311; 'The Cluniac Giant Bible and the Ordo librorum ad legendum: A Reassessment of Monastic Bible Reading and Cluniac Customary Instructions', in *From Dead of Night to End of Day: The Medieval Customs of Cluny*, ed. Susan Boynton and Isabelle Cochelin, Disciplina Monastica 3 (Turnhout, 2005), pp. 163–89.

41 On the size of Late Medieval Bibles: Miriello, 'Bibbia portabile', and in brief: Schnurman, 'Studies in the Medieval Book Trade', pp. 49–67. The manuscript is described in: Ker, *Medieval Manuscripts*, i:380.

42 Albert Derolez, *The Palaeography of Gothic Manuscript Books: From the Twelfth to the Early Sixteenth Century* (Cambridge, 2003), especially p. 100; Rouse and Rouse, 'Wandering Scribes'; de Hamel, *The Book*, pp. 118–19.

43 Appendix; Miriello, 'Bibbia portabile', Tabelle I and II, pp. 61–9; Schnurman, 'Studies in the Medieval Book Trade', pp. 49–63.

44 David L. d'Avray, *The Preaching of the Friars: Sermons Diffused from Paris before 1300* (Oxford, 1985), pp. 56–60; 'Portable Vademecum Books Containing Franciscan and Dominican Texts', in *Manuscripts at Oxford*, pp. 60–4.

45 '(Those) going to exercise the office of preaching or other itinerants will neither accept nor carry gold, silver, wealth or gifts but for sustenance and necessary clothes and books', Raymond Creytens, 'Les constitutions des frères prêcheurs dans la rédaction de s. Raymond de Peñafort', *Archivum Fratrum Praedicatorum* 18 (1948), 5–68 (65–6). See also: Simon Tugwell, OP, 'The Evolution of Dominican Structures of Government III: The Early Development of the Second Distinction of the Constitutions', *Archivum Fratrum Praedicatorum* 71 (2001), 5–182 (138); William A. Hinnebusch, *The History of the Dominican Order: vol. II Intellectual and Cultural Life to 1500* (New York, 1973), p. 215.

46 Explicit in the Franciscan Regula: *Bullarium Franciscanum Romanorum pontificium: Constitutiones, epistols, ac diplomata continens …*, 4 vols, ed. Johannes H. Sbaralea (Rome, 1759, repr. 1983), i:16, col. 2.

47 This was noted by Miriello, 'Bibbia portabile', pp. 56–7; Schnurman, 'Studies in the Medieval Book Trade', p. 63.

48 Miriello, 'Bibbia portabile', p. 56; Derolez, *Palaeography of Gothic Manuscript Books*, pp. 34–9.

49 Rouse and Rouse, 'Statim invenire', pp. 205–9, 221.

50 Smalley, *Study of the Bible*, pp. 222–4; de Hamel, *The Book*, 124–5; Light, 'French Bibles', 168–72 (with a full bibliography on *capitula*, p. 168 n. 69); Saenger, 'British Isles'; Saenger and Bruck, 'Anglo-Hebraic Origins'.

51 A connection between chapter divisions and lectures at Paris University was made by Smalley (*Study of the Bible*, pp. 222–4), who, while acknowledging Langton's role in the integration of the chapter division, nevertheless noted their lack in Langton's own references, concluding those that were possibly introduced towards the end of his teaching, *c.* 1203. This attribution was challenged by Saenger and Bruck, 'Anglo-Hebraic Origins', to suggest an earlier twelfth-century appearance of the chapter division, which rose to facilitate monastic readings, and was influenced by Jewish practice.

52 John Locke, *An Essay for the Understanding of St Paul's Epistles, by Consulting St Paul himself* (London: Awnsham and John Churchill, 1707), pp. 14–15; discussed by: D. F. McKenzie, *Bibliography and the Sociology of Texts: The Panizzi Lectures 1985* (London, 1986, reprinted in *Bibliography and the Sociology of Texts*, Cambridge, 1999), pp. 7–76 (55–7). I thank John Moreland for this reference.

53 This manuscript has evaded the attention of scholars of the medieval Bible. It was described in *A Descriptive Catalogue of the Manuscripts in the Library of St John's College, Cambridge*, ed. M. R. James (Cambridge, 1913), pp. 1–2.

54 The most detailed work on subdivisions of biblical chapters (but not of the Carthusian division preceding them) is Saenger, 'British Isles', which also identifies the rare use of verse numbers in late medieval England. It builds upon his 'The Impact of the Early Printed Page on the Reading of the Bible', in *The Bible as Book: The First Printed Editions*, ed. Kimberly Van Kampen and Paul Saenger (London, 1999), pp. 31–51 (35–6); *A Catalogue of the Pre-1500 Western Manuscript Books at the Newberry Library*, ed. Paul Saenger (Chicago, 1989), pp. 35–6, 38. Other important works are: Richard H. Rouse and Mary A. Rouse, 'Verbal Concordance of Scriptures', *Archivum Fratrum Prædicatorum* 44 (1974), 5–30 (22–3, for the A–G subdivision in Dominican concordance); *Preachers, Florilegia and Sermons: Studies on the 'Manipulus florum' of Thomas of Ireland*, Studies and Texts 47 (Toronto, 1979), pp. 9–13; Michael Albaric, 'Hugues de Saint-Cher et les concordances bibliques latines (XIIIe–XVIIIe siècles)', in *Hugues de Saint-Cher (d. 1263) bibliste et théologien*, ed. Louis-Jacques Bataillon et al., Bibliothèque d'histoire culturelle du moyen âge 1 (Turnhout, 2004), pp. 467–79 (472, suggesting a fourth revision of the concordance, utilising an A–D subdivision). An example of preachers' handbooks which incorporates such subdivision is: Servus of Sint Anthonis, 'Preaching in the Thirteenth Century: A Note on MS Gonville and Caius 439', *Collectanea Franciscana* 32 (1962), 310–24 (311).

55 *Western Illuminated Manuscripts: A Catalogue of the Collection in Cambridge University Library*, ed. Paul Binski and Patrick Zutshi, with the collaboration of Stella Panayotova (Cambridge, 2011), pp. 90–1. The Carthusian attribution appears to rely solely on its subdivisions.

56 Paul Needham associates this division in printed Bibles with the Carthusians: 'The Changing Shape of the Vulgate Bible in Fifteenth-Century Printing Shops', in *The Bible as Book: The First Printed Editions*, ed. Kimberly Van Kampen and Paul Saenger (London, 1999), pp. 53–70 (64).

57 Schnurman, 'Studies in the Medieval Book Trade', p. 83; Saenger and Bruck, 'Anglo-Hebraic Origins'.

58 Bo Johnson, 'Form and Message in Lamentations', *Zeitschrift für die alttestamentliche Wissenschaft* 97 (1985), 58–73.

59 On the importance of visual and spatial aspects to medieval mnemonics: Mary Carruthers, *The Book of Memory: A Study of Memory in Medieval Culture*, 2nd edn (Cambridge, 2008), and especially on the use of foreign alphabets to memorise a text, pp. 137–9.

60 Gilbertus Universalis, *Glossa ordinaria in Lamentatione Ieremie prophete, prothemata et liber I: A Critical Edition with an Introduction and a Translation*, ed. and tr. Alexander Andrée, Acta universitatis Stockholmiensis, Studia Latina Stockholmiensia 52 (Stockholm, 2005), especially pp. 52–4, 119–20.

61 E. Ann Matter, *The Voice of My Beloved: The Song of Songs in Western Medieval Christianity* (Philadelphia, 1992), briefly noting the medieval 'voices' on pp. 102–4, 157.

62 *Sommaires, divisions et rubriques de la Bible latine* (Namur, 1914), pp. 558–62.

63 Such as the *Biblia Sacra juxta vulgatam clementinam, editio electronica*, gen. ed. Michael Tuveedale (London, 2005 = http://vulsearch.sourceforge.net/gettext.html, accessed 27 May 2012). These are far from ubiquitous.

64 These are BL, Royal MS 1 D.i and BL, Arundel MS 303. Their nature and provenance are discussed below.

65 *The Book*, pp. 128–9.

66 For information on the manuscript: Alexander, *French or English*; Morgan, *Early Gothic Manuscripts*, §69, i:114–16. Illuminations assist in identifying its illuminator as William de Brailes, who worked in Catte Street, Oxford, at the beginning of the thirteenth century. On the basis of its calendar, the Bible seems to have been made for a Dominican, some time between the establishment of the Oxford House (1221) and the canonisation of St Dominic (1234). The Bible's lavish illuminations, rich in gold and blue, are slightly at odds with its Dominican provenance. Information on the workshop, and a detailed analysis of another of its products is: Clare Donovan, *The de Brailes Hours: Shaping the Book of Hours in Thirteenth Century Oxford* (London, 1991), with pp. 19–21 presenting the de Brailes Bible.

67 Van Dijk, 'The Bible in Liturgical Use', pp. 244–7; Susan Boynton, *Shaping a Monastic Identity: Liturgy and History at the Imperial Abbey of Farfa, 1000–1125* (Ithaca, NY, 2006), pp. 80–8 ('Psalms as Prophetic Song and Prayer').

68 *Les psautiers manuscrits latins des bibliothèques publiques de France*, 2 vols, ed. Victor Leroquais (Mâcon, 1940–41), i:i–cxxvi; Pierre-Marie Gy, 'La Bible dans la liturgie au Moyen Age', in *Le Moyen Age et la Bible*, pp. 537–52 (543–50) with charts for the division of Psalms in the Roman and Benedictine uses.

69 William M. Green, 'De tribus maximis circumstantiis gestorum', *Speculum* 18:4 (1943), 484–93 (489); The treatise is translated and examined in: Hugh of St Victor, 'The Three Best Memory Aids for Learning History', tr. and ed. Mary Carruthers, in *The Medieval Craft of Memory: An Anthology of Texts and Pictures*, ed. Carruthers and Jan M. Ziolkowski (Philadelphia, 2002), pp. 32–40. For the supremacy of visual memory: Carruthers, *Book of Memory* (with a discussion of the Psalms, pp. 121–7). I thank Mary Carruthers for pointing me in this direction.

70 This concurs with the interest in the Hebrew and Greek Psalter among the Oxford Dominicans, Saenger, 'British Isles', p. 80.

71 Terence Bailey, 'Psalm: II. Latin Monophonic Psalmody', in *Grove Music Online*, ed. L. Macy (www.oxfordmusiconline.com.catalogue.ulrls.lon.ac.uk/subscriber/article/grove/music/48161, accessed 27 May 2012). This can be discerned in the various melodies ascribed to Psalm 94 (*Venite exultemus*) in a thirteenth-century missal: BL Add. MS 35,285 fols 217v–221v. An early modern example for an antiphonal psalmody is to be found in the Hebrides of Scotland, where each verse was first read and then chanted antiphonally. These were expanded upon by Christopher Marsh, 'Music and Ritual in English Parish Churches 1550–1700 – Singing the Psalms', a paper delivered at the *Fourth Warwick Symposium on Parish Research 20 May 2006*. A modern recording was made at the Back Free Church on the Isle of Lewis, Scotland, as: *Salm: Gaelic Psalms from the Hebrides of Scotland*, CD 1–2 (Aberdeen: Ridge Records, 2004).

72 Paul Saenger, 'Impact of the Early Printed Page', pp. 41–2.

73 S. J. P. van Dijk, 'Medieval Terminology and Methods of Psalm Singing', *Musica Disciplina* 6 (1952), 7–26.

74 I have nevertheless preferred *superscriptions* to *tituli*, so as to distinguish these verses from their medieval substitutions. This concurs with early use of the word in English, as in the prologues to the Psalms in the Wycliffite Bible.

75 Briefly noting the superscriptions is: Richard W. Pfaff, 'The *Tituli*, Collects, Canticles, and Creeds', ch. iv of: *The Eadwine Psalter: Text, Image, and Monastic Culture in Twelfth-Century Canterbury*, ed. Margaret Gibson et al. (London and University Park, PA, 1992), pp. 88–107 (88).

76 Leslie McFall, 'The Evidence for a Logical Arrangement of the Psalter', *Westminster Theological Journal* 62:2 (2000), 223–56, based on: Bathja Bayer, 'The Titles of the Psalms: A Renewed Investigation of an Old Problem', *Yuval* 4 (1982), 29–123; Mowinckel, *Psalms in Israel's Worship*. For additional bibliography: McFall, 'Evidence for a Logical Arrangement', nn. 27–9.

77 Bruce K. Waltke, 'Superscripts, Postcripts, or Both', *Journal of Biblical Literature* 110:4 (1991), 583–96.

78 Pierre Salmon, *Les 'tituli psalmorum' des manuscrits latins*, Collectanea biblica latina 12 (Rome, 1959), pp. 18–26; *Gregory of Nyssa's Treatise on the Inscriptions of the Psalms*, ed. and tr. Ronald E. Heine, Oxford Early Christian Studies (Oxford, 1995).

79 Salmon, *Les tituli*, based on de Bruyne, *Sommaires, divisions et rubriques*, pp. 563–89. Cassiodorus's series appears, for example, in an early tenth-century Psalter with Old English glosses, BL, Royal MS 2 B.v (George H. Brown, 'The Psalms as the Foundation of Anglo-Saxon Learning', in *The Place of the Psalms in the Intellectual Culture of the Middle Ages*, ed. Nancy Van Deusen (Albany, NY, 1999), pp. 1–24). An alternative origin for Augustine's series is suggested by Pfaff, 'Tituli, Collects, Canticles', p. 89. For the appearance of these *tituli* in monastic Psalters: Boynton, *Shaping Monastic Identity*, pp. 82–3. For more information on the last series: Bonifatius Fischer, OSB, 'Bedae de titulis Psalmorum liber', in *Festschrift Bernhard Bischoff zu seinem 65. Geburtstag dargebracht von Freunden, Kollegen, und Schülern*, ed. Johanne Autenrieth and Franz Brunhölzl (Stuttgart, 1971), pp. 90–110.

80 'I. Christ's voice tells the Father about the Jews; II. Pertains to Christ's Passion; III. The Church speaks against the Jews and other heretics and the Gentiles; and Christ speaks of his Resurrection; IV. The Prophecy of David about what he endured; V. That he fell asleep in the sleep of death and rose again for us; VI. Christ tells the Father about his persecutors. The faithful nation is instructed not to fear death, because its advocate furnished them with the hope of true resurrection by resurrecting.'

81 Joseph Dyer, 'The Psalms in Monastic Prayer', *The Place of the Psalms in the Intellectual Culture of the Middle Ages*, pp. 59–89 (73–4). *Tituli* nevertheless appeared in some Psalters, and influenced their illuminations – Boynton, *Shaping Monastic Identity*, pp. 82–6.

82 I thank Regina Randhofer for sharing her knowledge of psalmody.

83 This applies also to the Jewish example, where Psalms were identified by their incipit rather than superscription: *Mishna*, Tractate *Tamid* 7:4 = *Mishnayot Mevo'arot* (in Hebrew), 21 vols, ed. Pinechas Kehati (Jerusalem, 1998), x:58–9.

84 I thank Cardinal Carlomaria Martini, SJ, for this observation.

85 *The Byble in Englyshe, that is to saye the Content of all the Holy Scrypture, bothe of ye Olde and Newe Testament, truly translated after the Veryte of the Hebrue and Greke Textes, by ye Dylygent Studye of Dyuerse Excellent Learned Men, Expert in the Forsayde Tonges* (London: Richard Grafton and Edward Whitchurch, 1539); Eyal Poleg, 'Memory, Performance and Change: The Psalms' Layout in English Bibles 1200–1600', in *Writing as Material Practice: Substance, Surface and Medium*, ed. Kathryn E. Piquette and Ruth Whitehouse, University College London Institute of Archaeology Publications (Walnut Creek, CA, 2013).

86 Olivier Szerwiniack, 'Les glossaires de noms hébreux dans les Bibles latines imprimées aux XVe et XVIe siècles: quelques jalons', in *Biblia: les Bibles en latin au temps des Réformes*, dir. Marie-Christine Gomez-Géraud (Paris, 2008), pp. 211–29.

87 Such as the Bible and concordance bequeathed by Thomas Farnylawe, Chancellor of York (d. 1379), to be chained at the the church of St Nicholas, or a Bible bequeathed by John of Ufford, canon of Sarum and Lincoln (d. 1375), to be chained at the church of St Andrew Hingham, Norfolk, where he served as rector (Cavanaugh, 'Study of Books', pp. 330, 890).

4

Preaching the Bible: three Advent Sunday sermons

Introduction

Christian preaching is rooted in the Bible itself. Medieval preachers emulated the Prophets in their moral admonitions and followed Christ's commandment to the Apostles: 'Go ye into all the whole world, and preach the Gospel to every creature' (Mk 16:15, an injunction celebrated expressly by members of the mendicant orders). Luke's description of Christ's own preaching (4:16–30) reverberated throughout the Middle Ages: it narrates Christ's entry into a synagogue in Nazareth on the Sabbath, and his reading from the Book of Isaiah; Christ then linked Isaiah's 'The Spirit of the Lord is upon me, because the Lord hath anointed me: he hath sent me to preach to the meek' (Is 61:1–2) to his own preaching. Alluding to the stories of Elijah and Elisha (1 Kings chapter 17; 2 Kings chapter 5), Christ claimed that prophets had never been accepted by their own communities. And nor was he; he incurred the wrath of his audience who drove him out of the synagogue and sought to take his life. This episode was seen by medieval preachers as a blueprint for their own works. Paul Ricoeur's understanding of written and spoken elements within the Bible, discussed in Chapter 1, sheds additional light on this episode and its medieval re-enactment.[1] As evident in Christ's reliance on Isaiah, it was the authority of the written word that substantiated the spoken act. Christ employed sacred narrative and object to endow his understanding of the present with meaning. Christ's sermon later became sacred on its own account; canonised as dogma to become part of the New Testament. Much like Christ, preachers preferred to combine authoritative use of Scripture with a certain degree of ingenuity: the former substantiating their message, the latter a prerequisite in order to make the Bible relevant to their audiences. This was done in tandem with other forms of biblical mediation: preachers acted within sacred time and space, with sermons traditionally being part of the celebration of the liturgy; preaching and exegesis were often practised by the same people for similar aims. The interplay between authority and contextualisation, between Bible, audience, and preacher, stands at the core of this chapter.

Preaching was a vital form of biblical mediation all through the Middle Ages. In the words of Nicole Bériou, 'Pour la plupart des fidèles, les sermons ont dû constituer le lieu principal, sinon exclusif, de leur initiation à ce qui était écrit dans la Bible.'[2] At a time when Bibles were written and read primarily in Latin, sermons presented the word of God to lay men and women in the vernacular; when improvisation and audience-awareness were the exception in the liturgy, the clergy were instructed to make their sermons palatable to their audience. Preachers incorporated contemporary imagery, humour, and tales of the natural world into their sermons, seeking new ways to ensure that their message came across. The Bible supplied preachers with authority, narrative, and structure. Biblical verses and images, at times in their dozens, were woven into the fabric of the sermon. Centrality, however, does not denote simplicity, and the link between Bible and sermon cannot be taken at face value. Was the Bible a means or an end, the ultimate goal of preachers or an authoritative tool to enable instruction in doctrine and dogma? How were biblical components woven together, and how did preaching engage in dialogue with other form of biblical mediation, with biblical manuscripts and the liturgy?

Preaching as a form of biblical mediation evolved in the Middle Ages, to alter both popular and elite perceptions of the Bible. The form of preaching most common in Late Antiquity and the early and high Middle Ages was the homily. It provides a line-by-line reading of the pericope, interspersed with commentaries, exempla, and biblical citations, and was used by preachers and biblical exegetes alike.[3] The biblical lesson thus structures the entire sermon and is elucidated in its course. The homilies of central Christian thinkers such as Augustine, Gregory, and the Venerable Bede were copied and read all through the Middle Ages, especially among monastic communities. At the end of the twelfth century, however, a new form of preaching emerged.[4] Rather than commenting upon the entire pericope, it employs only a segment of it, a line or even a single word, as the sermon's core. This biblical nucleus, known as a *thema*, is then developed in major and minor divisions, each verified by a biblical or extra-biblical quotation or allusion – the proof. This 'modern sermon' (also known as 'university sermon') adheres in theory to a highly rigid structure: it begins with the *protheme*, which provides an opportunity to comment upon the act of preaching in general; then comes the *thema*, sometimes accompanied by the headings of the major divisions; an appeal for divine assistance follows, known as *antetheme* or prologue; then a repetition of the *thema* and a short introduction precede the major divisions into which the *thema* has been broken, accompanied by their own subdivisions, each verified by a proof; the sermon concludes with a repetition of the *thema*, a short admonition, and a prayer.

These new and elaborate sermons emerged just as the Late Medieval Bible began to proliferate, at a time when the mendicant orders were formed and the first universities gained prominence. A dedicated cadre of preachers was thus equipped with new books and training opportunities to assist in the creation and dissemination of a novel form of preaching. Its novelty did not pass unnoticed, and such innovative use of the Bible was rebuked by church reformers in a strand of criticism which continued in the Reformation, and has attracted, until recently, the disapproval of modern scholars. Those critics lamented how the Bible had become like 'any hand-book of collected narrations or moralized Properties of Things [...] distorted or mutilated into mere passive conveniences for moral dilation'.[5] Beyond approval or rejection, the new form of preaching became an important means of biblical dissemination, one which opened new ways of engaging with the biblical text. As explored in this chapter, its rise evolved in tandem with changes in biblical manuscripts, and the novel features of Late Medieval Bibles, primarily chapter divisions and the *Interpretations of Hebrew Names*, appear time and again in model sermons and aids to preachers. This connection helps identify the audience for these biblical manuscripts; it also raises the possibility that the new form of preaching is indicative of the same shift from narrative to text, presented and discussed in the previous chapter.

The meeting point of sermons and biblical manuscripts is indicative of a problem in the sources available to modern scholar. Sermons were preached on different occasions, by clerics (and rarely by laity) of varying capacities. Most of these sermons are now lost, and extant manuscripts are anything but an accurate record of delivery. Sermon collections were not compiled to record, but rather as memory aids or to assist preachers in compiling their sermons.[6] Thus, they often provide only a skeletal structure for preachers to expand upon extemporaneously. Sermon collections were written in preparation for delivery, or as a perfected account, polished after the speech act took place. Even the few extant *reportationes* – shorthand accounts of the delivery of sermons, primarily of French and Italian origins – still reflect scribal conventions and education rather than a mere transcription.[7] The gap between oral event and textual testimony extends to the place of the Bible within sermons: biblical verses are often truncated in the manuscripts, accompanied by book and chapter number; it is possible that in delivery these were expanded and read aloud. Sermon collections were created primarily for other priests, whose reading was eased by following references in a Late Medieval Bible (a habit embraced by the laity with the rise of printed sermons in early modern times). The manuscript evidence can therefore be seen as an echo of a speech act but also as an independent testimony, which facilitated further use by a clerical audience, consulting books in preparation for future delivery. The truncation of biblical verses also blurs the division between old and new forms of preaching: although the new form of preaching utilised only a fragment of the pericope, there is evidence to suggest that the entire pericope was read and translated without leaving a reference in our sources.[8]

Some of the most accurate records of delivery are of sermons preached by renowned clergy. These are often embedded in contemporary events and give evidence of a time when preachers stood with the equivalent of 'a Bible in one hand and a newspaper in the other'.[9] Preaching at St Paul's cross on Quinquagesima Sunday 1387/8/9, Thomas Wimbledon explored how each of the three estates (knights, priests, and laity) would act on Judgement Day, making an implicit comparison between Rehoboam (1 Kgs 12) tormenting his people and Richard II replacing his counsellors with his friends. At the same place Thomas Brinton (d. 1389) depicted losses in the war with France as a manifestation of God's wrath at English arrogance; he later lamented the burning of churches and the execution of the Archbishop of Canterbury during the 1381 rebellion, equating the rebels with the Jews – both denied absolution following the magnitude of their crimes – and applying God's reaction to the murder of Abel ('the voice of thy brother's blood crieth to me from the earth', Gn 4:10) to that of the Archbishop.[10] Another *ad status* sermon immersed in biblical language was delivered by Henry de Harkeley (d. 1317), Chancellor of the University of Oxford, on 29 December 1314, the feast of Thomas Becket.[11] The Chancellor addressed the state of the Kingdom, likening himself to Jeremiah, St Thomas to Josiah, and the reign of Edward II to that of Rehoboam. These sermons presented an insoluble link between past and present, and offer a record of a delivery from a discernible time and place. They are, however, but a negligible fraction of the surviving evidence. Their presentist agenda is the very reason for their rarity. The vast majority of sermons extant nowadays were copied for practical reasons. Sermon collections had been kept primarily not as a historical record but rather as a tool for preachers (and later as a devotional manual for the laity). Most surviving sermons thus were intended to be useful for future generations of preachers; they followed the liturgical cycle and made only passing reference to historical events, whose usefulness on later occasions was most limited.

In order to present a faithful (though inevitably partial) account of thirteenth- and fourteenth-century preaching, this chapter engages with three sermons for the same liturgical occasion, all relying on the same pericope. These sermons range in date, style, language, author, and audience to present a variety of preaching strategies; their scriptural similarities, however, highlight the difference in technique and therefore help trace the aesthetics of biblical quotations and allusions embraced by individual preachers. The liturgical occasion of the three sermons is Advent Sunday, when the Gospel lesson of Mt 21:1–9 was read. This pericope assists in the analysis of biblical mediation in two ways: first, the same biblical narrative underpins the liturgy of Palm Sunday (analysed in the first chapter). On Advent Sunday, however, it did not support a literal rendering of the event (as in its re-enactment on Palm Sunday), but rather a more allegorical interpretation. Second, choosing a minor liturgical occurrence enables us to follow the mundane in sermon production and delivery. Rather than a singular sermon preached by a renowned preacher, these Advent Sunday sermons are part of a large corpus, indicative of the way the Bible was presented in parish churches, cathedrals, and schools throughout England in the later Middle Ages.

The first sermon under examination was written before 1219 by Odo of Cheriton (d. 1246), who studied to become a *magister* at the university of Paris and compiled several sermon collections (including the *Sermones de tempore* (*Dominicales*) from where this sermon is taken), a commentary on the Song of Songs, and a popular collection of animal fables (*Narrationes* or *Parabolae*). He travelled extensively in France and Spain before returning by 1232/3 to England, where he spent the rest of his life as heir to his father's estate of Farningham in west Kent.[12] The sermon itself – transcribed and presented by H. L. Spencer – provides a tropological interpretation of Christ's path, seen as the way of the righteous soul on its journey to the Heavenly Jerusalem.[13] The sermon adheres to the older homiletic form by expounding upon the entire pericope, but incorporates amplifications and divisions common to the new form of preaching. It begins with an allegorical interpretation of the names on Christ's path, assisted by the interpretation of place names; the Apostles' mission to retrieve the ass and colt is then expounded as an attack on the world of sin. Next, the common identification of the ass and colt as Jews and Gentiles is presented and then put aside in favour of the tension between flesh and spirit. A lengthy digression enumerates the qualities of the ass as signs of piety and is followed by an interpretation of the activities of crowd and Apostles. A comparison between liturgical processions, Christ's life, and the spiritual journey of the faithful serves as a coda to the sermon. Copies of this sermon were extant in libraries both in England and the Continent; its dissemination and popularity are attested by a late fourteenth- or early fifteenth-century rendering. Written in Middle English, possibly by an adherent of Wyclif, this version engages in dialogue with Odo's sermon through its choice of themes and words while serving as a rare witness to the afterlife of the Latin sermon.

The second sermon dates to the late thirteenth century, and its sole copy exists in an early fourteenth-century Franciscan collection. Little is known of its author and it was transcribed and commented upon by Alan Fletcher.[14] It follows the new form of preaching in utilising only a fragment of the pericope as its *thema*: 'Benedictus qui venit in nomine Domini' ('Blessed is he that cometh in the name of the Lord' Mt 21:9b). It identifies Christ as a messenger, with three main attributes: he had come from a great lord (*in nomine Domini*), brought good tidings (*Benedictus*), and his arrival has ushered in joyous times (*qui venit*). Christ the messenger is further identified by his clothing and the feast with which the great lord receives him. Understanding the great lord as God leads to a tripartite subdivision, in which each person of the Trinity is defined according to time (past, present, and future) and a quality (might, right, and light). This division is tied with Advent, and the copy of the sermon ends abruptly in a discussion of the Second Coming and the world's end. The sermon is written in a linguistic hybrid style, known as macaronic or code-switching, in which languages change in between passages or even mid-sentence. This is evident in the following example, in which I have given the Latin in italics to assist in differentiating the two:

> *Pater enim mittit appropriate loquendo* wit a selli miht, *Filius* wit a semli riht, *Spiritus sanctus* wyt a seli lyht. *Et correspondenter his venit Filius primo* onto mans kynd, *secundo* onto mans mind, *tercio* onto the demyng.[15]

The transition between Latin and Middle English is immediate. It preserves the rhyming of the English (*miht*, *riht*, *lyht*) alongside the religious terminology and the logical conjunctions of the Latin (*Pater*, *Filius*, *Spiritus sanctus*; *correspondenter*). In the past scholars saw in these sermons evidence for a decline of priestly education, but recently a more complex understanding of bilingualism has emerged in which clerics are seen as competent in both languages.[16] Whereas English sermons are a rarity before the end of the fourteenth century, this macaronic sermon supplies insight into the use of the vernacular in preaching; it is still debated, however, whether macaronic sermons were delivered in the same lingual hybrid, or wether this was an efficient means of recording sermons which were then carried in the vernacular.

The third sermon was written by John Waldeby (d. after 1372), an Augustinian friar, for use both on Advent Sunday and on Palm Sunday. It is part of a collection of sermons *De tempore – novum opus dominicale*, which exists only in manuscript form. After becoming a doctor of theology at Oxford, Waldeby spent most of his life at the Austin friary at York. While teaching theology there (*c.* 1365), he compiled a sermon collection for the benefit of his students, as made explicit in the first sermon of his collection ('pro introductione iuvenes qui mihi in studentes annotantur').[17] Waldeby wrote extensively, and among his other writings are homilies on the Apostles' Creed, the Paternoster, and the *Ave Maria*, a collection of sermons *de sanctis*, and commentaries on the Apocalypse and on the Penitential Psalms, most of which have not survived. The sermon's structure follows the modern form closely, apart from its choice of *thema*. As shown in Figure 7, it begins with a *protheme* which comments upon the value of preaching and hearing the Gospel, followed by the major divisions, a prayer (the *antetheme*), a repetition of the *thema* with its major and minor subdivisions – verified by a multitude of proofs – and ends with a short admonition and a prayer. While relying on the entire pericope rather than a shorter *thema*, the sermon presents a quadruple division that links moments in the pericope with their protagonists and moral qualities: generosity (*liberalitas*) – the quality of Christ's divinity as he approached Jerusalem; humility (*humilitas*) – the quality of Christ's humanity, as he rode an ass; the fire of love (*incendium amoris*) – the quality of the disciples as they placed garments on the ass; the proclamation of honour (*preconium honoris*) – the quality of the crowd as it welcomed Christ. The first major division, Christ's generosity, is further developed into a tripartite subdivision (in ascending order): mercy (*misericordia*), freely (*gratis*) and harmony (*concordia*). The fourth major division, the crowd's proclamation of honour, is also divided in three: external praises in deeds (*exterior exemplario conversatio*), internal in recollection of God's gifts (*interior donorum dei recordatio*), and elevation by prayer (*per orationem mentis elevatio*).

These three sermons serve as the backbone for this chapter. It begins with an exploration of preachers' own understanding of sermons as biblical media, which draws also on *ars praedicandi* treatises to question the link

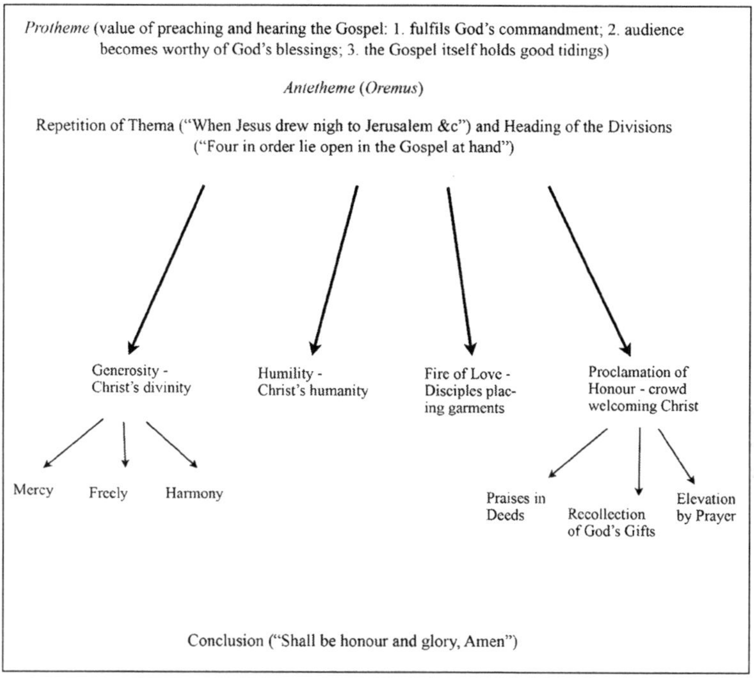

Figure 7 Waldeby's Advent Sunday sermon

between Bible, preacher, and audience. Elements in the day's pericope then assist in unearthing means of constructing entire sermons: Christ's route to Jerusalem demonstrates how the *Interpretation of Hebrew Names* was put in practice; the village from where the ass and colt were retrieved suggests the incorporation of extra-biblical narratives; the internal contradictions and conundrums of riding both ass and colt exemplify the role of the difficult biblical readings in medieval preaching. Moving to the smaller units of sermon construction, the biblical building-blocks of the proofs are explored for their complex techniques of quotation and allusion. The chapter ends with a discussion of the role of liturgy in late medieval sermons: supplying preachers with text, context, and rationale.

The Bible in sermons: the preachers' view

Preaching necessitates a degree of initiative and innovation. While liturgical manuscripts laid down texts, music, and ritual activities, priests were expected to compose their own sermons with a degree of creativity often hesitantly endorsed by church authorities. They were assisted in this task by preachers' aids, sermon collections, and treatises on preaching, which combined theoretical insights with practical advice. Among the pages of these treatises, as in medieval sermons themselves, one finds a high degree of self-awareness. Unlike liturgical rites, which seldom gave occasion for self-reflexiveness, preachers often commented on their own practice; they questioned what parts of the Bible were best preached, and how one should address different audiences, and explored innovative means of weaving biblical episodes and texts into a sermon. In all three sermons there are reflections on the act of preaching. For Odo and for the author of the macaronic sermon, Christ's coming provided an opportunity to demonstrate that their own acts were rooted in the Bible. In the macaronic sermon this is done through the image of the banquet with which Christ the messenger is received: the banquet is seen as devotional deeds (including 'herkening of Goddes worde', 'listening to the word of God'); its fourth subdivision explicitly presents the supremacy of hearing God's words and its centrality to spiritual wellbeing: 'Quartum, quia: "qui ex Deo est verba Dei audit" (Jn 8:47). Nota: casus appetitus est signum infirmitatis.'[18] The sermon itself, an occasion for the laity to hear the word of God, is seen as the spiritual feast, in an allegorical interpretation of Christ's Advent. Anyone displaying a lack of interest in this spiritual nourishment, as offered by the preacher, is therefore suspected of ill faith. In Odo's sermon it is rather Christ's commandment to the Apostle to retrieve the ass and colt that opens up a view of medieval preaching. Odo compares this injunction with another of Christ's commandments, found in Mark 16:15: 'And he said to them: Go ye into the whole world, and preach the Gospel to every creature'. The mission of the Apostles is thus developed beyond merely bringing the animals to Christ. It is rather the very act of preaching: the sermon presents this as the biblical origins of preaching, with its carrier thus merely following in the footsteps of Christ and the Apostles.

The most elaborate discussion of preaching appears in Waldeby's sermon. It presents the *protheme* – a specific part in which preachers reflect upon their own practice in the modern form of preaching – as an opportunity to discuss the value of preaching and hearing the Bible:

> Evangelium est laycis exponendum & predicandum triplici de causa: primo quod talis implet dei preceptum, secundo audiens meretur dei benedictiones, tertio ipsum evangelium continet bonum nuntium. Primum patet marci ultimo 'predicate evangelium omni creature' (Mk 16:15). Secundum lucas .12. 'Beati qui audiunt verbum dei et custodiunt

> illud' (Lk 11:28). Tertium patet quod evangelium interpretatur bonum nuntium lucas 2 'evangelizo vobis gaudium magnum &c' (Lk 2:10). Igitur evangelium illud quod describit adventum Christi in carnem est nobis bonum nuntium, ideo ut nobis presit ad salvationem'.[19]

At the beginning of the sermon, Waldeby assures his audience that the value of preaching is embedded in the biblical text itself. He employs well-known references (including the very same one used by Odo) to reveal that there is no distinction between Scripture and the admonition of one's audience. Rather, moral injunction is the Bible's very essence, evident in the etymology of the word *Gospel*. The audience, by hearing the sermon and adhering to its articles of faith, is assured of its future salvation; preachers follow Christ's injunction to the Apostles. Such division implies a moral boundary, elevating priests over laity: while the latter pursue physical or spiritual gains, the former are presented as seeking merely to follow the commandment of Christ.

These sermons touch upon questions of authority and use, Bible and admonition, which are key to the medieval sermon. They follow a well-trodden path in their explorations. Reflections on preaching and biblical mediation date back to first centuries of Christianity, and likewise address questions of biblical authority, dissemination, and the goal of preaching. An early work is the fourth book of Augustine's *De doctrina Christiana*.[20] This book is divided in two, interpretation and communication (*modus inveniendi* and *modus proferendi*), a division that mirrors the perennial link between preaching and exegesis. Preachers are expected to engage in both simultaneously, to analyse the text and disseminate it widely. They are to be aware of text and audience alike, immersing themselves in the study of exegesis and rhetoric. While biblical exegesis was widely employed by Augustine's contemporaries, he laid a special emphasis on eloquence. Augustine warns Christian orators of the danger of boring their audiences, and advocates the value of the Pagan *artes*, predominantly rhetoric, in making the Christian message palatable. Anticipating objections he goes to a great length in assuring his readers that both form and content, rhetorics and eloquence, are to be found in the Bible, especially in the words of the Prophets. For Augustine the truth on its own does not ensure a successful sermon, and the mark of a good Christian orator is his ability to transform his audience into a receptacle for sacred words. Two centuries later the value of Christian eloquence and audience-awareness was reaffirmed by Gregory the Great (d. 604). In his *Cura pastoralis*, Gregory advances the means of dissemination available to Christian orators. Breaking away from classical rhetoric, he highlights the importance of accommodating one's message to specific audiences and provides examples of themes appropriate for discrete groups.[21]

The treatises of Augustine and Gregory were immensely popular in the Middle Ages, copied and read extensively, and later serving as the basis for the compilation of *ars praedicandi* treatises, which emerged at the end of the twelfth century.[22] An early work is Alain of Lille's *Summa de arte praedicatoria* of *c.* 1199. It follows Gregory in recommending an appropriate message for specific audiences and provides an array of typical audiences alongside their corresponding themes: the poor are to be told of the praises of poverty, the rich of almsgiving; the young are to be instructed with parables, while virgins are offered the praises of purity, et cetera.[23] Alain then discusses the role of the Bible in sermons through the image of Jacob's Ladder (Gn 28:12 'And he (Jacob) saw in his sleep a ladder standing upon the earth, and the top thereof touching heaven: the Angels also of God ascending and descending by it'). At first its rungs are likened to man's ascent in faith: from confession to prayer, to thanksgiving, then the study of Scripture, of the church fathers, of biblical exegesis, and lastly preaching the Bible.[24] Preaching becomes the culmination of Christian life, and the link between exegesis and preaching is presented as one of dependency and progression; biblical study of both text and exegesis becomes a prerequisite for oral dissemination.

The second time Alain invokes the image of Jacob's ladder, however, raises doubts regarding the link between Bible and sermon. It describes preaching thus: 'quod significatur per angelos ascendentes et descendentes: angeli enim hi sunt prædicatores, qui tunc ascendunt cum cœlestia prædicant; descendunt, quando per moralia se inferioribus conformant'.[25] In a memorable image, angels are presented as the quintessential mediators, bridging the gap between heaven and earth.[26] Preachers, their earthly counterparts, likewise move between the two realities (with the implied moral and sacral parallels) teaching of divine truths and moral values. The place of the Bible in this image is far from evident. Is it the 'heavenly matters' to which the ascending angels are drawn or the ladder which enables the connection between the two realities? Alain's own definition of preaching provides an answer. At the opening of the treatise he supplies a definition of the sermon which was common among his contemporaries and is still used by modern scholars of medieval preaching: 'Praedicatio est manifesta et publica instructio morum et fidei, informationi hominum deserviens, ex rationum semita, et auctoritatum fonte proveniens'.[27] In this definition the Bible takes a second place. Preachers aspired to the expansion of faith, to the presentation of doctrinal matters and moral teaching rather than to expound biblical narratives. The Bible is thus cast in the figure of Jacob's Ladder, on which medieval preachers climbed in their moral admonitions.

Not all books of the Bible carry the same weight for Alain, and a subtle hierarchy arose from their usefulness in sermons. He argues that *themata* – the biblical nuclei at the core of the sermon – are to be taken solely from parts of the Bible whose ethics enable preachers to instruct in faith and morality: the Gospels, Psalms, Paul's Epistles, and the Books of Solomon. Proofs, on the other hand, can be taken from all books of the Bible, as well as from church fathers or even pagan writers. For Alain morality is the yardstick for the use of the Bible in sermons. This view was shared by his contemporary, Alexander of Ashby (d. 1208/14) in his *De artificioso modo predicandi*.[28] Alexander relies heavily on Augustine and Gregory in an appeal for the use of the pagan *artes* and the importance of audience-awareness for the Christian preacher. Much in tune with Alain's *Summa*, the sermon's objective is seen as the admonition of sins, with the Bible a means for achieving this goal. Alexander then advises his readers to divide their sermons into four parts: a prologue, in which the audience was rendered docile, benevolent, and attentive; the division of the biblical *thema*; the confirmation of each part of the division, either with authorities or with reason; and a conclusion with a brief recapitulation, admonition, and prayer.

Alain of Lille and Alexander of Ashby mark the beginning of a new era in Christian preaching. The rise of the new form of preaching, complex and highly rhetorical, was accompanied by a multitude of *ars praendicandi* treatises. Although not officially part of the university curriculum, these treatises were studied in grammar schools, mendicant *studia*, and possibly in the newly formed universities themselves.[29] They were firmly connected to the newly established mendicant orders, leading Briscoe to conclude that 'It is not surprising, then, that after Alan [*sic*], almost all the identified medieval authors of *artes praedicandi* were members of one or another of the new mendicant orders'.[30] Rather than seeing the Bible as extraneous to late medieval sermons, some *ars praedicandi* treatises present the Bible as the fountainhead of all sciences, including rhetoric, thus masking their innovativeness in biblical authority.[31] A widespread English treatise takes such authority even further. Little is known of the composition of the treatise, possibly compiled at Oxford in 1322, apart from an acrostic identifying its author as Robert of Basevorn and its addressee as the Abbot of Basingwerk in Flintshire.[32] The treatise presents the Bible as a template for preaching, and concludes a discussion of a variety of preaching techniques with the assertion that all forms of preaching are exemplified in the ministry of Christ, as evident in Matthew 4:17 ('From that time Jesus began to preach, and to say: Do penance, for the kingdom of heaven is at hand'). Much like a medieval preacher, so goes Basevorn's argument, Christ compiled a brief sermon taking 'Do penance, for the kingdom of heaven is at hand' as his *thema*. The *thema*, as required, is a biblical quotation. These are the exact words of John the Baptist, quoted earlier in the Gospel (Mt 3:2). Basevorn takes this as an opportunity to teach his readers the value of humility and accuracy. Christ's willingness to rely on the words of his inferior teaches preachers not to let their pride stand in the way of quoting their predecessors – first and foremost Christ, Paul, Augustine, Gregory, and Bernard (implicitly making Christ a link in a chain of preachers). Christ's reliance on John the Baptist also advocates verbatim quotation: throughout the treatise Basevorn rejects any alteration to the biblical *thema*, dismissing even minor alterations that do not affect meaning. Thus, *veni* ('I have come') should not be altered to *veniendi* ('have been coming') nor *Domine* ('Lord' i.e. Christ) to *Salvator* ('the Saviour'). This argument furthers Alain of Lille's dichotomous view of the Bible in sermons. The *thema* is to be taken solely from the Bible, without even the smallest alteration; proofs, on the other hand, may be taken from the Bible as well as from liturgy, exempla, syllogisms, or natural phenomena. The centrality of biblical proofs is nevertheless maintained by Basevorn's limitation of extra-biblical elements to three of a kind in each sermon, a restriction that does not apply to the Bible.

Basevorn explicitly rejects Alain of Lille's understanding of Bible and preaching. Rather than Alain's restrictive view of biblical books suitable for *themata* based on their moral applicability, Basevorn argues that all genuine biblical books are divinely inspired and can serve for *themata*. Rather then rhetoric, his analysis employs authority and exegesis as a yardstick. Following Jerome's prologues and medieval exegetes, Basevorn questions the authority of Third and Fourth Ezra, some of the Psalms, the Shepherd of Hermas (*Liber pastoris*), Paul's Epistle to the Laodiceans, Ecclesiasticus, and the Epistle of Jude. He also raises doubts concerning the Prayers of Manasseh and Jeremiah, Judith, and Tobit, and the Greek influence in Wisdom and the Books of Maccabees. This in-depth exploration ends by asserting the applicability of all biblical books for *themata*, apart from Third and Fourth Esdras, the said Psalms, Hermas's Shepherd, and Paul to the Laodiceans. Such engagement with the Christian canon reflects the sequence and layout of Late Medieval Bibles, which likewise put parts of the canon and their authority in question.[33]

The twenty-first chapter of Basevorn's treatise identifies the role of preachers as expanding the mysteries of the biblical text: 'Clausa est enim Sancta Scriptura per secretorum mysteria, sed aperta per praedicatorum ministeria, quia "decleratio sermonis Dei illuminat et intellectum dat parvulis" (loosely based on Ps 118:130)'.[34] Much like the introduction to the *Interpretations* in the Arsenal manuscript (above, Chapter 3, p. 122), the Bible is presented as a locked secret, to be accessed only by qualified ministers. Basevorn does not state the exact nature of these mysteries, nor their keys. However, the context of his discussion points the reader in an unexpected direction. The very same chapter addresses single-word *themata*, which led preachers to construct an entire sermon from a single word of Scripture. Basevorn advises his readers to be cautious in choosing the right word, implying that the mysteries of the Bible lie in its each and every word. Basevorn then proceeds to address the difficult task of constructing an entire sermon from such a minute biblical nucleus, offering in effect the keys to its mysteries. He suggests using the word's definition, dividing a word according to its multiple meanings, or relying on concordances and on verbal agreement. Such ways of expanding the *thema*, known as means of amplification, highlight the textual qualities of the biblical *thema* and lead to an in-depth analysis of biblical language, etymology, and genre. Similar methodologies underpin means of amplification in other treatises as well: an anonymous thirteenth-century Franciscan treatise concurs with Basevorn and presents structural elements such as division and argument, alongside a careful reading of the biblical text (i.e. interpreting every word in the *thema* or alluding to its context), relying on biblical exegesis through the four senses of Scripture, or integrating extra-biblical sources, such as church fathers and hagiography.[35]

The new form of preaching led preachers to build elaborate structures comprised of biblical building blocks. Despite Basevorn's assurances that the new style was biblical in nature, its use of the Bible became a cause of strife in late medieval England. The tension between biblical and extra-biblical elements stands at the core of two sermons of John Wyclif (d. 1384) which share the same *thema*: 'The seed is the word of God' (Lk 8:11b).[36] Following Christ's Parable of the Sower, Wyclif sees preachers' negligence and pride as the reason for the Gospel's seed falling on barren land. He laments that the Word of God has become riddled with fables, apocrypha, lightheartedness, or falseness; that the biblical text, which is best spoken openly and plainly, has turned into the object of rhetorical devices. These originate in the vainglory of preachers and the pride of audience, the root of all evil. Wyclif's strong words follow his assertion that preaching is key to the instruction of faith and doctrine, because 'spiritualissimum actum edificandi ecclesiam qui est predicatio verbi Dei'.[37] For Wyclif, as for Christian writers from the time of Augustine, preaching is rooted in the Bible; and much like his contemporaries he sees the ultimate goal of sermons as spiritual edification, which was seen as an integral part of the Bible by Wyclif as by Waldeby. Despite Wyclif's strong stand against rhetoric, the tension between form and content, between biblical and extraneous elements, is less evident in Wyclif's sermon than one might expect. An examination of the two sermons reveals that Wyclif's negation of the modern form of preaching with its use of rhetoric, extra-biblical elements, and modifications of biblical words, is not reflected in his own practice. The structure of both these sermons follows the new form of preaching to the letter, with a *protheme*, *thema*, heading of major divisions, *antetheme*, repetition of *thema* followed by the major and minor divisions (enumerating the types of seeds and soil). Moreover, although his sermons rely heavily on the Bible, they also incorporate elements from Augustine, Gregory the Great, Chrysostom, Robert Grosseteste, and even, while advocating the necessity of an exemplary lifestyle for preachers, the story of a serpent that can kill with its gaze.[38] These sermons thus employ the new form of preaching to advocate a return to the unmediated Word of God.

The Interpretations of Hebrew Names in practice

> And when they drew nigh to Jerusalem,
> and were come to Bethphage, unto mount Olivet. (Mt 21:1a)

The methods of expanding a *thema* to an entire sermon provide us with a glimpse into preachers' use of Late Medieval Bibles.[39] In *ars praedicandi* treatises the definition of words and their etymology are presented as important means of amplification.[40] This opportunity is taken up in the Advent Sunday sermons examined, as the day's pericope presents two place names: Jerusalem and Bethphage, a small village on Mount of Olives. These places are noted in the *Interpretations of Hebrew Names*, the most common glossary in Late Medieval Bibles (above, Chapter 3, pp. 118–24), whose entries in the *Aaz* rendering read: 'pacifica vel visio pacis', for the former, and 'domus oris vel domus bucce seu domus oris vallium aut domus maxillarum, Syrum est non Hebreum' for the latter.[41]

The interpretation of place names supplies Odo with an allegorical understanding of Christ's path. In order to elaborate this understanding, he adds another place to his narrative: Bethany, a village on Mount of Olives which appears in Christ's entry to Jerusalem in Mark (11:1) and Luke (19:29), and on Christ's return in Matthew (21:17). Its entry in the

Interpretations reads: 'Bethania – domus obedientie vel domus afflictionis eius seu domus doni Dei aut domus gratificata domino'.[42] Odo locates the two villages at the foot of Mount of Olives and follows Luke in depicting Christ's entry to Jerusalem:

> In pede montis Oliveti erant due civitates: Betphage et Bethania. Betphage interpretatur domus bucce, vel maxillarum; Bethania domus obedientie. Primo venit de Bethania per Betphage in Ierusalem, ut narrat Lucas, instruens nos per quam viam incedendum est ad supernam Ierusalem. De Bethania namque, id est de obedientia, transire debemus ad Betphage, id est ad oris confessionem [...] ut a Bethania per Betphage ad visionem pacis transire valeamus.[43]

Christ's path is seen as an allegory of the course of the righteous soul. The spiritual journey from obedience through confession to eternal salvation unfolds through the interpretation of place names on Christ's route; a historical journey is rendered pertinent for each and every believer by detaching places from their geographical context. A similar reckoning appears in another late medieval sermon. An anonymous Advent Sunday sermon from the Midlands presents Bethany (in a slight misreading of biblical etymology) as the house of disobedience and Bethphage as a symbol of confession, with the itinerant soul progressing from the one to the other.[44]

The Middle English rendering of Odo's sermon sends the soul in another direction, through a different understanding of Bethphage:

> And so he came by Betphage, that is to seye an hous of teerus, from betphanie, that is buxumnesse, techinge us what weye we schulen wende to the citee of hevenly pees. First by buxumnesse to do the wille of God and to kepe hise heestus [...] And so, fro buxumnesse, that is meke knowlechynge of synne, armen schulden weende by Bethphage, that is teerus and wepynge, with Criste to the mounte of Olyvete.[45]

As shown by Spencer, such a modification is indicative of the adherents of Wyclif and their negation of the centrality of oral confession.[46] A slight modification in biblical definition assisted the Middle English redactor to steer the sermon, and the allegorical journey of each believer, into a different path. Following Christ's journey, whose obedience to the Father led him to accept the cross and led to his Passion, the believer is expected to acknowledge his sins and proceed through tears of repentance. Unlike Odo's account, in which Bethphage is seen as a *house of the mouth*, exploring the village as a *house of tears* enables one to avoid the emphasis on oral confession. Both alternatives are found in the *Interpretations*. Such a shift of meaning therefore exemplifies the value of the multiple interpretations underpinning the success of the *Aaz* rendering; a glossary that contains several alternatives to each entry was thus most useful for medieval preachers, seeking to accommodate place names for different aims.

A very different use of the interpretation of place names is presented by Waldeby. In a discussion of Christ's generosity, as extended to the Kiss of Peace (following *freely* – the second subdivision of the first major division), the definition of Bethphage is put into use: '"& venisset bethfage" qui interpretatur domus bucce, id est uterus virginis in quo fuit unum nature humane ad verbum tanquam pacis osculum. Sicut exponit Bernardus super illud cantico primo "osculetur me osculo oris sui &c" (Sg 1:1)'.[47] Waldeby's understanding of the biblical narrative and its allegorical interpretation follows the relevant entry in the *Interpretations* and fits perfectly with the liturgical occasion of the sermon (as with his own Marian devotion).[48] Nevertheless, the connection between mouth, kiss, and womb is nebulous, to say the very least. Christ's entry to Jerusalem is linked to the Incarnation through the identification of Bethphage with Mary's womb. This connection relies upon the common interpretation of Bethphage as mouth, which is then linked with another biblical mouth – that of the first verse of the Song of Songs. This transition is far from explicit, as Mary does not appear in that Old Testament book, nor in the account of Matthew 21. However, the biblical kiss was understood by medieval exegetes, including Bernard of Clairvaux, as an allegory of the First Advent, with reference to the Kiss of Peace. Philip of Harveng's (d. 1183) commentary on the Song of Songs fits Waldeby's argument even better, as it links the kiss with Mary's womb and the coming together of the two natures ('Haec assumptio, haec junctura qua deus sibi voluit hominem personaliter counire, et naturam cum natura foedus pacis in utero virginis ferire vel unire').[49] Among the pages of Late Medieval Bibles such connection is displayed graphically. The initial O of *Osculetur*, the opening word of the Song of Songs, is frequently illuminated with an image of Mary and Christ the child (Figure 8).[50] Waldeby thus follows exegesis and visual narratives to connect the kiss of the lovers from the Song of Songs to Mary, and the kiss of the mouth to the Advent of Christ: the place of the kiss, the mouth, is ascribed to the place of the Incarnation, Mary's womb; the womb is then connected, through the mouth, to Bethphage – a place on Christ's path in the day's pericope. Unlike Odo's seamless incorporation of the *Interpretations* into his sermon, Waldeby went to great lengths to accommodate the definition of Bethphage into his understanding of the connection between the Kiss of Peace and Christ's Advent. His troubles exemplify the importance of the

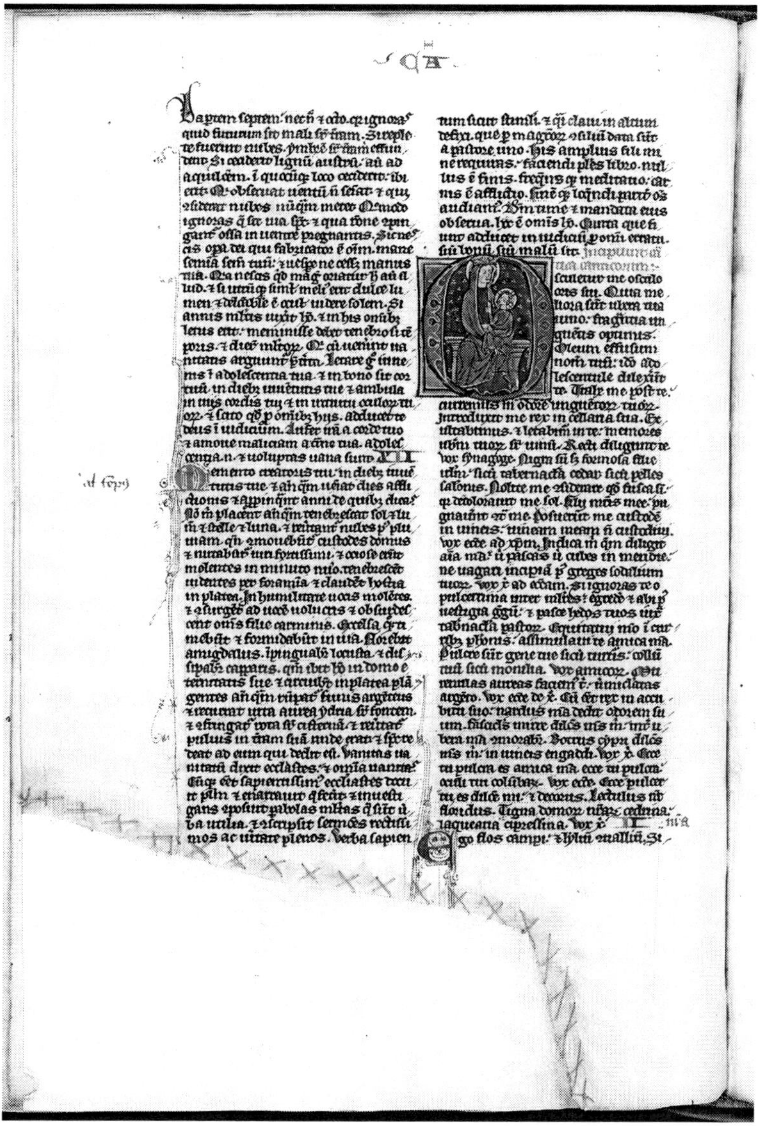

Figure 8 Song of Songs, Edinburgh University Library, MS 2, fol. 229v

Interpretations of Hebrew Names for a medieval preacher, who was so keen on integrating this definition into his sermon that he ended up supplying additional layers of biblical texts and exegesis.

Two other types of name exegesis appear briefly in these sermons. One is the interpretation of proper names, the other of Latin names. On the basis of the *Interpretations*, Odo presents an allegorical understanding of the crowd's exclamation of *Hosanna* as 'save me' ('Obsecro salva'), of Jews as those who confess (*confitentes*) and of Hebrews as those who traverse (*transeuntes*), all following the entries in the *Interpretations* (*Aaz* rendering) as well as Jerome.[51] Other place names follow the Latin, rather than transliterated Hebrew, but are still deemed worthy of expansion. Odo sees the Mount of Olives as exemplifying righteous living, as well as standing for Mary; both understandings derive from the mount's qualities of stability, of height, and of being the first landmark to receive the rays of sunlight. Waldeby's attention is captured rather by the olives. In the third subdivision of the first major division (*Harmony*), olives are seen to illuminate, nourish, and heal. So too is Christ, as the light of the world, the bread of life, and the conveyor of everlasting salvation.[52] Thus, biblical names became an important tool for medieval preachers in weaving new narratives and complex allegorical interpretations. Seeking new means of expanding short biblical nuclei into entire sermons, they were aided by the *Interpretations of Hebrew Names*, a quintessential part of the Late Medieval Bible. This provides the modern scholar with a glimpse into the glossary's reception and use.

Extra-biblical narratives

> then Jesus sent two disciples. Saying to them:
> Go ye into the village that is over against you, and immediately you shall find an ass tied, and a colt with her: loose them and bring them to me.
> (Mt 21:1b–2)

Medieval preachers sought to expand biblical episodes in ways significant to their audience. Images and sources outside the immediate remit of the Bible enabled them to tap into the 'here and now' of their audience. Aided by the medieval proliferation of saints' lives, exempla, and fabulae, proofs in sermons often included animal fables, natural anecdotes, historical episodes, and daily events. In the sermons under investigation these are taken from exegetical works (on the Psalms and Bernard on the Song of Songs), church fathers (Gregory the Great and Augustine), and saints' lives, as well as numerous animal fables and natural phenomena.

The incorporation of extra-biblical materials into the fabric of the sermon sometimes met with disapproval, as in Wyclif's explicit rejection (above, pp. 165–6), or that of Basevorn:

> 'et hoc modo [a variation of the school of Paris] magis acceptatur narratio Augustini, dummodo sit nova et inusitata, quam Bibliae; et magis Helinandi vel alicuius alterius qui raro habetur, quam Augustini vel Ambrosii. Cuius ratio non est alia nisi vana curiositas hominum.[53]

Basevorn's lament for the decline of the Bible in sermons was probably exaggerated. The array of proofs in the three sermons concur with surveys of late medieval sermons to show that biblical proofs remained the most common biblical proofs.[54] Like Wyclif, Basevorn was following a fashion by lamenting the state of the Bible among his colleagues; and, like Wycilf, the first paragraph of Basevorn's prologue follows a biblical quotation with a quote from Boethius. In doing so, however, he did not necessarily succumb to hypocrisy. Rather, such proofs enabled him and other preachers to catch the attention of their audiences and link a remote past to their present.

Quotations from the classics, church fathers, or natural phenomena enabled preachers to captivate their audiences while showing off their education. Beyond such short and discernible allusions, preachers filled gaps within the Bible or expanded upon minor elements by subjecting the biblical narrative to contemporary stories, well-known and easily understood by their audience. In Matthew's pericope, as is common in the Bible, the extreme brevity of the narrative leaves much room for imagination and creativity. This opportunity was embraced by medieval preachers, who saw in it an opportunity to link Bible and audience, past and present. In the macaronic sermon, between the division of the *thema* and the qualities of the Trinity, Christ's Advent is seen as the coming of a messenger from a great lord. This image presents the Incarnation in terms easily understood by lay men and women, and its minute details are then further explored. Mundane elements, such as Christ's clothes and the banquet with which the messenger is welcomed, provide familiar grounding for complex subdivisions. Christ's clothes are not luxurious, but each of them (*serk* (undergarment), *kirtil* (tunic), surcoat and mantle) stands for his chastity, humility, charity, and the truth of the Trinity. Of little connection with the clothes of the day's pericope, these garments nevertheless brought home the preacher's message of moral admonition. Similarly, with no basis in the day's pericope, the banquet welcoming Christ mirrors medieval feasts; the delicacies of the medieval table are briefly explored, appealing to and exerting the imagination of audience members. The dishes of meat and fish are then put aside in favour of an allegorical interpretation: 'This mangeries nes nouther flesly daynte ne fysly plente, sed devocioun and orisoun, huselyng at God(d)es borde and herkening of Goddes worde'.[55] This is a feast of devotion and prayer. Its vivid imagery then serves as the basis of a quadruple division: sacred times of sacred deeds; a time when God is kind to humanity, as a noble on his feast day; the ancient custom of celebrating thrice a year; God's people can hear the word of God. These divisions draw from ancient history and from contemporary customs, and contextualise the link between Bible and doctrine through the well-known habits of the nobility, accompanied by the contemporary medical diagnosis, addressed above.

The image of Christ the rider furnishes Odo with ample grounds for integrating equestrian images into his exploration of the biblical episode. He takes the opportunity to paint an absurd picture of an ass which rides its master to market, and brings the tension inherent in the biblical pericope (Christ, a deity, riding an ass) into a new level of easily visualised and highly memorable absurd.[56] Another contemporary image, one most familiar to Odo's audience, underpins an entire section of the sermon. In the Gospel narrative Christ instructs the Apostles to retrieve the ass and colt from a nearby village (*castellum*). The only biblical reference to the actual mission is the statement of its fulfilment ('And the disciples going, did as Jesus commanded them', Mt 21:6). For Odo this incident provides fertile ground for weaving an allegorical interpretation into the narrative. At first the two Apostles, anonymous in the biblical narrative, are named as Peter and Philip, or Peter and Andrew – the most righteous of Christ's entourage. The attention given the Apostles, expanded through use of Mark 16:15 ('And he said to them: Go ye into the whole world, and preach the Gospel to every creature'), extends beyond a mere biblical echo: in medieval England a pair of humble preachers taking to the road was visible to all; the friars, whose oath of poverty led them to walk the roads in pairs and preach whenever possible, were intentionally imitating this very same biblical verse.[57]

In their newly devised mission, the Apostles' arena is transformed from the village to the entire world. This new identification is not immediate, and relies on equating Christ's commandment to the Apostles in Luke with a Parable in Ecclesiastes 9:14–16 and its allegorical interpretation (discussed below, pp. 183–4). The Apostles are then to venture into the world of sin, confront the devil and retrieve the ass and colt – the souls of the righteous. The word *castellum*, a small village in the Vulgate but also

Table 2 The Divisions of the Castle of Odo of Cheriton's Sermon

	One	*Two*	*Three*	*Four*
Sin	Teaching of Falseness	Earthly Power	False Righteousness	Carnal lust
Inhabitants	Idolaters & Heretics	Mighty Men & Covetous	Hypocrites & Deceivers	Self-indulgents & Lecherouses
Engines	Faith	Hope	Charity	Chastity

meaning a fortress, furnishes Odo with an opportunity to expand upon the struggle between good and evil within one's soul. The world of sin, in the image of a fortress, is divided into four turrets, each inhabited by its own residents – a variety of sinners. The approaching Apostles are to assail each turret with a siege engine – an act of charity. Table 2 illustrates this information. The success of the image rests on the juxtaposition of catechism with medieval warfare. The siege ties together the variety of sins and acts of charity, in a way that could be easily visualised by its medieval audience. An array of proofs links sins and acts of charity – turrets and siege engines – to present the battle for one's soul. Thus, for example, the third turret – false righteousness – is assailed by charity, based on a verbal echo from Paul's Epistle to the Romans: 'Contra terciam, caritatem: ubi nam est dilectio, recedit omnis simulatio' (cf. Rom 12:9a 'Dilectio sine simulatione').[58] The success of this digression and its appeal to medieval audiences is attested by the incorporation of this lengthy section in its entirety into the Middle English rendering. The image of the *castellum*, however, with its turrets, defendants, and assailants is completely foreign to the biblical narrative. It is a far cry from any attempt to simplify the biblical text, as it complicates a minor element of the pericope almost beyond reckoning. In tune with *ars praedicandi* treatises, the Bible sets the scene for further elaboration, achieving the doctrinal goal of chastising one's audience through a highly elaborate, and highly familiar, image.[59]

The end of the narrative opens a window into the origin of Odo's image. Following the Apostles' victory, the devil's castle is razed to the ground. Another castle is constructed in its place. While the first is of the devil, the second is God's, with acts of charity to guard its walls and fend off sin. The new castle was not foreign to Odo's audience. Understanding one's soul as God's castle with its elaborate array of virtues (only implied in the sermon) was common in late medieval England and made explicit in the Middle English rendering of the sermon 'And thus thorouh vertues schulde mannes soule be made the castel of God'.[60] Figure 9, from

Figure 9 The Tower of Wisdom, BL, Arundel MS 83 II, fol. 135r

the *De Lisle Psalter* (South East England, *c.* 1310) is a visual representation of the Tower of Wisdom (*turris sapientiae*).[61] The image, which is presented here from a manuscript of a lay and pious lord (who became a Franciscan near the end of his life), is based on a treatise by the same name of the thirteenth-century Franciscan John of Metz (though it circulated independently as well). It presents a complex understanding of virtues and acts of charity through the minute details of the tower's architecture: its foundation, steps, door, windows, walls, crenellations, and defenders. A similar image is that of the Castle of Love, depicted in several Middle English translations all based on Robert Grosseteste's sermon, in which the Incarnation and Mary's womb are likened to a castle, with its minute details representing a variety of virtues.[62] Much like the Heavenly Jerusalem, the Tower of Wisdom and the Castle of Love became the epitomes of pious living; and much like the cities of Babylon, Sodom and Gomorrah, its obverse manifested the dwelling of evil, as in Odo's sermon. This and similar images enabled preachers to connect the Bible to their audience and make plain complex theological notions; they took preacher and listeners far beyond the biblical text to transform minor moments in the biblical narrative into complex and challenging stories, full of vivid images and contemporary landscape. In this endeavour, preachers preferred images that could be easily broken to divisions and subdivisions (akin to the ones employed in medieval *ars memorativa* treatises). Such use is indicative of the aesthetics of the late medieval sermon and its elaborate structures; it can also explain the existence of similar images, such as the candelabrum or the cherub's wing, among the pages of Late Medieval Bibles, where they could have assisted preachers in the compilation of their sermons.[63]

Application of biblical difficulties

> Tell ye the daughter of Sion: Behold thy king cometh to thee, meek, and sitting upon an ass, and a colt the foal of her that is used to the yoke.
>
> (Mt 21:5)

The Bible is a complex book. The conflation of minor biblical elements, described above, demonstrates how preachers gladly filled biblical silences with contemporary imagery and extra-biblical materials. Contradictions, misinterpretations, and conundrums likewise are frequent in the Bible. For the modern scholar these are signs of the Bible's prolonged evolution, of generations of scribes and editors resulting in a composite text with its diverse historical strata and genres. For medieval preachers and exegetes these elements were also mysteries, which opened up the depths of the biblical text. They supplied preachers with ample opportunities to weave church doctrine, interpretations, and admonitions into the biblical narrative. These were not seen as extraneous to the biblical text, nor was their incorporation viewed as artificial. Rather, as seen in *prothemes* and exegetical works alike, these were the very essence of the Bible. Advent Sunday's pericope incorporates several such elements, which were consequently embraced by medieval preachers. The description of two animals, the ass and the colt, in Matthew's account is an example of one such difficult reading. While all other canonical Gospels refer to a single animal, Matthew presents two. The origin of this confusion lies in a misinterpretation of Zechariah 9:9b, which provides the New Testament scene with its rationale. The synonymous parallelism of Zechariah's Hebrew describes a single animal twice, as can be seen in modern biblical translations (e.g. in the *World English Bible*: 'Tell the daughter of Zion, behold, your King comes to you, humble, and riding on a donkey, on a colt, the foal of a donkey').[64] This repetition led to vagueness in the Septuagint and was subsequently altered in Jerome's translation from an 'ass's colt' to 'an ass and a colt'. It created a conundrum – the existence of two animals where only one was needed – which enhances the contradictory elements already existing in Matthew's account. Zechariah's prophecy of a king riding a lowly animal, magnified tenfold when applied to Christ, was further muddled up in Jerome's translation.

Medieval exegetes, unlike their modern counterparts, did not seek to undermine Jerome's translation or to amend Matthew's account via a re-evaluation of its dependency on Zechariah (the latter preserving the ambiguity of the Hebrew). Rather, they approached this conundrum as a biblical mystery, worthy of further exploration and dissemination. Following Jerome, the *Glossa ordinaria* provides an interpretation of the two animals in the light of the two Apostles, sent to retrieve them. Philip and Peter, named by exegetes and preachers alike, were the ones who brought the Samaritans and Cornelius into the Christian faith. The retrieved animals were identified accordingly: the ass with the Jews and the colt with the Gentiles.[65] Matthew's misinterpretation thus became a symbolic representation of the future of the Christian faith and its appeal to diverse nations: the ass, which was placed under a yoke, was under the yoke of the laws and commandments kept by the Jews; the colt, free to err, represented the Gentiles. Some exegetes linked the ass with Matthew, who allegedly wrote in Hebrew and retained hopes for the conversion of the Jews; the colt represented Mark, who approached a Gentile audience. Jerome also addressed the practicalities of the problem: which animal was actually employed by Christ? He concluded that, owing to the shortness of the road, only the ass was ridden while the colt remained free.

Debates over the identity of the animals and their function made their way into medieval sermons. In Odo's sermon (though not in its later reduction), the biblical conundrum is presented and discussed at length:

> Per asinam (intelligitur) sinagogam, que iugo legis erat edomita; per pullum, populum gentilem, que sine lege lascivus et indomitus diversos deos colebat. [...] Notandum quod Dominus non simul super ambos, sed mistice per fidem utrique populo insedit. Multi enim (de) Iudeis, (multi de gentibus) conversi sunt, (et factum) est *unum ovile et unum pastor* (Jn 10:16). Item probabile (est) quod Dominus prius equitavit asinam, postea pullum, ut istoria rei significate respondeat.[66]

Odo follows the common identification of ass and colt with Jews and Gentiles and explicitly addresses the problem of which animal was actually ridden. Two solutions follow: the first is a mystical interpretation which draws the scene away from the world of mundane riding and audience experience and into a realm beyond nature. Although Christ did not ride the animals together in practice, he ruled the two nations by faith. The second solution is a common historical allegorisation, with the animals ridden in sequence of conversion. The audience is left with two conflicting views, free to choose between them. It is possible, however, that Odo intended this understanding for the eyes of preachers, in preparation of their sermons, and that in oral delivery such alternatives would have been simplified, on the basis of the preacher's needs and aims. As the sermon unfolds, the mystery of the two animals is put aside in favour of a single animal. Zechariah's original conundrum – a king riding a lowly animal – is implicitly presented as a hierarchy of body and soul, with the latter's supremacy a clear lesson for the morality of audience members.

The difference between the two animals is commented upon in Waldeby's sermon:

> '& ibi invenientis asinam et pullum cum ea' (Mt 21:2b), id est gentem iudaicam onere legis gravatam ... et gentem paganam nullius legis oneri assuetam. 'Solvite et adducite mihi' (Mt 21:2c), Supple per veram doctrinam vel per asinam, nitetur natura humana verbo unita, quin sessor superior est, asinus inferior; sessor regit et ducit, asinus regitur et ducitur; sessor quiescit, asinus vexatur; sic fuit de natura divina quod ipsa fuit superior et alterius nature regitiva id est ductiva & in summa dilectione quieta. Ecce ergo in exemplum humilitatis quomodo Christus prophetiam illam implevit: 'ecce rex tuus venit tibi mansuetus sedens

> super asinam &c' (Mt 21:5). Et non solum semel, se Christus humiliavit sed continue, sic se humiliavit sedendo super asinam id est super humanam animam. Quia ecclesiastici, 'anima iusti sedes est sapientie'.[67]

After briefly presenting the common identification of ass and colt, the question of the two animals is quickly dismissed. In its stead, Waldeby engages with Zechariah's original contradiction – the juxtaposition between ass and regality. The tension between rider and animal exerted the imagination of the audience through a familiar image of a man riding an unruly ass (with implied comic possibilities for *in situ* delivery). This image does not convey a moral understanding, as did Odo's account, but rather presents the complex theological notion of Christ's two bodies in a memorable and familiar image, one in which audience members could picture themselves. Such theological expounding in mundane guise supports the discussion of Christ's humility – the subject of the second major division of Waldeby's sermon. It employs Zechariah's contradictory description to present Christ, whose great humility led him to adopt a human form. This moment of humility, taking place on the road to Jerusalem, is extended to the Incarnation at large, through a verbal echo of *sedens* in a common proverb, mistakenly attributed to Proverbs 10:25b.[68]

Waldeby's emphasis on the tension between the lofty status of the rider and his humble animal echoes the liturgy of Palm Sunday. There, the second versicle of the first station in the Sarum use followed Isaiah 63:1 in presenting Christ's humility: 'gradiens virtutibus non in equis bellicosis nec in altis curribus'.[69] Liturgy, however, strongly diverges from preaching in regards to difficult biblical readings. While sermons addressed biblical conundrums explicitly, highlighting contradictions and expanding upon possible solutions, liturgical chants made only sparing reference to the contrast between Christ and ass. No reference was made to the existence of two animals (apart from in the biblical lesson itself), and the question of which animal had been ridden by Christ was completely avoided. In Germany such a simplification became tangible in the form of the *Palmesel*, a life-size sculpture of a single animal which was employed in Palm Sunday processions. Visual images took their cue from the liturgy and images of Christ's entry to Jerusalem commonly depict a single animal (Plate 1, Figures 3–4); the few images to present two animals (e.g. Figure 2) raise no doubts regarding the hierarchy between the animals, as well as their role in carrying Christ. This stands in stark contrast to Advent Sunday sermons, which not only noted the number of animals but celebrated their importance and wrestled with its logic.

On biblical quotations

Interpretations of place names, expansion of the biblical difficult readings, or integration of extra-biblical narratives enabled preachers to expand upon the biblical *thema* and to structure their sermons. The vast majority of biblical components in sermons, however, are not taken from the pericope, but rather employed as proofs to substantiate each of the preacher's arguments. Dozens of biblical allusions appear in a single sermon and recent studies have demonstrated how some preachers employed on average thirty-seven or even eighty-three quotations within a single sermon.[70] This profusion of biblical quotations and allusions was far from accidental. Medieval sermons were deemed to be a fabric woven (*texitur*) from biblical materials, an image traced by Simon Tugwell to Bernard of Clairvaux (d. 1153) and Humbert of Romans (d. 1277), the fifth Master General of the Dominican order.[71] Such an image allows for a seamless transfer of authority from Bible to sermon; it exemplifies how proofs were envisioned as means of assuring that each and every part of the sermon is rooted in the Bible, rather than a clerical invention. The ways in which medieval preachers wove biblical proofs together are far from evident. A close analysis reveals that biblical verses were truncated and removed from their original context; that preachers' choices and flexible understanding of the Bible assisted in linking Bible, doctrine, and audience.

The modern theory of allusions can assist – to a degree – in the study of biblical proofs. Literary scholars have employed the following definitions: a *marker* is the textual element by which an allusion is evoked (as in the few biblical words in a sermon); a referent is the original text (the biblical verse or chapter, from which the marker is taken); and *key qualities* are elements within the referent that are to be identified and appreciated by the audience. Thus, the marker is meant to evoke the memory of the referent, in order to retrieve key qualities.[72] The interaction of marker, referent, and key qualities is applicable to medieval sermons; the playfulness in identifying and retrieving allusions is likewise key in the construction and the reception of sermons. Still, medieval preachers often did not expect their audience to retrieve the biblical referent, especially when addressing the laity. Rather, biblical proofs were primarily a source of authority, whose exact context was of secondary value. In many cases, especially when addressing a lay audience, the most important – if not only – key quality of the referent was its sacrality. Biblical allusions nevertheless reveal the aesthetics of preachers and their engagement with their audience. A typical biblical proof appears in Waldeby's third major division ('Fire of Love', as the Apostles placed garments on the ass): '"vestimenta sternebant in via" (Mt 21:8), id est virtutum opera ostenderunt ad bonum exemplum proximorum et non ad vanam gloriam iuxta id quod precipitur Mt. quinto: "nesciat sinistra tua &c." [Mt 6:3]'.[73] Waldeby's marker, a truncation of the biblical verse 'nesciat sinistra tua' (with added 'quid faciat' in B), is taken from Mt 6:3 'Te autem faciente eleemosynam, nesciat sinistra tua quid faciat dextera tua' ('But when thou dost alms, let not thy left hand know what thy right hand doth'). It retains a few biblical words, but renders it meaningless on its own. The marker suffices to identify the biblical quotation, but in order to fully grasp Waldeby's aim one needs to acknowledge the verse in full. Only then the necessary morality, the anonymity of almsgiving, is revealed. Preachers, reading the manuscript in preparation for future sermons, could have followed the biblical reference in a Late Medieval Bible with its newly integrated chapter division. In the course of oral delivery, preachers could then expand such an allusion without leaving any trace in the manuscript. The popularity of the Sermon on the Mount, however, suggests that a clerical audience, such as Waldeby's students at York, were able to identify the verse and integrate its moral into the sermon's fabric even upon oral delivery of the truncated marker. The way the marker is truncated retains a memorable device from Matthew's account – a hand lacking knowledge – further supporting this possibility. The role of the marker is not to verify the preceding biblical verse of the pericope, as it needs no authorisation. Rather, it supports the preacher's own interpretation of it, in this case Waldeby's emphasis on the anonymity of charity in contrast with vainglory. The allusion serves to present the preacher's ingenuity as rooted in the Bible, marginalising his interpretative role as biblical mediator. By the truncation of the marker, readers are left to seek the original biblical verse, either in manuscript or from memory. Having done that, they can then turn back to the sermon and acknowledge the authority of the preacher's argumentation, in a process reminiscent of modern scientific experiments.

Proofs refer to biblical narratives, as well as to biblical texts. In the macaronic sermon an allusion is made to Noah's Flood, but without relying directly on the text of Genesis: 'Ista enim persona Christi incarnata est signum federis quod posuit Dominus cum Noe quando benedixit ei. Cuius tres colores sunt tres nature, quod et bis curvatur ad terram et in medio elevatur ad celum, quia in ingressu est humilitatus ad carnem, in egressu autem in mortem, cuius cum tota conversatio est in celis per iugem Dei contemplationem.'[74] The marker is the rainbow, which is taken from the story of the Flood. It brings to mind both the biblical promise and the natural phenomenon. Thus, for an audience familiar with the biblical story, the marker reminds of God's covenant; for those deprived of such knowledge, the marker portrays the natural phenomenon, whose shape is key in the preacher's description of pious life.

Noah's Flood and the Sermon on the Mount are examples of popular biblical stories that appeared in visual images, biblical drama, and liturgical chants. Other proofs employ less well-known stories. In the macaronic sermon the two Advents (the Incarnation and the Second Coming) are explained using a verse from the Book of Judges[75]:

Macaronic (Fletcher p. 227)	*Jgs 1:15*
Unde in figura huius, Axa filia Caleb accepit in benedictionem irriguum superius and inferius: hoc est gratiam in presenti et gloriam in futuro.	At illa [Axa filia Caleb] respondit: Da mihi benedictionem, quia terram arentem dedisti mihi: da et irriguam aquis. Dedit ergo ei Caleb irriguum superius, et irriguum inferius.

The blessing of Caleb (a companion of Joshua) to his daughter cannot be construed as a major biblical event, nor one that even those fluent in the biblical text would have identified effortlessly. Knowledge of the story and its connection to the conquest of the Promised Land is irrelevant for the preacher's argument. Only the juxtaposition of 'upper' and 'lower' is of value to the analysis of the two Advents. Unlike the previous examples, the importance of this biblical referent lies not with its content but rather with its wording. The Bible serves here merely as a source of authority, acknowledged, if not identified, by members of the audience. Such use of the biblical text is highly functional, and is indicative of the rhetoric that incurred the criticism of reformers and modern scholars alike, who saw in it the neglect of the biblical text and its spirit.

The removal of biblical allusions from their context led to the creation of chains of seemingly unrelated elements. These demonstrate a unique form of biblical aesthetics, as evident in Waldeby's third major division[76]:

Waldeby (D 27v–28r; B 79va–b)	*Bible*
Non enim dominus dignatur nudo sedere equo vel asino quia in contemptum ductus ad suspendium taliter cogitur sedere	

Waldeby (D 27v–28r; B 79va–b)	*Bible*
Apocalypse ultimo: 'Beatus qui custodit vestimenta sua ne nudus ambulet'.	Ecce venio sicut fur. Beatus qui vigilat, et custodit vestimenta sua, ne nudus ambulet, et videant turpitudinem ejus (Rv 16:15)
Quasi diceret equivalenter 'beatus qui audit verbum dei et custodit illud'.	at ille dixit Quinimmo beati qui audiunt verbum Dei et custodiunt (Lk 11:28)
De hiis vestibus locutio apostolus ad Ephes. 5 dicens 'induite vos sicut electi dei misericordias et benignitatem &c'	Induite vos ergo, sicut electi Dei, sancti, et dilecti, viscera misericordiæ, benignitatem, humilitatem, modestiam, patientiam (Col 3:12)

Waldeby employs three separate biblical verses to explain why the Apostles placed garments on the ass ridden by Christ. This closely knit array of proofs immediately follows Waldeby's argument, and is made up of a true biblical fabric, a chain of allusions preceded only with a few of the preacher's words.As the readers progress through the array of biblical allusions and quotations, the preacher's meaning unfolds. All proofs rationalise adorning the ass and its symbolism. The first proof is linked to the pericope through the repetition of a single word – *vestimenta*. It is then linked to the second in a verbal echo – *beatus qui* – while the third is applied again to the theme of garments through the image of dressing oneself. The proofs enable Waldeby to present the Apostles' act as an allegory for hearing God's words and performing acts of charity. The biblical verses are modified in their new environment, with truncation, change of case, and a move between plural and singular. Such modifications cannot be accorded to lack of biblical knowledge, as Waldeby had access to biblical manuscripts and aids, and some of his other proofs are made from immaculate biblical quotations.[77] The juxtaposition of Mt 21:7–8 and Rv 16:15 even relies on the appearance of a single word in both (*vestimenta*), a connection which fits perfectly with the use of a biblical concordance such as the one available to Waldeby at York. It is therefore important to note that Waldeby's modifications of the biblical text are not random: the verbal echo connecting the first and second proofs relied on the modification of the biblical verse, from *beati qui* to *beatus qui*.

The accuracy of biblical quotations varies significantly. As a rule they follow the translation of the Vulgate, and, when supplied, chapter numbers match the Langtonian division (albeit with minor variations). Waldeby's degree of freedom with the biblical text was shared by other preachers, as can be seen in Odo's analysis of the ass's tough skin which prevents it from feeling the devil's wounds:[7]

Odo (Spencer p. 654)	*Proverbs 23:35*	*Song of Songs 5:7*
Unde salomon 'Perces-serunt me et non dolui, vulneraverunt me et non sensi'	Et dices: Verberaverunt me, sed non dolui; traxerunt me, et ego non sensi. Quando evigilabo, et rursus vina reperiam	invenerunt me custodes qui circumeunt civitatem percusserunt me vulner-averunt me tulerunt pallium meum mihi custodes murorum

The vagueness of the referent, alluding to Solomon rather than to a specific book, constitutes a surprisingly accurate depiction. The proof draws simultaneously on the Song of Songs and Proverbs, both attributed to Solomon. It preserves the wording of both verses, as well as the division and parallelism of Proverbs. Odo's use of the biblical text is quite liberal but retains enough key words to enable identification by an educated audience. These two examples are but the tip of an iceberg in the variety of modifications of biblical proofs. Proofs are altered constantly in sermons, as plural is changed to singular, singular to plural, cases transformed, adverbs and conjunctions omitted, and verses truncated. Such modifications enabled preachers to integrate biblical quotations into the fabric of their sermons and helped endow their arguments with biblical authority.

The modification of biblical proofs stands in stark contrast to the use of the *thema*.[79] In tune with *ars praedicandi* treatises, whenever a pericope or *thema* is evoked in the sermon, it takes the form of a verbatim quotation, keeping close to the biblical text. *Themata* were taken solely from the Bible, and there is evidence to suggest the audience's disapproval at a preacher's breaking this custom.[80] Furthermore, as evident in numerous means of amplification and ways of expanding themata into sermons, elements such as case and suffix in the *thema* were deemed of the utmost importance, and merit further analysis. Addressing the goal of the Apostles' mission – the village or fortress (*castellum*) – Odo remarks: 'Castellum dim(i)nutive … Mistice per castellum intellige mundum, quia "Diminute sunt veritates a filiis hominum" (Ps 11:2). Ideo potius "castellum" quam "castrum" vocatur, unde in Ecclesiaste mundus civitas parva dicitur (cf. Eccl 9:14).'[81] The biblical diminutive of *castellum* (rather than the noun *castrum*) assists Odo in his interpretation of the village or castle as the world. In this he highlights the suffix of the biblical word, taken up by the 'diminutive' of the Psalms and the smallness of the city in Ecclesiastes.[82] Such use underscores the injunctions of *ars praedicandi* treatises not to change or modify the biblical *thema*. The attention to every minute detail of the *thema* is in sharp contrast to the modifications that enabled preachers to accommodate proofs into their sermons; the gap between the two attests once more to the creativeness of preachers, and to their utilitarian use of the Bible.

Conclusion: beyond preaching the liturgy

In the macaronic sermon, at the third division of the Trinity (the Holy Spirit, as manifested in light and leading to the Last Judgement), the same biblical quotation appears twice within a short space of time:[83]

Macaronic (Fletcher, pp. 226, 227)	*Luke 1:35*
Lyht, dico, non ab illuminando, sed a condescendendo. Quia 'Spiritus sanctus superveniet in te, et virtus Altissimi obumbrabit tibi.'	Et respondens angelus dixit ei: Spiritus Sanctus superveniet in te, et virtus Altissimi obumbrabit tibi. Ideoque et quod nascetur ex te sanctum, vocabitur Filius Dei
...	
Nisi enim Sancti Spiritus gratia corda nostra visitando preveniat et ad nos condescendendo perveniat, nequaquam corda nostra Dei Filius inhabitat. Et hoc est quod angelus ad Mariam querentem quomodo Dei Filium nedum carne sed et corde conciperet, respondit 'Spiritus Sanctus superveniet in te' et sic 'quod nascetur ex te Sanctum vocabitur Filius Dei.'	

Luke's angelic response to Mary helped the preacher stress the need to receive the Holy Spirit into the heart of each and every believer. Its place within the sermon receives a new meaning when we consider the time for the sermon's delivery. Advent Sunday, with its commemoration of the First Coming, entailed several chants that elaborated upon this biblical theme. One of these was 'Hail Mary, full of grace', the fourth responsory (liturgical chant often sung as a sequence of versicles and responsories) of the second nocturn (part of the night office) in the Sarum use: 'Ave Maria gratia plena: dominus tecum. Spiritus Sanctus superveniet in te, et virtus Altissimi obumbrabit tibi. Quod enim ex te nascetur sanctum: vocabitur filius dei.'[84]

The Holy Spirit is thus presented through the figure of Mary (after the sermon has elaborated on the Father and the Son). Although appearing at first to be a clear biblical allusion, this comparison echoes the day's liturgy and blurs the distinction between the Bible and its liturgical re-enactment.

In Odo's sermon a comparison between the qualities of Mary and the Mount of Olives relies on a clear liturgical proof: 'Alta per eminentiam vite, quoniam *Super choros angelorum exaltata est ad celestia regna*'.[85] The versicle 'Super choros angelorum' was chanted on the Feast of the Assumption, and ties in perfectly with the Marian emphasis in this part of the sermon. Unlike other biblical and non-biblical proofs, the liturgical text is not preceded by a reference, and a certain degree of audience familiarity is assumed. The proof was retained by the Middle English redactor, who supplied both the Latin and a translation of the versicle, alluding to the way the liturgy was known as a chanted text, whose Latin was integral to its performance. The Marian emphasis of the two liturgical proofs is of little wonder. Mary's centrality in the Middle Ages, appealing especially during the season of Christ's Advent, is at odds with her minor appearance in the Bible. Preachers, seeking an authoritative text to substantiate their Marian emphases, found in the liturgy an invaluable resource.

Beyond textual allusions, sermons made reference to the practice of the liturgy. In Odo's sermon a detailed comparison is made between three liturgical processions: the feast of Purification, Palm Sunday, and Ascension. An allegorical interpretation of these feasts ensues with regard to their time (an astronomical view of the dragon's tail of Revelation 12:4), their paraphernalia (lights, branches and flowers, flags and crosses), the receivers of Christ (the Elder Simeon, children, angels), and the vehicle on which Christ was carried (Mary and Joseph's arms, ass, cloud). This lengthy comparison is reminiscent of extra-biblical narratives in the way it employs well-known imagery to support an elaborate division. It once more blurs the boundaries between Bible and liturgy in presenting liturgical re-enactment as part of the biblical narrative and in highlighting elements foreign to the biblical narrative, such the liturgical paraphernalia of Purification and Ascension or the children of Palm Sunday.

The link between liturgy and preaching runs deep, and one can discern an intentional blurring of the two. Beyond proofs and divisions sermons embedded liturgical echoes and prayers. Early medieval sermons ended with benedictions, and the new form of preaching prescribed an additional prefatory prayer, known as prologue or *antetheme*, as well as a concluding prayer. Basevorn, who commented upon these initial and final prayers, also suggested integrating a vocal echo from the *thema* into the prayer, deepening the connection between sermon and liturgy and between preaching and praying.[86] The blurring of the boundaries was not foreign to preachers in Late Antiquity and the early Middle Ages. Augustine even punned on the Latin word *orator*, which can mean both an orator and one who prays: 'sit orator antequam dictor'.[87] The link between the two media was firmly ingrained. Liturgy gave sermons not only content, but provided their context as well. Sermons were typically preached during Mass, between the Gospel reading (which was expounded in the sermon) and the canon of the Mass. The sermon was thus surrounded by liturgical actions, space, and actors: the priest, administering the sacraments, was also responsible for preaching; traditionally sermons were preached within the confines of the church, from pulpits, or from sacred locations on its outskirts (such as the churchyard cross, a sacred location for the procession of Palm Sunday discussed in Chapter 1).

Liturgical time influenced the very essence of the sermon. It dictated which biblical books were used most commonly as *themata*: the Gospels and Epistles, the biblical books most frequent as lessons for the Mass.[88] This move not only prescribed texts but carried with it an important undercurrent. Pericopes were linked to liturgical occurrence by an implicit allegorical interpretation.[89] Thus, for example, Advent Sunday was tied to Christ's Entry to Jerusalem, both manifestations of Christ's arrival; the Feast of the Holy Maccabees (1 August) employed Luke chapter 12 and Psalm 132, addressing themes of martyrdom and brotherhood pertinent for the torture and death of the seven brothers (2 Maccabees chapter 7). The pericopes cannot therefore be taken at face value as mere biblical episodes. They supplied preachers with a biblical excerpt alongside an inherent tension between text and liturgical occurrence. Preachers thus commented upon both biblical text and its occasion, the timing of the sermon. Preaching continued the exegetical impulse that had linked pericopes and liturgical worship. This link is evident in the construction of individual sermons. It also underpins the structure of entire sermon collections, which commonly follow the sequence of the liturgical year, rather than that of the Bible.[90]

The removal of biblical texts from their immediate context is evident in the liturgical nature of the pericope, as in the 'liberal' use of biblical proofs, or the deployment of definitions and extra-biblical materials. It emerged from the need to accommodate the Bible into a very different environment from that of ancient Israel, the same need that made allegorical interpretation a necessity. By juxtaposing biblical names and their definitions, as well as by linking pericope and feast, preachers created an interpretative gap. They opened up cracks within the biblical episodes, which were then filled with their own exploration of doctrinal elements (deemed the true essence of the Bible). The story of Christ's entry to Jerusalem does not contain any reference to his Advent, and preachers had to find creative ways of connecting the villages on the slopes of Mount of Olives, or the ass on which he had ridden, with the Incarnation and Last Judgement. Typological understanding and the use of allegories, an integral part of the Christian mindset already from the time of the New Testament, were paramount to medieval preachers.

Cracks within biblical narratives were often found in the complex readings of the biblical text. Such contradictory readings and conundrums, happily disregarded in the liturgy and visual images, joined extra-biblical elements and forced interpretation of words to present a very specific view of the Bible. Sermons were not constructed primarily to elucidate the biblical text. Rather, preachers employed the Bible to support their dissemination of church doctrine, typically moral admonition. As in Alain of Lille's image, the Bible became Jacob's ladder, on which preachers climbed seeking to transmit sacred truths and moral admonitions. Seeing the Bible as means, rather than an end, concurs with what was expected of the laity in the Middle Ages. Church councils and legislation stressed the need for lay knowledge of morality, but marginalised any grasp of the Bible expected of them.[91] This led to a very particular reading of the Bible. In providing moral and doctrinal lessons preachers presented conflicting readings and employed major and minor divisions to transform even the shortest biblical reference into an elaborate narrative, interspersing seemingly disconnected biblical quotes and allusions on their way. Such use of the Bible, however, should not lead us down the path of medieval and modern reformers lamenting the decline of the Bible in late medieval sermons. Medieval preachers did not consider their tropological understandings to be superimposed on the Bible, but rather saw them as intrinsic to the biblical text, the means of unveiling its innermost mysteries. Furthermore, such functional use of the Bible had unexpected results for biblical knowledge. The need to identify conundrums and inconsistencies, means of amplification that relied on definitions and etymologies, and the constant desire to conflate even the smallest of biblical episodes led preachers to scrutinise each and every word of the Bible, to employ innovative biblical aids and concordances, and to question time and again the links between the Bible and their own environment.

The laments of reformers are indicative of the transformation biblical mediation underwent in the new form of preaching. Biblical pericopes are typically units of narrative, liturgical readings of clearly demarcated biblical episodes. Their line-by-line exploration in homilies preserved much of this narrative sense. In the new form of preaching, on the other hand, the use of *themata*, means of amplification, and the major and minor divisions led preachers to put aside the biblical narrative in favour of its textual essence. The aesthetics of division, permeating late medieval sermons, led to a shift of emphasis, removing biblical stories, texts, and images from their original context. The rainbow was no longer necessarily tied to the Flood, nor Axa to the story of her inheritance. The latter example demonstrates the ramifications of such use of the Bible. As verbal and formal agreements became important means of amplification, the entire Bible was regarded as a pool of words and sentences. Biblical proofs were chosen from the most minor of biblical episodes, truncated and modified in their new setting. This function enabled preachers to weave a biblical fabric, which sanctioned (and camouflaged) their own message. The new paratext of Late Medieval Bibles was thus put into practice, enabling quick identification and retrieval of textual divisions. In this context the reason for the overwhelming popularity of the *Interpretations of Hebrew Names* becomes evident. That biblical glossary, especially in its most popular rendering (*Aaz*), enabled preachers to destabilise a biblical narrative through the elaboration of a single word. By supplying several definitions for a single word, it assisted preachers to accommodate the Bible to their own argument. Thus, place names on Christ's path to Jerusalem supported the value of oral confession, tears, or repentance, or became an allegory for the Incarnation. In a time of changes in biblical knowledge and dissemination, preachers drew from the depths of the biblical text in order to accommodate the Bible to the tenets of Christian faith and to chastise their audience. The three sermons analysed here are but the tip of an iceberg that is still mostly obscured by the dearth of critical editions of sermons (whether in print or in digital forms). On other liturgical feasts preachers wrestled with different biblical texts, but the sermons they produced are still indicative of the same form of mediation. Sermons for saints' days, exploring a non-biblical event through a biblical *thema* and array of proofs, or *ad status* sermons with their strong links between biblical past and medieval present, employed similar strategies in rendering the Bible relevant for their audience. Preachers engaged time and again with the Bible in their exploration of the biblical text. In doing so they developed an understanding of the Bible as a complex and fascinating text, an understanding worthy of sharing with their clerical – as well as lay – audiences.

Notes

1 Above, Chapter 1, pp. 48–9.

2 Bériou, *L'avènement des maîtres*, i:480.

3 Louis-Jacques Bataillon, 'Similitudines et exempla dans les sermons du XIIIe siècle', in *The Bible in the Medieval World: Essays in Memory of Beryl Smalley*, ed. Katherine Walsh and Diana Wood, Studies in Church History, Subsidia 4 (Oxford, 1985), pp. 191–205; 'De la lectio à la praedicatio. Commentaires bibliques et sermons au XIIIe siècle', *Revue des sciences philosophiques et théologiques* 70 (1986), 559–75; 'Early Scholastic and Mendicant Preaching as Exegesis of Scripture', in *Ad Litteram: Authoritative Texts and Their Medieval Readers*, ed. Mark D. Jordan and Kent Emery, Jr, Notre Dame Conferences in Medieval Studies 3 (Notre Dame, IN, 1992), pp. 165–98.

4 For an overview see: John W. O'Malley, SJ, 'Introduction: Medieval Preaching', in *De ore Domini: Preacher and the Word in the Middle Ages*, ed. Thomas L. Amos, Eugene A. Green, and Beverly Mayne Kienzle (Kalamazoo, 1989), pp. 1–11. On the *protheme*: Johannes Baptist Schneyer, *Die Unterweisung der Gemeinde über die Predigt bei scholastischen Predigern: Eine Homiletik aus scholastischen Prothemen* (Munich, Paderborn, and Vienna, 1968).

5 Owst, *Literature and Pulpit*, p. 66.

6 Towards the end of the Middle Ages, and especially in the early modern period, sermons began also to circulate as devotional literature, devised for private contemplative reading.

7 Nicole Bériou, 'Latin and the Vernacular: Some Remarks About Sermons Delivered on Good Friday During the Thirteenth Century', in *Die deutsche Predigt im Mittelalter. Internationales Symposium am Fachbereich Germanistik der Freien Universität Berlin vom 3.–6. Oktober 1989*, ed. Volker Mertens and Hans-Jochen Schiewer (Tübingen, 1992), pp. 268–84; Malcolm B. Parkes, 'Tachygraphy in the Middle Ages: Writing Techniques Employed for "Reportationes" of Lectures and Sermons', *Medioevo e Rincascimento* 3 (1989), 159–69 (reprinted in *Scribes, Scripts and Readers: Studies in the Communication, Presentation and Dissemination of Medieval Texts*, London, 1991, pp. 19–34).

8 Bériou, *L'avènement des maîtres*, i:504.

9 Lawrence T. Martin, 'The Two Worlds in Bede's Homilies: The Biblical Event and the Listeners' Experience', in *De ore Domini*, pp. 27–46 (27–8). A similar statement, again with reference to modern preachers, was made by d'Esneval, 'Instrument de travail', p. 164.

10 Patrick J. Horner, 'Preachers at Paul's Cross: Religion, Society, and Politics in Late Medieval England', in *Medieval Sermons and Society: Cloister, City, University, Proceedings of International Symposia at Kalamazoo & NY*, ed. Jaqueline Hamesse et al. (Louvain-la-Neuve, 1998), pp. 261–82; *Wimbledon's Sermon. Redde rationem villicationis tue: A Middle English Sermon of the Fourteenth Century*, ed. Ione Kemp Knight, Duquesne Studies, Philological Series 9 (Pittsburgh, PA, 1967), pp. 80–3; Wenzel, *Latin Sermon Collections*, pp. 45–9 (Brinton), 171–4 (Wimbledon); *The Sermons of Thomas Brinton, Bishop of Rochester, 1373–1389*, 2 vols, ed. Mary A. Devlin, Camden Soc. 3rd ser. 85–6 (London, 1954), i:42–8 (Sermon 12), ii:454–8 (Sermon 99).

11 E. W. Kemp, 'History and Action in the Sermons of a Medieval Archbishop: The Bishop of Chichester', in *The Writing of History in the Middle Ages: Essays Presented to Richard William Southern*, ed. R. H. C. Davis and J. M. Wallace-Hadrill (Oxford, 1981), pp. 349–65.

12 Brian J. Levy, 'Cheriton, Odo of (1180s–1246)', in DNB.

13 'Middle English Sermons', in *The Sermon*, dir. Beverly Mayne Kienzle, Typologie des sources du Moyen Age occidental, Fasc. 81–3 (Turnhout, 2000), pp. 597–660.

14 Alan J. Fletcher, '"Benedictus qui venit in nomine Domini": A Thirteenth-Century Sermon for Advent and the Macaronic Style in England', *Mediaeval Studies* 56 (1994), 217–45; reprinted with a revised discussion in: Fletcher, *Late Medieval Popular Preaching in Britain and Ireland: Texts, Studies, and Interpretations*, Sermo: Studies on Patristics, Medieval, and Reformation Sermons and Preaching 5 (Turnhout, 2010), pp. 33–66.

15 'The Father sends, appropriately speaking, with wonderful might, the Son with pure right, the Holy Ghost with blessed light. Correspondingly by this went the Son, at first into mankind, secondly into man's mind, thirdly into Judgment' (Fletcher, 'Benedictus qui venit', 225).

16 Linda E. Voigts, 'What's the Word? Bilingualism in Late-Medieval England', *Speculum* 71:4 (1996), 813–26; Siegfried Wenzel, *Macaronic Sermons: Bilingualism and Preaching in Late-Medieval England* (Ann Arbor, MI, 1994).

17 'for introducing the youth, who are attached to me as students.' (D fols 2r–2v). Waldeby's sermon collection was analysed by: Yuichi Akae, 'A Study of the Sermon Collection of John Waldeby, Austin Friar of York in the Fourteenth Century' (PhD dissertation, University of Leeds, 2004), with an abridged version published as: 'A Library for Preachers: The Novum opus dominicale of John Waldeby OESA and the Library of the Austin Friars at York', *Medieval Sermon Studies* 49 (2005), 5–26. The collection was already alluded by Owst, *Preaching in Medieval England*, pp. 64–6, and discussed at length by: Wenzel, *Latin Sermon Collections*, pp. 40–4 (general), 625–30 (contents of the *dominicale*). For information on Waldeby's life: Jeremy Catto, 'Waldeby ,John (d. after 1372)', DNB. The sermon is extant in two manuscripts: Oxford, Bodleian Library, MS Laud misc. 77, fols 26r–28v (= D) and Oxford, Bodleian Library, MS Bodley 687, fols 79r–80r (= B). Indication for the use of the sermon on Palm Sunday appears on D, fol. 84v and B, fol. 99v.

18 'Fourth, that "He that is of God, heareth the words of God" (Jn 8:47). Note: failing appetite is a sign of sickness' (Fletcher,'Benedictus qui venit', 224).

19 'The Gospel is to be elucidated and preached to the laity for three reasons: first as this fulfils God's commandment; second, the audience becomes worthy of God's blessings; third, the Gospel itself holds good tidings. First we find in the last chapter of Mark: 'preach the Gospel to every creature' (Mk 16:15); second Luke 12: 'blessed are they who hear the word of God and keep it' (Lk 11:28); third we find that the Gospel is interpreted as good tidings – Luke 2: 'I bring you good tidings of great joy &c' (Lk 2:10). Therefore this Gospel, which describes the Advent of Christ in the flesh is for us good tidings, to such a degree that it shall lead us to salvation' (D, fols 26r–26v; B, fol. 79ra).

20 Augustine, *De Doctrina Christiana*, ed. and tr. R. P. H. Green (Oxford, 1995), pp. 196–285.

21 *The Book of Pastoral Rule and Selected Epistles of Gregory the Great Bishop of Rome*, ed. and tr. James Barmby (Oxford and New York, 1895), 24–71.

22 Marianne G. Briscoe, *Artes praedicandi* (with Barbara H. Jaye, *Artes orandi* = Typologie des sources du Moyen Age occidental fasc. 61, Turnhout 1992). These were described by: Th. M. Charland, *Artes praedicandi: Contribution à l'histoire de la rhétorique au moyen âge*, Publications de l'Institut d'Etudes Médiévales d'Ottawa 7 (Paris and Ottawa, 1936); James J. Murphy, *Rhetoric in the Middle Ages: A History of Rhetorical Theory from St Augustine to the Renaissance* (Berkeley, 1974, repr. Tempe, AR, 2001), especially ch. VI 'Ars Predicandi', pp. 269–355. Advocating caution in relying on the *artes* for the study of sermons is: David L. d'Avray, *The Preaching of the Friars: Sermons Diffused from Paris before 1300* (Oxford, 1985), pp. 178, 206. The use of *artes praedicandi* in the compilation of sermons was recently substantiated by: Yuichi Akae, 'Between *artes praedicandi* and Actual Sermons: Robert of Basevorn's *Forma praedicandi* and the Sermons of John Waldeby, OESA', in *Constructing the Medieval Sermon*, ed. Roger Andersson, Sermo 6 (Turnhout, 2008), pp. 9–32. Akae's detailed comparison between the sermons of John Waldeby and Robert Basevorn's *Forma praedicandi* assists in contextualising the works of these two English authors, which are discussed at length (though separately) in the present chapter.

23 Alanus de Insulis, *Summa de arte prædicatoria*, PL 210:109–98 (especially the Preface (col. 111), cap. 1 'de prædicatione' (111–14) and cap. 39 'Quibus proponenda sit prædicatio' (cols 184–5)); translated as: Alain of Lille, *The Art of Preaching*, tr. Gillian R. Evans (Kalamazoo, MI, 1981).

24 PL 210:111; Alain of Lille, *The Art of Preaching*, pp. 15–16.

25 'This is what is meant by the angels ascending and descending. Preachers are the angels who ascend when they preach about heavenly matters, and descend when they bend themselves to earthly things in speaking on behavior', PL 210:111; *The Art of Preaching*, pp. 17–18.

26 The image is evoked in: Claire M. Waters, *Angels and Earthly Creatures: Preaching, Performance, and Gender in the Later Middle Ages* (Philadelphia, 2004), pp. ix, 1–7; the applicability of angels to the study of mediation was raised, without referring to this image, by Debray, *Transmettre*, pp. 53–71 (*Transmitting Culture*, pp. 31–44).

27 'Preaching is an open and public instruction in faith and behavior, whose purpose is the forming of men; it derives from the path of reason and from the fountainhead of the "authorities"', §1 (PL 210:111, *The Art of Preaching*, pp. 16–17); Mark A. Zier, 'Sermons of the Twelfth Century Schoolmasters and Canons', in *The Sermon*, pp. 325–62 (325–7).

28 *Alexandri Essebiensis opera theologica*, ed. Franco Morenzoni and Thomas H. Bestul, CCCM 188:1 (Turnhout, 2004), pp. 29–30.

29 James J. Murphy, 'Rhetoric in Fourteenth-Century Oxford', *Medium Aevum* 34 (1965), 1–20 (= *Latin Rhetoric and Education in the Middle Ages and Renaissance*, Ashgate, 2005, §ix); Martin Camargo, 'Tria sunt: The Long and the Short of Geoffrey of Vinsauf's Documentum de modo et arte dictandi et versificandi', *Speculum* 74:4 (1999), 935–55; 'Beyond the Libri Cantoniani: Models of Latin Prose Style at Oxford University ca. 1400', *Mediaeval Studies* 56 (1994), 165–87 (182–3); John O. Ward, 'Rhetoric in the Faculty of Arts at the Universities of Paris and Oxford

in the Middle Ages: A Summary of the Evidence', *Bulletin Du Cange: Archivum Latinitatis Medii Aevi* 54 (1996), 159–231. I thank Rita Copeland for her assistance in this matter.

30 Briscoe, *Artes praedicandi*, p. 29 (expounded on pp. 58–60).

31 Thomas of Chobham, *Summa de arte praedicandi*, ed. Franco Morenzoni, CCCM 82 (Turnhout, 1988), p. 267 (ch. 7).

32 Latin: Robert of Basevorn, 'Forma praedicandi', in *Artes praedicandi*, ed. Charland, pp. 227–323; translation: Robert of Basevorn, 'The Form of Preaching', tr. Leopold Krul, in *Three Medieval Rhetorical Arts*, ed. James J. Murphy (Berkeley, 1971), pp. 109–215.

33 Above, Chapter 3, pp. 129–30.

34 'For sacred Scripture is closed by the mysteries of secrets, but opened through the ministries of preachers, because "the declaration of the word of God illumines and gives understanding to the little ones"', §21 ('Forma praedicandi' p. 256; 'Form of Preaching', p. 141).

35 Servus of Sint Anthonis, 'Preaching in the Thirteenth Century: A note on MS Gonville and Caius 439', *Collectanea Franciscana* 32 (1962), 310–24. I thank Bill Campbell for this reference.

36 Sermons 30, 31: *Iohannis Wyclif Sermones*, iv:256–62, 262–75.

37 'Preaching God's Word is the most spiritual act of edification of the church' (iv:256).

38 iv:257 (serpent), 261 (Gregory the Great, Chrysostom), 263 (Augustine), 270 (Grosseteste).

39 This follows in the footsteps of Dahan, 'Lexiques Hébreu-Latin', pp. 503–11, where the use of the *Interpretations* is discussed from an exegetical point of view.

40 As in the anonymous Franciscan treatise (above, p. 165) or in the treatise of William of Auvergne (d. 1249), Briscoe, *Artes praedicandi*, p. 31.

41 'pacific or the vision of peace; house of mouth or house of jaw, house at valley's mouth or house of jaws, Syriac not Hebrew' (BL, Additional MS 39,629, fols 585ra, 571rb).

42 'Bethany: a house of obedience, that of his suffering, if not the house of God's offering or the house of kindness offered to the Lord' (BL, Additional MS 39,629, fol. 571ra).

43 'At the foot of Mount of Olives there were two cities: Bethphage and Bethany. Bethphage is interpreted as the house of the mouth, or of jaws; Bethany the house of obedience. At first he came from Bethany, through Bethphage to Jerusalem, as Luke relates, instructing us through which way one should rise with fire to Heavenly Jerusalem. Of Bethany certainly, that is of obedience, we ought to pass to Bethphage, that is to oral confession [...] so that we shall be able to cross from Bethany through Bethphage to the vision of peace' (Spencer, 'Middle English Sermon', pp. 642–3).

44 *Preaching in the Age of Chaucer: Selected Sermons in Translation*, ed. and tr. Siegfried Wenzel, Medieval Texts in Translation (Washington, DC, 2008), p. 57.

45 'And so he came by Bethphage, that is to say a house of tears, from Bethany, that is humility, teaching us (in) what way we should travel to the City of Heavenly Peace (i.e. Heavenly Jerusalem). First by humility to do the will of God and to keep

his commandments [...] And so from humility, that is humble knowledge of sin, armed we should go by Bethphage, that is tears and weeping, with Christ to the Mount of Olives' (Spencer, 'Middle English Sermon', pp. 640–1).

46 Spencer, 'Middle English Sermon', p. 640 n 5. On the rejection of oral confession: J. Patrick Hornbeck II, *What Is a Lollard? Dissent and Belief in Late Medieval England* (Oxford 2010), pp. xvii, 61, 93, 142; Anne Hudson, *The Premature Reformation: Wycliffite Texts and Lollard History* (Oxford, 1988), pp. 294–9, for Lollard documents, and 'John Purvey: A Reconsideration of the Evidence for his Life and Writing', *Viator* 12 (1981), 355–80 (= *Lollards and Their Books*, London, 1985, §6), for an article on oral confession abjured by John Purvey.

47 '"and he came to Bethphage" (Mt 21:1), which is interpreted as house of the mouth, that is the Virgin's womb, in which a union was made of the human nature to the Word, just as the kiss of peace. As Bernard expounded this on the first Canticle "Let him kiss me with the kisses of his mouth etc."' (D 26v; B 79ra).

48 On Waldeby's marian devotion: Margaret J. Morrin, *John Waldeby, O.S.A., c.1315–c.1372, English Augustinian Preacher and Writer: With a Critical Edition of His Tract on the Ave Maria*, Studia augustiniana historica 2 (Rome, 1975 = *Analecta augustiniana* 35 (1972), 7–80; 36 (1973), 5–79; 37 (1974), 162–98).

49 'That Assumption, that joining in which God wanted to come together himself personally to a man, and to make the treatise of peace in the Virgin's womb or to unite nature with nature', Philippus de Harvengt, *Commentaria in Cantica Canticorum*, book 1, cap. 1 (PL 203:192). See also *Glossa ordinaria*, ii:708.

50 Similar images are: BL, Additional MS 15,253, fol. 172vb; BL, Royal MS 1 D.iv, fol. 249va; BL, Royal MS 1 D.i, fol. 272rb. The proximity between Mary and Christ is most visible in BL, Egerton MS 2867, fol. 282v.

51 Spencer, 'Middle English Sermon', pp. 657, 659.

52 'Et sicut oleum illuminat, pastit et sanat, sic Christe erat lux mundi, panis vite et medicus salvis eterne' (D 26v, B 79ra).

53 'In this method a tale from Augustine is more acceptable than a story from the Bible, provided it is novel and unusual. One from Helinandus, or from an author rarely considered, is more acceptable than one from Augustine or Ambrose. The reason for this is nothing else but the vain curiosity of men', §49 ('Forma praedicandi', p. 316; 'Form of Preaching', p. 207). For an analysis of this statement as evidence for a growing popularity for the study of the classics: Smalley, *English Friars*, p. 42.

54 Larissa Taylor, *Soldiers of Christ: Preaching in Late-medieval and Reformation France* (New York and Oxford, 1992), pp. 73–6. Similar conclusions were reached by Hervé Martin, *Le métier de prédicateur en France septentrionale à la fin du moyen âge (1350–1520)* (Paris, 1988), p. 246.

55 'This banquet is neither of fine meats not of an abundance of fish, but devotion and prayer, receiving Communion at God's table [also altar] and hearing the word of God' (Fletcher, 'Benedictus qui venit', p. 224).

56 Spencer, 'Middle English Sermon', p. 651.

57 D'Avray, *Preaching of the Friars*, pp. 43–4.

58 'Against the third, charity: for where there is love, all dissimulation recedes' (Rom 12:9a 'Let love be without dissimulation'), Spencer, 'Middle English Sermon', p. 646.

59 A similar strategy had guided Bernardino of Siena (d. 1444) to employ the image of a trousseau – a bridal box containing jewellry, pearls and a ring – in expounding the mystical union with Christ to the women of Florence. Bernardino da Siena, *Le Prediche volgari inedite, Firenze 1424, 1425, Siena 1425*, ed. P. Dionisio Pacetti, I Classici Cristiani 56 (Siena, 1935), p. 413. This metaphor is provided in parts by Adrian W. B. Randolph, 'Performing the Bridal Body in Fifteenth-Century Florence', *Art History* 21:2 (1998), 182–200. Many other visual images in Bernardino's sermons are analysed by Lina Bolzoni, *The Web of Images: Vernacular Preaching from Its Origins to St Bernardino da Siena* (orig. *La rete delle immagini: Predicazione in volgare dalle origini a Bernardino da Siena* (Turin, 2001), tr. Carole Preston and Lisa Chien (Aldershot, 2004), pp. 120–95. I thank Suzy Knight for bringing this to my attention.

60 'And thus through virtues should man's soul be made the castle of God', Spencer, 'Middle English Sermon', p. 646.

61 Lucy Freeman Sandler, *The Psalter of Robert de Lisle: In the British Library*, 1st paperback edn (London, 1999), pp. 84–5, 107–15; 'John of Metz, the Tower of Wisdom', in *The Medieval Craft of Memory: An Anthology of Texts and Pictures*, ed. Mary Carruthers and Jan M. Ziolkowski (Philadelphia, PA, 2002), pp. 215–25.

62 Jane Zatta, 'The "romance" of the Castle of Love', *Chaucer Yearbook: A Journal of Late Medieval Studies* 5 (1998), 163–85, at pp. 178–9. For the Castle of Love as means of amplification in medieval sermons see: Fletcher, *Late Medieval Popular Preaching*, pp. 166–71.

63 Above, Chapter 3, pp. 116–17; Carruthers, 'Ars oblivionalis'.

64 Foster, 'The Use of Zechariah'.

65 *Sancti Hieronymi presbyteri Opera. Pars I, Opera exegetica. 7, Commentariorum in Matheum libri IV*, ed. D. Hurst and M. Adriaen, CCSL 77 (Turnhout, 1969), p. 183; *Glossa ordinaria*, iv:66.

66 'By the ass (is understood) the synagogue, that was tamed completely under the yoke of law; in the colt the gentile people, that wanton without the law and untamed worshipped sundry gods [...] Note that the Lord did not sit on both at the same time, but mystically by faith on each nation. Many of the Jews (and many of the Gentiles) were converted, and (were made) one sheepfold and one shepherd (Jn 10:16). Similarly it is credible that God first rode the ass, afterwards the colt, as the history of the event signified shall advise' (Spencer, 'Middle English Sermon', pp. 647–50).

67 '"And there you shall find an ass and a colt with her" (Mt 21:2b) that is the Jewish nation weighted down under the burden of the law and the Pagan nation accustomed to no burden of law. "Loose them and bring them to me" (Mt 21:2c), Supply by true doctrine (or by the ass): the human nature will be united through the word. Verily the rider is superior, the ass inferior; the rider governs and leads, the ass is governed and led; the rider is calm, the ass agitated; such was of the divine nature that was superior and of the other nature regulated (that is led and is calm in the highest love). Behold therefore in the example of humility how much Christ fulfilled that prophecy: "Behold thy king cometh to thee, meek and sitting upon an ass &c." (Mt 21:5). And not only once, but Christ has humiliated himself continu-

ously in such a way that he has humiliated himself in sitting on the ass, that is on the human soul. Therefore Ecclesiast, "the soul of the just is the seat of wisdom"' (D 26v–27r; B 79rb).

68 The attribution is found in Augustine (e.g. *Enarrationes in Psalmos: Sermo I. De prima parte Psalmi* – PL 36:324) and Pseudo-Bede (*Liber proverbium*, PL 90:1091).

69 'walking in the greatness of his strength; not on war horses, nor in lofty chariots', see above, Chapter 1, pp. 29–30.

70 The former is presented in Thomas Falmagne's analysis of the mid-fourteenth-century sermons of the Cistercian Jean de Villers in Paris: 'Les instruments de travail d'un prédicateur cistercien', in *De l'homélie au sermon: Histoire de la prédication médiévale*, ed. Jacqueline Hamesse and Xavier Harmand, Publications de l'Institut d'études médiévales: Textes, études, congrès 14 (Louvain-la-Neuve, 1993), pp. 183–236 (197); the latter is based on Taylor's examination of 1,337 late medieval sermons (*Soldiers of Christ*, pp. 73–6).

71 Simon Tugwell, '*De huiusmodi sermonibus texitur omnis recta predicatio*: Changing Attitude towards the Word of God', in *De l'homélie au sermon*, pp. 159–68.

72 Carmela Perri, 'On alluding', *Poetics* 7:3 (1978), 289–307; Michael Leddy, 'Limits of Allusion', *The British Journal of Aesthetics* 32:2 (1992), 110–22; William Irwin, 'What Is an Allusion?', *The Journal of Aesthetics and Art Criticism* 59:3 (2001), 287–97.

73 '"(they) spread their garments in the way" (Mt 21:8), that is they displayed acts of virtue for the good example of neighbours, and not for vain glory, like that which is instructed in Mt 5: "let not thy left hand know, etc." [Mt 6:3]' (D 28r; B 79vb).

74 'Therefore that incarnated person of Christ is a sign of the treaty that God made with Noah when he blessed him. Its three colours are three natures, which are twice curved to the ground and in the middle elevated to the heaven, for in entry he is humiliated to the flesh, in exit to death, but all his manner of life is in heaven by the continual contemplation of God' (Fletcher, 'Benedictus qui venit', p. 226).

75

Macaronic (Fletcher p. 227)	*Jgs 1:15*
Therefore in that figure, Axa the daughter of Caleb accepted in blessing the upper and the nether watery ground: that is the grace in the present and the glory in the future.	But she [Axa] answered: Give me a blessing, for thou hast given me a dry land: give me also a watery land. So Caleb gave her the upper and the nether watery ground

76

Waldeby's Advent Sunday Sermon	*Bible*
The Lord did not think (it) fitting to sit on a naked horse or ass, because on such he was forced to sit, led in contempt, to his (own) hanging.	

Waldeby's Advent Sunday Sermon	*Bible*
Last (chapter) of the Apocalypse 'Blessed is he that watcheth his garments, lest he walk naked'	Behold, I come as a thief. Blessed is he that watcheth, and keepeth his garments, lest he walk naked, and they see his shame (Rv 16:15)
As though he was to say similarly 'blessed is he that hears the word of God and keeps it'.	But he said: Yea, rather, blessed are they who hear the word of God, and keep it (Lk 11:28)
About these vestments spoke the Apostle, Ad Epes. 5, 'put on as the elect of God mercies and kindness etc.'	Put ye on, therefore, as the elect of God, holy, and beloved, the bowels of mercy, benignity, humility, modesty, patience (Col 3:12)

77 Akae, 'Library for Preachers'. For accurate quotations see for example his use of Is 1:3 (D 27r–v; B 79rb–79va).

78

Odo (Spencer p. 654)	*Prv 23:35*	*Sg 5:7*
Therefore Solomon 'they struck me and I was not sensible of pain, they wounded me and and I felt not'	And thou shalt say: They have beaten me, but I was not sensible of pain: they drew me, and I felt not: when shall I awake, and find wine again?	The keepers that go about the city found me: they struck me: and wounded me: the keepers of the walls took away my veil from me

79 This distinction was explored by Bériou, *L'avènement des maîtres*, i:503.

80 Spencer, *English Preaching*, pp. vi–vii.

81 '*Castellum* (is) a diminutive [...] mystically you should understand *castellum* to be the world as 'truths are decayed (*diminute*) from among the children of men' (Ps 11:2/12:1). Therefore it is called *castellum* rather than *castrum* (castle), hence in Ecclesiastes the world is called a small town' (Spencer, 'Middle English Sermon', p. 644).

82 The link between the small city and the world relies on an additional layer of exegesis: *Glossa ordinaria*, ii:704.

83

Macaronic (Fletcher, pp. 226–7)	*Luke 1:35*
Light, I say, not by illumination, but by descent, since 'The Holy Ghost shall come upon thee, and the power of the most High shall overshadow thee'. ... Therefore the grace of the Holy Ghost shall not enter our hearts by visitation and arrive in us by descent, unless	And the angel answering, said to her: The Holy Ghost shall come upon thee, and the power of the most High shall overshadow thee. And therefore also the Holy which shall be born of thee shall be called the Son of God.

Macaronic (Fletcher, pp. 226–7)	*Luke 1:35*
God's son inhabits our hearts. And that is what the angel responded to Mary's complaint concerning the way she might conceive the son of God still less in the flesh but in her heart: 'The Holy Ghost shall come upon thee' and thus 'the Holy which shall be born of thee shall be called the Son of God'.	

84 *Breviarium ad usum insignis ecclesiae Sarum*, ed. Francis Procter and Christopher Wordsworth, Fasc. I (Cambridge, 1882), col. xxiv; cursus: http://cursus.uea.ac.uk/ms/stalbans#Alb2.01011000, accessed 3 March 2010; for other occurrences: Legg, *The Sarum Missal*, pp. 216 n. 1, 259. The responsory was chanted at the first nocturn in St Albans and at vespers in Ely.

85 'High through excellence of life, since *over the choirs of angels she was exulted to the heavenly kingdom*', Spencer, 'Middle English Sermon', p. 642 (n. 9 supplies the entry in the Sarum breviary). For the spread and variation of the Antiphon see also *Cursus*, Antiphon c2762 (http://cursus.uea.ac.uk/ed/c2762, accessed 3 March 2010).

86 Basevorn, §25; §47 ('Forma praedicandi', pp. 262–4, 307–10; 'The Form of Preaching', pp. 148–50, 198–200).

87 'he (the preacher) must be a man of prayer (orator) before becoming a man of words', Augustine, *De doctrina Christiana*, pp. 234–5.

88 For a detailed survey of high medieval sermons according to their biblical theme see *Repertorium der lateinischen Sermones des Mittelalters für die Zeit von 1150–1350*, 11 vols, ed. Johannes Baptist Schneyer (Münster, Westfalen, 1969–1990). An analysis based on mendicant preaching and liturgy can be found in Louis-Jacques Bataillon, 'Early Scholastic and Mendicant Preaching'.

89 Gy, 'La Bible dans la liturgie'. Events such as Palm Sunday, when the biblical pericope is re-enacted in the liturgy, are the exception rather than the rule.

90 For survey and analysis of late-medieval sermon collections: Siegfried Wenzel, *Latin Sermon Collections*.

91 Norman Tanner and Sethina Watson, 'Least of the Laity: The Minimum Requirements for a Medieval Christian', *Journal of Medieval History* 32:4 (2006), 395–423.

CONCLUSION

Digital editions, evoked in this book's introduction, have proved invaluable for the current analysis of Bibles and related texts. Search engines, scanned glosses, and virtual Bibles have assisted in the identification and retrieval of biblical snippets and allusions, in tracing chant variations and iconographic traditions. This, however, is a mixed blessing. The digital era has ushered in an unprecedented ease in consulting the Latin Bible, a change comparable to that of the Late Medieval Bible and its later dissemination in manuscript and print. Bibles and a universe of scholarly tools are now at one's fingertips, in a hitherto unknown immediacy. Such proximity has its own perils. The new technology brings one closer to the biblical text, but at the same time can remove the layers of mediation that have evolved around it for centuries. I do not wish to invoke here John Locke's lament for the introduction of verse and chapter division. Locke feared that the new technology detached readers from the earliest strata of the Bible. Currently, the opposite is taking place. Websites enable readers to tap into levels of biblical scholarship which have hitherto been the prerogative of a few. Users can now quickly compare episodes in the synoptic and apocryphal Gospels, consult a multitude of translations, or browse digital images of the earliest known Bibles in a quality that is imitating (and at times surpasses) that of an *in situ* examination.[1] In this new environment one can too easily create a boundary between the Bible and extra-biblical elements; the quick and easy identification of biblical snippets can exclude the strata of sensual qualities attached to its performance and depiction, drawing one away from the Bible as it was known and disseminated over the centuries. The current study of biblical mediation has revealed that channels of transmission were part and parcel of the medieval Bible, embedded into the understanding of the biblical text itself. Trying to differentiate between liturgical and biblical echoes, or between the 'pure' Bible and preachers' rhetoric, is therefore futile, as well as against the grain of medieval biblical knowledge. When sacred books were judged by their covers, and manuscripts encoded a very specific form of biblical knowledge, it was the medium that contributed associations, emphases, sensory and emotional experiences, in dialogue with the complexity and multiple layers of the Bible itself.

The shift of emphasis from origins to mediation reveals the unique characteristics of individual channels of transmission. Different media transmitted the Bible in very different ways. Liturgy and preaching were two of the most strongly connected forms of biblical mediation. They shared performative and textual elements, as well as a need to bring the Bible to life. Their perennial link did not, however, lead to a similar deployment of the Bible. The creation of a quasi-biblical language rendered biblical and liturgical texts inseparable, while the biblical fabric of sermons was woven with clearly demarcated proofs, relying on identifiable biblical references and quotation formulae. This distinction is reflected in the two media's manuscript culture: in sermons collections biblical components are singled out, clearly demarcated by quotation formulae and references (at times with a touch of colour or marginal notes directing readers to these allusions); in liturgical manuscripts, on the other hand, all texts – biblical or extra-biblical – are written similarly. Sermons presented biblical conundrums and contradictions, elements foreign to liturgical rites; preachers celebrated in the complexity of the biblical text, only glanced upon in liturgical spectacles. The crowd welcoming Christ on the outskirts of Jerusalem was too similar to that at Jesus's trial five days later. In the performance of Palm Sunday this was silently resolved by bringing in the children from the subsequent episode at the Temple. Preachers, on the other hand, celebrated such difficulties, at times complicating even the simplest biblical narrative almost beyond reckoning. The exact identity of the Apostles sent to retrieve the ass, the occurrences on their way, and the route taken by Christ were all explored by preachers at length, witnesses to the deep mysteries of the Bible. The existence of two animals on Christ's path to Jerusalem – emanating from Jerome's misinterpretation of the biblical text – exemplifies a bone of contention between liturgy and preaching. Whereas liturgical texts and performances made little reference to this difficult duality, preachers saw in it an opportunity to weave their own interpretation into the biblical narrative. These differences are at the core of the two media: the aesthetics of late medieval preachers had led them to employ an array of divisions and subdivisions, transforming biblical texts and narratives; biblical text and narratives assumed a new life in the liturgy, with their performance becoming an integral part of the biblical episode, a seamless unity of a quasi-biblical language, tunes and paraphernalia, actors and locations.

Different media transmitted the Bible differently. Yet, none functioned in a vacuum. The layout of biblical manuscripts conveyed a specific understanding of the biblical text, at times complemented by historiated initials, which often accompanied biblical books with an allegorical interpretation, akin to the prologues which preceded these book. Biblical manuscripts engaged in dialogue with other forms of mediation, primarily liturgy and preaching. Addenda such as the *Interpretations of Hebrew Names* and visual images of the Tower of Wisdom and the Wings of the Cherub befitted late medieval sermons and tied in with preachers' exploration of the biblical text. The same manuscripts often display elements of liturgical performance, as in the layout of the Psalms and church hymns, or in the incorporation of calendars, tables of readings, chants, and Mass-texts. Similarly, the red marks in a thirteenth-century Bible from Worcester (Cambridge University Library MS Kk.2.6, fols 81vb–84va) facilitated the dramatic reading of the Passion according to Matthew on Palm Sunday, placing this Bible at the heart of liturgical celebration. The joining of media is evident in other places as well. Middle English texts were an important means of transmitting biblical knowledge to less-Latinate audiences. These literary narratives convey liturgical traits alongside preaching techniques, demonstrating how different forms of biblical aesthetics came together. Thus, in *Piers Plowman* the latter is evident in the divisions of the Tower of Truth and the Castle of Care (Passus 1 and 5), as in the portrayal of biblical events in their medieval attire (e.g. the dubbing of Christ in Passus 18), and the former is evident in the profusion of liturgical spectacles, as in Christ's entry to Jerusalem.

The ways in which discrete media influenced one another are intricate and nuanced. The appearance of Late Medieval Bibles and the explorations of the new form of preaching came into being at the same time, both celebrating the textual qualities of the Bible. In liturgy and preaching, on the other hand, one can detect a certain directionality. Liturgical words and acts, prayers and allusion, were embedded into sermons. The opposite was not the case. Sermons were preached on the outskirts of liturgical performance, but did not permeate the very essence of the liturgy. Liturgical techniques and emphases were addressed by preachers; the aesthetics of the new form of preaching was not integrated into chant. This directionality is a testimony to the enduring powers of the liturgy, whose language and customs were deemed at times as ancient and as authoritative as the Bible itself. Performance and Bible became one, rendering the liturgy an extension of the Bible, rather than a separate entity. Sacrality and antiquity became the emblems of liturgical performance, and can thus explain the use of *textus*, whose iconic appearance and ancient bearings were at its very essence. The power of the liturgy shaped the way the Bible was retained in the memory of clerics and lay persons. This unique form of mnemonics influenced the appearance of biblical manuscripts, in which the Psalms did not undergo the changes initiated in the twelfth-century classroom.

Liturgical traits in Late Medieval Bibles were a remnant from an earlier era. The innovative features of these manuscripts were embraced by preachers, who found in them an extremely useful handbook. The new chapter division appears in preachers' aids and model sermons; some Bibles preserve marginal annotations made by preachers, typically depicting the divisions of biblical *themata*, indicative of the new form of preaching. The *Interpretations of Hebrew Names* was the standard addendum to biblical manuscripts, and its entries received a place of honour in late medieval sermons. The study of this glossary demonstrates the need to link origins and reception in the history of the medieval Bible. The link between biblical manuscripts and preaching explains the popularity of this glossary and its evolution. As the glossary came to incorporate more and more entries, and its definitions grew shorter and detached from the biblical text, its appeal to medieval preachers grew. The Middle English redactor of Odo of Cheriton, wishing to avoid the latter's emphasis on oral confession, simply replaced one entry in the *Interpretations* with the other, thus steering the path of the righteous soul in a direction more favourable to the adherents of Wyclif. Such a shift of meaning exemplifies the success of the last rendering of the *Interpretations*, whose succinct and multiple entries did not dictate a single strand of interpretation, but rather opened up numerous possibilities for preachers and exegetes to explore. The link between Late Medieval Bibles and the new form of preaching runs deeper than the practicalities of biblical access and interpretation. Both are witnesses to a significant shift in the nature of biblical knowledge and mediation – the move from narrative to text underpinning such textual divisions and etymologies. As lamented by Locke, the new textual divisions modified biblical reading and truncated earlier narratives. This was joined by the entries of the *Interpretations* in the *Aaz* rendering, which dissociated biblical words from their literary context. Changes in biblical manuscripts corresponded to the rise of the new form of preaching. The move from pericope to *thema* served to marginalise biblical narratives at the expense of biblical texts; means of amplifications and the conflation of a minor biblical component (a verse or even a single word) into a full sermon through major and minor divisions led preachers to scrutinise the biblical text, employing etymologies, exploring contradictory readings, and identifying verbal echoes. Lamented by contemporaries and later reformers as witnesses to the decline of biblical preaching, these sermons employed biblical proofs in a way that often dissociated them from their context.

Nevertheless, in weaving their ever-elaborate structures, preachers celebrated in the Bible's conflicting narratives its semitic origins, and explored its 'hypertext' qualities, in which each word could potentially be tied to any other. Late Medieval Bibles and sermons thus evolved in tandem and bear witness to a new form of engagement with the biblical text.

Preachers' explorations of biblical difficult readings and their deployment of biblical etymology are similar to the re-incorporation of the Psalms' superscriptions into biblical manuscripts. All are manifestations of the textual instability and ambiguity of the Bible, elements that have exerted the minds of medieval exegetes and modern scholars alike. One of the unexpected facets of the study of biblical mediation is the usefulness of questions and methodologies from the field of biblical criticism. Wilfred Cantwell Smith argued against the separation of biblical studies from religious history, and for the side-by-side study of origins and reception.[2] This assertion is most pertinent to the study of biblical mediation. Only by adopting the tools of modern biblical scholars can we become attuned to the intricacies of biblical texts and narratives. As demonstrated time and again (with the theoretical support of Ricoeur's study and its modification), the complexity of the biblical text is tied in with its mediation and reception. Inner biblical quotations and allusions are rife, and have influenced the appearance and use of Bibles. The four Gospels, each presenting a different account of Christ's life, were often read in parallel. The early use of the Eusebian canons enabled readers to navigate quickly between parallel episodes, and marginal references in Late Medieval Bibles filled a similar function. Matthew's description of Christ's entry relies on Zechariah's prophecy; this has been studied by modern scholars as the rationale for that entire New Testament episode, and by medieval exegetes as exemplifying Christ's messianic role and its Old Testament prefiguration. The link between the two texts, explored by medieval preachers, is infrequently depicted in marginal annotations in Late Medieval Bibles, and is even alluded to in the performance of the liturgy (*En rex venit*, in the first station of Palm Sunday).

Biblical criticism raises our awareness of the complexity of the biblical text, its different strata, and its genres. This diversity has affected its mediation, with discrete elements explored by exegetes, others transformed in chant, or depicted through a distinct layout in biblical manuscripts. A most striking example is the Psalms' superscriptions. These unique elements (almost completely unnoticed by modern scholars of the medieval Bible) have been studied for nearly two millennia. Their instability and distinct vocabulary have made them one of the least stable elements of the Bible, a peculiarity which renders them a useful yardstick in assessing how the Bible's appearance has fluctuated over time and facilitated discrete reading strategies. Distinctly different from the body of the Psalms, they were replaced or singled out, and manifest a tension between written and chanted texts. Different genres within the Bible have been mediated differently. Poetic elements, such as the body of the Psalms or the hymns of the Gospels, have appeared time and again in the liturgy; the layout of Lamentations in Late Medieval Bibles reflects its mnemonic roots. Many of these devices' original use and rationale was lost in translation. The verses of Lamentations no longer followed an alphabetical sequence, nor was the superscriptions' editorial role visible. Still these unique elements and their origins influenced their graphic depiction and further mediation. The beginning of the Gospel of John differs considerably from that of the Synoptic Gospels (Matthew, Mark and Luke, all presenting similar structures and narratives). It echoes tensions within the primitive church, pertaining to the divinity of Christ. Its strong messianic tone reverberates in enigmatic imagery and vocabulary. Such uniqueness ties in perfectly with its later use, when it became the cornerstone of talismanic uses of the Bible, inscribed in amulets or oath-books and used in incantations. The *longue durée* history of biblical compilation and reception thus assists in identifying how certain books (or elements within them) were more prone to appear in chant, others were mined for biblical role-models, while specific parts of the Bible befitted talismanic use, in traditions that could be traced to the very compilation of the biblical canon.

The complexity of biblical mediation warns against drawing a boundary too sharply between the experience of clergy and laity. The shadow cast by the Reformation's emphasis on *Sola scriptura* and the importance of lay biblical reading still influences studies of the medieval Bible. In assuming that the Reformation and its vernacular translations restored direct access to the Bible, one implies that such access had been denied and heavily guarded by the Catholic Church throughout the Middle Ages. Vernacular translations, moveable-type print, and rising levels of literacy did have an important impact on biblical knowledge. Yet, placing too much emphasis on the link between biblical translation and biblical knowledge is misleading. It suggests that while the medieval laity had no true knowledge of the Bible, the clergy enjoyed direct access to the 'naked text' of the Bible. Such a view relies on two underlying assumptions: the control embedded in biblical mediation and the existence of an unmediated biblical text – neither fully true for the medieval case. Church murals, liturgical rites, or vernacular sermons were a far cry from mere simplifications of the biblical text; rather, they often presented an intricate notion of biblical texts and stories, one that drew from the depth of its narratives while wrestling to convey its stories to a non-Latinate audience. Non-textual means of transmission presented complex and challenging views of the Bible, at times with delicate undertones and exegetical traces not far from those open to the clergy. The messianic undertones of the versicle *Hic est qui Edom venit*, chanted at the first station of Palm Sunday in the Sarum use, opened only to a narrow clerical audience the links between the First and Second Comings, between Isaiah's prophecy and the Passion. However, this understanding was evident for all to experience at that very moment in the procession, standing in the midst of a graveyard, awaiting the arrival of Christ in a liturgical moment that merged past, present, and future. Biblical mediation did not apply only to the laity. Priests were even more exposed to oral, textual, and material media, and came to rely on them in their understanding of the Bible. The Bible punctuated the life of the religious, as biblical lessons were read during Mass, in refectories, and in infirmaries, while Psalms were chanted day and night in monasteries and cathedrals. Educated priests knew the Psalter by heart, and such knowledge was steeped in the liturgy with its musical and performative strata. Biblical stories were likewise approached through a typological understanding evoked in exegetical works and taken up in manuscript illuminations, church murals, or stained glass windows. Thus, the narratives of the Song of Songs, a favourite reading among monastic communities, were seen as a map of salvation history, the route of the righteous soul, rather than the 'naked text' they convey. The existence of an unmediated text of the Bible is equally deceptive. Even the Latin-literate clerical elite who enjoyed access to biblical manuscripts, experienced the Bible through a carefully executed plan of layout and addenda. Subtle modifications of ink and script, glossaries, and summaries dictated a very specific understanding of the biblical text contained in these manuscripts.

Biblical mediation did not affect all audiences alike. The messianic undertones at the public performance of the first station of Palm Sunday were similar to those of glosses to Isaiah. The sensory experience of waiting for Christ in a graveyard nevertheless differed considerably from that of the *Glossa ordinaria*. The explicit fascination of exegetes with allegorical interpretation and their engagement with the literal sense of Scripture was an academic pursuit and an intellectual engagement. The laity, on the other hand, physically re-lived that biblical moment. At times the two worlds came into conflict. An argument on adorning the naked cross prior to the Mass reveals the tension between joy and mourning embedded into the liturgy of Palm Sunday. At times, different audiences were engaged simultaneously. Sermon collections presented a priestly audience with a manuscript form that enabled active readers to follow biblical references in biblical manuscripts; a lay audience was presented with a modified version of the same message, with preachers instructed in the need to accommodate their words to suit their audiences. The speech of Caiphas was part liturgical performance, part sermon; its lighthearted use of Latin and Middle English reveals how lay and clerical audiences were approached simultaneously, but also how each was presented with a different understanding of Bible and liturgy. While the laity was given a single tropological explanation of the palms, the address to the clergy followed Durand to the letter in expounding the wider variety of liturgical paraphernalia employed on the day. Such a mixed reality was evident for all in the distribution of palms earlier on that day. 'Real' palms were given to the high clergy while 'indigenous' ones were distributed to the rest. Gestures and objects likewise aggrandised the clergy in Masses and oath-rituals. Lay people touched oath-books attesting to the truth of their words, while priests were required only to acknowledge the book's existence. An inversion of these activities in the liturgy re-inforced the same social boundary. Priests enjoyed direct contact with Gospel books in the course of the liturgy, when lay men and women could only watch them from afar. Such a proximity, accompanied by liturgical activities which culminated in the intimacy of a kiss, endowed the priest with an aura of sacrality for the reading of the lesson and for its expansion in the subsequent sermon. It sanctioned the message of the priest and rendered his words truly biblical.

A prerequisite in the successful dissemination of the Bible, authority was a closely guarded key. It was employed primarily not to prevent the laity from unearthing the mysteries of the Bible (often regarded as the inherent truths of the Church) but rather to counter what were regarded as wrong interpretations and, worse still, to prevent the application of biblical authority outside official hierarchy. When John Ball, a renegade priest and leader of the 'Peasants' Revolt', preached 'when Adam delved (dug) and Eve span, who was then a gentleman' at the outskirts of London on June 1381, he drew on a common trope, used by preachers of impeccable orthodoxy.[3] For the thousands of rebels who descended on London the following day wishing to reform English church and society, his sermon grounded their claims in biblical authority. That revolt served as a catalyst, a reminder of the dangers of unsanctioned biblical mediation and lay theology. In its aftermath the Council of Blackfriars was convened in May 1382 to mark a new era in the fight against John Wyclif and his followers.

Although Wyclif had little to do with the revolt, his negation of the established church (a common trope among church reformers all through the Middle Ages) was seen in a different light after 1381. The radical transformation of the English church sought by the rebels, leading to their execution of the Archbishop of Canterbury (Simon Sudbury, also chancellor at the time), influenced attitudes to Wyclif's theology. The Council of Blackfriars therefore condemned Wyclif and was an early step in the identification and persecution of the Lollards, in a move that came to endorse a dichotomous view of biblical access in late medieval England and sought to safeguard biblical authority and mediation.

Lollards were commonly accused of refusing to swear upon the Gospels. Their negation of oaths and sacred books earned them the wrath of civic and ecclesiastical authorities, as it touched the very core of authority in churches and courts of law. The link between ritual activities and material Bibles underpinned religious and secular rituals. It reveals the similarities between the two systems. Legal and liturgical spectacles employed similar books to ascertain the truth of speech-acts, whether Gospel lessons or the testimony of witnesses and litigants. These sacred books, whose contents were secondary to their appearance, demonstrate not only parallels between these two highly analogous systems but also how law and liturgy converged in matter and custom. The few surviving oath-books from secular courts contain oath formulae and legal treatises, alongside quires from liturgical manuscripts, and boast an impressing crucifix on their binding. They were the secular equivalent of a *textus*, a book also judged by its binding, whose sacred texts were often accompanied by deeds, charters, and oath-formulae. The supply of oath-books to secular courts, mostly unmentioned in our sources, was a collaboration between religious communities and secular authorities, as in the Chester 'Jurybook', the oath-book of Mere, or the books and scrolls supplied by the Jewish community of York. Such merging of civic and religious spheres pertained also to the re-enactment of biblical scenes. The royal entry of Henry V after the Battle of Agincourt mirrored Christ's entry to Jerusalem (in its liturgical guise) and linked King and Christ, London and Jerusalem. Such uses combined the pious with the mundane, and, as evident in the *textus* bequeathed by Hubert de Burgh and adorned by Henry III, reflected both a temporal and a spiritual balance of power. Their study demonstrates the value and the need for further examination of law and liturgy, both in their parallel rituals and in points of convergence.

The rise of biblical pandects at the beginning of the thirteenth century revolutionised the appearance of Bibles ever since. The change they ushered in rendered many earlier manuscripts obsolete. Nevertheless, a unique class of earlier Bibles was still employed in the medieval rite. Gospel books, ancient and hallowed, were used as icons within the medieval church. Their legibility was secondary. Instead, their antiquity became an integral part of their sacrality, as evident in Chaucer's depiction of the 'Britoun book' or in the books used to facilitate the oaths of archbishops and canons in York Minster. Such talismanic use of *textus* in liturgy and oath-rituals has an unexpected outcome, and can explain the high survival rates of Anglo-Saxon Gospel books. Richard Marsden's survey of Anglo-Saxon Bibles gives evidence for 107 biblical manuscripts, out of which seventy-nine (over 73 per cent) are Gospel books.[4] Recalling the talismanic use of these books, we can now better understand this survival rate, which relied less on the practicalities of consultation, and more on sanctity and antiquity. This is exemplified in the York Gospels, the sole survivor of its kind from the Minster, which was kept through the turbulent years of the Dissolution owing to its role as the Minster's oath-book, in a custom that by now extends nearly a millennium. The modern custom, in which the book's glorious past is the reason for its use rather than its applicability to Anglican rite, is indicative of the medieval rite, when these books were superseded textually, but still employed as talismans.

The current synchronic investigation looks to a plateau of biblical mediation, a period of relative stability which followed the rapid changes of the early thirteenth century. Tranquillity, however, is always relative. Beneath the surface biblical mediation was slowly changing. Patterns of book ownership and use transformed gradually. The mass-production of Late Medieval Bibles created a vibrant markets of first- and second-hand books, many linked to the universities of Paris, Oxford, and Bologna. As these Bibles changed hands, they spread beyond monasteries, friaries, and cathedrals. From the mid-fourteenth century a gradual trickle of Bibles made its way to parish churches and private hands. The professional scribes and lay scriptoria that were primarily responsible for its creation sought new markets. With the rise of an educated laity, lay literacy and piety, new types of books appeared. Books of Hours offered the laity an experience akin to the monastic office (and its unique form of biblical mnemonics), while vernacular literature merged biblical imagery, liturgical traits, preaching and exegetical techniques. The move of biblical mediation into the lay sphere was partly the outcome of the rise of cities, changes in economy and society; in part it was caused by the friars, whose preaching disseminated the biblical word far and wide, into the cities and villages of medieval England. Against this background one should view the proliferation of Wycliffite Bibles at the close of the fourteenth century and the beginning of the fifteenth. These vernacular Bibles, which emulated the Late Medieval Bible in appearance and production, marked an important moment of transition, not necessarily in their heterodoxy, but rather in the shift of biblical dissemination and discourse beyond the confines of the church.

The Reformation and moveable-type print marked the end of the Middle Ages. They have influenced the afterlife of discrete biblical media. The trickle of Late Medieval Bibles and their Wycliffite counterparts became a flood of parish Bibles and family Bibles in the sixteenth century. Biblical paratext survived the advent of print and the Reformation to influence the appearance and use of Bibles ever since; other features, such as the new form of preaching or the *Interpretations of Hebrew Names*, quickly disappeared. The reception of biblical media did not follow their origins, but rather their adaptability and usefulness to a new environment. The same reformers who rejected medieval scholasticism were also the ones to employ the appearance of the Late Medieval Bible, which was the product of medieval classrooms and the biblical engagement typical of the mendicant orders. For them, elements such as running titles, chapters, and subdivisions (the latter becoming the norm in printed Bibles) furnished their attempt to put the Bible in every ploughboy's hand. These features, which had once worked in tandem with preachers' aids and concordances, were now seen also as providing access to the uninitiated. Other media followed a different course. The preservative powers of the liturgy have influenced its reception. As seen in the use of ancient *textus* or the unique layout of the Psalms, liturgical customs die hard. More perennial in nature, they appeal to the senses and lead to a unique form of biblical mnemonics which is slow to change. Much like the civic emulation of Christ's entry into Jerusalem, whose origins in *adventus* processions had long ceased to exist, the medieval use of palms lingered into modernity. Long after a steady influx of 'real' palms from the East was established, 'indigenous' palms were still employed and known as palms in nineteenth-century England; medieval psalmody, with its unique mnemonics, still influenced the way the Psalms were known and recalled, and English Bibles, as well as books of common prayer, had identified the Psalms by their Latin incipits for centuries after the Reformation.

Beyond individual components, biblical mediation at large did not end with the Middle Ages. Moveable-type print and the Reformation altered the dissemination of Bibles and the nature of biblical access, but did not eradicate the need for bridging the gap between Scripture and society in an ever-changing attempt to make that remote book present in lives of the clergy and the laity. Rather than the outcome of a specific time and place, biblical mediation is key to scripturalist religions at large. In every society where texts are codified and venerated, the need for mediation emerges. Mediation was a vibrant aspect of medieval religious culture. And, as this book has demonstrated, its innovativeness was often masked. The sacrality of new creations, whether in ritual, sermon, or chant, was rendered on a par with that of the sacred text itself. Successful mediation therefore necessitates rendering a medium truly 'biblical' – inseparable from the sacred scriptures it draws upon. This is accomplished by textual modifications, ritual spectacle, or the sanctity endowed on books and priests (the self-proclaimed mediators). It makes successful mediation dependent on a smooth transition of authority from Bible to message, rendering the mediators and their creativity invisible to the audience. On *Yom Kippur*, the most sacred day in the Jewish calendar, the cantor introduces his prayers with the words: 'here I am, poor in deeds to recommend me'. This chant, much like Augustine's answer to the challenge of the Donatists with the theology of *ex opere operato*,[5] makes the personal qualities of the minister of little relevance. And such is biblical mediation at large. When it is done effectively, it is all but invisible. Successful mediation constitutes a transfer of authority from Bible to audience, without suggesting that this relies on the personal qualities of an individual mediator. It was not the attributes of a court clerk that vouchsafed the oath's veracity, nor the personal worldview of a priest that sanctioned a chant or a sermon. The nature of biblical mediation influences its study. Its embedded anonymity makes tracing acts, often repetitive and evident for mediators and audience, all the more complicated for the modern scholar. However, every once in a while something went astray – a new priest employed the wrong *thema* or an abbot failed to supply an oath-book – offering the historian a precious glimpse into the function of the complex and innovative religious practices of biblical mediation.

Notes

1 *The Five Gospels Parallels*, ed. John W. Marshall, http://www.utoronto.ca/religion/synopsis/syn-ini.htm (accessed 14 May 2012); multiple translations appear on a multitude of websites, as well as in designated softwares such as *Logos*, www.logos.com (accessed 14 May 2012). Exemplary high-quality digital images are *The Codex Sinaiticus Project*, http://codexsinaiticus.org/en/ (accessed 14 May 2012), which provides transcription, translation, and high-resolution digital images in standard light and raking light; or *The Digital Dead Sea Scrolls*, http://dss.collections.imj.

org.il/ (accessed 14 May 2012), whose tagging of the digital scrolls links image and text with much ease.

2 'The Study of Religion and the Study of the Bible', *Journal of the American Academy of Religion* 39:2 (1971), 131–40 (reprinted in *Rethinking Scripture: Essays from a Comparative Perspective*, ed. Miriam Levering (Albany, NY, 1989), pp. 18–28).

3 *The St Albans Chronicle, Volume I 1376–1394: The Chronica Maiora of Thomas Walsingham*, ed. John Taylor, Wendy R. Childs, and Leslie Watkiss, Oxford Medieval Texts (Oxford, 2003), pp. 546–7. The sermon reverberates in earlier versions of *Piers Plowman* (Steven Justice, *Writing and Rebellion: England in 1381* (Berkeley and Los Angeles, 1994), p. 234). Earlier versions of the proverb were employed to chastise the nobility, as in Brinton's sermon 44 (Devlin ed., i:194).

4 '"Ask What I am Called": The Anglo-Saxons and Their Bibles', in *The Bible as Book: The Manuscript Tradition*, ed. John L. Sharpe III and Kimberly Van Kampen (London, 1998), pp. 145–76 (169–76).

5 'by the very fact of the action's being performed', in the phrasing of the Council of Trent, 1545–63. The Donatists questioned the ability of lapsed priests to perform the sacraments. Augustine rejected this, arguing against linking the efficacy of the sacraments with the individual qualities of an individual priest.

APPENDIX

A survey of Late Medieval Bibles

Notes

To assist in appreciating the paratext of Late Medieval Bibles (discussed in Chapter 3), this Appendix provides a list of fifty-six randomly chosen manuscripts, primarily of English or French origins, which date to the thirteenth and fourteenth centuries.

Date and provenance

Most information is an estimation based on artistic elements, calendars, sequence of books and chapter numbers. Estimated dates and provenance are in italics. The few colophons are noted in 'Additional Material'. When a date range can be inferred it is supplied either as half-century (with superscript 1, 2) or as quarter-century (superscript ¼, ¾)
G indecisive dating between 1230 and 1350
EF uncertain location, northern France or England.

Size

The size of the manuscript is of the folios, rather than binding, and is measured in centimetres.

Running titles

+ alternating blue and red abbreviated titles, written in two parts on two facing leafs

Chapter numbers

i integral Langtonian chapter division (identified by paragraph breaks and/or integral chapter numbers), alternating blue and red
c *capitula* marks and/or lists

t transitory (marks of *capitula* and chapters side by side, or partial integral chapter division)

Song of Songs (rubrics)

- – no special features
- VE Vox ecclesie (de Bruyne series A–L)
- AS Adulescentulis sponsa narrat de sponso ... (modification of de Bruyne series S)
- VA Vox adulescentialarum (modification of de Bruyne series S)
- VC Vox ecclesie ... sponsus de sacta cruce (de Bruyne series D)
- VP Vox ecclesie ... vox patriarchi (combination of de Bruyne series A and B)

Large initials for key Psalms

For Psalms 1, 26, 38, 52, 68, 80, 97 and 109 (with infrequent tripartite division of Psalms 51 and 101)

Chapter number (Psalms)

– (l) added by later hand
+ (s) written as part of superscriptions

Superscriptions (Psalms)

G Generic superscriptions
n.r. space provided but not filled by rubricator

Additional materials

Tr Table of reading
K Calendar

§1 Cambridge University Library MS Dd.8.12 – Additional material: capitula lists; chart of Gospels; Baruch IV; chart of biblical exegetes; Jerome's prologues; Theological treaties; Recipe for ink; calendar; canon of lessons; Song of Gospels; treatise and diagrams of biblical genealogy.

§2 Cambridge University Library MS Ee.6.26 – Transitional MS. Although first line written underneath ruling line, chapter numbers and titles appear to be added at a later date in red ink. The text is written in one column until the Psalms, and from then in the standard two column.

Press-mark	Provenance		Layout (General)					Layout (Psalms)					Addenda	
	Date	Place	*Full Bible*	*Size*	*Running titles*	*Chapter numbers*	*Song of Songs (Rubrics)*	*Large initials for Key Psalms*	*Running Title*	*Chapter number*	*Verse coloured initials*	*Superscriptions*	*Interpretationes*	*Additional materials*
Cambridge University Library														
Dd.1.14	14²⁄₄	England (London? Queen Mary Psalter Workshop)	Full	42.5 × 26	+	i	–	+	–	–	+	+	Aaz (truncated)	–
Dd.5.52	G	Devon	Full (quires lacking)	21 × 14	+	t	–	excised?	–	–	+	–	–	–
Dd.8.12	1210–30	North Midlands	Full (parallel Psalter)	38 × 25.5	+ (orig. Black)	c (add. Subdivision)	VE	+	–	+ (s)	+	+	Aaz	§1
Dd.10.29	13¾	England	Full (quires lacking)	23.5 × 15.7	+	i	n/a	+	–	–	+	+	–	Tr (later hand)
Dd.12.47	G	EF	– Ps and other quires	15 × 10.5	+	i	–	n/a					Aaz	short prayers

Dd.13.6	*$13^{2/4}$*	England	Full	38 × 25	+	t	+ (red marks identify voices)	+	+ (liber psalmorum)	–	+	+	–	Eusebian canon, Tr
Ee.1.9	*$13^{2/4}$*	St Albans	– Ps	21 × 15	+	c	VE	n/a					–	Tr
Ee.1.16	G	EF	Full (quires lacking)	20.8 × 15	+	i	–	+	–	+	+	n.r.	Aaz	Tr, K, scolia
Ee.2.23	*$13^{2/4}$*	SW England, possibly for an English charter-house	Full	33.3 × 21	+	i (liturgical sub-div.)	AS	+	+ (Psalter)	– (l)	+	+	–	partial summary (beginning with Aggei)
Ee.6.26	*1220s*	by 15 in England	Full	20 × 14	§2		–	+	–	–	+	–	Aaron (Partial, beg. Cicilia)	K
Hh.1.3	*$13^{3/4}$*	England	Full	19.8 × 15	+	i	–	+	–	–	+	–	Aaz	notes, Canon of Mass (different hand)
Mm.1.2	G	EF	Full	24.3 × 16.5	+	i	–	+	–	– (l)	+	–	Aaz	–
Mm.3.2	*$13^{3/4}$*	England	Full	33.5 × 22	+	i	–	+	–	– (l)	+	–	–	Tr, K, Song of Gospels, notes

St John's, Cambridge														
C24	G	Ginsburne Priory, York	Full	37.3 × 23	+	i	–	+	+ (psalterium)	–	+	+ (from Ps 32 n.r.)	Aaz	Prologues, Esdra IV, list of books
I28	G	EF	Full (parallel Psalter)	20 × 14.5	+	t	–	+	–	–	+	n.r.	Aaz	Tr, classification of sins
N1	1240	England – Gilbertine House.	Full	25.5 × 18	+	i	VE	+	–	–	+	+	Aaz	prefaces and canon of mass; Joachim's prophecies
N8	13¾	EF	Full	16.3 × 11.5	+	i	VA	+	–	–	+	+	Aad	hymns, prologues, Tr
N11	G	By 15 at the Austin Abbey of Southwark	Full	15.2 × 9.7	+	i	–	+	–	+	+	+ G (Psalmus David)	Aaz	–
Edinburgh University Library														
EUL 2	G	EF	Full	29.9 × 20.4	+	i	–	+	–	–	+	+	Aaz	none
EUL 4	G	Northern France	Full	14.1 × 10.9	+	i	–	+	–	+	+	+	removed (rubric at end of Revelation)	none

London, The British Library

Add. 5,160	G	England	Full	11.2 × 7.8	+	i	–	+	–	– (l)	+	+	Aaz	–
Add. 11,842	G	England	Full	29.4 × 19.5)	+ (Red)	t	–	+	+ (Psalterium)	– (l)	+	–	–	Tr (later hand)
Add. 15,253	*1210–20*	Paris	Full	48 × 32	+	t	–	+	–	– (l)	+	+	–	Paritial Glossa ordinaria; capitula lists preceding books
Add. 15,452	G	France	Full (parallel Psalter)	21 × 15.3	+ (black, apart from Nehemiah to Ezra)	t	–	+	+ (Romanum/ hebraicum)	–	+	+	Aaz	Eusebian canon (earlier hand)
Add. 35,085	*13²*	Dominican, Clermont Abbey, France	Full	12.6 × 8	+	i	–	+	+ (Psalterium)	+	+	+	Aaz	K, Tr
Add. 39,629	G	France	Full	14.6 × 9.8	+	i	–	+	–	–	+	+	Aaz	few notes on canon law and recipe (15 hand)
Arundel 78	1230	France	Full	32.7 × 22.7	+	t	–	+	+ (Psalmus David)	–	+	–	–	–

Arundel 303	1228–1234	Dominican, England	Full	14 × 9.5	+	i	–	–	+ (David)	+	–	–	Aaz	Tr, K
Arundel 311	G	France	Full	11.5 × 8	+	i	–	+	–	–	–	n.r.	Aaz	K (partial, erased)
Burney 1	1220–30	England (by 14 in Franciscan convent, Worcester)	Full	31 × 21	+	t	–	+	–	– (l)	+	+	–	–
Burney 2	13^2	France	Full	29.2 × 19	+	i	–	+	–	– (l)	+	+	Aaz	exegesis (different hand)
Burney 5	1220–30	by 14 at Bury St Edmunds (Reginald, a priest, and the Franciscan convent of Babwell)	Full (ends abruptly in Lk 3:31)	25.5 × 19	+ (red, abbr.)	t	+ (red marks identify voices)	+	+ (Liber Psalmorum)	–	+	+	–	–
Burney 6	$13^{2/4}$	England	Full	20.7 × 14.3	+	i	–	+	+ (Psalterium)	+	+	+	Aaz	–
Burney 7	G	EF	Full	15.5 × 11	+	i	VE (modified, in margin)	+	–	– (l)	+	–	–	Legales; names of biblical books (15 hand)

Burney 9	G	France	Full (ends abruptly in Rom 16:20)	16.7 × 11.4	+	i	–	+	–	– (l)	+	+	–	Tr (brief)
Burney 10	G	France	Full	15.8 × 10.2	+	i	–	+	–	– (l)	+	+	Aaz (truncated)	–
Burney 11	1230	Oxford	–Ps	12.8 × 9	+	t	–	n/a					Aaz	Table of contents; Table of Psalms, and incipits of the six ferial canticle, *modus predicandi* (Later hands)
Egerton 2867	1230–1247	St Martin Dover (Priory of Canterbury)	Full (Single column)	21 × 14.5	+	i	–	+	–	–	+	G (Psalmus David)	–	Table of contents (later hand);K; preaching themes with biblical references; Tr
Harley 613	1220–30	England	Full (parallel Psalter, partial NT)	43 × 32	+ (Black)	c	VE	+	–	–	+	from Ps. 45 n.r.	–	–

Harley 1661	G	EF	–Ps	17.4 × 12	+	i	separation of voices by spaces	n/a					Aaz (later hand)	–
Harley 2813	13^{1}	Oxford	Full	18.2 × 13.1	+	i	VE	+	–	–	+	–	Aaz	Table of contents (later hand); Gallican canticles with reference (following Psalms); list of biblical books; Missal
Lansd. 438	1225–1275	England (Oxford Dominicans?)	Full	33 × 24	+	t	voices and exegesis added interlinear for part of first chapter by early reader	+	–	–	+	–	Aaz	*Liber sompniorum*, Tr
Lansd. 453	13¼	England	Full	36 × 26.3	+ (red)	c	VC	+	–	–	+	G (Psalmus David)	–	–

Royal 1 A.xix	13¾	by 14 at Monkbretton (York)	Full	15.5 × 17.3	+	i	–	+	–	–	+	–	Aaz	chart of exegetes; Latin hexameters; scholia (later hands)
Royal 1 B.iii	G	England	Full	27 × 18.5	+	i	–	+	–	– (l)	+	+	Aaz	–
Royal 1 B.viii	13¾	England	– Ps	29.2 × 19	+ (not abbr.)	i	VP	n/a					Aaron	–
Ryal 1 B.xii	1254	Salisbury (William de Hales for Thomas de la Wile)	Full	30.5 × 20.5	+ (Blue)	i (Blue)	VP	+	–	–	+	–	Aaz	Colophon
Royal 1 D.i	1260–70	Oxford (William of Devon)	Full	31.3 × 20.3	+	i	–	+	+ (Psalterium)	+	–	–	Aaz	colophon
Royal 1 D.iv	G	England	Full	31.8 × 22	+	i	VP	+	–	– (l)	+	+	Aaz	–
Royal 1 E.i	1220–30	England	Full (– some NT epistles)	39.6 × 27	+ (not abbreviated)	c	VE	+	–	– (l)	+	+	*Liber interpretationis* (later hand)	–

Royal 1 E.ix	15[1]	London	Full	63 × 45	+	i	VE	+	+ (liber psalmorum)	–	+	+	Aaz	Gospel of Nicodemus, capitula list
Stowe 1	G	Paris	Full	30 × 20	+	i	–	+	–	–	+	+	Aaz	*Glose divinorum librorum*
London, Lambeth Palace Library														
533	G	Dominicans, England	Full (Ps. inserted later)	16.5 × 10.5	+	i (subdividion)	–	+	–	–	+	+	–	K; Song of Gospels (later hand)
534	G	Dominicans, Ireland (Arklow)	Full	17 × 11.4	+	i	–	+	–	– (l)	+	+	Aaz	Tr, *Summarium Biblicum*, Table of contents, liturgical notes
756	G	EF	Full	23 × 15.9	+	i	–	+	–	– (l)	+	+	–	Recipes for blindeness (15 hand)
London, Victoria and Albert Museum														
Reid 21 (A.L. 1710–1902)	G	England	Full	16.3 × 11.3	+	i (a–g sub division)	–	+	–	– (l)	+	+	Aaz	–

BIBLIOGRAPHY

Catalogues, reference books, and dictionaries

Catalogue of Dated and Datable Manuscripts, c.700–1600 in the Department of Manuscripts, the British Library, ed. Andrew G. Watson (Oxford, 1979)

Catalogue of Dated and Datable Manuscripts c.435–1600 in Oxford Libraries, ed. Andrew G. Watson (Oxford, 1984)

Catalogue of Dated and Datable Manuscripts c.737–1600 in Cambridge Libraries, ed. Pamela R. Robinson (Cambridge, 1988)

'Catalogue of the Library of the Priory of St Andrew, Rochester, AD 1202', ed. W. B. Rye, *Archaeologia Cantiana* 3 (1860), 47–64

A Catalogue of the Pre-1500 Western Manuscript Books at the Newberry Library, ed. Paul Saenger (Chicago, 1989)

A Descriptive Catalogue of the Manuscripts in the Library of St John's College, Cambridge, ed. M. R. James (Cambridge, 1913)

A Dictionary of Biblical Tradition in English Literature, gen. ed. David L. Jeffrey (Grand Rapids, MI, 1992)

Dover Priory, ed. William P. Stoneman, Corpus of British Medieval Library Catalogues 5 (London, 1999)

Early Gothic Manuscripts, 1250–1285, 2 vols, ed. Nigel Morgan, A Survey of Manuscripts Illuminated in the British Isles 4 (London, 1988)

English Benedictine Libraries: The Shorter Catalogues, ed. Richard Sharpe et al., Corpus of British Medieval Library Catalogues 4 (London, 1996)

The Friars' Libraries, ed. K. W. Humphreys, Corpus of British Medieval Library Catalogues 1 (London, 1990)

Glossarium meidae et infimae latinitatis, 10 vols, ed. Charles du Fresne du Cange et al., new edn (Paris, 1883–87)

Gothic Manuscripts, 1285–1385, 2 vols, ed. Lucy Freeman Sandler, A Survey of Manuscripts Illuminated in the British Isles 5 (London, 1986)

Guide to Medieval and Renaissance Manuscripts in the Huntington Library, ed. C. W. Dutschke with the assistance of R. H. Rouse et al. (San Marino, 1989, available online http://sunsite.berkeley.edu/hehweb/HM26061.html, accessed 27 May 2012)

Inventories of Christchurch Canterbury, ed. J. Wickham Legg and W. H. St John Hope (London, 1902)

The Inventories of St George's Chapel, Windsor Castle, 1384–1667, ed. Maurice F. Bond (Windsor, 1947)

Inventory of Church Goods temp. Edward III, 2 vols, ed. Dom Aelerd Watking, Norfolk Record Society XIX, I–II (Norwich, 1947–48)

Mediae latinitatis lexicon minus, ed. Jan F. Niermeyer and Co van de Kieft, 2nd rev. edn by J. W. J. Burgers (Leiden, 2002)

Medieval Libraries of Great Britain: A List of Surviving Books, ed. Neil R. Ker, 2nd edn, Royal Historical Society Guides and Handbooks 3 (London 1964), supplemented by: *Supplement to the Second Edition*, ed. Andrew G. Watson (London, 1987)

Medieval Manuscripts in British Libraries, 4 vols, ed. Neil Ker (Oxford, 1969–92); vol. 5, *Indexes and Addenda*, ed. I. C. Cunningham and A. G. Watson (Oxford, 2002)

Middle English Dictionary, gen. ed. Hans Kurath (Ann Arbor, MI, *c.* 1952–*c.* 2001 = http://quod.lib.umich.edu/m/med, accessed 10 June 2012)

Oxford Dictionary of Medieval Latin from British Sources, gen. ed. D. R. Howlett (Oxford, 1975–)

Oxford Dictionary of National Biography, ed. H. C. G. Matthew and Brian Harrison (Oxford, 2004 = http://oxforddnb.com, accessed 10 June 2012)

The Oxford Dictionary of the Christian Church, ed. F. L. Cross and E. A. Livingstone, 3rd edn (Oxford, 1997)

The Oxford English Dictionary, 3rd edn (Oxford, 2005 =http://oed.com, accessed 10 June 2012)

Les psautiers manuscrits latins des bibliothèques publiques de France, 2 vols, ed. Victor Leroquais (Mâcon, 1940–1941)

Repertorium Biblicum Medii Aevi, 11 vols, ed. Friedrich Stegmüller (Madrid, 1950–80)

Repertorium der lateinischen Sermones des Mittelalters für die Zeit von 1150–1350, 11 vols, ed. Johannes Baptist Schneyer (Münster, Westfalen, 1969–90)

Western Illuminated Manuscripts: A Catalogue of the Collection in Cambridge University Library, ed. Paul Binski and Patrick Zutshi, with the collaboration of Stella Panayotova (Cambridge, 2011)

Manuscript sources

The information supplied adjacent to the each entry is a short description of part most relevant to the book, rather than an exhaustive description. Manuscripts which were consulted only in their electronic form are supplied alongside their URL.

Cambridge

Cambridge University Library

Dd.1.14 Late Medieval Bible

Dd.1.15 Sarum missal

Dd.5.52	Late Medieval Bible
Dd.8.12	Late Medieval Bible
Dd.10.29	Late Medieval Bible
Dd.12.47	Late Medieval Bible
Dd.13.6	Late Medieval Bible
Ee.1.9	Late Medieval Bible
Ee.1.16	Late Medieval Bible
Ee.2.3	Sarum pontifical
Ee.2.23	Late Medieval Bible
Ee.6.26	Late Medieval Bible
Ff.2.31	Sarum missal
Hh.1.3	Late Medieval Bible
Ii.6.22	Late Medieval Bible
Mm.1.2	Late Medieval Bible
Mm.3.2	Late Medieval Bible

Emmanuel College

252	Psalter fragment

St John's College

A1	Hebrew Bible
B14	Legal treatise
C24	Late Medieval Bible
I28	Late Medieval Bible
N1	Late Medieval Bible
N8	Late Medieval Bible
N11	Late Medieval Bible

Trinity College

O.1.71	Legal treatise

Canterbury

Canterbury Cathedral

olim Law Society 3	Late Medieval Bible

Edinburgh

Edinburgh University Library

MS 2	Late Medieval Bible
MS 4	Late Medieval Bible

Glasgow

Glasgow University Library

Gen 999	Gradual fragment

London

The British Library

Additional 5,160	Late Medieval Bible
Additional 11,842	Late Medieval Bible
Additional 15,253	Late Medieval Bible
Additional 15,452	Late Medieval Bible
Additional 22,573	Oath book
Additional 24,142	Early Medieval Bible
Additional 35,085	Late Medieval Bible
Additional 35,285	York missal (Augustinian Priory of Gisburne)
Additional 39,629	Late Medieval Bible
Additional 43,380	York missal
Additional 49,598	Early medieval benedictional
Additional 57,534	Sarum processional (Norwich)
Arundel 78	Late Medieval Bible
Arundel 303	Late Medieval Bible
Arundel 311	Late Medieval Bible
Arundel 324	Late Medieval Bible
Burney 1	Late Medieval Bible
Burney 2	Late Medieval Bible
Burney 5	Late Medieval Bible
Burney 6	Late Medieval Bible
Burney 7	Late Medieval Bible
Burney 9	Late Medieval Bible
Burney 10	Late Medieval Bible
Burney 11	Late Medieval Bible
Cotton Galba E.iv	Library catalogue, Christ Church, Canterbury
Cotton Titus D.vii	Sacristy record, Glastonbury
Cotton Vespasian A.xxii	List of bequests, Rochester Cathedral
Egerton 656	Legal treatise
Egerton 2867	Late Medieval Bible
Harley 613	Late Medieval Bible
Harley 1661	Late Medieval Bible
Harley 2787	Sarum missal
Harley 2813	Late Medieval Bible
Harley 2911	Sarum ordinal
Harley 2942	Sarum processional

Harley 2945	Sarum processional
Harley 2983	Hereford ordinal
Harley 4919	Sarum missal
Lansdowne 438	Late Medieval Bible
Lansdowne 453	Late Medieval Bible
Royal 1 A.xix	Late Medieval Bible
Royal 1 B.iii	Late Medieval Bible
Royal 1 B.viii	Late Medieval Bible
Royal 1 B.x	Late Medieval Bible
Royal 1 B.xi	Gospel book
Royal 1 B.xii	Late Medieval Bible
Royal 1 D.i	Late Medieval Bible
Royal 1 D.iii	Gospel book
Royal 1 D.iv	Late Medieval Bible
Royal 1 E.i	Late Medieval Bible
Royal 1 E.ix	Late Medieval Bible
Royal 1 E.vii–viii	Early medieval Bible
Royal 2 B.v	Psalter
Royal 2 F.iv	Gospel book
Royal 9 A.vii	Oath-book
Royal 9 A.xii	Oath-book
Sloane 2478	The speech of Caiphas
Stowe 1	Late Medieval Bible
Stowe 15	Oath-book

Guildhall Library

04645	Oath-book
4158A	Late Medieval Bible (the parish church of St Peter-upon-Cornhill, on permanent deposit)

Lambeth Palace Library

371	Letter on theft of Bible, Reading Abbey
533	Late Medieval Bible
534	Late Medieval Bible
756	Late Medieval Bible

Register of Thomas Arundel, Archbishop of Canterbury, i

Victoria and Albert Museum

L. 2060–1948	Late Medieval Bible
Reid 21	Late Medieval Bible
Reid 22	Late Medieval Bible

New York

Pierpont Morgan Library

M. 708	Gospel book. Accessed online (http://utu.morganlibrary.org/medrenpass_page_through_images_initial.cfm?ms_letter=msm&msnumber=0708&totalcount=9&current=1, accessed 8 June 2012)

Oxford

The Bodleian Library

Bodley 637	Sarum processional (Winchester)
Bodley 687	John Waldeby, *Novum opus dominicale*
Lat. bibl. e.7	Late Medieval Bible
Lat. liturg. d. 42	Breviary
Laud Misc. 77	John Waldeby, *Novum opus dominicale*
Laud Misc. 291	Peter Comestor, *Lecture on Matthew*
Misc. Lit. 408 (= Add. B20)	Sarum processional
Rawlinson Liturgical e.47	Sarum processional

New College Archives

3914	Manor court records

San Marino (CA)

Huntington Library

HM 26061	Late Medieval Bible. Accessed online (http://sunsite.berkeley.edu/hehweb/HM26061.html, accessed 8 June 2012)

Printed sources

Alan of Lille (Alanus de insulis), *Summa de arte prædicatoria*, PL 210:109–98

Alain of Lille, *The Art of Preaching*, tr. Gillian R. Evans (Kalamazoo, MI, 1981)

Pseudo-Alcuin, *Liber de divinis oficiis*, PL 101:1173–286

Alexandri Essebiensis opera theologica, ed. Franco Morenzoni and Thomas H. Bestul, CCCM 188:1 (Turnhout, 2004)

Die älteste Teutsche so wol allgemeine als insonderheit Elsassische und Strassburgische Chronicke. Von Jacob von Königshofen … von Anfang der Welt biss ins Jahr … 1386 beschrieben, ed. Johann Schiltern (Strassburg, 1698)

Amalarii episcopi opera liturgica omnia, ed. Jean-Michel Hanssens, vol. 2, Studi e testi 139 (Vatican City, 1948)

An Apology for Lollard Doctrines Attributed to Wicliffe; Now First Printed from a Manuscript in the Library of Trinity College, Dublin, ed. James Henthorn Todd, Camden Soc. 1st ser. 20 (London, 1842)

Augustine (Augustinus Hipponensis), *De Doctrina Christiana*, ed. and tr. R. P. H. Green (Oxford, 1995)

— *Enarrationes in Psalmos: sermo I, de prima parte Psalmi*, PL 36:322–33

Bacon, Roger, *Opus minus*, ed. John S. Brewer, RS 15 (London, 1859)

Bede's Ecclesiastical History of the English People, ed. Bertram Colgrave and R. A. B. Mynors (Oxford 1969, repr. 1992)

Pseudo-Bede, *Liber proverbium*, PL 90:1089–113

Bernardino da Siena, *Le Prediche volgari inedite, Firenze 1424, 1425, Siena 1425*, ed. P. Dionisio Pacetti, I Classici Cristiani 56 (Siena, 1935)

Biblia latina cum glossa ordinaria: Facsimile Reprint of the editio princeps Adolph Rusch of Strassburg 1480/81, ed. Karlfried Froehlich and Margaret T. Gibson (Turnhout, 1992)

Biblia Sacra iuxta Vulgatam Versionem, ed. Robert Weber (Stuttgart, 1969)

The Byble in Englyshe, that is to saye the Content of all the Holy Scrypture, bothe of ye Olde and Newe Testament, truly translated after the Veryte of the Hebrue and Greke Textes, by ye Dylygent Studye of Dyuerse Excellent Learned Men, Expert in the Forsayde Tonges (London: Richard Grafton and Edward Whitchurch, 1539)

The whole Byble. that is the holy scripture of the Olde and Newe testament faythfully translated into Englyshe by Myles Couerdale, and newly ouersene and correcte (Zurich: C. Froschouer, for Andrewe Hester, London, 1550)

The Book of Margery Kempe, ed. Barry Windeatt (Harlow, 2000)

The Book of Pastoral Rule and Selected Epistles of Gregory the Great Bishop of Rome, ed. and tr. James Barmby (Oxford and New York, 1895)

Breviarium ad usum insignis ecclesiae Sarum, ed. Francis Procter and Christopher Wordsworth, Fasc. I (Cambridge, 1882)

Bullarium Franciscanum Romanorum pontificium: Constitutiones, epistols, ac diplomata continens …, 4 vols, ed. Johannes H. Sbaralea (Rome, 1759, repr. 1983)

Calendar of the Charter Rolls preserved in the Public Record Office: Vol. I Henry III A.D. 1226–1257 (London, 1903)

Ceremonies and Processions of the Cathedral Church of Salisbury, edited from the Fifteenth Century ms. no. 148, with Additions from the Cathedral Records and Woodcuts from the Sarum Processionale of 1502, ed. Christopher Wordsworth (Cambridge, 1901)

Chaucer, Geoffrey, *The Canterbury Tales: A Verse Translation*, tr. David Wright, new edn (Oxford, 2011)

— *The Riverside Chaucer*, gen. ed. Larry D. Benson, 3rd edn (Boston, MA, 1988)

Concilia magnae Britanniae et Hiberniae, a synodo Verolamiensi A.D.

CCCXLVI ad Londinensem A.D. (MDCCXVII): Accedunt constitutiones et alia ad historiam Ecclesiae Anglicanae spectantia, ed. David Wilkins (London, 1737)

Corpus Iuris Canonici, 2 vols, ed. Emil Friedberg (Leipzig, 1879, 1881, repr. Graz, 1959)

Councils and Synods, with other Documents Relating to the English Church, vol. 2, A.D. 1205–1313, ed. Frederick M. Powicke and Christopher R. Cheney (Oxford, 1964)

Curia Regis Rolls of the Reigns of Richard I and John preserved in the Public Record Office: vol. 6: 11–14 John, ed. C. T. Fowler (London, 1932)

Cursor Mundi (the Cursor of the World): A Northumbrian Poem of the XIVth Century in Four Versions, vol. 2, ed. Richard Morris, EETS OS 62 (London, 1876)

The Customary of the Benedictine Abbey of Eynsham in Oxfordshire, ed. Antonia Gransden (Siegburg, 1963)

The Customary of the Cathedral Priory Church of Norwich: Ms 465 in the Library of Corpus Christi College, Cambridge, ed. J. B. L. Tolhurst, HBS 82 (London, 1948, repr. 2010)

Decrees of the Ecumenical Councils: Vol. i, Nicaea I to Lateran V, ed. Norman P. Tanner, SJ (London, 1990)

Early English Versions of the Gesta Romanorum, ed. Sidney J. H. Herrtage (London, 1879)

Egeria's Travels to the Holy Land, ed. and tr. John Wilkinson, rev. edn (Jerusalem and Warminster, 1981)

English Economic History: Select Documents, ed. A. E. Bland, P. A. Brown, and R. H. Tawney (Norwich, 1914)

Extracts from the Account Rolls of the Abbey of Durham, from the Original mss, 2 vols, ed. Joseph T. Fowler, Surtees Society 99–100 (Durham, 1898–99)

Gesta Henrici Quinti: The Deeds of Henry the Fifth, ed. and tr. Frank Taylor and John S. Roskell (Oxford, 1975)

Gilbertus Universalis, *Glossa ordinaria in Lamentatione Ieremie prophete, prothemata et liber I: A Critical Edition with an Introduction and a Translation*, ed. and tr. Alexander Andrée, Acta universitatis Stockholmiensis, Studia Latina Stockholmiensia 52 (Stockholm, 2005)

'Glose divinorum librorum', ed. Giovanni Stefano Menochio, in *Commentarii totius Sacræ Scripturæ ex optimis quibusque auctoribus collecti ...*, tom. 3 (Venice, 1758), pp. 429–40

Gregory of Nyssa's Treatise on the Inscriptions of the Psalms, ed. and tr. Ronald E. Heine, Oxford Early Christian Studies (Oxford, 1995)

Guillelmi Duranti Rationale divinorum officiorum, 3 vols, ed. A. Davril and T. M. Thibodeau, CCCM 140, 140A, 140B (Turnhout, 1995, 1998, 2000)

Historia Monasterii S. Augustini Cantuariensis by Thomas of Elmham, *formerly Monk and Treasurer of that Foundation*, ed. Charles Hardwick, RS 8 (London, 1858)

Hooper, John, 'A Declaration of the Ten Holy Commandments of Almighty God', in *Early Writings of John Hooper, D.D., Lord Bishop of Gloucester and Worcester, Martyr, 1555*, ed. Samuel Carr, Parker Soc. 11 (Cambridge, 1843)

Hugh of St Victor, 'The Three Best Memory Aids for Learning History', tr. and ed. Mary Carruthers, in *The Medieval Craft of Memory: An Anthology of Texts and Pictures*, ed. Mary Carruthers and Jan M. Ziolkowski (Philadelphia, 2002), pp. 32–40

Innocent III, *De sacro altaris mysterio*, PL 217:773–915

Iohannis Beleth Summa de Ecclesiasticis officiis, 2 vols, ed. Herbert Douteil, CCCM 41, 41A (Turnhout, 1976)

Iohannis Wyclif Sermones: Now First Edited from the Manuscripts, 4 vols, ed. Iohann Loserth (London, 1887–90)

Itineraria et alia geographica, ed. A. Franceschini and A. Weber, CCSL 175–6 (Turnhout, 1965)

Jacobus a Voragine, *Legenda aurea: Vulgo historia lombardica dicta*, ed. Th. Grässe (Dresden and Leipzig, 1846)

Jerome (Eusebius Sophronius Hieronymus), *Sancti Hieronymi presbyteri Opera. Pars I, Opera exegetica. 7, Commentariorum in Matheum libri IV*, ed. D. Hurst and M. Adriaen, CCSL 77 (Turnhout, 1969)

— 'Liber interpretationis Hebraicorum nominum', ed. Paul de Lagarde, in *S. Hieronymi Presbyteri Opera. Pars I, Opera Exegetica. 1*, CCSL 72 (Turnhout, 1959), pp. 57–161

The Jew in the Medieval World: A Source Book, 315–1791, ed. Jacob R. Marcus (New York, 1938), rev. edn with introduction and updated bibliographies by Marc Saperstein (Cincinnati, 1999)

John of Bologna (Iohannes Bononiensis), 'Summa notarie de hiis que in foro ecclesiastico coram quibuscumque iudicibus occurunt notariis conscribenda', in *Briefsteller und Formelbücher des elften bis vierzehnten Jahrhunderts*, 2 vols, ed. Ludwig Rockinger, Quellen und Erörterungen zur bayerischen und deutschen Geschichte 9 (Munich, 1863–64, repr. New York, 1961), ii:593–712

Langland, William, *Piers Plowman: A Parallel-Text Edition of the A, B, C and Z Versions*, ed. A. V. C. Schmidt (London, 1995)

— *Piers Plowman: A New Translation of the B-Text*, tr. A. V. C. Schmidt (Oxford, 1992)

— *The Vision of Piers Plowman: A Critical Edition of the B-text Based on Trinity College Cambridge MS B.15.17 with Selected Variant Readings*, ed. A. V. C. Schmidt (London and New York, 1978)

The Lay-Folks Mass-Book or the Manner for Hearing Mass, with Rubrics and

Devotions for the People, in Four Texts and Office in English According to the Use of York from Manuscripts from the Xth to the XVth Century with Appendix, Notes, and Glossary, ed. Thomas F. Simmons, EETS OS 71 (London, 1879)

Liber Eliensis, ed. E. O. Blake, Camden Soc. 3rd ser. 92 (London, 1962)

Liber Eliensis, A History of the Isle of Ely from the Seventh Century to the Twelfth, Complied by a Monk of Ely in the Twelfth Century, tr. and ed. Janet Fairweather (Woodbridge, 2005)

Liber pontificalis Christopheri Bainbridge, archiepiscopi Eboracensis, ed. William G. Henderson, Surtees Society 61 (Durham, 1875)

Lincoln Cathedral Statutes, ed. H. Bradshaw and C. Wordsworth, part i (Cambridge, 1892)

Maimonides, *The Mishneh Torah: Edited according to the Bodleian (Oxford) Codex*, ed. Moses Hyamson (New York, 1949)

The Metz Pontifical: A Manuscript Written for Reinhald von Bar, Bishop of Metz (1302–1316), and now Belonging to Sir Thomas Brooke, Bart., F.S.A., ed. E. S. Dewick (London, 1902)

The Middle English Breton Lays, ed. Anne Laskaya and Eve Salisbury (Kalamazoo, 1995 = www.lib.rochester.edu/camelot/TEAMS/erltofrm.htm, accessed 24 May 2012)

The Middle-English Harrowing of Hell and Gospel of Nicodemus, ed. William H. Hulme, EETS ES 100 (London, 1907, repr. Oxford, 1961)

Middle English Metrical Romances, ed. Walter Hoyt French and Charles Brockway Hales (New York, 1930)

Middle English Sermons Edited from British Museum MS. Royal 18B. xxiii., ed. Woodburn O. Ross, EETS OS 209 (London, 1940)

Mishnayot Mevo'arot (in Hebrew), 21 vols, ed. Pinechas Kehati (Jerusalem, 1998)

Missale ad usum ecclesie Westmonasteriensis, 3 vols, ed. J. W. Legg, HBS 1, 5, 12 (London, 1891, 1893, 1897)

Missale ad usum insignis ac preclare ecclesie Sarum (London: Richard Pynson, 1512)

Missale ad usum insignis ecclesiae Eboracensis, ed. W. G. Henderson, Surtees Soc. 59 (Durham, 1874)

Missale ad usum percelebris ecclesiae Herfordensis, ed. W. G. Henderson (Leeds, 1874, repr. Farnborough, 1969)

Der mittelenglische Versroman über Richard Löwenherz: Kritische Ausgabe nach allen Handschriften mit Einleitung, Anmerkungen und Deutscher Übersetzung, ed. Karl Brunner, Wiener Beiträge zur englischen Philologie 42 (Vienna and Leipzig, 1913)

The Monastic Constitutions of Lanfranc, ed. and tr. David Knowles (London, 1951); rev. edn, ed. Christopher N. L. Brooke (Oxford, 2001)

Monasticon anglicanum: A History of the Abbies and Other Monasteries, Hospitals, Frieries, and Cathedral and Collegiate Churches ..., 6 vols, ed. William Dugdale, 2nd edn (London, 1817–30)

The Ordinal and Customary of the Abbey of St Mary York, 3 vols, ed. J. B. L. Tolhurst and Abbess of Stanbrook, HBS 73, 75, 84 (London, 1936–37, 1951)

The Ordinale and Customary of the Benedictine Nuns of Barking Abbey, 2 vols, ed. J. B. L. Tolhurst, HBS 65–6 (London, 1927–8)

Pecock, Reginald, *The Repressor of Over Much Blaming of the Clergy*, 2 vols, ed. Churchill Babington, RS 19 (London, 1860)

Philippus de Harvengt, *Commentaria in Cantica Canticorum*, PL 203:181–490

The Plea Rolls of the Exchequer of the Jews, Preserved in the Public Record Office, vol. V: Edward I, 1277–1279, ed. Sarah Cohen (London, 1992)

Preaching in the Age of Chaucer: Selected Sermons in Translation, ed. and tr. Siegfried Wenzel, Medieval Texts in Translation (Washington, DC, 2008)

'Private Indentures for Life Service in Peace and War 1278–1476', ed. Michael Jones and Simon Walker, *Camden Misc.* 22, Camden Soc. 5th ser. 3 (London, 1994), pp. 1–190

The Register of Walter de Stapeldon, Bishop of Exeter (A.D. 1307–1326), ed. F. C. Hingeston-Randolph (London, 1892)

Registrum Roffense: Or a Collection of Ancient Records, Charters and Instruments of Divers Kinds Necessary for Illustrating the Ecclesiastical History and Antiquities of the Diocese and Cathedral Church of Rochester, ed. John Thorpe (London, 1769)

'Relics at Glastonbury in the Fourteenth Century: An Annotated Edition of British Library, Cotton Titus D.vii, fols 2r–13v', ed. James P. Carley and Martin Howley, *Arthurian Literature* 16 (1998), 83–129

Reliquiæ Antiquæ: Scraps from Ancient Manuscripts, Illustrating Chiefly Early English Literature and the English Language, 2 vols, ed. Thomas Wright (London, 1845)

Robert of Basevorn, 'Forma praedicandi', in *Artes praedicandi: Contribution à l'histoire de la rhétorique au moyen âge*, ed. Th. M. Charland, Publications de l'Institut d'Études Médiévales d'Ottawa 7 (Paris and Ottawa, 1936), pp. 227–323

— 'The Form of Preaching', tr. Leopold Krul, in *Three Medieval Rhetorical Arts*, ed. James J. Murphy (Berkeley, 1971), pp. 109–215

— *Fratris Rogeri Bacon, ordinis minorum, Opus majus ad clementem quartum*, ed. Samuel Jebb (London, 1733)

The Roman Imperial Coinage, Vol. II Vespasian to Hadrian, ed. Harold Mattingly and Edward A. Sydenham (London, 1926)

Ruperti Tuitiensis liber De divinis officiis, ed. Hrabanus Haacke, CCCM 7 (Turnhout, 1967)

The St Albans Chronicle, Volume I 1376–1394: The Chronica Maiora of Thomas Walsingham, ed. John Taylor, Wendy R. Childs, and Leslie Watkiss, Oxford Medieval Texts (Oxford, 2003)

The Sarum Missal: Edited from Three Early Manuscripts, ed. J. Wickham Legg (Oxford, 1916, repr. 1969)

The Sarum Missal in English, 2 vols, tr. Frederick E. Warren, The Library of Liturgiology and Ecclesiology for English Readers 8–9 (London, 1911)

Select Pleas, Starrs, and Other Records from the Rolls of the Exchequer of the Jews, A.D. 1220–1284, ed. J. M. Rigg, Selden Soc. 15 (London, 1902)

Sir Perceval of Galles and Ywain and Gawain, ed. Mary Flowers Braswell (Kalamazoo, MI, 1995, = www.lib.rochester.edu/camelot/teams/ywnfrm.htm, accessed 23 May 2012)

Sommaires, divisions et rubriques de la Bible latine, ed. Donatien de Bruyne (Namur, 1914)

The Sermons of Thomas Brinton, Bishop of Rochester, 1373–1389, 2 vols, ed. Mary A. Devlin, Camden Soc. 3rd ser. 85–6 (London, 1954)

Testamenta Eboracensia: A Selection of Wills from the Registry of York. vol. 2, ed. James Raine the Younger, Surtees Soc. 30 (Durham 1855)

Thomas of Chobham, *Summa de arte praedicandi*, ed. Franco Morenzoni, CCCM 82 (Turnhout, 1988)

Tracts on the Mass, ed. J. Wickham Legg, HBS 27 (London, 1904)

The Use of Salisbury, vol. 1: The Ordinary of the Mass, ed. Nick Sandon (Amersham, 1984)

The Use of Salisbury, vol. 4: The Masses and Ceremonies of Holy Week, ed. Nick Sandon (Newton Abbot, 1996).

Vetus liber archdiaconi Eliensis, ed. C. L. Feltoe and Ellis H. Minns, Cambridge Antiquarian Soc. Octavo Ser. 48 (Cambridge, 1917)

Vetus registrum sarisberiense, alias dictum Registrum S. Osmundi episcopi: The register of S. Osmund, 2 vols, ed. W. H. Rich Jones, RS (London, 1883–84)

Visitations of Churches belonging to St Paul's Cathedral in 1297 and in 1458, ed. W. Sparrow Simpson, Camden Soc. NS 55 (London, 1895)

Wills and Inventories Illustrative of the History, Manners, Language, Statistics, etc. of the Northern Counties of England, from the Eleventh Century Downwards, ed. James Raine, Surtees Soc. 2 (London, 1835)

Wimbledon's Sermon. Redde rationem villicationis tue: A Middle English Sermon of the Fourteenth Century, ed. Ione Kemp Knight, Duquesne Studies, Philological Series 9 (Pittsburgh, PA, 1967)

The York Gospels: A Facsimile with Introductory Essays by Jonathan Alexander, Patrick McGurk, Simon Keynes & Bernard Barr, ed. Nicholas Barker (London, 1986)

The York Plays, ed. Richard Beadle (London, 1982)

Secondary sources

Adams, Robert, 'Langland and the Liturgy Revisited', *Studies in Philology* 73:3 (July 1976), 266–84

Akae, Yuichi, 'Between *artes praedicandi* and Actual Sermons: Robert of Basevorn's *Forma praedicandi* and the Sermons of John Waldeby, OESA', in *Constructing the Medieval Sermon*, ed. Roger Andersson, Sermo 6 (Turnhout, 2008), pp. 9–32

— 'A Library for Preachers: The Novum opus dominicale of John Waldeby OESA and the Library of the Austin Friars at York', *Medieval Sermon Studies* 49 (2005), 5–26

Albaric, Michael, 'Hugues de Saint-Cher et les concordances bibliques latines (XIIIe–XVIIIe siècles)', in *Hugues de Saint-Cher (d. 1263) bibliste et théologien*, ed. Louis-Jacques Bataillon et al., Bibliothèque d'histoire culturelle du moyen âge 1 (Turnhout, 2004), pp. 467–79

Alexander, Jonathan J. G., 'English or French? Thirteenth Century Bibles', in *Manuscripts at Oxford: An Exhibition in Memory of Richard William Hunt (1908–1979), Keeper of Western Manuscripts at the Bodleian Library Oxford, 1945–1975*, ed. A. C. de la Mare and B. C. Barker-Benfield (Oxford, 1980), pp. 69–71

Alford, John A., 'Bible in Middle English Literature', in *Medieval England: An Encyclopedia*, ed. Paul E. Szarmach et al. (New York and London, 1998), pp. 126–8

— *Piers Plowman: A Guide to the Quotations* (Binghamton, NY, 1992)

Anderson, M. D., *Drama and Imagery in English Medieval Churches* (Cambridge, 1963)

Aston, Margaret, 'Devotional Literacy', in *Lollards and Reformers: Images and Literacy in Late Medieval Religion*, ed. Margaret Aston (London, 1984), pp. 101–33

d'Avray, David, 'Printing, Mass Communication and Religious Reformation: The Middle Ages and After', in *The Uses of Script and Print, 1300–1700*, ed. Julia Crick and Alexandra Walsham (Cambridge, 2004), pp. 50–70

— *The Preaching of the Friars: Sermons Diffused from Paris before 1300* (Oxford, 1985)

— 'Portable Vademecum Books Containing Franciscan and Dominican Texts', in *Manuscripts at Oxford: An Exhibition in Memory of Richard William Hunt (1908–1979), Keeper of Western Manuscripts at the Bodleian Library Oxford, 1945–1975*, ed. A. C. de la Mare and B. C. Barker-Benfield (Oxford, 1980), pp. 60–4

Bailey, Terence, 'Psalm: II. Latin Monophonic Psalmody', in *Grove Music Online*, ed. L. Macy (www.oxfordmusiconline.com.catalogue.ulrls.lon.ac.uk/subscriber/article/grove/music/48161, accessed 27 May 2012)

Bale, John, *Illustrium maioris Britanniae, scriptorum, hoc est, Angliae, Cambriae, ac Scotiae summarium …* (Wesel, 1548)

Barr, Bernard, 'The History of the Volume', in *The York Gospels: A Facsimile with Introductory Essays by Jonathan Alexander, Patrick McGurk, Simon Keynes & Bernard Barr*, ed. Nicholas Barker (London, 1986), pp. 101–17

Bataillon, Louis-Jacques, 'La Bible au XIIIe siècle. Un incitation aux recherches de demain', in *La Bibbia del XIII secolo. Storia del testo, storia dell'esegesi: Convegno della Società Internazionale per lo studio del Medioevo Latino (SISMEL) Firenze, 1–2 Giugno 2001*, ed. Giuseppe Cremascoli and Francesco Santi (Florence, 2004), pp. 3–11

— 'Early Scholastic and Mendicant Preaching as Exegesis of Scripture', in *Ad Litteram: Authoritative Texts and Their Medieval Readers*, ed. Mark D. Jordan and Kent Emery, Jr, Notre Dame Conferences in Medieval Studies 3 (Notre Dame, IN, 1992), pp. 165–98

— 'De la lectio à la praedicatio. Commentaires bibliques et sermons au XIIIe siècle', *Revue des sciences philosophiques et théologiques* 70 (1986), 559–75

— 'Similitudines et exempla dans les sermons du XIIIe siècle', in *The Bible in the Medieval World: Essays in Memory of Beryl Smalley*, ed. Katherine Walsh and Diana Wood, Studies in Church History, Subsidia 4 (Oxford, 1985), pp. 191–205

Bayer, Bathja, 'The Titles of the Psalms: A Renewed Investigation of an Old Problem', *Yuval* 4 (1982), 29–123

Beckerman, John S., 'Procedural Innovation and Institutional Change in Medieval English Manorial Courts', *Law and History Review* 10:2 (1992), 197–252

Berger, Samuel, *Les préfaces jointes aux livres de la Bible dans les manuscripts de la Vulgate* (Paris, 1902)

— *Histoire de la Vulgate pendant les premiers siècles du moyen âge* (Paris, 1893)

— *De l'histoire de la Vulgate en France: Leçon d'ouverture faite à la Faculté de Théologie Protestante de Paris le 4 Novembre 1887* (Paris, 1887)

Bériou, Nicole, *L'avènement des maîtres de la Parole: La prédication à Paris au XIIIe siècle*, 2 vols (Paris, 1998)

— 'Latin and the Vernacular: Some Remarks About Sermons Delivered on Good Friday During the Thirteenth Century', in *Die deutsche Predigt im Mittelalter. Internationales Symposium am Fachbereich Germanistik der Freien Universität Berlin vom 3.–6. Oktober 1989*, ed. Volker Mertens and Hans-Jochen Schiewer (Tübingen, 1992), pp. 268–84

— *L'avènement des maîtres de la Parole: La prédication à Paris au XIIIe siècle*, 2 vols (Paris, 1998)

La Bibbia del XIII secolo. Storia del testo, storia dell'esegesi: Convegno della Società Internazionale per lo studio del Medioevo Latino (SISMEL) Firenze, 1–2 Giugno 2001, ed. Giuseppe Cremascoli and Francesco Santi (Florence, 2004)

The Bible as Book: The First Printed Editions, ed. Kimberly Van Kampen and Paul Saenger (London, 1999)

The Bible as Book: The Manuscript Tradition, ed. John L. Sharpe III and Kimberly Van Kampen (London, 1998)

The Bible in the Middle Ages: Its Influence on Literature and Art, ed. Bernard S. Levy (Binghamton, NY, 1992)

Bishop, Edmund, 'Holy Week Rites of Sarum, Hereford and Rouen Compared', in *Liturgica Historica: Papers on the Liturgy and Religious Life of the Western Church*, ed. Edmund Bishop (Oxford, 1918)

Blench, John W., *Preaching in England in the Late Fifteenth and Sixteenth Centuries: A Study of English Sermons 1450–c.1600* (Oxford, 1964)

Bloomfield, Morton W., 'The Magic of *In principio*', *Modern Language Notes* 70 (1955), 559–65

Bolzoni, Lina, *The Web of Images: Vernacular Preaching from its Origins to St Bernardino da Siena* (orig. *La rete delle immagini: Predicazione in volgare dalle origini a Bernardino da Siena* (Turin, 2001), tr. Carole Preston and Lisa Chien (Aldershot, 2004)

Bossy, John, 'The Mass as a Social Institution, 1200–1700', *Past and Present* 100 (1983), 29–61

Boynton, Susan, 'The Bible and the Liturgy', in *The Practice of the Bible in the Middle Ages: Production, Reception, and Performance in Western Christianity*, eds Susan Boynton and Diane J. Reilly (New York, 2011), pp. 10–33

— *Shaping a Monastic Identity: Liturgy and History at the Imperial Abbey of Farfa, 1000–1125* (Ithaca, NY, 2006)

— 'The Liturgical Role of Children in Monastic Customaries from the Central Middle Ages', *Studia Liturgica* 28:2 (1998), 194–209

Bradshaw, Paul F., 'The Use of the Bible in Liturgy: Some Historical Perspectives', *Studia Liturgica* 22:1 (1992), 35–52

Brand, Paul, *Kings, Barons and Justices: The Making and Enforcement of Legislation in Thirteenth-Century England* (Cambridge, 2003)

Branner, Robert, *Manuscript Painting in Paris during the Reign of St Louis: A Study of Styles* (Berkeley, 1977)

Briscoe, Marianne G., *Artes praedicandi* (with Barbara H. Jaye, *Artes orandi* = Typologie des sources du Moyen Age occidental fasc. 61, Turnhout 1992)

Brown, Carleton, 'Caiphas as a Palm Sunday Prophet', in *Anniversary Papers by Colleagues and Pupils of George Lyman Kittredge*, Boston, 1913, pp. 105–17

Brown, George H., 'The Psalms as the Foundation of Anglo-Saxon Learning', in *The Place of the Psalms in the Intellectual Culture of the Middle Ages*, ed. Nancy Van Deusen (Albany, NY, 1999), pp. 1–24

Bruyne, Donatien de, *Sommaires, divisions et rubriques de la Bible latine* (Namur, 1914)

Caenegem, R. C. van, *Legal History: A European Perspective* (London, 1991)

Camargo, Martin, 'Tria sunt: The Long and the Short of Geoffrey of Vinsauf's Documentum de modo et arte dictandi et versificandi', *Speculum* 74:4 (1999), 935–55

— 'Beyond the Libri Cantoniani: Models of Latin Prose Style at Oxford University ca. 1400', *Mediaeval Studies* 56 (1994), 165–87

Caplan, Harry, 'The Four Senses of Scriptural Interpretation and the Mediaeval Theory of Preaching', *Speculum* 4 (1929), 282–90 (= *Of Eloquence: Studies in Ancient and Mediaeval Rhetoric*, ed. Anne King and Helen North, Ithaca and London, 1970, pp. 93–104)

Carpenter, David, *The Reign of Henry III* (London 1996, repr. 2006)

Carragáin, Éamonn Ó, 'At Once Elitist and Popular: The Audiences of the Bewcastle and Ruthwell Crosses', in *Elite and Popular Religion: Papers Read at the 2004 Summer Meeting and the 2005 Winter Meeting of the Ecclesiastical History Society*, ed. Kate Cooper and Jeremy Gregory, Studies in Church History 42 (Woodbridge, 2006), pp 18–40

Carré, Yannick, *Le baiser sur la bouche au Moyen Age: Rites, symboles, mentalités, à travers les textes et les images XIe–XVe siècles* (Paris, 1992)

Carruthers, Mary, 'Ars oblivionalis, ars inveniendi: The Cherub Figure and the Arts of Memory', *Gesta* 48:2 (2010), 1–19

— *The Book of Memory: A Study of Memory in Medieval Culture*, 2nd edn (Cambridge, 2008)

Catto, Jeremy, 'Waldeby, John (d. after 1372)', DNB (www.oxforddnb.com.catalogue.ulrls.lon.ac.uk:80/view/article/53112, accessed 10 June 2012)

Cazel, Fred A. Jr, 'Intertwined Careers: Hubert de Burgh and Peter des Roches', *The Haskins Society Journal* 1 (1989), 173–81

Chadd, David, 'The Ritual of Palm Sunday: Nidaros in Context', in *The Medieval Cathedral of Tronheim: Architectural and Ritual Constructions in Their European Context*, ed. Margrete Syrstad Andås et al. (Turnhout, 2007), pp. 253–78

Chambers, John David, *Divine Worship in England in the Thirteenth and Fourteenth Centuries, Contrasted with and Adapted to that in the Nineteenth*, rev. edn (London, 1877)

Charland, Th. M., *Artes praedicandi: Contribution à l'histoire de la rhétorique au moyen âge*, Publications de l'Institut d'Études Médiévales d'Ottawa 7 (Paris and Ottawa, 1936)

Cheney, Christopher R., *Notaries Public in England in the Thirteenth and Fourteenth Centuries* (Oxford, 1972)

— 'The So-Called Statutes of John Pecham and Robert Winchelsey for the Province of Canterbury', *Journal of Ecclesiastical History* 12 (1961), 14–34

Clanchy, Michael T., *From Memory to Written Record: England 1066–1307*, 2nd edn (Cambridge, MA, 1993)

Clarkson, Christopher (with an introduction by John Sharpe), 'Some

Representations of the Book and Book-Making, from the Earliest Codex Forms to Jost Amman', in *The Bible as Book: The Manuscript Tradition*, ed. John L. Sharpe III and Kimberly Van Kampen (London, 1998), pp. 197–203

Clerck, Paul de, '"In the Beginning was the Word": Presidential Address', *Studia Liturgica* 22:1 (1992), 1–16

Coates, Alan, *English Medieval Books: The Reading Abbey Collections from Foundation to Dispersal* (Oxford, 1999)

Cohen, Jeremy, 'The Jews as Killers of Christ in the Latin Tradition, from Augustine to the Friars', *Traditio: Studies in Ancient and Medieval History, Thought, and Religion* 39 (1983), 1–27

Consitt, Frances, *The London Weavers' Company, vol. 1: From the Twelfth Century to the Close of the Sixteenth Century* (Oxford, 1933)

Cook, G. H., *The English Mediaeval Parish Church*, 3rd edn (London, 1961)

Courtenay, William J., 'The Bible in the Fourteenth Century: Some Observations', *Church History* 54:2 (1985), 176–87

Creytens, Raymond, 'Les constitutions des frères prêcheurs dans la rédaction de s. Raymond de Peñafort', *Archivum Fratrum Praedicatorum* 18 (1948), 5–68

Dahan, Gilbert, *L'exégèse chrétienne de la Bible en Occident médiéval: XIIe–XIVe Siècle*, Patrimoines christianisme (Paris, 1999)

— 'Lexiques Hébreu-Latin? Les recueils d'interprétations des noms hébraïques', in *Les manuscrits des lexiques et glossaires, de l'Antiquité à la fin du moyen âge*, ed. Jacqueline Hamesse, Textes et études du moyen âge 4 (Louvain-la-Neuve, 1996), pp. 481–526

Daniell, David, *The Bible in English: Its History and Influence* (New Haven and London, 2003)

Daniélou, Jean, *The Bible and the Liturgy* (Notre Dame, IN, 1956, orig. *Bible et Liturgie* (Paris, 1951)).

Deansely, Margaret, *The Lollard Bible and Other Medieval Biblical Versions* (Cambridge, 1920, repr. 1966)

Debray, Régis, *Transmettre* (Paris, 1997), translated as: *Transmitting Culture*, European Perspectives, tr. Eric Rauth (New York, 2000, with a comprehensive bibliography)

Dennison, Linda, '"Liber Horn", "Liber Custumarum" and Other Manuscripts of the Queen Mary Psalter Workshops', in *Medieval Art, Architecture and Archaeology in London*, ed. Lindy Grant, The British Archaeological Association 10, Conference Transactions for the Year 1984 (Leeds, 1990), pp. 118–34

Derolez, Albert, *The Palaeography of Gothic Manuscript Books: From the Twelfth to the Early Sixteenth Century* (Cambridge, 2003)

van Dijk, S. J. P., 'The Bible in Liturgical Use', in *The Cambridge History of the Bible: Vol. 2, The West from the Fathers to the Reformation*, ed. G. W. H.

Lampe (Cambridge, 1969), pp. 220–52
— 'Medieval Terminology and Methods of Psalm Singing', *Musica Disciplina* 6 (1952), 7–26.

Dobson, Barrie, 'The Medieval York Jewry Reconsidered', in *Jews in Medieval Britain: Historical, Literary and Archaeological Perspectives*, ed. Patricia Skinner (Woodbridge, 2003), pp. 145–56

Doležalová, Lucie, 'Biblia quasi in sacculo: Summarium Biblie and Other Medieval Bible Mnemonics', *Medium Aevum Quotidianum* 56 (2007), 5–35

Donovan, Clare, *The de Brailes Hours: Shaping the Book of Hours in Thirteenth Century Oxford* (London, 1991)

Dove, Mary, *The First English Bible: The Text and Context of the Wycliffite Versions*, Cambridge Studies in Medieval Literature 66 (Cambridge, 2007)

Duffy, Eamon, *Marking the Hours: English People and Their Prayers 1240–1570* (New Haven and London, 2006)
— *The Stripping of the Altars: Traditional Religion in England c.1400–c.1580*, 2nd ed. (New Haven and London, 2005)

Dugas, Don-John, 'The Legitimization of Royal Power in Chaucer's "Man of Law's Tale"', *Modern Philology* 95:1 (1997), 27–43

Dyer, Joseph, 'The Psalms in Monastic Prayer', in *The Place of the Psalms in the Intellectual Culture of the Middle Ages*, ed. Nancy Van Deusen (Albany, NY, 1999), pp. 59–89

The Early Medieval Bible: Its Production, Decoration and Use, ed. Richard Gameson (Cambridge, 1994)

Edwards, E., *Memoirs of Libraries*, 2 vols (London, 1859)

Edwards, Owain Tudor, 'Dynamic Qualities in the Medieval Office', in *Liturgy and the Arts in the Middle Ages: Studies in Honour of C. Clifford Flanigan*, ed. Eva L. Lillie and Nils Holger Petersen (Copenhagen, 1996), pp. 36–63

Eliade, Mircea, *The Sacred and the Profane*, tr. Willard R. Trask (Harcourt, 1959, repr. 1987)

Elich, Tom, 'Using Liturgical Texts in the Middle Ages', in *Fountain of Life: In Memory of Niels K. Rasmussen, O.P.*, ed. Gerard Austin (Washington, DC, 1991), pp. 69–83

Erler, Mary C., 'Palm Sunday Prophets and Processions and Eucharistic Controversy', *Renaissance Quarterly* 48:1 (1995), 58–81

d'Esneval, Amaury, 'Le perfectionnement d'un instrument de travail au début du XIIIe Siècle: Les trois glossaires bibliques d'Etienne Langton', in *Culture et travail intellectuel dans l'Occident médiéval*, ed. Geneviève Hasenohr and Jean Longère (Paris, 1981), pp. 163–75

Evelyn-White, C. H., *The Churches of Cambridgeshire and the Isle of Ely*, Country Churches (London, 1911)

Falmagne, Thomas, 'Les instruments de travail d'un prédicateur cistercien', in *De l'homélie au sermon: Histoire de la prédication médiévale*, ed. Jacqueline

Hamesse and Xavier Harmand, Publications de l'Institut d'études médiévales: Textes, études, congrès 14 (Louvain-la-Neuve, 1993), pp. 183–236

Feasey, Dom H. Philibert (Henry J.), 'Palm Sundays', *American Ecclesiastical Review* 38:4 (1908), 361–81

— *Ancient English Holy Week Ceremonial* (London, 1897)

Fischer, Bonifatius, OSB, 'Bedae de titulis Psalmorum liber', in *Festschrift Bernhard Bischoff zu seinem 65. Geburtstag dargebracht von Freunden, Kollegen, und Schülern*, ed. Johanne Autenrieth and Franz Brunhölzl (Stuttgart, 1971), pp. 90–110

Fletcher, Alan J., *Late Medieval Popular Preaching in Britain and Ireland: Texts, Studies, and Interpretations*, Sermo: Studies on Patristics, Medieval, and Reformation Sermons and Preaching 5 (Turnhout, 2010)

— '"Benedictus qui venit in nomine Domini": A Thirteenth-Century Sermon for Advent and the Macaronic Style in England', *Mediaeval Studies* 56 (1994), 217–45

Forrest, Ian, *The Detection of Heresy in Late Medieval England* (New York and Oxford, 2005)

Foster, Paul, 'The Use of Zechariah in Matthew's Gospel', in *The Book of Zechariah and Its Influence*, ed. Christopher Tuckett (Aldershot, 2003), pp. 65–85

Fowler, David C., *The Bible in Middle English Literature* (Seattle, 1984)

— *The Bible in Early English Literature* (London, 1976)

— 'A Middle English Bible Commentary (Oxford, Trinity College, Ms 93)', *Manuscripta* 12:2 (1968), 67–78

Gameson, Richard, 'The Gospels of Margaret of Scotland and the Literacy of an Early Medieval Queen', in *Women and the Book: Assessing the Visual Evidence*, ed. Lesley Smith and Jane H. M. Taylor (London, 1996), pp. 149–71

Gee, Stacey, 'Parochial Libraries in Pre-Reformation England', in *Learning and Literacy in Medieval England and Abroad*, ed. Sarah Rees Jones (Turnhout, 2003), pp. 199–222

Genette, Gérard, *Paratexts: Thresholds of Interpretation* (orig. *Seuils*, Paris 1987), tr. Jane E. Lewin (Cambridge, 1997)

Ghosh, Kantik, *The Wycliffite Heresy: Authority and the Interpretation of Texts* (Cambridge, 2001)

Gibson, Margaret T., 'The Place of the Glossa ordinaria in Medieval Exegesis', in *Ad Litteram: Authoritative Texts and Their Medieval Readers*, ed. Mark D. Jordan and Kent Emery, Jr, Notre Dame Conferences in Medieval Studies 3 (Notre Dame, IN, 1992), pp. 5–27

Glunz, Hans H., *History of the Vulgate in England from Alcuin to Roger Bacon: Being an Inquiry into the Text of Some English Manuscripts of the Vulgate Gospels* (Cambridge, 1933, repr. 2010)

Graham, William A., *Beyond the Written Word: Oral Aspects of Scripture in the History of Religion* (Cambridge, 1987)

Green, Richard Firth, *A Crisis of Truth: Literature and Law in Ricardian England* (Philadelphia, 1999)

Green, William M., 'De tribus maximis circumstantiis gestorum', *Speculum* 18:4 (1943), 484–93

Gy, Pierre-Marie, 'La Bible dans la liturgie au Moyen Age', in *Le Moyen Age et la Bible*, ed. Pierre Riché and Guy Lobrichon, Bible de tous les temps 4 (Paris, 1984), pp. 537–52

Hamel, Christopher de, *The Book: A History of the Bible* (London, 2001)

Haney, Kristine Edmondson, *The Winchester Psalter: An Iconographic Study* (Leicester, 1986)

Hanna, Ralph III, 'On the Versions of Piers Plowman', in *Pursuing History: Middle English Manuscripts and Their Texts* (Stanford, 1996), pp. 203–43

Harbert, Bruce, 'Langland's Easter', in *Langland, the Mystics and the Medieval English Religious Tradition: Essays in Honour of S. S. Hussey*, ed. Helen Phillips (Cambridge, 1990), pp. 57–70

Heinz, Andreas, 'Gloria, laus et honor', in *Lexikon für Theologie und Kirche*, 3rd edn, gen. ed. Michael Buchberger and Walter Kasper, vol. iv (Freiburg, 1995)

Hiley, David, *Western Plainchant: A Handbook* (Oxford, 1993)

Hill, Francis, *Medieval Lincoln* (Cambridge, 1948, repr. 1965)

Hinnebusch, William A., *The History of the Dominican Order: vol. II Intellectual and Cultural Life to 1500* (New York, 1973)

Hody, Humphrey, *De Bibliorum textibus originalibus, versionibus Græcis et Latina Vulgata libri IV* (Oxford, 1705)

Holdsworth, Christopher, 'Stephen Langton', DNB (www.oxforddnb.com.catalogue.ulrls.lon.ac.uk/view/article/16044, accessed 10 June 2012)

Holsinger, Bruce W., 'Langland's Musical Reader: Liturgy, Law, and the Constraints of Performance', *Studies in the Age of Chaucer* 21 (1999), 99–141

Hornbeck, J. Patrick II, *What Is a Lollard? Dissent and Belief in Late Medieval England* (Oxford, 2010)

Horner, Patrick J., 'Preachers at Paul's Cross: Religion, Society, and Politics in Late Medieval England', in *Medieval Sermons and Society: Cloister, City, University, Proceedings of International Symposia at Kalamazoo & NY*, ed. Jaqueline Hamesse et al. (Louvain-la-Neuve, 1998), pp. 261–82

'Hospitals: SS Lazarus, Mary & Martha, Sherburn', in *A History of the County of Durham*, ed. William Page, Victoria County History, Durham 2 (London, 1907), pp. 115–17 (www.british-history.ac.uk/report.asp?compid=39888, accessed 10 June 2012)

Hudson, Anne, *The Premature Reformation: Wycliffite Texts and Lollard History* (Oxford, 1988)

— 'John Purvey: A Reconsideration of the Evidence for His Life and Writing', *Viator* 12 (1981), 355–80 (= *Lollards and Their Books*, London, 1985, §6)

Hughes, Andrew, *Medieval Manuscripts for Mass and Office: A Guide to Their Organization and Terminology* (Toronto, 1995)

Hutton, Ronald, 'The English Reformation and the Evidence of Folklore', *Past and Present* 148:1 (Aug. 1995), 89–116

Ilnitchi, Gabriela, 'Music in the Liturgy', in *The Liturgy of the Medieval Church*, ed. Thomas J. Heffernan and E. Ann Matter, 2nd edn (Kalamazoo, MA, 2005), pp. 589–612

Irwin, William, 'What Is an Allusion?', *The Journal of Aesthetics and Art Criticism* 59:3 (2001), 287–97

Johannot, Yvonne, *Tourner la page: Livres, rites et symboles*, 2nd edn (Grenoble, 1988)

Johnson, Bo, 'Form and Message in Lamentations', *Zeitschrift für die alttestamentliche Wissenschaft* 97 (1985), 58–73

Jörns, Klauss-Peter, 'Liturgy: Cradle of Scriptures?', *Studia Liturgica* 22:1 (1992), 17–34

Jungmann, Joseph A., *The Mass of the Roman Rite: Its Origin and Development* (orig. *Missarum Solemnia*, Vienna, 1949), 2 vols, tr. Francis A. Brunner (New York, 1951)

Justice, Steven, *Writing and Rebellion: England in 1381* (Berkeley and Los Angeles, 1994)

Kantorowicz, Ernst H., *Laudes Regiae: A Study in Liturgical Acclamations and Medieval Ruler Worship* (Berkeley, 1946)

— 'The King's Advent and the Enigmatic Panels in the Doors of Santa Sabina', *Art Bulletin* 26:4 (1944), 207–31

Kauffmann, C. M., *Biblical Imagery in Medieval England, 700–1550* (London, 2003)

Kelly, Eamonn P., 'The Lough Kinale Book Shrine: The Implications for the Manuscripts', in *The Book of Kells: Proceedings of a Conference at Trinity College Dublin, 6–9 September 1992*, ed. Felicity O'Mahony (Aldershot, 1994), pp. 280–9

— 'The Lough Kinale Book Shrine', in *The Age of Migrating Ideas: Early Medieval Art in Northern Britain and Ireland*, ed. R. Michael Spearman and John Higgit (Edinburgh, 1993), pp. 168–74

Kemp, E. W., 'History and Action in the Sermons of a Medieval Archbishop: The Bishop of Chichester', in *The Writing of History in the Middle Ages: Essays Presented to Richard William Southern*, ed. R. H. C. Davis and J. M. Wallace-Hadrill (Oxford, 1981), pp. 349–65

Ker, Neil R., *Books, Collectors and Libraries: Studies in the Medieval Heritage*, ed. Andrew G. Watson (London, 1985)

Kipling, Gordon, *Enter the King: Theatre, Liturgy, and Ritual in the Medieval Civic Triumph* (Oxford, 1998)

Krochalis, Jeanne E. and Matter, E. Ann, 'Manuscripts of the Liturgy', in *The Liturgy of the Medieval Church*, ed. Thomas J. Heffernan and E. Ann Matter, 2nd edn (Kalamazoo, MA, 2005), pp. 393–430

Leddy, Michael, 'Limits of Allusion', *The British Journal of Aesthetics* 32:2 (1992), 110–22

Levy, Brian J., 'Cheriton, Odo of (1180s-1246)', DNB

Life, Death and Art: The Medieval Stained Glass of Fairford Parish Church, A Multimedia Exploration, ed. Sarah Brown and Lindsay MacDonald (Stroud, 1997)

Light, Laura, 'The Thirteenth-Century Pandect and the Liturgy: Bibles with Missals', in *Form and Function in the Late Medieval Bible*, ed. Eyal Poleg and Laura Light, Library of the Written Word: The Manuscript World (Leiden, 2013), pp. 185–215

— 'Roger Bacon and the Origin of the Paris Bible', *Revue bénédictine* 111 (2001), 483–507

— 'French Bibles c. 1200–30: A New Look at the Origin of the Paris Bible', *The Early Medieval Bible: Its Production, Decoration and Use*, ed. Richard Gameson (Cambridge, 1994), pp. 155–76

— 'The New Thirteenth-Century Bible and the Challenge of Heresy', *Viator* 18 (1987), 275–88

— 'Versions et révisions de texte biblique', in *Le Moyen Age et la Bible*, Bible de tous les temps 4, ed. Pierre Riché and Guy Lobrichon (Paris, 1984), pp. 55–93

Lim, Timothy H., 'Deuteronomy in the Judaism of the Second Temple Period', in *Deuteronomy in the New Testament: The New Testament and the Scriptures of Israel*, ed. Steve Moyise and Maarten J. J. Menken, Library of New Testament Studies (London, 2007), pp. 6–26

Limor, Ora, *Holy Land Travels: Christian Pilgrims in Late Antiquity* (in Hebrew, Jerusalem, 1998)

Lincoln, F. A., 'The non-Christian Oath in English Law', *The Jewish Historical Society of England – Transactions* 16 (1945/51), 73–6

Lipton, Emma, 'Language on Trial: Performing the Law in the N-Town Trial Play', in *The Letter of the Law: Legal Practice and Literary Production in Medieval England*, ed. Emily Steiner and Candace Barrington (Ithaca, NY, 2002), pp. 115–35

Lobrichon, Guy, 'Les éditions de la Bible latine dans les universités de XIIIe siècle', in *La Bibbia del XIII secolo. Storia del testo, storia dell'esegesi: Convegno della Società Internazionale per lo studio del Medioevo Latino (SISMEL) Firenze, 1–2 Giugno 2001*, ed. Giuseppe Cremascoli and Francesco Santi (Florence, 2004), pp. 15–34

Locke, John, *An Essay for the Understanding of St Paul's Epistles, by Consulting St Paul himself* (London: Awnsham and John Churchill, 1707)

MacCormack, Sabine, 'Change and Continuity in Late Antiquity: The Ceremony of Adventus', *Historia: Zeitschrift für alte Geschichte* 21:4 (1972), pp. 721–52

McFall, Leslie, 'The Evidence for a Logical Arrangement of the Psalter', *Westminster Theological Journal* 62:2 (2000), 223–56

McGurk, Patrick and Rosenthal, Jane, 'The Anglo-Saxon Gospelbooks of Judith, Countess of Flanders: Their Text, Make-Up and Function', *Anglo-Saxon England* 24 (1995), 251–308 (= Patrick McGurk, *Gospel Books and Early Latin Manuscripts*, Ashgate, 1998, §15)

McHardy, A. K., 'Church Courts and Criminous Clerks in the Later Middle Ages', in *Medieval Ecclesiastical Studies in Honour of Dorothy M. Owen*, ed. M. J. Franklin and Christopher Harper-Bill, Studies in the History of Medieval Religion 7 (Woodbridge, 1995), pp. 165–84

McIhagga, Donald, '*Hosanna*: Supplication and Acclamation', *Studia Liturgica* 5:3 (1966), 129–50

McKenzie, D. F., *Bibliography and the Sociology of Texts: The Panizzi Lectures 1985* (London, 1986, reprinted in *Bibliography and the Sociology of Texts*, Cambridge, 1999)

Maitland, S. R., *The Dark Ages: A Series of Essays, Intended to Illustrate the State of Religion and Literature in the Ninth, Tenth, Eleventh, and Twelfth Centuries. Reprinted from 'The British Magazine', with Corrections and Some Additions* (London, 1844)

Malone, Carolyn Marino, *Façade as Spectacle: Ritual and Ideology at Wells Cathedral*, Studies in Medieval and Reformation Thought 102 (Leiden, 2004)

Marrow, James H., *Passion Iconography in Northern European Art of the Late Middle Ages and Early Renaissance: A Study of the Transformation of Sacred Metaphor into Descriptive Narrative* (Kotrijk, 1979)

Marsden, Richard, '"Ask What I am Called": The Anglo-Saxons and Their Bibles', in *The Bible as Book: The Manuscript Tradition*, ed. John L. Sharpe III and Kimberly Van Kampen (London, 1998), pp. 145–76

— 'Cain's Face, and Other Problems: The Legacy of the Earliest English Bible Translations', *Reformation* 1 (1996), 29–51 (available on http://www.tyndale.org/Reformation/1/rmarsden.html, accessed 10 April 2012)

Martin, Hervé, *Le métier de prédicateur en France septentrionale à la fin du moyen âge (1350–1520)* (Paris, 1988)

Martin, Lawrence T., 'The Two Worlds in Bede's Homilies: The Biblical Event and the Listeners' Experience' in *De ore Domini: Preacher and the Word in the Middle Ages*, ed. Thomas L. Amos, Eugene A. Green, and Beverly Mayne Kienzle (Kalamazoo, 1989), pp. 27–40

Martin, P., 'Le texte Parisien de la Vulgate Latine', *Le Muséon* 8 (1889), 444–66; 9 (1890), 55–70, 301–16

— 'La Vulgate latine au treizième siècle d'après Roger Bacon', *Le Muséon* 7 (1888), 88–107, 169–96, 278–91, 381–93

Matter, E. Ann, *The Voice of My Beloved: The Song of Songs in Western Medieval Christianity* (Philadelphia, 1992)

Mayeski, Marie Anne, 'Reading the Word in a Eucharistic Context: The Shape and Methods of Early Medieval Exegesis', in *Medieval Liturgy: A Book of Essays*, ed. Lizette Larson-Miller (New York, 1997), pp. 61–84

Miriello, Rosanna, 'La Bibbia portabile de origine italiana del XIII secolo. Brevi considerazioni e alcuni esempi', in *La Bibbia del XIII secolo. Storia del testo, storia dell'esegesi: Convegno della Società Internazionale per lo studio del Medioevo Latino (SISMEL) Firenze, 1–2 Giugno 2001*, eds Giuseppe Cremascoli and Francesco Santi (Florence 2004), pp. 47–77

Morey, James H., *Book and Verse: A Guide to Middle English Biblical Literature* (Urbana and Chicago, 2000)

Morgan, Nigel J., 'The Introduction of the Sarum Calendar into the Dioceses of England in the Thirteenth Century', in *Thirteenth Century England VIII*, ed. Michael Prestwich, Richard Britnell, and Robin Frame (Woodbridge, 2001), pp. 179–206.

Morrin, Margaret J., *John Waldeby, O.S.A., c.1315–c.1372, English Augustinian Preacher and Writer: With a Critical Edition of his Tract on the Ave Maria*, Studia augustiniana historica 2 (Rome, 1975 = *Analecta augustiniana* 35 (1972) 7–80; 36 (1973), 5–79; 37 (1974), 162–98)

Morris, Richard, *The Church in British Archaeology*, Council for British Archaeology Research Report 47 (London, 1983)

Mowinckel, Sigmund, *The Psalms in Israel's Worship* (orig. *Offersang og Sangoffer*, Oslo, 1951), tr. D. R. Ap-Thomas (Oxford, 1962, with several reprints)

Mullarkey, Paul, 'Some Observations on the Form and Date of the Soiscéal Molaise Book Shrine', in *Irish Art Historical Studies in Honour of Peter Harbison*, ed. Colum Hourihane (Dublin, 2004), pp. 124–40

Murano, Giovanna, 'Chi ha scritto le *Interpretationes hebraicorum nominum*', in *Etienne Langton, prédicateur, bibliste, théologien*, ed. Louis-Jacques Bataillon et al., Bibliothèque d'histoire culturelle du Moyen Age 9 (Turnhout, 2010), pp. 353–71

Murphy, James J., *Rhetoric in the Middle Ages: A History of Rhetorical Theory from St Augustine to the Renaissance* (Berkeley, 1974, repr. Tempe, AR, 2001)

— 'Rhetoric in Fourteenth-Century Oxford', *Medium Aevum* 34 (1965), 1–20 (= *Latin Rhetoric and Education in the Middle Ages and Renaissance*, Ashgate, 2005, §ix)

Needham, Paul, 'The Changing Shape of the Vulgate Bible in Fifteenth-

Century Printing Shops', in *The Bible as Book: The First Printed Editions*, ed. Kimberly Van Kampen and Paul Saenger (London, 1999), pp. 53–70

— *Twelve Centuries of Bookbindings, 400–1600* (New York, 1979)

Newman, Hillel I., 'Jerome's Judaizers', *Journal of Early Christian Studies* 9:4 (2001), 421–52

Nichols, Bridget, *Liturgical Hermeneutics: Interpreting Liturgical Rites in Performance* (Frankfurt am Main, 1996)

Nixon, Howard M. and Foot, Mirjam M., *The History of Decorated Bookbinding in England* (Oxford, 1992)

Nolan, Maura, '"Acquiteth yow now": Textual Construction and Legal Disclosure in the Man of Law's Introduction', in *The Letter of the Law: Legal Practice and Literary Production in Medieval England*, ed. Emily Steiner and Candace Barrington (Ithaca, NY, 2002), pp. 136–53

Nolcken, Christina von, 'Lay Literacy, The Democratization of God's Laws and the Lollards', in *The Bible as Book: The Manuscript Tradition*, ed. John L. Sharpe III and Kimberly Van Kampen (London, 1998), pp. 177–95

Notes and Queries (1st Ser.) 8:210 (Nov. 5 1853), 447–8; (2nd Ser.) 5:124 (May 15 1858), 391–2

O'Malley, John W., SJ, 'Introduction: Medieval Preaching', in *De ore Domini: Preacher and the Word in the Middle Ages*, ed. Thomas L. Amos, Eugene A. Green, and Beverly Mayne Kienzle (Kalamazoo, 1989), pp. 1–11

Owst, G. R., *Literature and Pulpit in Medieval England: A Neglected Chapter in the History of English Letters and of the English People*, 2nd edn (Oxford, 1961)

— *Preaching in Medieval England: An Introduction to Sermon Manuscripts of the Period c.1350–1450* (Cambridge, 1926)

Palazzo, Eric, *A History of Liturgical Books: From the Beginning to the Thirteenth Century* (orig. *Le Moyen Age: Des origines au XIIIe siécle*, Paris, 1993), tr. Madeleine Beaumont (Collegeville, MN, 1998)

— 'Le livres dans trésors du Moyen Age: Contribution à l'histoire de la Memoria médiévale', *Annales: Histoire, Sciences Sociales* 52:1 (1997), 93–118

Pantin, W. A., *The English Church in the Fourteenth Century, Based on the Birkbeck Lectures, 1948* (Cambridge, 1955)

Parker, William, *The History of Long Melford* (London, 1873)

Parkes, Malcolm B., 'Tachygraphy in the Middle Ages: Writing Techniques Employed for "Reportationes" of Lectures and Sermons', *Medioevo e Rincascimento* 3 (1989), 159–69 (reprinted in *Scribes, Scripts and Readers: Studies in the Communication, Presentation and Dissemination of Medieval Texts*, London, 1991, pp. 19–34)

Penn, Michael, 'Ritual Kissing, Heresy and the Emergence of Early Christian Orthodoxy', *Journal of Ecclesiastical History* 54:4 (2003), 625–40

Perella, Nicolas J., *The Kiss Sacred and Profane: An Interpretative History of*

Kiss Symbolism and Related Religio-Erotic Themes (Berkeley, 1969)

Perkins, Nicholas, 'Reading the Bible in Sawles Warde and Ancrene Wisse', *Medium Aevum* 72:2 (2003), 207–37

Perri, Carmela, 'On Alluding', *Poetics* 7:3 (1978), 289–307

Pfaff, Richard W., *The Liturgy in Medieval England: A History* (Cambridge, 2009)

— 'Bihop Baldock's Book, St Paul's Cathedral, and the Use of Sarum', in *Liturgical Calendars, Saints, and Services in Medieval England* (Aldershot, 1998), §xi

— 'Why Do Medieval Psalters Have Calendars?'in *Liturgical Calendars, Saints, and Services in Medieval England* (Aldershot, 1998), §vi

— 'The *Tituli*, Collects, Canticles, and Creeds', ch. iv of: *The Eadwine Psalter: Text, Image, and Monastic Culture in Twelfth-Century Canterbury*, ed. Margaret Gibson et al. (London and University Park, PA, 1992), pp. 88–107

Poleg, Eyal, 'Memory, Performance and Change: The Psalms' Layout in English Bibles 1200–1600', in *Writing as Material Practice: Substance, Surface and Medium*, ed. Kathryn E. Piquette and Ruth Whitehouse, University College London Institute of Archaeology Publications (Walnut Creek, CA, forthcoming)

— 'Wycliffite Bibles as Orthodoxy', in *Instructing the Soul, Feeding the Spirit and Awakening the Passion. Cultures of Religious Reading in the Late Middle Ages*, ed. Sabrina Corbellini, Utrecht Studies in Medieval Literacy (Turnhout, 2013), pp. 71–91

Powicke, Frederick M., 'The Oath of Bromholm', *English Historical Review* 56:224 (1941), 529–48

Quentin, Henry, *Mémoire sur l'établissement du texte de la Vulgate: 1ère partie Octateuque*, Collectanea Biblical Latina 6 (Rome and Paris, 1922).

Randolph, Adrian W. B., 'Performing the Bridal Body in Fifteenth-Century Florence', *Art History* 21:2 (1998), 182–200

Rawcliffe, Carole, *Medicine for the Soul. The Life, Death and Resurrection of an English Medieval Hospital: St Giles's, Norwich, c. 1249–1550* (Stroud, 1999)

Reilly, Diane J., 'The Cluniac Giant Bible and the Ordo librorum ad legendum: A Reassessment of Monastic Bible Reading and Cluniac Customary Instructions', in *From Dead of Night to End of Day: The Medieval Customs of Cluny*, ed. Susan Boynton and Isabelle Cochelin, Disciplina Monastica 3 (Turnhout, 2005), pp. 163–89

— 'French Romanesque Giant Bibles and Their English Relatives: Blood Relations or Adopted Children?' *Scriptorium* 56:2 (2002), 294–311

Retelling the Bible: Literary, Historical, and Social Contexts, ed. Lucie Doležalová and Tamás Visi (Frankfurt am Main, 2011)

Reynolds, Roger E., 'Image and Text: The Liturgy of Clerical Ordination in Early Medieval Art', *Gesta* 22:1 (1983), 27–38

Ricoeur, Paul, 'Herméneutique philosophique et herméneutique biblique', in *Du text à l'action: Essais d'herméneutique II* (Paris, 1986), pp. 133–49 (translated as 'Philosophical Hermeneutics and Biblical Hermeneutics', in *From Text to Action: Essays in Hermeneutics II*, tr. Kathleen Blamey, London, 1991, pp. 89–101)

Roberts, C. H. and Skeat, T. C., *The Birth of the Codex* (Oxford, 1987)

Rosenthal, Jane and McGurk, Patrick, 'Author, Symbol, and Word: The Inspired Evangelists in Judith of Flanders's Anglo-Saxon Gospel Books', in *Tributes to Jonathan J. G. Alexander: The Making and Meaning of Illuminated Medieval & Renaissance Manuscripts, Art & Architecture*, ed. Susan L'Engle and Gerald B. Guest (Turnhout, 2006), pp. 185–202

Ross, Marvin C., 'An Eleventh-Century English Bookcover', *The Art Bulletin* 22:2 (1940), 83–5

Rouse, Richard H. and Rouse, Mary A., *Manuscripts and Their Makers: Commercial Book Producers in Medieval Paris, 1200–1500; Illiterati et uxorati*, 2 vols (Turnhout, 2000)

— 'Wandering Scribes and Traveling Artists: Raulinus of Fremington and His Bolognese Bible', in *A Distinct Voice: Medieval Studies in Honor of Leonard E. Boyle, O.P.*, ed. Jacqueline Brown and William P. Stoneman (Notre Dame, IN, 1997), pp. 32–67

— 'Statim invenire: Schools, Preachers, and New Attitudes to the Page', in *Renaissance and Renewal in the Twelfth Century*, ed. Robert. L. Benson et al. (Oxford, 1982), pp. 201–25 (= *Authentic Witnesses: Approaches to Medieval Texts and Manuscripts*, Publications in Medieval Studies 17, Notre Dame, IN, 1991, pp. 191–219)

— *Preachers, Florilegia and Sermons: Studies on the 'Manipulus florum' of Thomas of Ireland*, Studies and Texts 47 (Toronto, 1979)

— 'Verbal Concordance of Scriptures', *Archivum Fratrum Prædicatorum* 44 (1974), 5–30

Rubin, Miri, *Corpus Christi: The Eucharist in Late Medieval Culture* (Cambridge, 1991)

Russell, Henry G., 'Lollard Opposition to Oaths by Creatures', *The American Historical Review* 51:4 (1946), 668–84

Ryan, J. Joseph, 'Pseudo-Alcuin's *Liber de divinis officiis* and the *Liber 'Dominus vobiscum'* of St Peter Damiani', *Mediaeval Studies* 14 (1952), 159–63

Saenger, Paul, 'The British Isles and the Origin of the Modern Mode of Biblical Citation', *Syntagma* 1 (2005), 77–123

— 'The Impact of the Early Printed Page on the Reading of the Bible', in *The Bible as Book: The First Printed Editions*, ed. Kimberly Van Kampen and Paul Saenger (London, 1999), pp. 31–51

Saenger, Paul and Bruck, Laura, 'The Anglo-Hebraic Origins of the Modern

Chapter Division of the Latin Bible', in *La fractura historiográfica: Las investigaciones de Edad Media y Renacimiento desde el tercer milenio*, dir. Javier San José Lera (Salamanca, 2008), pp. 177–202

Salmon, Pierre, *Les 'tituli psalmorum' des manuscrits latins*, Collectanea biblica latina 12 (Rome, 1959)

Sandler, Lucy Freeman, 'John of Metz, the Tower of Wisdom', in *The Medieval Craft of Memory: An Anthology of Texts and Pictures*, ed. Mary Carruthers and Jan M. Ziolkowski (Philadelphia, PA, 2002), pp. 215–25

— *The Psalter of Robert de Lisle: In the British Library*, 1st paperback edn (London, 1999)

Savage, Ernest A, *Old English Libraries: The Making, Collection, and Use of Books during the Middle Ages* (London, 1911)

Schapiro, Meyer, 'The Religious Meaning of the Ruthwell Cross', *Art Bulletin* 26:4 (December 1944), 232–45

Schiller, Gertrud, *Iconography of Christian Art* (orig. *Iconographie der christliche Kunst*, Gütersloh, 1968), tr. Janet Seligman, *vol. II The Passion of Jesus Christ* (London, 1972)

Schmoeckel, Mathias, 'Proof, Procedure, and Evidence', in *Christianity and Law: An Introduction*, ed. John Witte, Jr and Frank S. Alexander (Cambridge, 2008), pp. 143–62

Schneyer, Johannes Baptist, *Die Unterweisung der Gemeinde über die Predigt bei scholastischen Predigern: Eine Homiletik aus scholastischen Prothemen* (Munich, Paderborn, and Vienna, 1968)

Schreiner, Klaus, 'Das Buch im Nacken: Bücher und Buchstaben als zeichenhafte Kommunikationsmedien in rituellen Handlungen der mittelalterlichen Kirche', in *Audiovisualität vor und nach Gutenberg: zur Kulturgeschichte der medialen Umbrüche*, ed. Horst Wenzel et al., Schriften des Kunsthistorischen Museums, Band 6 (Vienna, 2001), pp. 59–103

Sheerin, Daniel J., 'Sonus and Verba: Varieties of Meaning in the Liturgical Proclamation of the Gospel in the Middle Ages', in *Ad Litteram: Authoritative Texts and Their Medieval Readers*, ed. Mark D. Jordan and Kent Emery, Jr, Notre Dame Conferences in Medieval Studies 3 (Notre Dame, IN, 1992), pp. 29–69

Shinners, John, 'Parish Libraries in Medieval England', in *A Distinct Voice: Medieval Studies in Honour of Leonard E. Boyle, O.P.*, ed. Jacqueline Brown and William P. Stoneman (Notre Dame, IN, 1997), pp. 207–30

Sint Anthonis, Servus of, 'Preaching in the Thirteenth Century: A Note on MS Gonville and Caius 439', *Collectanea Franciscana* 32 (1962), 310–24

Skemer, Don C., *Binding Words: Textual Amulets in the Middle Ages* (University Park, PA, 2006)

Smalley, Beryl, *The Study of the Bible in the Middle Ages*, 3rd rev. edn (Oxford, 1983)

— *English Friars and Antiquity in the Early Fourteenth Century* (Oxford, 1960)

Smith, Lesley, 'The Theology of the Twelfth- and Thirteenth-Century Bible', in *The Early Medieval Bible: Its Production, Decoration and Use*, ed. Richard Gameson (Cambridge, 1994), pp. 223–32

Smith, Wilfred Cantwell, 'The Study of Religion and the Study of the Bible', *Journal of the American Academy of Religion* 39:2 (1971), 131–40 (reprinted in *Rethinking Scripture: Essays from a Comparative Perspective*, ed. Miriam Levering, Albany, NY, 1989, pp. 18–28)

Somerset, Fiona, *Clerical Discourse and Lay Audience in Late Medieval England* (Cambridge, 1998)

Spencer, H. L., 'Middle English Sermons', in *The Sermon*, dir. Beverly Mayne Kienzle, Typologie des sources du Moyen Age occidental, Fasc. 81–3 (Turnhout, 2000), pp. 597–660

— *English Preaching in the Late Middle Ages* (Oxford, 1993)

Spurr, John, '"The Strongest Bond of Conscience": Oaths and the Limits of Tolerance in Early Modern England', in *Contexts of Conscience in Early Modern Europe, 1500–1700*, ed. Harald E. Braun and Edward Vallance (Basingstoke, 2004), pp. 151–65

Spurrell, Mark, 'The Procession of Palms and West-Front Galleries', *Downside Review* 119:415 (2001), 125–44

Steenbock, Frauke, *Der Kirchliche Prachteinband im frühen Mittelalter: von den Anfängen bis zum Beginn der Gotik* (Berlin, 1965)

Steiner, Emily and Barrington, Candace, 'Introduction', in *The Letter of the Law: Legal Practice and Literary Production in Medieval England*, ed. Emily Steiner and Candace Barrington (Ithaca, NY, 2002), pp. 1–11

Steward-Brown, R., 'The "Jurybook" of the County Court of Chester', *The English Historical Review* 48:190 (1933), 268–9

Stock, Brian, *Listening for the Text: On the Uses of the Past* (Baltimore, 1990)

— *The Implications of Literacy: Written Language and Models of Interpretation in the Eleventh and Twelfth Centuries* (Princeton, 1983)

Swanson, Robert N., 'Medieval Liturgy as Theatre: The Props', in *The Church and the Arts*, ed. Diana Wood, Studies in Church History 28 (Oxford, 1991), pp. 239–53

Swarzenski, Hanns, *The Berthold Missal, the Pierpont Morgan Library ms 710 and the Scriptorium of Weingarten Abbey* (New York, 1943)

Szerwiniack, Olivier, 'Les glossaires de noms hébreux dans les Bibles latines imprimées aux XVe et XVIe siècles: quelques jalons', in *Biblia: les Bibles en latin au temps des Réformes*, dir. Marie-Christine Gomez-Géraud (Paris, 2008), pp. 211–29

Tanner, Norman and Watson, Sethina, 'Least of the Laity: The Minimum Requirements for a Medieval Christian', *Journal of Medieval History* 32:4

(2006), 395–423

Taylor, Larissa, *Soldiers of Christ: Preaching in Late-Medieval and Reformation France* (New York and Oxford, 1992)

Thurston, Herbert, *Lent and Holy Week: Chapters on Catholic Observance and Ritual*, 2nd edn (London, 1914)

— 'Palms', *The Month: A Catholic Magazine and Review* 86 (1896), 373–87

Tristram, E. W., *English Wall Painting of the Fourteenth Century* (London, 1955)

Tugwell, Simon, 'The Evolution of Dominican Structures of Government III: The Early Development of the Second Distinction of the Constitutions', *Archivum Fratrum Praedicatorum* 71 (2001), 5–182

— '*De huiusmodi sermonibus texitur omnis recta predicatio*: Changing Attitude towards the Word of God', in *De l'homélie au sermon: Histoire de la prédication médiévale*, ed. Jacqueline Hamesse and Xavier Harmand, Publications de l'Institut d'études médiévales: Textes, études, congrès 14 (Louvain-la-Neuve, 1993), pp. 159–68

Turner, Denys, *The Darkness of God: Negativity in Christian Mysticism* (Cambridge, 1995)

Valkenberg, Pim, 'Readers of Scripture and Hearers of the Word in the Mediaeval Church', in *The Bible and Its Readers*, Concilium 233:1, ed. Wim Beuken, Sean Freyne, and Anton Weiler (London, 1991), pp. 47–57

Vezin, Jean, 'Les livres utilisés comme amulettes et comme reliques', in *Das Buch als Magisches und als Repräsentationsobjekt*, ed. Peter Ganz, Wolfenbütteler Mittelalter-Studien 5 (Wiesbaden, 1992), pp. 101–15

Vincent, Nicholas, 'Edmund of Almain, Second Earl of Cornwall (1249–1300)', DNB (www.oxforddnb.com.catalogue.ulrls.lon.ac.uk:80/view/article/ 8505, accessed 6 June 2012)

Vitz, Evelyn Birge, 'Liturgical Versus Biblical Citation in Medieval Vernacular Literature', in *Tributes to Jonathan J. G. Alexander: The Making and Meaning of Illuminated Medieval & Renaissance Manuscripts, Art & Architecture*, ed. Susan L'Engle and Gerald B. Guest (Turnhout, 2006), pp. 443–9

— 'The Liturgy and Vernacular Literature', in *The Liturgy of the Medieval Church*, ed. Thomas J. Heffernan and E. Ann Matter, 2nd edn (Kalamazoo, MA, 2005), pp. 503–63

Voigts, Linda E., 'What's the Word? Bilingualism in Late-Medieval England', *Speculum* 71:4 (1996), 813–26

Waltke, Bruce K., 'Superscripts, Postcripts, or Both', *Journal of Biblical Literature* 110:4 (1991), 583–96

Ward, John O., 'Rhetoric in the Faculty of Arts at the Universities of Paris and Oxford in the Middle Ages: A Summary of the Evidence', *Bulletin Du Cange: Archivum Latinitatis Medii Aevi* 54 (1996), 159–231

Waters, Claire M., *Angels and Earthly Creatures: Preaching, Performance, and Gender in the Later Middle Ages* (Philadelphia, 2004)

Wenzel, Siegfried, *Latin Sermon Collections from Later Medieval England: Orthodox Preaching in the Age of Wyclif*, Cambridge Studies in Medieval Literature 53 (Cambridge, 2005)

— *Macaronic Sermons: Bilingualism and Preaching in Late-Medieval England* (Ann Arbor, MI, 1994)

Witte, John Jr, 'Introduction', in *Christianity and Law: An Introduction*, ed. John Witte Jr and Frank S. Alexander (Cambridge, 2008), pp. 1–32

Wordsworth, Christopher and Littlehales, Henry, *The Old Service-Books of the English Church*, 2nd edn (London, 1910)

Zatta, Jane, 'The "romance" of the Castle of Love', *Chaucer Yearbook: A Journal of Late Medieval Studies* 5 (1998), 163–85

Ziegler, Joseph, 'Oath, Jewish', in *Medieval Jewish Civilization: An Encyclopedia*, ed. Norman Roth, Routledge Encyclopedias of the Middle Ages 7 (New York, 2003), pp. 483–7

— 'Reflections on the Jewry Oath in the Middle Ages', in *Christianity and Judaism*, ed. Diana Wood, Studies in Church History 29 (Oxford, 1992), pp. 209–20

Zier, Mark A., 'Sermons of the Twelfth Century Schoolmasters and Canons', in *The Sermon*, dir. Beverly Mayne Kienzle, Typologie des sources du Moyen Age occidental, Fasc. 81–3 (Turnhout, 2000), pp. 325–62

Unpublished sources

Akae, Yuichi, 'A Study of the Sermon Collection of John Waldeby, Austin Friar of York in the Fourteenth Century' (PhD dissertation, University of Leeds, 2004)

Cavanaugh, Susan H., 'A Study of Books Privately Owned in England 1300–1450' (PhD Thesis, University of Pennsylvania, 1980)

Schnurman, Josephine Case, 'Studies in the Medieval Book Trade from the Late Twelfth to the Middle of the Fourteenth Century with Special Reference to the Copying of Bibles' (B.Litt. Thesis, St Hilda's College, Oxford, 1960)

Electronic sources

The electronic resources provided below are only those whose virtual rendering has an additional value beyond their paper equivalent, or sources without any printed version. Printed sources which have been uploaded to the Word Wide Web are classified according to their printed version.

On the World Wide Web

Biblia Sacra juxta vulgatam clementinam, editio electronica, gen. ed. Michael Tuveedale, http://vulsearch.sourceforge.net/gettext.html (accessed 10 June 2012)

Cantus: Database of Latin Ecclesiastical Chant, dir. Terence Bailey, http://publish.uwo.ca/~cantus (accessed 10 June 2012)

Cursus: An Online Resource of Medieval Liturgical Texts, dir. David Chadd, www.cursus.uea.ac.uk (accessed 13 April 2010)

Digitalisierung des Repertorium Biblicum, dir. Klaus Reinhardt, *in a preliminary stage, but contains search facilities beyond those of the printed edition*, http://repbib.uni-trier.de/cgi-bin/rebihome.tcl (accessed 10 June 2012)

The Five Gospels Parallels, ed. John W. Marshall, www.utoronto.ca/religion/synopsis/syn-ini.htm (accessed 6 June 2012)

Medieval Wall Painting in the English Parish Church: A Developing Catalogue, ed. Anne Marshall, http://paintedchurch.org/subinx2.htm (accessed 10 June 2012)

A Repertorium of Middle English Prose Sermons, dir. Veronica O'Mara, www.hull.ac.uk/middle_english_sermons/index.php (accessed 10 June 2012)

Digital recordings

Salm: Gaelic Psalms from the Hebrides of Scotland, CD 1–2 (Aberdeen:Ridge Records, 2004)

BIBLICAL INDEX

MANUSCRIPT INDEX

GENERAL INDEX

CPSIA information can be obtained at www.ICGtesting.com
Printed in the USA
BVOW05s0310140616

451907BV00003B/4/P